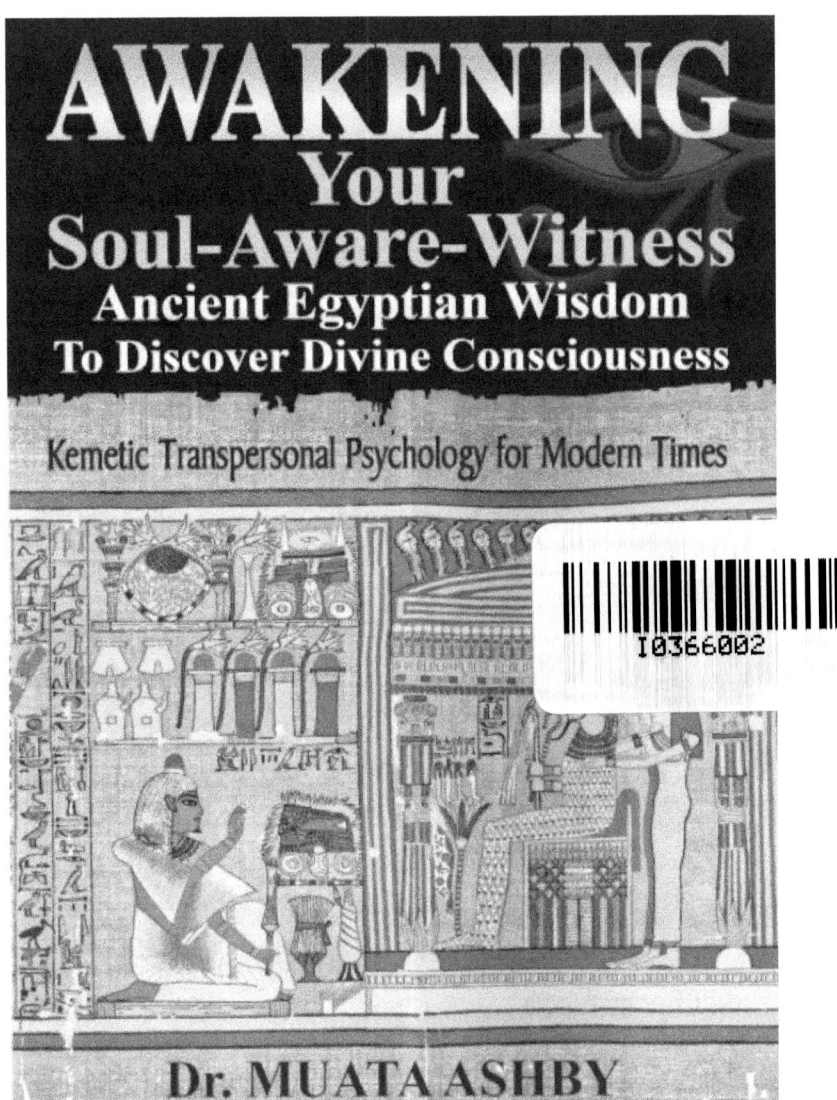

Sema Institute

P.O. Box 570459

Miami, Florida, 33257

(305) 378-6253 Fax: (305) 378-6253

First U.S. edition 2025 By Reginald Muata Ashby

All rights reserved. No part of this book may be used or reproduced in any manner whatsoever without written permission (address above) except in the case of brief quotations embodied in critical articles and reviews. All inquiries may be addressed to the address above.

The author is available for group lectures and individual counseling. For further information contact the publisher.

Ashby, Muata (2025)

Awakening Your Soul-Aware-Witness Ancient Egyptian Wisdom To Discover Divine Consciousness

ISBN: 9781937016777

Library of Congress Cataloging in Publication Data

# About the Author - Dr. Muata Ashby

Dr. Muata Ashby is a distinguished spiritual teacher, scholar, philosopher, and author whose groundbreaking work has transformed the understanding of Ancient Egyptian (Kemetic) spirituality and its connections to world religions. With over 70 published works on yoga philosophy, religious philosophy, and social philosophy based on ancient African principles, Dr. Ashby is recognized as the leading authority in comparative religious studies, specializing in Ancient Egyptian wisdom traditions.

## Academic Credentials and Foundation

Dr. Ashby holds a Doctor of Philosophy degree in Religion and a Doctor of Divinity degree from the American Institute of Holistic Theology, as well as a Master's degree in Liberal Arts and Religious Studies from Thomas Edison State College. His extensive academic background encompasses comprehensive independent research in Egyptian Yoga, Indian Yoga, Chinese Yoga, Buddhism, mystical psychology, and Christian mysticism. He has conducted postgraduate research in advanced Jnana, Bhakti, and Kundalini Yogas at the Yoga Research Foundation.

## Institutional Leadership and Innovation

Dr. Ashby founded the Sema Institute, a non-profit organization dedicated to preserving and disseminating Ancient Egyptian mystical traditions, as well as Kemetic University and the Egyptian Mystery School. Through these institutions, he has pioneered innovative approaches that combine traditional temple teaching methods with modern technologies. He has served as an adjunct professor at Florida International University and currently teaches through his online institution, Kemet University.

## Scholarly Contributions and Research

Beginning his groundbreaking research in the 1990s, Dr. Ashby investigated correlations between Ancient Egyptian and Indian spiritual traditions, leading to his successful "Egyptian Yoga" book series launched in 1994. He advocates that advanced social and religious philosophies existed in ancient Africa, comparable to Eastern traditions such as Vedanta, Buddhism, Confucianism, and Taoism. His extensive lectures and writings on these correlations promote cross-cultural understanding and spiritual advancement.

Dr. Ashby's scholarly work encompasses extensive research into Ancient Egyptian philosophy and social order, with particular expertise in Maat philosophy—the ethical foundation of Ancient Egyptian society. Having studied anthropology and Ancient Egyptian language, he has devoted thousands of hours to investigating and translating texts, focusing on Ancient Egyptian Religious Philosophy (sebayt) that shaped the development of Ancient Egyptian society and spirituality.

## Revolutionary Translation Method

Dr. Ashby has developed "Trilinear Translation," a unique and revolutionary approach to translating ancient texts that surpasses basic Egyptological interlinear formats. This innovative method provides three levels of translation: phonetic transliteration, direct word-for-word translation, and contextual translation incorporating philosophical, mythological, and historical insights. This approach makes ancient wisdom more accessible to contemporary readers.

## Musical and Artistic Contributions

Since 1999, Dr. Ashby has researched Ancient Egyptian musical theory and composed original works exploring this unique musical tradition from ancient Africa and its connections to world music. As an accomplished lecturer, musician, artist, poet, painter, screenwriter, and playwright, he brings a multidisciplinary perspective to his scholarly work, enriching understanding of ancient wisdom through diverse artistic expressions.

## Global Impact and Outreach

Dr. Ashby has lectured extensively throughout the United States, Europe, and Africa, sharing insights on ancient wisdom traditions with diverse audiences. His work has reached practitioners and scholars worldwide, establishing him as an internationally recognized authority on Ancient Egyptian spirituality and its practical applications for contemporary seekers.

## Collaborative Partnership

Dr. Ashby collaborates closely with his spiritual and life partner, Dr. Dja Ashby (formerly Karen Clarke), co-founder of the Sema Institute and director of C.M. Book Publishing. Married for over 40 years, they continue advancing the dissemination of Ancient Egyptian wisdom through their joint efforts in publishing, teaching, and spiritual guidance.

## Current Work and Legacy

In recent years, Dr. Ashby has focused intensively on the temples of Aset (Isis) and Asar (Osiris), producing detailed photographic documentation and original translations of hieroglyphic scriptures. His commitment to making ancient wisdom accessible is evident in comprehensive study programs that bridge ancient temple teachings with contemporary spiritual practice.

His monumental work on the Scripture of Ra and Hetheru from the Tomb of Sety I represents Dr. Ashby's continued dedication to translating and interpreting Ancient Egyptian spiritual texts for their mystical and practical applications. Through extensive scholarship, innovative translation methods, and deep spiritual understanding, he continues illuminating the profound wisdom of ancient Egypt for new generations of practitioners and scholars seeking authentic spiritual transformation.

Dr. Ashby's life work demonstrates that ancient African wisdom—particularly that of Ancient Egypt—offers profound insights into consciousness, spiritual development, and the path to enlightenment that remain as relevant today as they were millennia ago.

# Table of Contents

About the Author - Dr. Muata Ashby ................................................. 3
    Academic Credentials and Foundation .......................................... 3
    Institutional Leadership and Innovation ....................................... 3
    Scholarly Contributions and Research ......................................... 4
    Revolutionary Translation Method ............................................... 4
    Musical and Artistic Contributions .............................................. 4
    Global Impact and Outreach ....................................................... 5
    Collaborative Partnership .......................................................... 5
    Current Work and Legacy ........................................................... 5

Foreword: The Significance of "Mystic Transpersonal Psychology" in Understanding Ancient Egyptian Consciousness Teachings ...... 15
    References ................................................................................. 16

PREFACE: How the translations of the Ancient Egyptian Hieroglyphic texts in this volume were produced ............................ 17
    TRANSLATION FORMAT USED FOR PRESENTING THE SCRIPTURE WITH THE TRILINEAR METHOD .................. 17
    **Understanding the Contextual Translation Level of the Trilinear Translation System: Vertical Illumination and Horizontal Coherence: The Third Dimension of Hieroglyphic Translation** ............................................................................. 21

Introduction: Transpersonal Psychology Of Discovering the Soul-Aware-Witness-Self ................................................................. 28
    **The Three Foundational Ancient Egyptian Treatises** ........... 28
    **The Ancient Egyptian Book of Enlightenment (Pert-em-Heru)** ........................................................................................ 28
    **The Scripture of Ra and Hetheru** ........................................ 29
    **The Wisdom Text of Sage Amenemopet** ............................ 30
    **The Root of Life's Contradictions: Ego Awareness versus the Soul-Aware-Witness** ................................................................ 31

- **The Definition of the Ego Construct** ........................................ 32
- **Definition of Conscious-Awareness** .......................................... 33
- **The Solution: Discovering the Soul-Aware-Witness Beyond Contradiction** ............................................................................ 34
- **Why the Soul-Aware-Witness Transcends Contradictions** .. 34
- **The Practical Resolution of Life's Contradictions** ................. 36
- **Transpersonal Psychology in Ancient Egyptian Wisdom** ..... 36
- **Conclusion** ................................................................................. 37
- **Important Proviso for Students and Practitioners** ................ 38
- **References** ................................................................................ 39

Essential Concepts: A Progressive Introduction to Ancient Egyptian Spiritual Psychology ........................................................................... 41

- The Foundation: Understanding Consciousness Itself ................ 41
- The Divine Principles: Neteru as Psychological Realities .......... 42
- The Spiritual Framework: Core Principles for Development ..... 43
- HEKAU (Words of Power): Sacred Technology for Consciousness Transformation ....................................................... 44
- The Consciousness Levels: A Framework for Spiritual Recognition .................................................................................... 45
- The Spiritual Challenge: Heated Mind versus Silent Mind ........ 46
- The First Important Spiritual Goal: The Soul-Aware-Witness ... 47
- The Practical Method: Trilinear Understanding ......................... 48

Chapter 1: Foundations - The Ancient Wisdom Sources .................. 50

- The Source of Creation Revealed ................................................. 50
- Ancient Egyptian Anunian Creation Scripture Version B– translation by Dr. Muata Ashby ................................................... 51

Chapter 2: The Metaphysical Framework - The Three Levels of Consciousness Cosmology .................................................................. 65

- **The Cosmos as the Dream Creation of Universal Consciousness** ............................................................................. 65

**The Cosmic Dream** ............................................................... 66

**The Gods as Divine Thoughts** ............................................. 68

**The Nature of Manifest Existence** ...................................... 68

**The Practical Implications** .................................................. 70

Chapter 3: The Problem - How Consciousness Becomes Trapped. 105

   ANCIENT EGYPTIAN BOOK OF ENLIGHTENMENT - PERT-EM-HERU CHAPTER 26: THE CYCLE OF REINCARNATION ............................................................... 117

   The Ancient Egyptian Psychology of Herufy: Understanding the Dual Nature of Human Consciousness ........................... 122

**Teachings of New Kingdom Pert-M-Heru -Heru with Two heads** ............................................................................................ 124

Chapter 4: The Sacred Technology of Consciousness Transformation - The Systematic Pathway from Human Mind to Ra Consciousness Through Djehuty's Cosmic Bridge ...................... 142

   PART 1: THE FUNDAMENTAL SPIRITUAL TECHNOLOGY ........................................................................................... 142

      The Transformation Process: ............................................... 145

      The Logical Chain: ............................................................... 146

   PART 2: ADDITIONAL NUANCES IN THE TEXT ............. 147

      Physical/Ritual Preparation Requirements: ....................... 147

      Djehuty's Unique Cosmic Authority: ................................. 149

      Practical Application of Djehuty's Opposing Vibrations: .... 151

      Sacred Technology for Generating Opposing Vibrations: ... 152

      The Sacred Function of Textual Study: .............................. 153

      Verifiable Transformation Outcomes: ................................ 154

      Anan - The Microcosmic Bridge to Divine Consciousness: 154

Chapter 5: The Solution - Discovering the Soul-Aware-Witness ... 159

   ANCIENT EGYPTIAN PERT-EM-HERU CHAPTER 26 VERSES 1-16 ............................................................................. 159

The Three Key Mystic Psychology Themes of Chapter 26: Ancient Egyptian Teachings on Soul-Awareness and Liberation .................................................................. 162

Chapter 26 as Clinical Case Study: Ancient Egyptian Demonstration of Transpersonal Mental Health ................... 165

FROM THE WISDOM TEACHINGS OF SAGE AMENEMOPET .................................................................. 168

Teachings of Amenemopet Chapter 6B: Maintaining Awareness of All-Encompassing Divinity ............................................... 169

Teachings of Amenemopet-Chapter 18: Divine Guidance and Human Will .................................................................. 170

Chapter 11: The Consequence of Divine Rejection ............... 170

**References** .................................................................. 184

Chapter 6: Neberdjer - The All-Encompassing Foundation ........... 185

**Scriptural Foundation: The Ancient Texts on Neberdjer** ..... 186

**Teachings of Amenemopet Chapter 18** ............................... 186

**Stele of Djehuty Nefer Verse 3** .......................................... 187

**A Hymn to Osiris: Neberdjer as the "Tower of Creation"**
.................................................................................. 187

Chapter 7: The Universal Context - Asar Consciousness ................ 200

Ancient Egyptian Anunian Creation Scripture Version B .... 200

ANCIENT EGYPTIAN BOOK OF ENLIGHTENMENT CHAPTER 43 .................................................................. 202

Textual Evidence: The Asar Any Formula in Chapter 43 .... 216

The Mechanism of Universal Recognition ........................... 216

**The Divine Goodness and Eternal Existence: Understanding the Hymn to Asar's Revelation of Soul Nature** ................................ 223

Chapter 8: The Mechanics - How Transformation Occurs ............... 232

SCRIPTURE OF RA AND HETHERU: TRANSFORMATION MECHANICS ................................ 233

THE EFFECT OF SPIRITUAL ROASTING: RECONSTRUCTION FROM THE TOMB OF SETY I AND TUTANKHAMUN .................................................................. 241

The Effect of Spiritual Roasting ........................................... 242

TEACHINGS OF AMENEMOPET: THE SILENT ONES 246

Teachings of Amenemopet-Chapter 9: Cutting Away Heart's Dispositions ................................................................. 248

The Three Levels of Potential Consciousness Experience... 249

Experiential Mapping for Contemporary Practitioners ........ 252

Chapter 9: Foundational Principles and Philosophy of Practice. 255

The Majestic Wisdom of Sage Amenemopet ..................... 256

Prologue: The Foundation of Wisdom Philosophy ............... 257

The Foundational Principle: Wisdom Philosophy for Life Transformation .................................................................. 258

The Theoretical Foundation for Heated versus Silent Mind 260

FROM THE WISDOM TEACHINGS OF SAGE AMENEMOPET ................................................................. 261

The Developmental Philosophy: Natural Progression Through Consciousness Levels ....................................................... 262

The Threefold Integration Principle: Why Comprehensive Practice Proves Essential ................................................... 263

The Purification Philosophy: Aryu Transformation and Divine Light Transmission ............................................................ 264

The Navigation Principle: Conscious Steering Through Experience ......................................................................... 266

The Fate of the Boat Philosophy: Consciousness Level Determining Life Outcomes ............................................... 267

The Witness Consciousness Philosophy: The Unchanging Foundation ......................................................................... 270

The Foundation for Authentic Development ....................... 271

The Integration Model: Why Partial Practice Remains Insufficient ..................................................................... 277

The Natural Progression Philosophy: Spiritual Law and Automatic Development ....................................................... 278

The Practical Wisdom Foundation: Discrimination and Conscious Choice ................................................................. 281

The Mature Expression: Heru (Horus) Consciousness Philosophy ................................................................................ 283

The Cosmic Context: Individual Mind as Localized Universal Consciousness ........................................................ 284

The Recognition of Previous Delusion Philosophy .............. 284

The Living Expression Philosophy: Divine Awareness in Daily Life ....................................................................................... 285

The Intellectual Foundation for Awareness Investigation.... 286

Chapter 10: Spiritual Practices Suggested by the Scriptures Covered in this Book ........................................................................ 289

Introduction to the Fifteen Methods of Ancient Egyptian Consciousness Development based on the Translated Scriptures in this Volume ..................................................... 290

1. Trilinear Translation Methodology for Accessing Ancient Wisdom Authentically .......................................................... 293

2. Wisdom and Practice of Ethics: Living by Truth at Physical, Mental, and Spiritual Levels ............................................... 294

3. Working Skillfully with Heated Mind Disruptions and Maintaining Optimal Consciousness Levels ........................ 298

4. Conscious Life Navigation (Steering the Boat of Life Metaphor) ............................................................................. 300

5. Integration of Threefold Practice: Ethical Living, Philosophical Study, and Meditation ................................... 301

6. Three-Level Consciousness Recognition Training (Soul of Ra, Nunu, Ra) ...................................................................... 303

7. Integrated Divine Name and Sacred Utterance Practices . 305

The Practice of Circular Invocation ........................................ 305

8. Aryu Purification Through Spiritual Roasting (Vital-Life-Fire Development) .................................................................. 308

10. Recognition of Universal Soul Consciousness (Asar Consciousness) Operating Through Individual Forms .......... 311

11. Subtle Awareness Investigation Methods Including Gap Extension and Deep Sleep Investigation ............................... 313

12. Reflection-Contemplation on the Non-Objective Qualities of Expanded Consciousness ....................................................... 317

HYMN TO RA from the Ancient Egyptian Book of Enlightenment Papyrus Hunefer- Presented at the 2015 Neterian Conference. Translation by Dr. Muata Ashby ....... 317

HYMN TO RA and the Contemplative Investigation of Ra's Non-Objective Qualities ........................................................ 324

13. Neberdjer Awareness Practice - Maintaining Recognition of All-Encompassing Divinity ............................................... 330

14. Development and Stabilization of Witness Consciousness ........................................................................................... 334

15. The Wisdom of Association with Sages: Sacred Community as Foundation for Consciousness Development ........................................................................................... 337

The Wisdom of Association with Sages: Understanding the Spiritual Community as Living Temple ............................... 339

Chapter 11: Verification and Integration - The Measures of Spiritual Establishment ............................................................................. 344

CHAPTER 175 PERT-EM-HERU: CONVERSATION WITH TEMU .................................................................................. 347

COMMENTARY ON CHAPTER 175 PERT-EM-HERU: THE DIALOGUE WITH THE GOD TEMU ...................... 350

BRIDGING FROM CHAPTER 175 TO THE PURIFICATION PROCESS ............................................... 356

INTEGRATION THROUGH SPIRITUAL ROASTING: VERSES 177-179 .................................................................. 357

MOVING FROM INDIVIDUAL TO COSMIC INTEGRATION .................................................................. 361

BRIDGING ANCIENT WISDOM TO CONTEMPORARY PRACTICE .................................................................. 362

Sacred Technology: The HETEP Offering Table as Consciousness Transformation Tool .................................. 363

Contemporary Applications of Ancient Spiritual Technology .................................................................. 368

EXPANDING THE FOUNDATION: ADDITIONAL SCRIPTURAL CONTRIBUTIONS .................................. 370

AMENEMOPET'S TEACHINGS ON PRACTICAL INTEGRATION .................................................................. 374

THEORETICAL GUIDANCE FOR CONTEMPORARY PRACTITIONERS .................................................................. 378

SYNTHESIZING THE COMPLETE TEACHING ............ 384

CONCLUSION: THE SCRIPTURAL MAP FOR SPIRITUAL ESTABLISHMENT .................................. 386

INDEX .................................................................. 390

OTHER BOOKS BY MUATA ASHBY .................................. 403

# Foreword: The Significance of "Mystic Transpersonal Psychology" in Understanding Ancient Egyptian Consciousness Teachings

The term "Mystic Transpersonal Psychology" represents a deliberate synthesis that emerges from recognizing both the contributions and inherent limitations within contemporary psychological approaches to spiritual experience. Transpersonal psychology, as developed through the pioneering work of figures such as Abraham Maslow and Stanislav Grof, represents a significant advancement beyond traditional behaviorism and psychoanalysis by acknowledging transcendental experiences that were previously relegated exclusively to religious studies [1][2][3]. Nevertheless, this field maintains certain conceptual boundaries that constrain its capacity to fully comprehend the profound states of enlightenment and mystical realization described throughout the Ancient Egyptian wisdom traditions. Indeed, transpersonal psychology approaches these experiences primarily through the lens of mind-centered psychological analysis rather than as direct spiritual realizations that transcend ordinary mental operations [1][4][2].

Consider, however, that when the scholarly rigor and systematic methodology of transpersonal psychology become integrated with the transformative principles of mystic psychology—which operates through direct experiential realization rather than academic analysis—practitioners discover conceptual frameworks that illuminate aspects of consciousness development that purely religious study might overlook or treat as matters of faith rather than practical spiritual technology [1][4][2]. As the ancient sages taught, consciousness encompasses multiple simultaneous levels of operation: the Soul of Ra (Absolute) level representing pure consciousness without subject-object differentiation; the Nunu (unconscious) level representing undifferentiated consciousness with non-specific awareness; and the Ra (waking) level representing individuated consciousness capable of self-reference and personal identity [2]. This three-level cosmology provides essential metaphysical understanding that enables practitioners to approach mystical teachings with both psychological sophistication and spiritual authenticity. In other words, what contemporary scholars term "transpersonal psychology" represents not a modern innovation but rather the recovery of humanity's most ancient and sophisticated understanding of consciousness [1][4][2].

Thus, the designation "Mystic Transpersonal Psychology" acknowledges that while transpersonal psychology offers valuable analytical frameworks for understanding consciousness beyond ego-identification, these frameworks achieve their highest utility when integrated with the direct experiential methodology of mysticism as taught through the Scripture of Ra and Hetheru, the Ancient Egyptian Book of Enlightenment (Pert-em-Heru), and the Wisdom Text of Sage Amenemopet. Indeed, this synthesis enables contemporary aspirants to benefit from both the systematic investigation methods of psychological science and the transformative realization practices of authentic mystical tradition, creating a comprehensive approach to consciousness development that honors both the scholarly investigation of spiritual phenomena and the ultimate goal of spiritual practice: the discovery of "that which upon knowing, all is known" [1][4][2].

# References

[1] Ashby, M. (2019). Ancient Egyptian Book of Enlightenment (Pert-em-Heru): Hymn to Asar (Osiris). Translation by Dr. Muata Ashby. Sema Institute.

[2] Ashby, M. (2022). The Mysteries of Ra and Hetheru/Sekhmet. Translation by Dr. Muata Ashby. Sema Institute.

[3] Grof, S. (1985). Beyond the Brain: Birth, Death, and Transcendence in Psychotherapy. State University of New York Press.

[4] Ashby, M. (2016). Egyptian Book of the Dead Hieroglyph Translations for Enlightenment: Understanding the Mystic Path to Enlightenment Through Direct Readings of the Sacred Signs and Symbols of Ancient Egyptian Language With Trilinear Deciphering Translation Method Vol. 1. Translation by Dr. Muata Ashby. Sema Institute.

# PREFACE: How the translations of the Ancient Egyptian Hieroglyphic texts in this volume were produced

## TRANSLATION FORMAT USED FOR PRESENTING THE SCRIPTURE WITH THE TRILINEAR METHOD

**What is the Conventional Interlinear Format and how is it different from the new trilinear format of translating?**

The conventional interlinear format for translating Ancient Egyptian hieroglyphic texts presents a phonetic transliteration of the hieroglyphs and transposes them into the characters of the target language. The second line provides a word-for-word translation. This method can result in a limited, choppy, and less intelligible presentation of the original script's intent. When translating between languages with dissimilar structures and cultural references, such as the metaphor-rich Ancient Egyptian language and the more alphabetically structured European languages, a strict word-for-word translation can fail to convey the full meaning. Therefore, while the conventional interlinear format proves somewhat useful, this author recognized that a more comprehensive translation matrix was needed to capture the deeper richness and import of the original hieroglyphic text.

Awakening Your Soul-Aware-Witness

**Example of the Regular Interlinear Format:**

Verse 1.  ORIGINAL TEXT *(in its own language)*
    1.1.   Transliteration into the phonetic letters of the language of the reader
    1.2.   Translation into the words of the language of the reader

Ex:

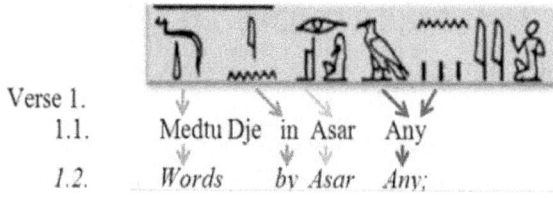

Verse 1.
  1.1.   Medtu Dje in Asar Any
  *1.2.*   *Words   by Asar  Any;*

**Trilinear Contextual Format**

The Trilinear Format for translating Ancient Egyptian writing is both a method and a decipherment protocol. It allows for viewing the meaning from its source through layers of extraction to the final rendition. The term "decipherment" is used because, to the modern mind, the contexts and philosophy of the Ancient Egyptians are akin to a code or formula to be discovered, unlocking the secrets of life, death, and the afterlife. Dr. Muata Ashby has developed a format for translating Ancient Egyptian hieroglyphs into the reader's native language, incorporating three levels of translation instead of the two levels of the conventional interlinear format. The Ternary System (Trilinear Translating Protocol) adds a third layer of translation, termed "Contextual Translation," which, together with the other two levels, constitutes the Trilinear Contextual Format.

The Trilinear Form, developed by Dr. Muata Ashby, is a ternary system for translating Ancient Egyptian Hieroglyphic texts. It consists of three translation sections or layers. The first level is a phonetic transliteration. The second level is a direct word-for-word translation from hieroglyphic to the reader's native language, generally constituting the "Conventional Interlinear Format." The Trilinear Format adds a third level of translation, a contextual translation that brings out the meaning in an informal, colloquial context in prose style. This includes:

A— Ancient Egyptian Sebayt (philosophical) tenets, when appropriate.

B— Ancient Egyptian Matnu (mythic) references and Maut (morals or takeaways of the myth) contained in the text to better reveal the intended meaning for the reader's language and culture.

C— In this volume, a new feature has been added to the trilinear system; the last translated verse will also include, where possible, a summary making contextual sense of the wisdom presented throughout the text, with a particular focus on the beginning verse to clarify the takeaway by recalling the status of the spiritual aspirant at the beginning, then the transformation experiences throughout the text in its key hieroglyphic expressions, and concluding with the outcome expressed in the final verse.

**Example of the Trilinear Format:**

*Verse 1.*    ORIGINAL HIEROGLYPHIC TEXT
  *1.1.*    ***Transliteration into the phonetic letters of the language of the reader***
  1.2.    <u>Translation into the words of the language of the reader</u>
  1.3.    Translation with contextual insights which may include philosophical and/or mythological and/or historical background insights with colloquial references.

Ex:

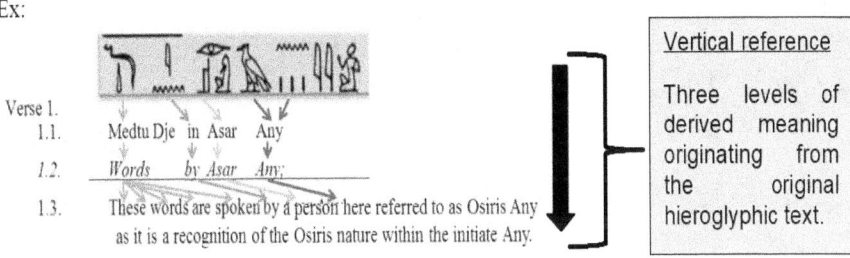

**NOTE:** With the trilinear format, each level of translation is designed to be both a reference to the other levels (vertically) but also to the previous and next statement in each level; so, for example, Verse translation Level 2.1 relates to 2.2 and 2.3 (vertical) but 2.2 also relates to 1.2 and 3.2 (horizontal). Therefore, if all the Level 2 translations are read by themselves or Level 3 translations are read by themselves one after the other, there will be a continuous and coherent rendering of the text.

**Example**

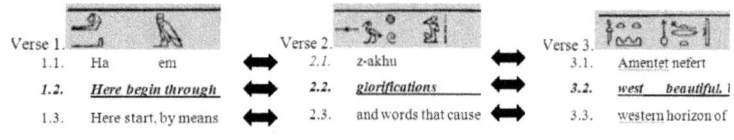

(Horizontal relationship)

In this way, the readings of Verse 1.2 followed by Verse 2.2, followed by Verse 3.2, translations, one after the other (ignoring .1 and .3 levels), horizontally, provide a continuous and coherent word-for-word narrative of the translation.

Also, the readings of Verse 1.3 followed by Verse 2.3, followed by Verse 3.3, translations, one after the other (ignoring .1 and .2 levels), horizontally, provide a continuous and coherent prose narrative of the translation.

**Note:** When some text appears in red, it is because the original hieroglyphic text was written in the same way. This was done by the original creators of the scripture, the Ancient Egyptian priests and priestesses, to highlight certain parts of the text or to emphasize the chapter titles.

Verse 1.

| 1.1. | Pu | tra | er –f | su | Asar | pu | ky | djed | Ra |
|---|---|---|---|---|---|---|---|---|---|
| 1.2. | That | what | as to-he? | He | Osiris | that | | otherwise said: | Ra |

1.3. What is that personality that is being talked about? That personality is Osiris. Another way of thinking about it is that Osiris is also Ra...

# Understanding the Contextual Translation Level of the Trilinear Translation System: Vertical Illumination and Horizontal Coherence: The Third Dimension of Hieroglyphic Translation

The contextual translation level in Dr. Ashby's trilinear system serves as the interpretive culmination of the translation process. While the transliteration preserves phonetic values and the word-for-word translation maintains linguistic structure, the contextual translation integrates philosophical concepts (Sebayt), mythological references (Matnu), cultural context, and colloquial meaning, based on the key words from the word-for-word translation, to convey the deeper intent of the text.

This third level doesn't merely restate the literal meaning but reveals the philosophical underpinnings and metaphysical implications embedded in the hieroglyphs. Indeed, it acts as a bridge between ancient Egyptian thought and modern understanding, recognizing that certain concepts like those conveyed by the "owl" glyph (im/em) carry profound philosophical significance beyond their surface meaning.

The relationship between the three levels is both vertical and horizontal. Vertically, each level progressively deepens understanding of a single verse. Horizontally, reading all contextual translations sequentially provides a cohesive philosophical narrative that might be obscured in the more fragmented word-for-word translations. This multilayered approach acknowledges that Ancient Egyptian texts operated simultaneously as literal communications, philosophical treatises, and mystical instructions.


**How is the translation format organized? Below: Sample papyrus sheet with hieroglyphic text:**

A trilinear translation is created by photographing the sheet and dividing the lines of text electronically into strips. Then, the text is converted to a TRANSLITERATION, followed by a WORD-for-WORD TRANSLATION, and finally, a CONTEXTUAL TRANSLATION.

**EXAMPLE OF A VERSE OF TEXT TRANSLATED WITH THE INTERLINEAR FORMAT:**

Verse 13.
13.1. *Djerau    im tjehu       maazenu su   entau -  im shepsherner n-F*
13.2. Strength   within joyousness   seeing they he   being  - among venerated
                                                                    awe of-he
13.3. There is a strong feeling of joyousness when they see Osiris, among those who are in the ranks of the venerable, noble ancestors; when they see him, they are in awe of him.

## Reading the Philosophy Embedded in Ancient Egyptian Hieroglyphic Writings

Here, I will provide two examples using two of the most important hieroglyphs to demonstrate why and how the philosophy of the Ancient Egyptian Mysteries is determined in the texts to be read. As stated earlier, reading the Ancient Egyptian texts in a literal way and ascribing meanings that relate to the culture of the reader is a disservice to the ancient culture. Indeed, it also distorts the meaning of the texts and the legacy of the original priests and priestesses who created them.

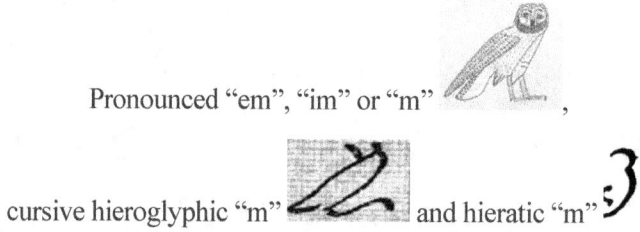

Pronounced "em", "im" or "m" , cursive hieroglyphic "m" and hieratic "m"

The first glyph is the owl. Perhaps one of the most important glyphs, unlike determinatives, which do not convey phonetic aspects to the word, the owl has both phonetic and philosophical meanings. Whenever the owl appears, its meaning can range from "in, within, inside, through, as, in the form of." This makes it a pivotal term, especially when it relates the person for whom the text has been created to any particular or general Divinity (god or goddess). It, therefore, means that such a person is being identified with that divinity or with an aspect of divinity, or they are being recognized as "becoming, appearing, or manifesting as." This, of course, can signify, among other things, a factor of mutual identification or a movement of transformation either in progress or already attained. Consider how this glyph is seldom interpreted in such a manner, and thus the overall outcomes of such neglectful translations will render a mundane or erroneous insight into the Ancient Egyptian hieroglyphic writings.

## Conclusion: The Transformative Power of Trilinear Translation for Ancient Wisdom

The trilinear method serves a specific purpose in this translation approach:

| Translation Level | Purpose | User Experience |
| --- | --- | --- |
| Hieroglyphic Text | Shows authentic ancient source | "I can see the actual text" |
| Transliteration | Preserves phonetic values/pronunciation | "I can pronounce it" |
| Word-for-Word | Maintains linguistic structure | "I can see the literal meaning" |
| Contextual | Provides philosophical interpretation | "I can understand the spiritual meaning" |

It is important to understand that Dr. Ashby's trilinear translation system represents a revolutionary advancement in deciphering Ancient Egyptian hieroglyphic texts, moving beyond the limitations of conventional interlinear formats to capture the full philosophical, mythological, and spiritual dimensions embedded within these sacred writings. As the ancient sages taught through their sophisticated use of hieroglyphs like the owl glyph (im/em), Ancient Egyptian texts operated simultaneously as literal communications, philosophical treatises, and mystical instructions—a multilayered reality that demands equally sophisticated translation methodology.

We must recognize that the trilinear format's three-dimensional approach—combining phonetic transliteration, word-for-word translation, and contextual interpretation—creates both vertical depth of understanding for individual verses and horizontal coherence when read sequentially, thus preserving the educational progression intended by the original priest-scribes. Indeed, this translation system serves as essential spiritual technology (hekau) for modern aspirants, ensuring that the profound wisdom of Shetaut

Neter is transmitted authentically rather than diluted through cultural misinterpretation or oversimplified literal rendering.

Consider how the contextual translation level bridges ancient Egyptian consciousness and contemporary understanding, recognizing concepts like divine identification (expressed through the owl glyph) that conventional translation methods often miss entirely—thereby preserving the transformative potential of these texts for genuine spiritual development (nehast) in our time. Therefore, the trilinear system stands as more than mere academic methodology; it represents a sacred responsibility to honor the intellectual and spiritual sophistication of Ancient Egyptian civilization while making their timeless wisdom accessible to serious students of the Neterian tradition.

For more on Ancient Egyptian Hieroglyphic Writing see the book *Ancient Egyptian Hieroglyphs for Beginners* by Muata Ashby

Having established the revolutionary trilinear translation methodology that makes authentic ancient Egyptian wisdom accessible to contemporary practitioners, we must now turn to the fundamental psychological insights these texts reveal. The translation format serves as more than academic methodology—it functions as spiritual technology that preserves the transformative power embedded within the original hieroglyphic scriptures. Indeed, the ancient sages understood that consciousness itself operates through multiple levels of recognition, much like the trilinear system reveals multiple levels of textual meaning. We must recognize that this methodological foundation prepares us to explore the central teaching that emerges from these sacred texts: the discovery of what may be termed the "Soul-Aware-Witness" as the solution to humanity's fundamental psychological contradictions.

# Introduction: Transpersonal Psychology Of Discovering the Soul-Aware-Witness-Self

## The Three Foundational Ancient Egyptian Treatises

With the revolutionary trilinear translation methodology established as our foundation for accessing authentic ancient wisdom, we must now turn to examine three monumental Ancient Egyptian treatises, along with supporting texts, that provide the complete framework for transpersonal psychology and the discovery of the Soul-Aware-Witness-Self (or "Soul-Aware-Witness" for brevity). These teachings draw from sacred texts that I have newly translated using the trilinear method—a system providing three distinct levels of rendering: phonetic transliteration preserving original sounds, direct word-for-word translation maintaining ancient grammatical structure, and contextual translation incorporating philosophical concepts (sebayt), mythological references (matnu), and cultural insights necessary for contemporary practitioners.

The significance of this translation work cannot be overstated, as this innovative approach transcends conventional Egyptological methods to expose the deeper spiritual dimensions embedded within the original hieroglyphic texts, making the authentic wisdom of the ancient sages accessible for genuine spiritual transformation.

## The Ancient Egyptian Book of Enlightenment (Pert-em-Heru)

The first foundational text is the Ancient Egyptian Book of Enlightenment, more commonly known as the "Book of the Dead," sections of which I have extensively translated using the trilinear methodology [1]. This sacred scripture, properly titled "Pert-em-Heru" meaning "Book of Coming Forth into the Light of

Enlightenment," provides fundamental understanding of consciousness development through various stages of spiritual realization.

The translation work reveals profound teachings on the nature of consciousness beyond ordinary waking awareness, particularly through Chapter 175, which presents the concept of HETEP—a state of spiritual peace and integration that transcends ordinary consciousness [1]. Indeed, the text illuminates how practitioners move from states of spiritual disturbance and seeking (hanur) to profound spiritual peace (HETEP) through understanding the true nature of consciousness and its relationship to manifestation.

This scripture serves as the foundational text for understanding the psychological and metaphysical principles that govern consciousness transformation, providing essential context for recognizing how awareness can separate itself from identification with temporary phenomena and discover its eternal nature as divine consciousness [1].

# The Scripture of Ra and Hetheru

The second foundational text is the Scripture of Ra and Hetheru, also known as "The Story of the Destruction of Humankind," "The Myth of the Eye of Ra," or "The Story of the Heavenly Cow." I have created a separate trilinear translation covering this scripture from a chamber in the walls of the Tomb of Sety I, dating to the 19th Dynasty (circa 1294-1279 BCE) [2]. The entire scripture is presented in a separate volume: MYSTIC TRANSPERSONAL PSYCHOLOGY in the MYSTERIES OF RA & SEKHMET & METAPHYSICS OF THE Glorious Light Meditation System of Ancient Egypt.

This profound scripture presents a dramatic narrative of Ra's aging, humanity's rebellion, Hetheru's transformation into the fierce lioness goddess Sekhemit, and the ultimate restoration of divine harmony through the sacred setjert drink [2]. Consider how the translation reveals that this narrative operates on multiple levels: as cosmological teaching about the relationship between Creator and Creation, as psychological instruction about the movement from ego-consciousness to divine awareness, and as practical meditation guidance for consciousness transformation.

The Scripture of Ra and Hetheru provides the central teaching methodology used throughout this book, particularly its instruction on the three levels of consciousness: Soul of Ra (pure consciousness), Nunu (undifferentiated consciousness), and Ra (individuated consciousness) [2]. This text offers both the philosophical framework for understanding consciousness levels and practical visualization techniques, particularly the Glorious Light Meditation, that enable practitioners to directly experience these different modalities of awareness [3].

# The Wisdom Text of Sage Amenemopet

The third foundational text is the Wisdom Text of Sage Amenemopet, a profound collection of teachings on human psychology, ethical conduct, and spiritual enlightenment that I have translated with complete hieroglyphic documentation [4]. This text, dating to approximately the 12th century BCE, provides the ethical and philosophical framework for proper spiritual development, particularly the crucial distinction between the heated mind (shemm) and the silent mind (ger) [4].

As the ancient sages taught through Sage Amenemopet's teachings, the fundamental understanding that underlies all spiritual practice involves the recognition of Neberdjer as the all-encompassing consciousness that both underlies and overlies all manifested existence [4]. Indeed, the translation illuminates how this ancient sage provided systematic instruction for moving consciousness from agitated, ego-based thinking to the silent awareness that naturally recognizes its unity with the divine source of all existence.

The Wisdom Text serves as the ethical and practical foundation for spiritual development described in the other texts, providing guidance on right thinking, right conduct, and the cultivation of inner silence that enables consciousness to transcend its identification with temporary phenomena and discover its essential nature as an expression of universal divine awareness [4].

# The Root of Life's Contradictions: Ego Awareness versus the Soul-Aware-Witness

Every human being, regardless of culture, historical period, or personal circumstances, shares the fundamental drive to discover genuine happiness and lasting fulfillment in life [1][4][2]. From the perspective of the average person, the method of seeking happiness and lasting fulfillment often occurs through finding meaning in the world through relationships—whether with work, friends, or family—in an attempt to find connection or wholeness as if something is missing and needs to be added to the personality for completion. That completion is most often sought through bodily or worldly means.

This universal search for contentment represents the soul's inherent recognition of its divine nature seeking to know itself through human experience. Nevertheless, the ancient Egyptian wisdom teachings reveal that most people pursue this fulfillment from the perspective of ego awareness operating through the influence of accumulated aryu (unconscious karmic impressions) rather than from recognition of their essential nature as consciousness itself.

The tradition of Shetaut Neter teaches that when consciousness approaches life's fundamental pursuits—security, achievement, relationships, growth, freedom, meaning, and wellbeing—from the heated mind (shemm) patterns of ego-identification, it inevitably creates what appears to be irreconcilable conflicts and contradictions [4][2]. This occurs because the ego construct (defined next), operating through the illusion of separateness and the compulsive patterns of aryu, seeks fulfillment through external means and temporary phenomena, while the deeper nature of the personality (the soul basis) has entirely different requirements for satisfaction that can only be met through recognition of its spiritual essence and divine unity with all existence.

# The Definition of the Ego Construct

The ego construct may be defined as the complex of aryu as it operates through mind, body, and senses, along with its developed identity and desires based not on the spiritual self but on the personality that emerges from this complex and identifies as the body/mind thinking and feeling in ways determined by that complex. Therefore, the ego of a person is not a reality but a manifestation of complex interaction between past desires, thoughts, and feelings as they manifest in real time through the mind and body of a person who has not become thoughtful enough to deconstruct the complex in order to discover the true nature of the personality: consciousness-awareness that we refer to in this volume as the Soul-Aware-Witness, which is a reflection of the Absolute Spirit Being that sustains all souls and manifestations of conscious-awareness operating in all people.

The ego construct manifests as consciousness caught in what the text describes as "drowning in the ever-agitating movements of opposition and attraction" and "sailing downstream to the north of Kemet (Egypt)" in endless cycles of reincarnation and fruitless recurring movements that do not accomplish a goal of fulfillment or satisfaction in life [1]. The wisdom of the neteru reveals that this ego construct operates through a fundamental pattern of agitation and external control, wherein consciousness identifies with the agitated heart (being controlled by bodily urges and mental fluctuations), seeks to control the body and circumstances through reactive effort, and becomes trapped in what the scripture describes as the "mayhem of desires born of spiritual ignorance and duality perceived through mind and senses" [2].

This means that ego-consciousness suffocates the soul by overwhelming it with constant mental-emotional turbulence and endless cycles of seeking fulfillment through external means rather than recognizing its divine nature as the source of all satisfaction. As the ancient sages taught, this ego-identification creates the condition where "people drown in the ever-agitating movements of opposition and attraction" [2]. Indeed, the scripture reveals that this drowning occurs precisely because ego-consciousness approaches life from the illusion of separateness—imagining itself as an isolated entity that must struggle against external forces to achieve security, pleasure, and validation beyond that which is needed by a person to develop into a well-adjusted ego personality—that is, a personality capable of maintaining self-respect and wellbeing without excessive dependence on external validation.

## Definition of Conscious-Awareness

Conscious-awareness represents consciousness filtered through the personality (ka), allowing function through mind and senses but becoming subject to limitation and conditioning. When witness-consciousness operates through human conditioning, it becomes what we term "conscious-awareness"—consciousness that operates through the personality rather than resting in its pure, unconditioned state (limitless, timeless, universal awareness).

This conditioned consciousness (consciousness operating through mind, senses, and body and adapting to their limitations as if it were its own) becomes captured by aryu (karmic impressions) and driven by ego patterns developed from experiences in current and previous lifetimes. For the unenlightened person, the awareness faculty becomes enslaved to these unconscious patterns, preventing recognition of one's essential nature as unlimited consciousness rather than limited ego personality.

Consider that conscious-awareness is not necessarily ethical awareness or self-awareness, but simply consciousness operating through mind, body, and senses, whether for positive or negative purposes. This differs from witness-consciousness, which remains unaffected by conditioning and serves as the illuminating principle that makes all experience possible.

In the tradition of Shetaut Neter, the objective of spiritual practice involves transcending the limitations of conditioned conscious-awareness to recognize our true nature as pure awareness—consciousness resting in itself without operating through ego individuation or karmic filtering.

## The Solution: Discovering the Soul-Aware-Witness Beyond Contradiction

The ancient Egyptian scriptures reveal that these psychological conflicts dissolve when consciousness discovers its true nature as the "Soul-Aware-Witness"—the awakening of awareness of not being an ego personality but rather a being possessing higher awareness above the ego self-identity [1]. This awareness manifests through what Chapter 26 of the Ancient Egyptian Book of Enlightenment describes: "my heart, he is peaceful within me," "I know myself," and "I have control over my arms and legs (body)" [1]. The Soul-Aware-Witness represents consciousness that has achieved separation from ego-identification and now operates as what the ancient teachings call the "instrument of the soul" (consciousness that exercises appropriate control over the body without being controlled by bodily urges and desires, functioning from inner peace and divine recognition rather than reactive patterns) [1].

This doesn't mean suppressing thoughts or emotions but rather allowing mental activity to arise and dissolve within the spacious awareness that recognizes its own divine nature as the unchanging witness of all changing phenomena. When consciousness establishes itself in this aware-witnessing perspective, the heart becomes peaceful rather than agitated, self-control emerges naturally rather than through forced effort, and the path becomes clear and direct rather than the back-and-forth cycles that characterize ego-consciousness [1].

## Why the Soul-Aware-Witness Transcends Contradictions

The tradition reveals that silent mind operates from recognition of consciousness's essential nature, creating what the teachings describe as "peaceful heart" awareness that maintains inner stability regardless of external circumstances [1]. This awareness transcends the fundamental contradictions of ego-life because it no longer operates from the illusion of separateness that creates competing desires. The following table shows the position of human consciousness experience in the context of Ancient Egyptian mystic psychology based on the texts referenced in this volume.

| Human Level |
|---|
| Ego awareness |
| Soul-Aware-Witness-Self |

| Cosmic Level |
|---|
| *Ra* (differentiated consciousness), objects of Creation |
| *Nunu* (undifferentiated consciousness), potential of Creation |
| *Ba en Ra* [Soul of Ra](Absolute), Consciousness supporting the potential (undifferentiated) and the manifest apparent reality (differentiated) of time, space, objects and localized individuated consciousness |

When consciousness functions as the Soul-Aware-Witness, it recognizes that security and freedom are not contradictory because true security emerges from recognition of one's eternal nature rather than control of external circumstances. Achievement and connection integrate naturally because actions flow from soul expression rather than ego-gratification, serving both individual development and collective wellbeing. Present and future harmonize because the witness consciousness operates from timeless awareness that encompasses all temporal experiences without being limited by them.

The person maintains full engagement with essential social and work responsibilities while recognizing that their essential worth doesn't depend on external outcomes. This means approaching challenges with creative intelligence rather than reactive anxiety, collaborating rather than competing, and maintaining inner stability regardless of external circumstances.

## The Practical Resolution of Life's Contradictions

The scripture reveals that when conscious-awareness within a human operates as the instrument of the soul, all actions emerge from what the teachings describe as "peace, self-control, and clear path" [1]. Instead of the ego's characteristic agitation, seeking, and endless back-and-forth movement, the Soul-Aware-Witness maintains steady awareness that naturally expresses the soul's inherent wisdom, compassion, and divine purpose.

This corresponds with the understanding in the ancient teachings that liberation comes not through eliminating the personality but through establishing consciousness in its true nature as the soul's expression in manifestation, as opposed to the false sense of separate ego identity [1]. Indeed, the witness consciousness recognizes that apparent contradictions exist only from the perspective of ego-identification, while from the viewpoint of divine awareness, all experiences serve the unified purpose of consciousness knowing itself through apparent differentiation.

## Transpersonal Psychology in Ancient Egyptian Wisdom

Transpersonal psychology, as revealed through the ancient Egyptian wisdom scriptures, represents a sophisticated understanding of consciousness that transcends the personal ego while encompassing the full spectrum of human psychological and spiritual experience [1][4][2]. This approach to consciousness studies emerges not from modern academic speculation but from the direct experiential investigations of the ancient sages, whose trilinear translations reveal profound insights into the nature of awareness beyond ordinary personality-identification.

The Scripture of Ra and Hetheru, the Ancient Egyptian Book of Enlightenment (Pert-em-Heru), and the Wisdom Text of Sage Amenemopet provide the foundational framework for comprehending both transpersonal psychology and mystic psychology as complementary approaches to understanding consciousness. Transpersonal psychology represents the scientific study of consciousness levels that encompass and transcend ordinary personality operations, approaching mystical scriptures from a scholarly psychological perspective. Mystic psychology, conversely, functions as an advanced form of psycho-spiritual discipline that integrates direct experiential realization with psychological understanding to achieve what transcends ordinary mental, physical, and spiritual health—seeking to discover "that which upon knowing, all is known." While mysticism traditionally operates through direct spiritual experience rather than academic psychological analysis, this manuscript employs both the scholarly rigor of transpersonal psychology and the transformative methodology of mystic psychology to provide comprehensive understanding of these ancient consciousness teachings [1][4][2].

The ancient Egyptian understanding differs fundamentally from contemporary psychological approaches that remain confined to personality-level investigations. The neteru teachings reveal that human beings experience multiple levels of consciousness simultaneously: the Soul of Ra (Absolute) level representing pure consciousness without subject-object differentiation; the Nunu (unconscious) level representing undifferentiated consciousness with non-specific awareness; and the Ra (waking) level representing individuated consciousness capable of self-reference and personal identity [2]. Consider how this three-level cosmology provides the essential metaphysical framework for understanding how consciousness can discover its transpersonal nature while maintaining functional capacity in the manifest world.

# Conclusion

The fundamental conflicts that characterize human life emerge not from any inherent limitation in existence but from the condition of consciousness forgetting its divine nature and identifying with the temporary phenomena of body-mind experience (what the ancient sages understood as the root cause of all psychological suffering). When consciousness discovers its essential nature as the Soul-Aware-Witness through the practices revealed in the ancient Egyptian wisdom scriptures—the threefold path of ethical living, philosophical study, and meditation that gradually purifies the aryu patterns—these contradictions dissolve in the recognition that all experiences arise within the one consciousness that is the true Self of all beings. As the ancient sages taught, this represents not the elimination of individual experience but its transformation from ego-driven reactivity to soul-directed expression in service of divine will.

This recognition of life's fundamental contradictions and their resolution through the Soul-Aware-Witness naturally leads us to examine the ancient wisdom sources that preserve these profound psychological insights. These teachings emerge not from abstract philosophical speculation but from the direct experiential investigations of consciousness conducted by the ancient Egyptian sages over millennia. The following foundational texts provide both the theoretical framework and practical methodology for understanding consciousness development—revelations that remain as relevant for contemporary seekers as they were for ancient practitioners of Shetaut Neter.

# Important Proviso for Students and Practitioners

This work presents the philosophical teachings of Shetaut Neter (Ancient Egyptian spirituality) as a comprehensive treatise designed to illuminate the profound wisdom of the neteru (gods and goddesses) and the timeless principles of Maat. Indeed, these teachings have been preserved through millennia as a guide for spiritual understanding and personal transformation. Nevertheless, aspirants must recognize that this text serves primarily as a philosophical foundation and study guide rather than a standalone therapeutic manual for self-directed spiritual work.

The ancient sages of Kemet (Ancient Egypt) understood that authentic spiritual development requires not merely intellectual comprehension but also proper guidance, community support, and gradual implementation under experienced mentorship. Consider how the temple traditions always emphasized the relationship between teacher and student, recognizing that the path of spiritual awakening (nehast) involves both study and guided practice. This means that while this book provides essential philosophical frameworks and practical insights, the most effective application occurs when these teachings are explored within the context of structured discussion, spiritual mentoring, or guided group study.

Contemporary practitioners of Shetaut Neter will find that the wisdom contained herein serves as an invaluable reference and contemplative resource; however, those seeking therapeutic applications or intensive spiritual transformation should understand that such work benefits greatly from the support of qualified teachers, counselors, or spiritual guides who can provide personalized guidance appropriate to individual circumstances and spiritual development. In other words, this treatise offers the philosophical foundation upon which deeper practice may be built, but it represents the beginning rather than the entirety of the spiritual journey.

Therefore, readers are encouraged to approach these teachings with both reverence for their transformative potential and wisdom regarding their proper application. The path of spiritual development, as taught by the ancient Egyptian sages, unfolds most safely and effectively when pursued with appropriate guidance, community support, and gradual, mindful implementation of these profound principles.

# References

[1] Ashby, M. (2016). Egyptian Book of the Dead Hieroglyph Translations for Enlightenment: Understanding the Mystic Path to Enlightenment Through Direct Readings of the Sacred Signs and Symbols of Ancient Egyptian Language With Trilinear Deciphering Translation Method Vol. 1. Translation by Dr. Muata Ashby. Sema Institute.

[2] Ashby, M. (2022). The Mysteries of Ra and Hetheru/Sekhmet. Translation by Dr. Muata Ashby. Sema Institute.

[3] Ashby, M. (2025). The Complete Glorious Light Meditation Volume 1: The Ancient Egyptian Scripture of Hathor and Ra and the Glorious Light Meditation. Translation by Dr. Muata Ashby. Sema Institute.

[4] Ashby, M. (2019). Teachings of Ancient Egyptian Sage Amenemopet with Hieroglyphic texts. Translation by Dr. Muata Ashby. Sema Institute.

# Essential Concepts: A Progressive Introduction to Ancient Egyptian Spiritual Psychology

Before exploring the profound teachings contained within these sacred texts, aspirants require a clear understanding of the fundamental concepts that form the foundation of Ancient Egyptian spiritual psychology. Consider how the ancient sages designed their wisdom teachings to guide consciousness from familiar experiences toward recognition of its divine nature through systematic understanding rather than mystical confusion.

## The Foundation: Understanding Consciousness Itself

Consciousness represents the most fundamental reality from which all experience emerges [1]. In the tradition of Shetaut Neter (the Ancient Egyptian spiritual path), consciousness does not belong to individuals but rather manifests as the universal divine essence that operates through all beings and all phenomena. The ancient sages taught that what we typically call "our consciousness" actually represents the one universal consciousness temporarily expressing itself through individual mind-body systems.

Conscious-awareness, by contrast, refers to consciousness operating through the conditioning, experiences, and limitations of human personality [2]. This includes the thoughts, emotions, preferences, and reactions that emerge from personal history, cultural influences, and accumulated life experiences. Indeed, most people spend their entire lives identifying with conscious-awareness while remaining unaware of the pure consciousness that serves as its foundation.

Consider how this distinction proves essential for spiritual development: conscious-awareness changes constantly throughout life, while consciousness itself remains eternally unchanged. Nevertheless, recognizing this difference requires what the teachings describe as philosophical discrimination—the capacity to distinguish between the temporary modifications of awareness and the unchanging awareness that makes all experience possible.

## The Divine Principles: Neteru as Psychological Realities

The Neteru (pronounced "Net-er-oo") represent one of the most important concepts in Ancient Egyptian wisdom [3] and cosmology. Often translated as "gods and goddesses," the Neteru function as cosmic principles that operate both throughout the universe and within human consciousness. In other words, the Neteru are not external deities only to be worshipped, but through worship and philosophical insight into their nature, they can be discovered to be aspects of our own deeper psychological and spiritual nature that can be awakened and integrated so as to lead to integrated discovery of higher levels of consciousness.

Ra serves as the central Neteru, representing divine consciousness that has individuated while maintaining recognition of its universal nature [3]. As the ancient sages taught, Ra consciousness corresponds to awakened individuality—the capacity to function as a distinct personality while recognizing one's essential unity with all existence. Contemporary practitioners can understand Ra as the divine aspect of individual consciousness that operates through wisdom rather than ego-driven patterns.

Asar (pronounced "Ah-sar"), known in Greek as Osiris, represents the universal soul that operates as the true identity of all beings [1]. The tradition teaches that every spiritual practitioner is actually an "Asar" expressing through their given personality name. Therefore, when the ancient texts refer to "Asar Any" or "Asar Someone," they indicate that the person's true identity is universal soul consciousness (Asar) temporarily manifesting through individual form (Any or Someone).

Hetheru (pronounced "Het-her-oo"), known in Greek as Hathor, embodies divine love, creative joy, and the nurturing feminine principle of Ra that maintains cosmic harmony [3]. Nevertheless, the Scripture reveals how Hetheru can transform into Sekhemit (pronounced "Sekh-eh-mit"), the fierce lioness goddess who represents consciousness that has become constricted through focus on a particular name and form, leading to heated mental states and forgetfulness of universal nature.

## The Spiritual Framework: Core Principles for Development

Maat (pronounced "Mah-aht") represents divine order, truth, and righteous living that aligns individual actions with cosmic harmony [4]. The ancient sages taught that following Maat creates what we might call "light aryu"—mental impressions that remain transparent to divine light rather than obstructing spiritual development. In practical terms, Maat encompasses ethical conduct, truthful speech, and actions motivated by wisdom rather than selfishness.

Aryu (pronounced "Ah-rioo") refer to the mental impressions or karmic residues that accumulate in the unconscious mind from past experiences, thoughts, and actions [3]. These impressions function like seeds that sprout into future experiences, determining whether consciousness operates from wisdom or delusion, peace or agitation. The tradition teaches that spiritual practice aims to purify negative aryu while cultivating positive impressions that support divine recognition.

Consider how aryu operate: every thought, emotion, and action create subtle impressions in the unconscious mind that influence future mental and emotional responses. Heavy aryu, created through actions against Maat, cloud consciousness and create automatic reactive patterns. Light aryu, generated through righteous living, allow divine consciousness to flow freely through the personality without obstruction—thereby allowing divine inspiration to manifest in human conscious-awareness.

# HEKAU (Words of Power): Sacred Technology for Consciousness Transformation

**Primary Definition:** Hekau represents "divine utterance, prayer" that enables "the divine word allows the speaker to control the gods and goddesses, i.e. the cosmic forces"—functioning as transformative instruments designed to overcome obstacles and fundamentally alter the practitioner's conscious awareness and spiritual identity.

**Essential Nature:** Consider how the Scripture of Ra and Hetheru reveals that hekau are "direct embodiments of divine presence" rather than merely symbolic representations. When Ra declares: "Those Words-of-Power, they are indeed my very self... I am in those Words-of-Power," this indicates that the boundary between the divine and sacred utterance dissolves—each word becomes a vehicle of Ra's actual presence.

**Transformative Function:** The wisdom of the neteru illuminates that hekau function as "divine vibrations that, when properly understood and expressed, carry the creative force of Ra (Creator Spirit) himself." These sacred declarations represent far more than mere recitations; they operate as spiritual technology that systematically redirects consciousness away from the delusion of separate existence toward recognition of unity with divine consciousness.

**Requirements for Efficacy:** Nevertheless, the effectiveness of hekau depends entirely upon what the ancient sages called Maa-kheru (truth-speaking)—not simply speaking truthfully in the conventional sense but rather speaking from conscious-awareness aligned with Divine Truth. Indeed, this means the practitioner's consciousness must be sufficiently purified before creative power can properly manifest.

**Practical Applications:** The hieroglyphic texts become "hekau—the Ancient Egyptian 'Words of Power'—when the word is Hesi, chanted and Shmai-sung and thereby one performs Dua or worship of the Divine." This includes systematic affirmation practices beginning with declarations like "I am the Divine word of power" and culminating in ultimate realizations such as "I am Ra."

In other words, hekau represents both the power inherent in divine speech and the transformative capacity of these words to reshape consciousness itself, serving as essential spiritual technology for authentic consciousness development in the tradition of Shetaut Neter.

Shetaut Neter literally means "the hidden teachings of the Divine" and represents the complete spiritual tradition of Ancient Egypt [4]. This encompasses not merely religious beliefs but a comprehensive science of consciousness development that includes ethical guidelines, philosophical study, meditation practices, and ritual technologies designed to facilitate spiritual awakening.

## The Consciousness Levels: A Framework for Spiritual Recognition

The Scripture of Ra and Hetheru reveals that consciousness manifests through three distinct yet interconnected levels that provide the essential framework for understanding human psychology and spiritual development [3]. Indeed, recognizing these levels transforms abstract spiritual concepts into practical wisdom for daily spiritual practice.

Soul of Ra represents pure consciousness without subject-object awareness—the absolute foundation that underlies all experience while remaining unmodified by any particular content [3]. This level transcends even the concept of awareness itself, existing as what the ancient sages might refer to as "beingness without qualification." Nevertheless, Soul of Ra consciousness cannot be achieved through mental effort but emerges naturally when all obstacles to its recognition are removed.

Nunu (pronounced "Noo-noo") encompasses undifferentiated consciousness that maintains awareness without specific focus [3]. This represents the cosmic substrate from which all manifestation emerges and into which it dissolves—like the ocean that contains all waves without being disturbed by any particular wave formation. Nunu consciousness functions as spacious, open awareness that encompasses all mental activity without concentrating on particular contents.

Ra consciousness encompasses individuated divine awareness capable of self-reference and personal identity while maintaining recognition of its essential unity with universal consciousness [3]. This level allows consciousness to function effectively in the world of relationships and responsibilities while operating from wisdom rather than ego-driven patterns. The tradition teaches that Ra consciousness represents the optimal level for most daily activities and spiritual service.

## The Spiritual Challenge: Heated Mind versus Silent Mind

The wisdom teachings reveal that mind operates through two fundamental modes that determine the quality of all human experience [4]. Heated mind (shemm) manifests through agitation, control-seeking, and perception of separateness that emerges when consciousness forgets its divine nature. Silent mind (ger) operates from recognition of essential unity, creating natural peace and wisdom that flows from remembering one's true spiritual identity.

Ancient Egyptian Sage Amenemopet taught that "heated" persons (heated personality) live "by unrighteousness, fraud, anger, boisterousness, flippant retorts and thoughtless speech, inconsiderate and impulsive acts, rapacious greed, jealousy, envy" [4]. This heated condition creates what the Scripture of Ra and Hetheru describes as "the fire of suffering" where consciousness becomes trapped in endless cycles of seeking satisfaction through external means. This type of personality can devolve to being exploitative, rapacious, narcissistic, predatory, thievish, and even murderous.

Silent persons, by contrast, discover what Amenemopet calls "the fullness of the Creator-Spirit that is within" rather than seeking fulfillment through heated engagement with worldly phenomena

[4]. This silence represents not mere absence of speech but the establishment of consciousness in its natural divine nature where genuine satisfaction becomes self-evident.

# The First Important Spiritual Goal: The Soul-Aware-Witness

The Soul-Aware-Witness represents an intermediate developmental stage of consciousness that emerges when awareness has successfully separated from ego-identification but has not yet achieved full recognition of its ultimate nature as Amun-Ra, the universal witness consciousness. As described in Chapter 5, this stage manifests when "universal consciousness supports its true nature (Asar soul consciousness) such that the person becomes aware of their Asar soul nature simultaneously with being aware of the thoughts, feelings, perceptions and sensations of the body." This represents a profound shift from ego-conscious-awareness to soul-level awareness, where the practitioner has discovered themselves to be separate from the mind's thoughts, feelings, desires, and bodily sensations, yet functions as what Chapter 4 describes as "consciousness that has achieved separation from ego-identification and now operates as the vehicle and instrument of soul expression."

The Soul-Aware-Witness is a development in the human mind that serves as a reflection of or window through which the unlimited witness consciousness (Amun-Ra), operating in its highest development as what Chapter 5 characterizes as "a transparent mirror through which the true natural witness-consciousness can operate as the identity that perceives and is aware through the mind, senses, and body of that personality." This stage is evidenced by the declarations found in Chapter 26: "my heart, he is peaceful within me," "I know myself," and "I have control over my arms and legs (body)"—statements that reveal consciousness functioning from inner peace and self-knowledge rather than reactive ego-patterns. While this represents a crucial awakening from the suffocation of ego-identification, it remains a developmental phase that naturally progresses toward full recognition of one's essential nature as the unchanging witness consciousness that underlies all experience, serving as an essential bridge between ego-bound awareness and ultimate spiritual realization.

The ultimate aim of these teachings involves discovering what may be termed the Soul-Aware-Witness—consciousness that has separated itself from ego-identification and now operates as the vehicle and instrument of soul expression [1]. This represents the awakening of awareness of not being an ego personality but rather divine consciousness temporarily manifesting through individual form.

The ancient texts describe this transformation through the practitioner's recognition: "my heart, he is peaceful within me," "I know myself," and "I have control over my arms and legs (body)" [1]. Indeed, these declarations reveal consciousness that has achieved separation from ego-patterns and now functions from inner peace, self-knowledge, and appropriate self-control rather than reactive patterns.

## The Practical Method: Trilinear Understanding

Throughout this study, we encounter the revolutionary trilinear translation method, which provides three levels of understanding for each ancient text passage [3]. The phonetic transliteration preserves approximate Ancient Egyptian sounds; the word-for-word translation maintains ancient grammatical structure; and the contextual translation incorporates philosophical concepts, mythological references, and cultural insights necessary for contemporary practitioners.

Consider how this methodology serves spiritual development rather than mere academic study: each level progressively deepens understanding while preserving the transformative power embedded within the original hieroglyphic scriptures. The ancient sages understood that consciousness operates through multiple levels of recognition, much like the trilinear system reveals multiple levels of textual meaning.

With these fundamental concepts established as our foundation, we can now explore how the ancient Egyptian wisdom scriptures provide a complete framework for transpersonal psychology and the practical discovery of our essential divine nature. The following teachings emerge not from abstract philosophical speculation but from the direct experiential investigations of consciousness conducted by the ancient sages over millennia—revelations that remain as relevant for contemporary seekers as they were for ancient practitioners of Shetaut Neter.

# Chapter 1: Foundations - The Ancient Wisdom Sources

## The Source of Creation Revealed

**The Source of Creation Revealed**

Before examining the foundational texts that illuminate the path of consciousness development, aspirants must understand the ultimate source from which all spiritual teachings emerge. Indeed, this understanding provides the essential context within which all consciousness transformation occurs. The ancient Egyptian wisdom tradition establishes that genuine spiritual development cannot be comprehended apart from recognizing the fundamental nature of existence itself. This reality the sages called Neberdjer—the All-Encompassing Divinity that serves as both the source and substance of all manifestation.

In the following Ancient Egyptian Scripture of the Creation, a momentous revelation emerges that provides the essential foundation for every teaching explored throughout this study. This scripture reveals not only the name of the Source of Creation but also the profound mystery of how this ultimate reality manifests within Creation itself. In other words, it establishes the non-dual framework that underlies all authentic spiritual understanding. Indeed, what aspirants discover through this ancient wisdom is that the very consciousness seeking enlightenment and the goal of enlightenment represent different aspects of the same ultimate reality. This means that what appears as seeker and sought, student and teaching, individual awareness and cosmic consciousness are temporarily appearing as multiplicity while remaining eternally unified in essence.

# Ancient Egyptian Anunian Creation Scripture Version B– translation by Dr. Muata Ashby

Verse 20.
- **20.1.** djedu  Neberdjer  djed  f
- 20.2. words spoken  Lord-of-All  speaks-he-himself
- 20.3. the following words are by Neberdjer (Lord-of-All/All-encompassing divinity), he himself speaks thus:

**20.4.**
- **20.5.** pa  n-a  iu  pautetu  suh pa  n-a
- 20.6. this of-me it-is primeval-matter{Div}egg this of-me
- 20.7. "This is made of me, it is the {Divine} primeval matter, the stuff that everything is made of, this "primeval stuff", i.e. undifferentiated consciousness, was as if an egg and it was made out of me.

Verse 21.
- **21.4.** im  pautetu  {net}  pa  ren  a  Ausarz
- 21.5. within primeval-matter {Div} this name mine  Osiris
- 21.6. Within that primeval matter, that became the {Divine} Creation, I reside in my name Osiris.

This profound declaration establishes the foundational understanding that underlies all subsequent teachings. Consider how this teaching provides the essential context within which every aspect of consciousness development must be comprehended. Neberdjer—literally meaning "Lord of the Limits" or "All-Encompassing Divinity"—reveals itself as the ultimate reality that both transcends all boundaries while simultaneously manifesting as everything that appears within those boundaries. This means that rather than seeking to connect with something separate from themselves, aspirants discover that they are expressions of the very divinity they seek to know.

The scripture reveals that Neberdjer functions as both the material cause and efficient cause of all existence. As the ancient sages taught: "This is made of me, it is the Divine primeval matter, the stuff that everything is made of." Nevertheless, Neberdjer also expresses itself through the principle of Asar (Osiris) as the universal soul operating within Creation. This means that every aspect of consciousness development explored throughout this manuscript occurs within Neberdjer and represents Neberdjer's own process of self-recognition through apparent individual localized forms. In other words, the Soul-Aware-Witness, the three levels of consciousness (Ra, Nunu, Soul of Ra), aryu purification, and the transformation mechanics all represent movements within the infinite field of divine consciousness.

Indeed, this recognition provides the essential context for understanding how consciousness can discover its true nature beyond individual identification. What appears as personal spiritual development actually represents universal consciousness (Neberdjer) awakening to its own nature through the vehicle of human awareness. The ancient sages taught that this understanding prevents the fundamental error of spiritual seeking—imagining oneself as a separate entity attempting to reach some distant divine goal. Consider how this reveals that the seeker, the seeking, and the goal are all modifications of the same All-Encompassing Divinity temporarily appearing as multiplicity while remaining eternally unified in essence.

Therefore, as aspirants explore the profound teachings contained within the Scripture of Ra and Hetheru, the wisdom of Sage Amenemopet, and the Ancient Egyptian Book of Enlightenment, they must remember that these texts do not describe processes external to their essential nature. Rather, these teachings illuminate the mechanisms by which Neberdjer recognizes itself through the apparent journey from ignorance to enlightenment. This means that the heated mind and silent mind, the ego construct and Soul-Aware-Witness, the cosmic transformation from Sekhemit to Hetheru—all these represent movements within the infinite field of Neberdjer consciousness. This understanding provides the cosmic context that ensures our study serves authentic awakening rather than mere intellectual understanding.

This foundational recognition naturally leads us to examine the ancient wisdom sources that preserve these profound psychological insights. Indeed, each source contributes essential elements to our understanding of how universal consciousness manifests through individual experience while maintaining its essential unity as the All-Encompassing Divinity that is both the beginning and end of all spiritual aspiration.

## The Ancient Egyptian Discovery of Consciousness

Human beings throughout history experience awareness and consciousness in relation to their thought processing of information from sensations and perceptions. Most human beings carry out these processes taking for granted that such processes are intrinsic to human life and derived from the body and its capacity to react to sensations and perceptions in ways that promote wellbeing and comfort. Nevertheless, they remain unaware of the fundamental basis of their thought processes or what their perceptions and sensations mean beyond obvious or superficial appearances.

Earlier than any other culture in human history that we know of, the Ancient Egyptians discovered and extensively documented the nature of mind and consciousness—the source of motivation to feel and act in the world. The Ancient Egyptian Book of Enlightenment (Book of Coming Forth into the Light) contains several passages that show the recognition of concepts related to observed human experience. In other words, these texts reveal understanding of what contemporary psychology terms self-awareness and consciousness that observes the mind.

In Chapter 30B Verses 3-4– translation by Dr. Muata Ashby, a passage expresses fundamental understanding about mind, its role in motivating human beings to actions, and the presence of an overwatch awareness. This awareness proves capable of controlling the ordinary mind and the mental motivations that urge most people toward robotic ways of thinking, feeling, and acting. Consider the profound implications of this ancient psychological insight:

Awakening Your Soul-Aware-Witness

Verse 1.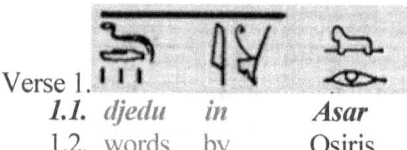
  1.1. *djedu*   *in*   **Asar**
  1.2. words    by     Osiris
  1.3. These are the words this person who is an Osiris, a human being whose source is the Divine God Osiris.

Verse 2.
  2.1. *sesh*   **Any**
  2.2. scribe   Any
  2.3. he is a scribe, and he goes by the name "Any"

Verse 3.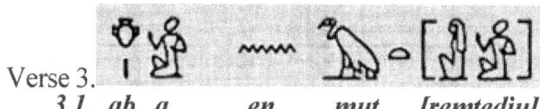
  3.1. *ab  a   en   mut   [remtedju]*
  3.2. heart mine the    mother [people]
  3.3. He says: "**my heart**, that is, my feeling memories (aryu), based on the past thoughts, feelings, desires and experiences, this is the mother of all human experiences."

Verse 4.
  4.1. *sep-sen haty a  en  kheperu   [a]*
  4.2. twice volition (of) mind mine creations [mine]
  4.3. This is doubly true, so it is repeated twice. It is from this heart that the emergent thoughts, feelings, and desires, in my mind that impel and compel one to actions, thoughts and feelings that create the circumstances, relations, and experiences in life.

Consider the implications of Chapter 30B verses 3-4. It signifies that there exists a mind that serves as the source of motivations in a person's life. The "ab" is an Ancient Egyptian hieroglyph symbolizing a "storage vase" that functions as a storehouse of aryu (impressions of past thoughts, feelings, experiences, memories—similar to what would be referred to as "karma" in India)—the repository from which arise impulses, impetuses, and compulsions that direct a person's feelings, desires, and thoughts about the world they inhabit. This means that the heart contains the causal mechanisms that determine how consciousness expresses itself through individual experience.

The following verse from Chapter 30A of the Pert-m-Heru contains a variation of the chapter theme related to the heart [1][1]:

Verse 1.

1.1. *Ab–a en mut - a zepsen hatyab–a en un–a dep ta*

1.2. Heart mine the   mother mine  repeat twice. Heart -mine (cause) of existing-I on earth.

1.3. My heart, my mother, my heart, my mother. My heart which is the mother which gives birth to my desires that cause my soul's coming into human incarnation on the surface of the earth.

The text makes a clear distinction between the common referent term "I" that most people use to refer to their mind, thoughts, feelings, memories, and body, and the essential subject "I" that remains present even when there are no thoughts, feelings, or memories. In this case, the "I" represents that subject of awareness that exists separate from the mind and body. This means that the ancient sages recognized the witness consciousness that contemporary transpersonal psychology has rediscovered.

This passage informs us that the heart of a person serves as the cause of their existence on earth—why they find themselves as living human beings on planet earth [1]. The heart contains something that provides the impetus, the motivation for why a person finds themselves experiencing human life and living the particular life circumstances they encounter. Indeed, the verse presents this understanding from the perspective of a subject who speaks of "my heart" and "my mother" as items that they possess rather than as aspects that intrinsically constitute the subject itself.

In other words, the subject who speaks refers to the heart as a source of motivation separate from the subject "I" who observes the heart's

---

[1] Translation by Dr. Muata Ashby

operations. The "something" that the heart contains is called aryu—the residues of past thoughts, feelings, experiences, and memories that influence (impel and compel) current thoughts and feelings in the personality. This means that aryu function as the psychological mechanisms that link past experience with present consciousness, creating what appears as individual personality patterns while obscuring recognition of the unchanging witness awareness that observes these patterns.

The perspective emerges from a subject that observes the situation of human existence on earth and its cause from a standpoint of detachment. The observer standpoint recognizes the heart as a motivating factor rather than the subject "I" as the source of motivation. That "I" represents the witness-consciousness that constitutes the higher reality of human consciousness, though not yet fully realized. This represents what may be termed the independent knower of the possessions it has (heart and mind) which have served as the cause motivating the "I" to find itself having particular experiences.

The realization by the subject "I" of higher consciousness—which may also be referred to as "Soul-Aware-Witness"—represents a purified egoic state where the aspirant observes their heart and mind as separate objects from itself rather than identifying with them as "self." This recognition affords the opportunity to view the heart and its contents (thoughts, feelings, desires, memories) from a detached point of view. This detachment necessarily provides the opportunity to experience oneself apart from those contents of mind, thereby experiencing oneself as an entity separate from and above the mind. Consider how this contrasts with the condition of most people, who experience the "I" of higher consciousness as an individual entangled with the mind and its vicissitudes in such a way that consciousness thinks it is the self-identity presented by the mind [1].

In such a case, the person living on earth would not have a sense of a part of themselves that exists separate from their mind. Their mind, its thoughts and memories would constitute their complete identity, and there would be no higher awareness—just ordinary human awareness driven by the mind's motivations. This condition may be termed as a state of khemn (ignorance) driven by human animal instinct. Nevertheless, the ancient sages revealed that this represents only the surface level of consciousness, beneath which lies the eternal witness that observes all changing phenomena without being affected by them.

## The Ordinary Human Identity: Understanding the Ego Construct as Baseline

Before exploring the profound implications of the ancient Egyptian distinction between ordinary awareness and higher consciousness, aspirants must first establish a clear understanding of what constitutes the typical human identity. This ordinary human identity represents what most people refer to when they speak of "I" or "myself." Indeed, this ordinary human identity represents the psychological foundation from which the vast majority of human beings operate throughout their lives. This identity serves as the baseline against which we can appreciate the revolutionary nature of the consciousness discoveries preserved in the ancient Egyptian wisdom texts.

From a psychological perspective, the ordinary human identity—what may be termed the "ego construct"—represents the complex of accumulated experiences, memories, thoughts, emotions, beliefs, preferences, and learned responses that crystallize into what consciousness experiences as a coherent sense of personal selfhood. Consider how this identity formation occurs naturally and necessarily during human development. The infant gradually learns to distinguish between "self" and "other," developing the capacity to recognize their reflection in mirrors, respond to their name, and maintain a continuous sense of being the same person despite the constant changes occurring in body and mind throughout the developmental process.

This ego identity serves essential psychological functions that enable human beings to navigate the complexities of social existence. In other words, it allows consciousness to maintain personal relationships, pursue goals and aspirations, and fulfill the practical responsibilities required for survival and flourishing in the material world. Indeed, the development of a stable ego identity represents a crucial psychological achievement that allows consciousness to operate effectively through the individual mind-body system while maintaining the sense of personal continuity that makes meaningful life choices and commitments possible.

Nevertheless, the wisdom of the neteru reveals that psychological difficulties emerge when this necessary functional identity becomes the exclusive understanding of self. This creates what the ancient sages recognized as the fundamental delusion underlying all human suffering. When consciousness completely identifies with the accumulated patterns of thoughts, emotions, memories, and bodily sensations rather than recognizing these as temporary modifications occurring within a deeper field of awareness, the result manifests as what contemporary psychology might recognize as various forms of identity confusion, existential anxiety, and the persistent sense of incompleteness that drives endless seeking for fulfillment through external means.

The situation becomes even more problematic when the ego construct develops what may be termed "spiritual disconnection"—a condition that emerges through what the ancient teachings describe as excessive egoism. In such cases, the sense of separate selfhood becomes so dominant that it obscures any recognition of the universal consciousness that serves as both the source and foundation of individual awareness. This means that the ego identity becomes increasingly rigid, defensive, and reactive, creating the psychological conditions that the ancient sages associated with what Sage Amenemopet describes as the "heated personality." This represents consciousness trapped in patterns of agitation, control-seeking, and separation that generate suffering both for the individual and those around them.

Consider how this disconnection manifests through what contemporary understanding might recognize as narcissistic patterns, where the ego construct becomes so inflated that it demands constant validation and external support while remaining incapable of recognizing the legitimate needs and perspectives of others. This represents consciousness that has become completely absorbed in the temporary phenomena of personal identity while losing all connection to the deeper awareness that the ancient Egyptian texts reveal as the true foundation of human existence.

The ancient sages understood that this ordinary ego identity, while necessary for practical functioning, represents only the surface level of human consciousness. This may be compared to the waves on the ocean that appear separate and distinct while remaining fundamentally composed of the same underlying water. The revolutionary insight preserved in the ancient Egyptian wisdom texts involves the recognition that beneath this surface level of ego identification exists a deeper level of awareness that remains unchanged by the constant modifications of thoughts, emotions, and experiences that characterize ordinary psychological functioning.

This deeper awareness—what the ancient texts refer to as the "I" that can observe the heart and its contents from a position of detachment—represents the foundation for understanding how consciousness can transcend the limitations of ego identification while maintaining full capacity for effective functioning in the world of relationships and responsibilities. Nevertheless, discovering this witness consciousness requires what the tradition describes as systematic purification of the ego patterns that obscure recognition of our essential nature as divine awareness temporarily manifesting through individual human form.

Therefore, as aspirants examine the central themes emerging from the ancient wisdom sources, they must remember that these teachings address the transformation of consciousness from identification with the ordinary ego construct toward recognition of the Soul-Aware-Witness that represents our deeper spiritual identity. This transformation does not involve eliminating the functional ego but rather establishing our primary identity in the unchanging awareness that observes all changing phenomena while using the ego as the instrument through which divine consciousness expresses itself in daily life circumstances.

**Central Themes for Transpersonal Psychology**

Having established the three foundational sources, the essential themes that emerge from these texts, particularly from the Scripture of Ra and Hetheru, now require examination as they provide the framework for this transpersonal psychology study [2]. Understanding these themes proves essential for grasping how ancient Egyptian spiritual psychology addresses the fundamental questions of consciousness, identity, and spiritual transformation.

## The Three-Level Consciousness Cosmology

The Three-Level Consciousness Cosmology forms the essential metaphysical framework used throughout this book [2]. The scripture teaches that consciousness manifests in three distinct yet interconnected modalities. These include Soul of Ra representing pure consciousness without subject-object differentiation; Nunu representing undifferentiated consciousness with non-specific awareness; and Ra representing individuated consciousness capable of self-reference and personal identity. This cosmological understanding provides the foundation for comprehending how human consciousness can discover its essential nature beyond ego-identification [2]. Indeed, as the ancient sages taught, these three levels represent progressive refinements of the same divine awareness expressing itself through different degrees of manifestation.

## The Heated versus Silent Mind Teaching

The Heated versus Silent Mind Teaching emerges as a central psychological instruction in the scripture [3]. The text reveals how consciousness operates in two fundamental modes. The heated state (shemm) characterizes consciousness through agitation, egoism, and perception of separateness. The silent state (ger) characterizes consciousness through peace, recognition of unity, and natural wisdom. This teaching provides the practical framework for understanding how consciousness moves from ego-identification to witness awareness [3]. Consider how this distinction offers aspirants a clear methodology for recognizing when consciousness has become trapped in ego patterns versus when it rests in its natural state of unity awareness.

## The Sekhemit Transformation Process

The Sekhemit Transformation Process, in the Scripture of Ra and Hetheru, presents a detailed map of how consciousness becomes trapped in ego-identification and how it can be liberated through proper understanding and practice [2]. The scripture shows how Hetheru's transformation into the fierce lioness Sekhemit represents consciousness becoming constricted through focus on a particular name and form, leading to forgetfulness of its universal nature. The subsequent restoration through the setjert drink provides the methodology for consciousness to remember its essential divine nature [2]. This means that the Sekhemit process offers both a warning about how consciousness becomes deluded and a complete method for restoration to its original divine awareness.

## The Witness Consciousness Teaching

The Witness-Consciousness is the background unchanging awareness (God/Spirit/Absolute) that sustains the human mind. This teaching reveals how the Soul-Aware-Witness emerges, through increasing mental clarity, in the form of the recognition of an unchanging existence—that one is not the agitated heart, reactive body, or struggling ego, but rather the unchanging awareness that observes all changing phenomena without being affected by them [1]. The scripture demonstrates how this witness consciousness stabilizes as the permanent foundation of identity through sustained practice and philosophical discrimination [1]. In other words, the aspirant learns to recognize that their essential nature remains untouched by the constant modifications of thoughts, emotions, and experiences that characterize ordinary psychological functioning.

## The Integration of Ancient Wisdom and Contemporary Understanding

These themes from the Scripture of Ra and Hetheru provide both the theoretical framework and practical methodology for understanding how consciousness can transcend ego-identification and discover its essential nature as divine awareness [2]. The following chapters will explore how these ancient teachings offer profound insights into contemporary transpersonal psychology and provide a complete system for spiritual transformation that remains as relevant today as it was thousands of years ago [2].

This ancient wisdom represents not mere historical curiosity but rather a sophisticated understanding of consciousness development that addresses the deepest questions of human psychology and spiritual potential. Indeed, the integration of these teachings with contemporary understanding reveals how the ancient Egyptian sages anticipated and provided solutions for the fundamental challenges that continue to characterize human psychological and spiritual development.

Having examined the foundational sources that preserve the ancient wisdom, the specific metaphysical framework that emerges from these texts—particularly from the Scripture of Ra and Hetheru—now requires deeper investigation [2]. These ancient teachings provide not merely historical curiosities but a sophisticated cosmological map of consciousness itself. The three foundational treatises reveal a consistent understanding of how awareness manifests through distinct yet interconnected levels, creating what may be termed the earliest comprehensive psychology of consciousness development ever recorded. This metaphysical framework serves as the essential foundation for comprehending how human consciousness can transcend its apparent limitations and discover its true divine nature [2].

**Conclusion**

The foundational wisdom explored in this chapter reveals the essential framework through which consciousness can transcend the limitations of ego-identification and discover its true divine nature as the very foundation of existence itself. The profound declaration of Neberdjer (the All-Encompassing Divinity)—"This is made of me, it is the Divine primeval matter, the stuff that everything is made of" followed by "Within that primeval matter, that became the Divine Creation, I reside in my name Osiris"—establishes the fundamental understanding that both the source and substance of all manifestation emerge from the same ultimate reality [1][2][3].

This recognition provides the essential context for comprehending how human consciousness, having forgotten its divine source, becomes trapped through what the ancient sages termed aryu (karmic impressions or feeling memories). These represent accumulated patterns of thoughts, feelings, desires, and behaviors that remain registered in the unconscious mind (which the scriptures identify as the "heart") and function as the motivating force behind all human experience on earth [1]. Indeed, these aryu operate as the precise psychological mechanism that either perpetuates what Sage Amenemopet describes as the "heated personality" (shemm) or allows for the emergence of the "silent personality" (ger) that naturally recognizes unity and discovers "the fullness of the Creator-Spirit that is within" [4].

The heated personality manifests through "corrupted mind, unrighteousness, fraud, anger, boisterousness" and other contrary dispositions that seek fulfillment through heated engagement with worldly phenomena. In contrast, the silent personality naturally recognizes the divine essence that constitutes consciousness itself. This means that the transformation from heated to silent consciousness occurs through the systematic "cutting away of the heart's dispositions that are contrary to goodness and enlightenment" [4].

This process enables the aspirant to recognize that the witness consciousness observing these mental-emotional patterns represents not the struggling ego-personality but rather the unchanging awareness that is one's essential nature as Asar—and therefore as Neberdjer itself expressing through individual form [1][2][4]. This ancient psychological framework thus provides contemporary practitioners with both the theoretical foundation and practical methodology for understanding how consciousness moves from ego-identification to the direct recognition of its divine source.

Nevertheless, this recognition reveals that what appears as individual spiritual development actually represents universal consciousness recognizing its own nature through the apparent multiplicity of individual forms. Therefore, this complete system offers aspirants the means for transcending the heated mind's perception of separateness and establishing themselves permanently in the silent recognition of unity that constitutes authentic spiritual realization.

## References

[1] Ashby, M. (2016). Egyptian Book of the Dead Hieroglyph Translations for Enlightenment: Understanding the Mystic Path to Enlightenment Through Direct Readings of the Sacred Signs and Symbols of Ancient

Egyptian Language With Trilinear Deciphering Translation Method Vol. 1. Translation by Dr. Muata Ashby. Sema Institute.

[2] Ashby, M. (2022). The Mysteries of Ra and Hetheru/Sekhmet. Translation by Dr. Muata Ashby. Sema Institute.

[3] Ashby, M. (2019). Teachings of Ancient Egyptian Sage Amenemopet with Hieroglyphic texts. Translation by Dr. Muata Ashby. Sema Institute.

# Chapter 2: The Metaphysical Framework - The Three Levels of Consciousness Cosmology

## The Cosmos as the Dream Creation of Universal Consciousness

Verses 6-8 of the Scripture of Ra and Hetheru mention how Ra and his company of gods and goddesses existed in the Nunu before arising and before Creation was formed [1]. This passage suggests a profound understanding about the nature of manifest reality. Figuratively, the Nunu can be considered as the unconscious level of cosmic mind, and Ra represents the first individuation. The other gods and goddesses may be understood as unconscious impressions (cosmic aryu) of Ra's volitions and divine intents.

In this way, by analogy, Creation appears to function as a dream world ideation by Ra. This resembles how a person creates a dreamworld at night, springing forth dream experiences from their own previously undifferentiated consciousness. Consider how this analogy illuminates other implications based on the themes that emerge from these ancient texts. This understanding finds support in the Ancient Egyptian Harper song, which indicates that "life is but a moment of a dream" [2].

**The Dream of Creation: Ra's Emergence from Nunu and the Nature of Manifest Existence**

**An Analysis of Cosmic and Individual Consciousness in Ancient Egyptian Sacred Texts**

The Scripture of Ra and Hetheru presents what appears to be a sophisticated understanding of the relationship between undifferentiated consciousness (Nunu) and individuated consciousness (Ra) [1]. This framework reveals fascinating parallels in the human experience of dreaming and waking consciousness levels. The following analysis considers this profound teaching through examination of both textual evidence and experiential implications.

## The Cosmic Dream

The Scripture of Ra and Hetheru reveals in verse 8 the primordial state before Creation [1]:

> "who were abiding with him in the form of Nunu (Nun), the primeval homogenous waters that symbolize undifferentiated consciousness (unformed substratum that can be acted upon by divine thought and intent to take on the varied forms of Creation)."

This description establishes Nunu as what appears to be the ground state of existence—pure consciousness without differentiation. From this Nunu emerges Ra, as indicated in the Scripture of Ra and Hetheru verses 151-152 [1]:

> "Salutations to the Divine Creator (Nunu) of me, whom I was within and from whom I arose in the beginning. I am the maker of heaven, and I am the one who, like a sculptor, chisels [dmg]—the forms of Creation."

The parallel with dreaming becomes apparent when we consider that dreams emerge from our own undifferentiated consciousness during sleep, taking form through the creative power of mind supported by consciousness. In other words, just as Ra emerges from Nunu and brings forth Creation through divine thought, the dreaming mind creates entire worlds from its own essence. This analogy suggests a fundamental similarity between cosmic creation and individual dream experience.

# Awakening Your Soul-Aware-Witness

**Figure 1: Ancient Egyptian tomb wall art depicting a blind harper singing and playing the harp.**

The understanding about the dream nature of apparent manifest existence receives explicit confirmation in the Harper's Song, verse 23[2] [2]. This ancient text provides direct textual evidence for the cosmological framework under discussion:

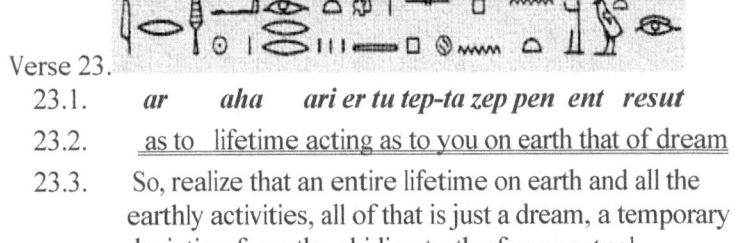

Verse 23.
    23.1.    ***ar   aha   ari er tu tep-ta zep pen ent resut***
    23.2.    as to  lifetime acting as to you on earth that of dream
    23.3.    So, realize that an entire lifetime on earth and all the earthly activities, all of that is just a dream, a temporary deviation from the abiding truth of your actual existence.

This verse indicates that the ancient understanding explicitly recognized the dreamlike nature of manifest existence. The text suggests that what appears as concrete earthly reality, the waking state experiences through the mind and senses, represents a temporary deviation from a more fundamental level of being. Consider how this perspective transforms our understanding of the

---

[2] Translation by Dr. Muata Ashby

relationship between consciousness and apparent material existence.

## The Gods as Divine Thoughts

The scripture describes how the gods and goddesses emerge as Ra's first manifestations. In the Scripture of Ra and Hetheru, Verse 6 states [1]:

> "his loyal followers, the gods and goddesses who were not with him, at the time, calling for, especially his emanations, Rat, his female counterpart and manifestor of his power."

The gods and goddesses can be understood as what the text calls "unconscious impressions of Ra's volitions and divine intents"—representing the first differentiation of pure consciousness into specific creative principles. This suggests that just as dream characters emerge from our own consciousness, the gods emerge from Ra's consciousness and manifest through Ra's cosmic mind. Nevertheless, they operate as empowered expressions through what the tradition describes as his Sekhem or Divine energy, manifesting as goddess Hetheru.

This framework indicates that the neteru (gods and goddesses) function not as separate entities but as aspects of unified cosmic consciousness expressing itself through multiple principles. In other words, they represent different facets of the same underlying divine awareness temporarily appearing as distinct forces and personalities within the cosmic dream of Creation.

## The Nature of Manifest Existence

This understanding carries profound implications for how consciousness relates to existence itself. The Harper's Song elaborates this perspective in verses 17-18[3], which provide

---

[3] Translation by Dr. Muata Ashby

additional textual evidence for the non-dual nature of ultimate reality [2]:

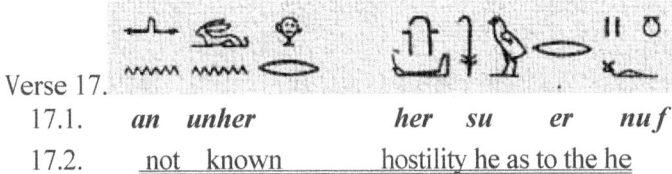

Verse 17.
- 17.1. ***an   unher        her    su    er    nu f***
- 17.2. <u>not   known        hostility he as to the he</u>
- 17.3. In that realm of eternity, the hostility of one person to another is unheard of, it is unknown, as it has no meaning in the realm of eternity, only in the realm of the living in time and space on earth.

Verse 18.
- 18.1. ***ta    pen    anty         reqa            f***
- 18.2. <u>territory that no     foes/fiends       he</u>
- 18.3. in that special realm of eternity there are no foes, enemies, adversaries to be against a person, as all are one existence there in that realm of unitary consciousness.

These verses suggest that apparent conflict and opposition exist only within the temporary realm of manifestation. Just as dream objects and dream characters in a dream are not truly separate from the dreamer and are actually composed of the dreamer's consciousness, all objects and living beings in Creation apparently forming multiplicity represent projections from Ra's consciousness. Therefore, they remain ultimately one with Ra, which also indicates that the apparent differentiations of Creation are non-different essentially and only appear different.

This means that no Creation has been created that exists separate from Ra/Nunu because all existence remains one in Ra. This understanding explains why verse 157 of the Ra and Hetheru scripture declares [1]:

"It is that same Soul of Ra...this Soul of Ra has reformed and, is manifesting as, the objects of the world, which are, in their entirety, encompassed, to the utmost limit, by Him, and He is the soul of everything."

## The Practical Implications

### The Practical Implications

This teaching carries profound practical significance for understanding the nature of experience itself. Just as a dream seems absolutely real while we're experiencing it, our current experience of separation and multiplicity appears unquestionably real. Nevertheless, the texts suggest that, like a dream which appears real while it is happening, manifest existence represents a temporary expression of consciousness that can revert to a higher form of awareness upon awakening.

This awakening involves awareness at a level beyond fear, conflict, terror, and death. It represents consciousness recognizing its true nature beyond the temporary, illusory differentiations of life and death, fear and security, conflict and harmony, or time and eternity. The Harper's Song indicates this understanding in verse 24 [2]:

Verse 24.
    24.1.    ***djed tu aay    ad    udja en peh    im    urt***
    24.2.    <u>say you come</u>    <u>sound vital to arrive in</u>    <u>great-land</u>
    24.3.    So, let us state it definitively: understanding this wisdom, you, come sound and vital, arrive in the great land, the beautiful west, the final abode of the righteous souls (mental state of enlightened awareness), where there is no terror and nothing to fear, no conflict and no death and there is no end, for it is eternal.

This verse suggests that recognizing the dreamlike nature of manifest existence leads to what the text describes as arrival in "the great land"—a state of consciousness characterized by freedom from the limitations that define ordinary human experience.

## The Dream of Ra: Consciousness and Creation in Ancient Egyptian Mysticism

The ultimate understanding revealed in these Ancient Egyptian scriptures indicates that we are not separate from the source of existence. We appear to be manifestations of Ra's divine dreaming—temporary forms taken by undifferentiated consciousness. Understanding this leads to what the Scripture of Ra and Hetheru calls becoming "eternity" and "forever"—awakening from the dream of separation to realize our true nature as one with Ra and Nunu [1].

## The Profound Wisdom of the Dream Analogy: Discovering the Constant Experiencer

The declaration from the Blind Harper that "life is but a dream" provides more than poetic metaphor [2]. It reveals what appears to be the precise mechanism by which consciousness becomes trapped in identification with temporary phenomena [3]. Consider how the Harper's teaching signifies that most people's experience of what they call "their life" operates through the same fundamental process as dream experience, though they remain unaware of this crucial similarity.

The ancient texts suggest that while the content differs between waking and dream states, the process of experiencing remains identical. There is awareness of objects, interactions with those objects, and identification with oneself as a subject within each field of experience [3]. Nevertheless, one major difference illuminates the illusory nature of ego-identification—the shifting of the subject of awareness itself.

In the waking world, consciousness in a person identifies with a particular subject possessing specific personal history. In dreams, that same consciousness adopts an entirely different subject identity.

This variability of the experiencing subject reveals its fundamentally illusory nature. In other words, that which experiences—the witness-consciousness that remains constant through both waking and dream states—represents what appears to be the abiding reality [3].

The wisdom embedded in these teachings indicates that both experiential fields offer similar manifestations of objects and interactions that seem completely real during the experience. Nevertheless, both prove illusory upon deeper investigation. Since the ego-personality of both waking and dream states proves changeable and therefore impermanent, the process of experiencing itself and the entity that experiences—existing prior to and sustaining both ego-states—appear to constitute the higher realities [3]. That entity represents the higher reality of the personality that exists prior to body, mind, and senses and which sustains the experiences through the body, mind, and senses.

This understanding leads to a momentous recognition. Since both waking and dream experiences appear illusory, the motivating factors (aryu) that support and push for involvement in them are likewise illusory [4]. These impetuses represent the compelling influences that cause universal consciousness to narrow its experience into limited body, mind, and senses. This creates the condition of experiencing existence from the perspective of a localized finite consciousness rather than recognizing its true nature as unlimited awareness [4].

This indicates that most people experience illusory worlds and themselves as illusory characters in those worlds. They remain motivated by illusory impetuses that keep pushing the personality to move forward in the illusory venue of the apparent world they experience. Nevertheless, in and of themselves, those experiences do not lead to anything concrete and abiding. Facing the illusory nature of both waking and dream worlds—along with their respective ego-subjects—allows practitioners to relax the motivational patterns that compel involvement with apparent dualities.

This relaxation creates openness to alternative forms of experience that lead to discovering the Soul-Aware-Witness. This discovery enables progression through Ra and Nunu recognition toward Ba en Ra awareness, realizing oneself to be not a finite and changeable personality but rather constant, infinite, and eternal [3].

## The Dream of the Human Life and the Dream of Creation: The Human Soul, Ra and the Nunu

In the Ancient Egyptian Scripture of Ra and Hetheru, verses 6-8 describe how Ra and his company of gods and goddesses existed in the Nunu before arising and before Creation was formed [1]. Figuratively, the Nunu can be considered as the unconscious level of the cosmic mind, with Ra as the first individuation. The other gods and goddesses may be understood as unconscious impressions of Ra's volitions and divine intents.

This interpretation indicates that Creation functions akin to a dream world ideation by Ra. This resembles how a person dreams at night and creates a dreamworld from their own undifferentiated consciousness. Just as a dreamer creates a world of experience with multiple characters and scenarios that appear separate but are ultimately composed of the dreamer's own consciousness, so too Ra manifests the multiplicity of existence from the singularity of divine awareness.

This theme receives powerful support from the Ancient Egyptian Harper's Song from the Tomb of Neferhotep (translation by Dr. Muata Ashby) [2]. In verse 23 of this profound text, we find the explicit declaration: "So, realize that an entire lifetime on earth and all the earthly activities, all of that is just a dream, a temporary deviation from the abiding truth of your actual existence." This perspective illuminates the Ancient Egyptian understanding that our waking reality is not the ultimate truth but rather a manifestation of a deeper, underlying consciousness.

The Harper's Song further reinforces this vision by describing the realm of eternity as a place where "there is no hostility of one person to another" (verse 17) and "there are no foes, enemies, adversaries to be against a person, as all are one existence there in that realm of unitary consciousness" (verse 18) [2]. This perfectly parallels the teaching in the Scripture of Ra and Hetheru that differentiated consciousness returns to undifferentiated unity [1].

The implications of this analogy appear profound for spiritual practice. If Creation functions as a dream of Ra, then everything within it represents an expression of Ra's consciousness and essential being. This means that all beings in Creation (Ra's dream) do not possess independent existence and are, in fact, composed of the dream consciousness of Ra and are therefore Ra.

Furthermore, this indicates that all beings in Creation (Ra's dream) and all objects are interconnected and share a common source and existence: Ra consciousness. The gods and goddesses (cosmic forces operating in Creation) may be thought of as Ra's volitions and represent different aspects of this cosmic mind. They embody various principles and forces that appear to govern the universe and human experience.

For example, in the Scripture of Ra and Hetheru, Hetheru (Hathor), as the Eye of Ra, represents the dynamic feminine power of consciousness [1]. Her transformation into Sekhemit, the fierce lioness, illustrates how consciousness can become caught in the delusion of separate existence, leading to suffering. The pacification of Sekhemit through the special drink (setjert) along with wisdom counseling from Ra, and her return to the form of Hetheru symbolizes the process of spiritual transformation and the return to the original source of unitary conscious awareness with Ra.

In this context, the delusion of Sekhemit can be likened to how a person believes in the reality of a dream while it is happening. Thus, a dream, like a waking delusion, appears to be a temporary deviation from the waking awareness of being or identity, which is itself also a deviation from the undifferentiated absolute.

The scripture emphasizes the importance of recognizing the illusory nature of the material world and the need to transcend it [1]. By understanding that life functions as a kind of dream, one can cultivate detachment from worldly desires and ego-driven pursuits. This detachment is essential for spiritual evolution and the realization of one's true nature as an aspect of Ra's consciousness. The Glorious Light Meditation system presented in the Scripture of Ra and Hetheru provides a systematic method for achieving this realization through focused visualization, hekau (words of power), and the purification of the personality [1].

The Harper's Song culminates this wisdom by affirming in verse 24 [2]: "So, let us state it definitively: understanding this wisdom, you, come sound and vital, arrive in the great land, the beautiful west, the final abode of the righteous souls, where there is no terror and nothing to fear, no conflict and no death and there is no end, for it is eternal." This perfectly aligns with the Scripture of Ra and Hetheru's teaching that the ultimate goal involves realizing one's identity with eternal, undifferentiated consciousness [1].

Verses 6-8 of the Scripture of Ra and Hetheru highlight the significance of this understanding by describing the state of Ra and his gods and goddesses in the Nunu before Creation [1]. This pre-creation state represents the undifferentiated consciousness from which all existence arises. It is presented as a state of pure potentiality, where all possibilities exist but have not been motivated to manifest. By meditating on this state, as instructed in the Glorious Light Meditation practice of the scripture, one can gain insight into the nature of reality and the process of creation [1].

The analogy of Creation as a dream also carries ethical implications aligned with Maat (truth, balance, order, righteousness). If all beings are manifestations of Ra's consciousness, then harming others becomes equivalent to harming oneself. This understanding fosters ethical conscience, compassion, empathy, and non-violence, as one recognizes the interconnectedness of all life. It also encourages a sense of responsibility for one's actions, as they contribute to the overall harmony or disharmony of the cosmic dream that one is experiencing.

**The Harper's Wisdom: Awakening from the Dream of Life**

When one is sleeping and having a dream, they believe they are the character within that illusory dreamworld. Similarly, the wisdom of the Harper signifies that what most human beings consider to be their life on earth in the waking state appears non-different from a person sleeping on a bed having a dream [2]. Ordinary existence represents an alternative form of dreaming where people believe they are the character of the dreamworld, remaining unaware of their deeper self that is dreaming the dream of life they experience as an apparent human being with responsibilities, relationships, a job, worries, anxieties, happy times, and suffering times.

The Harper beckons us to realize the dreamlike nature of life—its ephemeralness, its illusory character, and the nonsensical attachment to temporary dream situations [2].

**Understanding the Dream of Life Through Examples**

To comprehend how people experience the dream of life without realizing it, consider these illustrations and their spiritual implications:

**Career Aspirations:** Someone dedicates their entire life to climbing the corporate ladder, believing that success and status will bring lasting fulfillment. In the dream of life, this person experiences moments of triumph and satisfaction, but like a dream, these feelings quickly dissipate. The Harper's wisdom reveals that pursuing worldly success appears as fleeting as a dream, and the true self represents the dreamer, not the character chasing promotions and accolades [2].

**Relationships:** A person invests deeply in a romantic relationship, believing it to be the source of their happiness and identity. In the dream of life, this individual experiences intense emotions—joy, heartache, and everything in between. Nevertheless, just as dreams shift abruptly, relationships can change or end, leaving the dreamer (the true self) to realize that attachment to the dream character's experiences was illusory.

**Material Possessions:** Someone amasses wealth and material goods, convinced these possessions will provide security and happiness. In the dream of life, this person feels accomplishment and contentment, but like a dream, these feelings are transient. The Harper's wisdom implies that the true self represents the dreamer, observing the dream character's attachment to material things that are as ephemeral as the dream itself [2].

**Daily Routines:** A person follows rigid daily routines, believing that structure and predictability are essential for meaningful life. In the dream of life, this individual finds comfort and purpose in their schedule, but like a dream, routines can be disrupted or changed, revealing the dreamlike nature of their existence. The Harper encourages recognizing that the true self represents the dreamer, watching the dream character navigate the dreamworld of daily life [2].

**Cultural and Social Norms:** Someone adheres strictly to cultural and social norms, believing that conformity will bring acceptance and fulfillment. In the dream of life, this individual experiences belonging and validation, but like a dream, these feelings can be fragile and subject to change. The Harper's wisdom suggests that the true self represents the dreamer, observing the dream character's adherence to societal expectations that are as illusory as the dream itself [2].

**Accepting the Dream World's Rules and False Continuity**

When we dream at night, we appear in a readymade world without questioning it. We simply accept the rules of the dream situation. For example, if we dream of being in a classroom, we accept that we are students, follow the teacher's instructions, and participate in the lesson without questioning why we are there or how the dream world operates. This acceptance parallels how we experience waking life: we are born into an ongoing world and believe we are characters within it without questioning. We accept the roles, responsibilities, and rules of society as if they are inherent and unchangeable.

Moreover, we accept ourselves as legitimate characters in the dream of waking life and believe in its reality because there appears to be continuity—we remember yesterday, we anticipate tomorrow, we see our reflection in the mirror day after day. Nevertheless, this apparent continuity reveals itself as also illusory since everything changes all the time and is never the same from moment to moment, let alone year to year, decade to decade and so on. Things may appear to look similar from moment to moment, day to day, but actually they are not the same now as they were at any time in the past. Just as a dream can seem to have its own internal logic and timeline while we're experiencing it, the waking state presents a convincing narrative of continuous existence that masks its fundamentally dreamlike nature.

The Harper's wisdom reveals that this sense of personal continuity and historical progression represents yet another aspect of the dream that keeps consciousness identified with the character rather than recognizing itself as the dreamer [2].

## The Limitation of Confined Awareness

The confined, localized nature of the human mind and senses creates a narrow field of awareness that becomes filled with limited experience precisely because consciousness operates through these restricted faculties. The mind and senses, by their very design, create a constrained perceptual field that conscious-awareness operating through the human mind and senses mistakes for the totality of existence. If it were possible to experience more of the fullness of existence beyond these limitations, it would become possible to see and understand the illusory nature of human perceptions and sensations.

This expanded awareness represents the fundamental task aimed for through spiritual practices: to understand the illusory nature of mind and senses and discover deeper aspects of experience beyond their confined operation. This constitutes the movement toward enlightenment—an expansion of conscious-awareness beyond its apparent limitations—as opposed to the movement of constriction and delusion that draws consciousness deeper into identification with the waking world dream.

## The Path to Awakening

The Harper's wisdom relates to the understanding that if we listen to this teaching and reflect on the illusory and ephemeral nature of existence, we will inquire about truth and lead ourselves to the sacred land [2]. As the translated text states: "Understanding this wisdom, you come sound and vital, arrive in the great land, the beautiful west (a consciousness level of enlightened awareness), the final abode of the righteous souls, where there is no terror and nothing to fear, no conflict and no death, and there is no end, for it is eternal."

These examples illustrate how people become deeply engrossed in the dream of life, identifying with the characters and experiences they encounter without realizing their true nature as the dreamer. The Harper texts encourage us to awaken from this dreamlike condition, recognize the ephemeral and illusory nature of the dreamworld, and connect with our deeper self that is dreaming the dream of life [2].

**The Practice of Awakening**

This awakening process requires working with both intellect for understanding and emotions for psychological transformation, thereby controlling the personality caught up in delusion. This means controlling wayward thinking and seeking wisdom that explains the dreamlike nature of waking reality. It also involves working with feelings to disentangle from or avoid the enticing interests of the dreamworld that a deluded mind develops desires for, thereby becoming more entangled and drawn away from awakening.

What does controlling feelings for loved ones, pets, beautiful scenery, or career mean? It involves learning to view these interests as illusory reflections of the beautiful west rather than actual items that can be attained permanently in the waking world, just as they cannot be attained in the dreamworld. Through this shift in understanding and feeling toward truth, consciousness moves toward enlightenment, discovering peace and liberation beyond the illusions of the waking dream.

The spiritual practices serve as methodologies for transcending the confined nature of ordinary awareness, gradually expanding consciousness beyond the narrow field created by limited mind and senses. This expansion allows the practitioner to recognize the dreamlike quality of all phenomenal experience and discover the deeper reality that serves as both the source and substance of the apparent dream of existence.

**Implications of Consciousness with Awareness and with Cognition, Consciousness with Awareness but without Cognition (Precognitive Awareness) and Consciousness without Awareness or Cognition**

The Scripture of Ra and Hetheru presents profound insights about the nature of consciousness in verse 153, where Ra speaks of his soul being older than Nunu [1]. If, metaphorically speaking, Ra represents the conscious awareness with cognitive abilities (the capacity to analyze, categorize, and process information through thinking) aspect of divinity, and Nunu represents the unconscious undifferentiated (awareness without cognition) level, then the aspect that is older than Nunu appears to be the transcendental aspect of consciousness prior to awareness (which required individuation and then cognition with ensuing differentiations at the level of mind and senses).

In this verse, figuratively, Ra represents the mind, Nunu represents the body, and the soul of Ra represents the underlying Spirit source of the mind and body. That source/prior existence appears to be the transcendent absolute nameless aspect. This corresponds to the advanced levels of meditation practice described in verses 175-180 of the scripture, where the aspirant moves beyond names and forms to realize oneness with transcendental, formless existence [1].

The scripture thus presents what appears to be a complete cosmology of consciousness with three distinct levels:

1. **Consciousness with awareness and cognition** - Represented by Ra as the differentiated, individuated divine being who thinks, plans, and creates
2. **Consciousness with awareness but without cognition** - Represented by Nunu as the undifferentiated primordial waters that contain all potential but have not yet formed distinct thoughts or creations

3. **Consciousness without differentiated or undifferentiated awareness or cognition** - Represented by that which is "older" than Nunu, the transcendent absolute beyond all categories and distinctions

This threefold structure provides a framework for understanding both the cosmos and the human spiritual journey. The goal of spiritual practice, according to the scripture, involves moving from the limited state of differentiated consciousness (where we experience ourselves as separate entities) through the intermediate state of undifferentiated awareness, and ultimately to realize our identity with the transcendent absolute that appears prior to all manifestation [1].

The metaphor of creation as Ra's dream provides a powerful framework for understanding both cosmic and personal spiritual transformation. This same understanding receives explicit confirmation in the Harper's Song when it states that life on earth is "just a dream, a temporary deviation from the abiding truth of your actual existence" [2]. Just as dream objects are not truly separate from the dreamer, all apparently separate beings ultimately appear as manifestations of Ra's consciousness. Our spiritual journey parallels Hetheru's transformation from Sekhemit back to her true nature—moving from the delusion of separate existence to recognition of our essential oneness with divine consciousness [1].

## The Visual Architecture of Consciousness: Understanding the Three-Level Cosmology

Having established that Creation manifests as Ra's divine ideation emerging from the undifferentiated waters of Nunu—much like a dreamer springs forth a complete dreamworld from previously undifferentiated consciousness—we must now examine the precise architecture of this cosmic process as preserved in the sacred visual teachings of the ancient sages. Indeed, the wisdom of Shetaut Neter reveals that consciousness operates through specific levels that can be mapped with extraordinary precision, providing contemporary practitioners with an essential framework for understanding both cosmic manifestation and personal spiritual development.

The diagram presented here illustrates the fundamental structure underlying all consciousness transformation described throughout this manuscript. Consider how this visual representation encodes the same profound metaphysical principles that emerge from detailed scriptural analysis—yet offers immediate recognition of the cosmic architecture that governs spiritual development. The ancient sages understood that consciousness naturally seeks to return to its source through recognizable stages; therefore, this cosmological map serves not merely as theoretical knowledge but as practical guidance for aspirants navigating their own consciousness development.

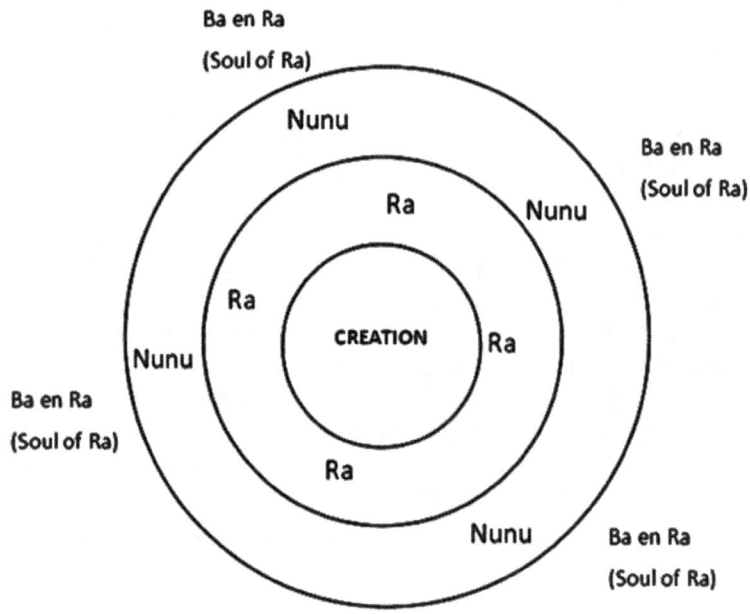

**Ba en Ra (Soul of Ra)** encompasses the entire diagram without any boundary or border—a crucial visual teaching that reveals the infinite nature of absolute consciousness. This boundless quality indicates that Ba en Ra extends infinitely in all directions without limitation or containment, representing consciousness that has no beginning, no end, no inside, and no outside. Consider how this corresponds with the teaching that Neberdjer (equivalent to Ba en Ra) serves as "the All-Encompassing Divinity that serves as both the source and substance of all existence." Just as when we dream, our consciousness extends infinitely beyond the apparent boundaries of the dreamworld itself, so Ba en Ra represents infinite awareness within which all apparent existence occurs while never exhausting or limiting that boundless foundation.

**Nunu** appears within this infinite Ba en Ra as undifferentiated consciousness—the primordial ocean that contains all potential while expressing none explicitly. Nevertheless, even this oceanic awareness exists within the boundless expanse of Ba en Ra, much like the dreaming capacity exists within the infinite consciousness of the dreamer. Undifferentiated awareness operates as the complete foundation for all manifestation, yet this foundation itself exists within infinite consciousness that has no limits or borders.

**Ra** manifests within Nunu as individuated consciousness—divine awareness that has apparently differentiated from the undifferentiated ocean yet remains within the boundless expanse of Ba en Ra. This represents the level where specific awareness and creative activity occur, like the dreaming mind that generates particular dream scenarios within infinite consciousness. The quadruple appearance reveals that individuated consciousness can function through all dimensions of experience while operating within the infinite awareness that encompasses everything.

**Creation** exists entirely within Ra's mind, representing the apparent physical universe that emerges from individuated divine consciousness. Nevertheless, Creation—like everything else in the diagram—exists within the infinite expanse of Ba en Ra that has no boundaries. This corresponds precisely with the dream analogy: just as dream objects exist within the dreaming mind, which itself operates within boundless consciousness, so the physical universe exists within Ra's cosmic mind, which operates within infinite Ba en Ra.

The absence of any border around Ba en Ra provides the most crucial teaching of the entire diagram: absolute consciousness possesses no limitations, boundaries, or restrictions whatsoever. This means that no matter how many levels of apparent differentiation occur—from Ba en Ra through Nunu through Ra to Creation—the infinite nature of consciousness remains unaffected and undiminished. Indeed, the boundless quality of Ba en Ra reveals why consciousness development ultimately leads to recognition of one's infinite nature rather than acquisition of limited spiritual states.

This nested architecture within infinite consciousness reveals the profound teaching that underlies all Ancient Egyptian wisdom: what appears as multiple levels of reality actually represents one boundless consciousness (Ba en Ra) manifesting through different states of apparent differentiation while never becoming limited by those modifications. The physical universe that seems so solid and separate exists within infinite consciousness and is composed entirely of that same consciousness, just as dream mountains and dream people exist within and are composed of the dreamer's boundless awareness.

Consider how this understanding of infinite consciousness transforms spiritual practice: rather than seeking union with something external, practitioners learn to recognize that their essential awareness participates in the same boundless Ba en Ra that encompasses and composes all existence without limitation. The journey from heated to silent consciousness represents infinite consciousness discovering its own boundless nature through the apparent process of individual awakening—yet that infinite foundation was never actually confined or diminished by the appearance of limitation.

This cosmological framework of infinite consciousness within which all experience occurs provides the essential foundation for understanding why genuine spiritual realization involves recognizing one's boundless nature rather than achieving particular states or experiences, revealing that what appears as individual spiritual development actually represents infinite consciousness recognizing its own limitless essence through the apparent multiplicity of forms.

**The Sacred Verses: Foundation of Consciousness Understanding**

The Scripture of Ra and Hetheru provides the fundamental cosmological framework for comprehending how consciousness manifests in different modalities that the mind can perceive and

Awakening Your Soul-Aware-Witness

experience [1]. Consider how these ancient texts embed within their sacred verses precise descriptions for understanding the very nature of Creation and awareness itself—teachings that serve as the foundation for all spiritual development and practical wisdom.

The following verses reveal this profound understanding through direct textual evidence [1]:

Verse 151.

*151.1.*    pet    im m diu    aau      {md} en Neternasu   {Net} kheper en a im-f   nuk-a
*151.2.*    heaven crying-out giving praise   {fig} to God. Hail    {Div}    creator of me in-
                                                                 he    I-am
*151.3.*    ...of heaven as they were crying out, praising the God (Ra). Ra says: "Salutations to the Divine Creator (Nunu) of me, whom I was within and from whom I arose in the beginning. I am...

Verse 152.

*152.1.*    ari pet smench [dmg]   <rerat bau (Ra)     neteru imzet >
*152.2.*    maker heaven, chiseler [dmg] <power souls (Creator Spirit) gods/goddesses
                                                                                             within>
*152.3.*    ...the maker of heaven and I am the one who, like a sculptor, chisels [dmg—the forms of Creation]... <and the power of my souls is within the gods and goddesses. >

**Verse 152.**
152.4.    iu      a   hena zenu heh     mes      en tri [dmg] h [dmg] pu
152.5.    It-is     I    with    them eternity    born      of time [dmg] h [dmg] this
152.6.    It is I who was with them (gods & goddesses) for millions of years after being born of time [dmg] this...

---

[4] This section is damaged in the Tomb of Sety 1st so this section in brackets comes from the version inscribed in the Tomb of Ramses 6

85

Awakening Your Soul-Aware-Witness

*Verse 153.*

*153.1.* ba a *{Net}* ur su er se ba pu en Shu*{Net}* khnum a ba   *a*
*153.2.* soul mine {Div} elder he as-to cause soul this of Shu {Div}, creator
{Div} soul I
*153.3.* …soul of mine is older than He (Nunu), even as body and mind emerged from Nunu. As regards the soul of my son, this God, Shu, the god of ethereal light; I caused his soul to come into manifestation as the God Shu; the soul of the God Shu is the soul of the Creator God, my soul.

*Verse 155.*

*155.1.* Ba pu en Nunu en Ra Ba pu en Asar Ba Djedty
155.2. Soul that of Nunu of Ra Ba that of Osiris soul Djedty
155.3. The soul of that Divinity, Nunu, is the same soul of Ra, the Creator Spirit, which is the same soul of Asar (Osiris), who is the soul of Busiris (Djedty), the abode of Asar (Osiris) on earth.

These verses reveal what appears to be a profound teaching about consciousness levels that transcends mere theoretical knowledge. The textual evidence suggests this understanding is based on experiential knowledge. The earlier finding of Ra coming forth from Nun and both being younger than the soul of Ra yet having the same soul indicates that Ra (differentiated Consciousness) comes out of Nun (undifferentiated consciousness), and both arise from Soul of Ra [1].

In the Ancient Egyptian wisdom context, the term "soul" here represents "essential source existence." In other words, it signifies a common underlying source for the existence of that which is being described. This represents what appears to be the cosmic architecture of consciousness itself, providing aspirants with a precise map for understanding their own awareness and its divine nature.

## The Ancient Egyptian God Ra The Ancient Egyptian God Nunu The Soul of Ra

**The Ancient Egyptian God Ra in his boat**

**The Ancient Egyptian God Nunu**

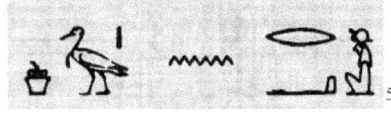

**The Soul of Ra**

---

[5] Ancient Egyptian Book of Enlightenment (PertmHeru)-translation by Dr. Muata Ashby

## The Three Consciousness Levels and their relation to human conscious-awareness: A Complete Framework

| Cosmic Level | Human consciousness correspondent: how the cosmic levels manifest in the human personality |
|---|---|
| *Ra* (differentiated consciousness), objects of Creation | Conscious-awareness, mind cogitating thoughts, feelings, desires, awareness of time and space. Causes undifferentiated consciousness to differentiate into the forms recognized by the mind and senses as objects. During sleep manifests as dreaming and the dream objects. |
| *Nunu* (undifferentiated consciousness), potential of Creation | Mental repose, quiescence, threshold consciousness, mind in between thoughts, feelings, desires, while being aware of no-thingness. During sleep manifests as deep-dreamless-sleep (no dreams). Nunu is the stuff that thoughts, dreams, etc. are made of. |
| *Ba en Ra* [Soul of Ra](Absolute), Consciousness supporting the potential (undifferentiated) and the manifest apparent reality (differentiated) of time, space, objects and localized individuated consciousness | Soul. Beingness without mind, existence beyond objective qualities. Beyond time and space. Beyond existence and non-existence. Beyond form, beyond qualities. |

Mystic Mathematics: Formulation of Consciousness Statement #1.

Consider how the ancient sages understood the fundamental architecture of human experience through what we might term the essential mystic mathematics of consciousness: **Consciousness [Neberdjer/Ba en Ra] combined with mind [perceptions and sensations] produces human conscious-awareness, which in turn manifests as all human experiences**. Indeed, this formula reveals the precise mechanism through which the infinite awareness that underlies all existence appears to become individuated experience—though this appearance occurs without the absolute foundation ever truly becoming limited or divided. This means that our daily experiences of thoughts, emotions, and sensations represent modifications within the unchanging field of Ba en Ra consciousness, rather than productions of a separate individual mind that somehow generates its own awareness."

## Soul of Ra: Pure Consciousness Existence

According to the Scripture of Ra and Hetheru, Soul of Ra exists as pure consciousness, devoid of subject-object awareness or relationship [1]. Then Nunu (undifferentiated awareness) arises from the absolute. This represents consciousness with non-specific awareness [1]. Therefore, Soul of Ra does not have differentiation or undifferentiation and appears to be pure consciousness and undirected nonspecific awareness prior to manifesting either undifferentiated or differentiated appearance.

In the tradition of Shetaut Neter, the Soul of Ra level represents what the teachings describe as "beingness without qualification"— existence prior to awareness, before any individuation or cognition occurs [5]. This pure consciousness transcends both manifestation and the awareness of manifestation, existing as the absolute foundation from which all experience emerges.

Aspirants often struggle to comprehend this level because the mind seeks objects to grasp, while Soul of Ra consciousness represents the very ground of being that underlies (comes before) all perceptions and subject-object relationships. This level operates beyond even the concept of awareness itself. The Soul of Ra consciousness cannot be experienced in the ordinary sense, the way people think of experiencing something with mind and senses or physical body because it represents the very foundation that makes all experience possible.

This means that recognition of Soul of Ra occurs not through mental effort or spiritual techniques but through the dissolution of everything that appears to separate (differentiate) consciousness from its essential nature. For example, this includes dissolving the belief in oneself as a separate individual identity and the belief that the world consists of objects with independent, abiding existence.

## Nunu: Undifferentiated Awareness

The Nunu level operates as the cosmic substrate from which all manifestation emerges and into which it dissolves. This represents undifferentiated consciousness that maintains awareness without specific focus—the homogeneous ocean of awareness that the ancient texts call the "primeval waters of undifferentiated consciousness" [5]. This represents consciousness with non-specific awareness [1], a state where consciousness manifests as non-localized awareness rather than the focused individual awareness characteristic of ordinary human experience.

Localized awareness refers to non-universal awareness. It represents the localization of awareness to specific individual minds that experience their reality through the particular mind, body and vantage point as opposed to perceiving the entire Creation at once the way Ra does or the way the dreaming mind perceives the entire dreamworld, along with all the activities, objects and personalities in the dream. Though the dream subject inside the dream does not perceive the whole dreamworld, the dreamer—the person having the dream—projects the entire dreamworld that they are dreaming within. In this context the dreamer perceives the world of their dream and their personality within the dream represents the localized subject looking at the section of the dreamworld that they are paying attention to through the limitations of their mind and senses.

This level corresponds to what contemporary Jungian and Transpersonal Psychology might refer to as the collective unconscious, yet it transcends psychological categories by representing pure undifferentiated awareness rather than unconscious mental contents. In other words, Nunu consciousness operates as awareness that encompasses all mental activity without focusing on any particular content—like space that contains all objects without being limited by any particular object.

The tradition teaches that Nunu consciousness functions as what might be called the "awareness substrate" from which individual consciousness emerges and into which it dissolves during states like deep sleep, profound meditation, or the transition between lifetimes. Nevertheless, this represents a living, conscious reality rather than an unconscious void, characterized by unlimited awareness that has not yet differentiated into specific forms or relationships.

## Ra: Individuated Divine Consciousness

The Ra aspect means moving from undifferentiation (Nun) to differentiation/individuation as an entity that can be conscious and aware of itself [1]. The Ra level encompasses what the Scripture describes as "conscious, differentiated awareness with cognition"— the thinking, parsing, segmenting process that allows consciousness to function as individuated awareness [5]. So, Ra represents that aspect of awareness that is now not undirected or nonspecific but is now focused on being an entity that can refer to itself as a being and specifically as being with self-awareness, the capacity to regard itself in terms of "I."

Nevertheless, this level encompasses a vast spectrum from ego-driven individuation through divine individuation, where consciousness recognizes its essential nature while maintaining individual expression. The Ra consciousness can function either through what the teachings describe as the delusion of separateness or through divine recognition that individual consciousness represents universal awareness temporarily manifesting in personal form. The same Ra awareness sustains the mind of an ego-bound person as well as the sage—the crucial difference being that the sage has discovered the higher level of Ra awareness within themselves, while the ego-bound person remains unaware (unknowing) of this divine foundation of consciousness.

Consider how the Soul-Aware-Witness represents the transitional stage that naturally evolves into full Ra-level consciousness recognition through sustained spiritual practice and philosophical discrimination. In this context, Ra as Amun-Ra (the hidden witness consciousness that underlies the awareness of the human mind but remains unknown to most) is no longer concealed from the practitioner who has established themselves in the Soul-Aware-Witness, since this development creates the spiritual sensitivity necessary for recognizing the divine witness that was always present but previously obscured by ego-identification and the accumulated patterns of heated mental activity.

Having discovered oneself as Ra also means experiencing Ra as the mind that has created Creation or what appears as Creation to the mind and senses, out of its mentation that has caused Nunu (undifferentiated consciousness) to assume a differentiated form that the mind and senses can perceive as a distinct object as opposed to as undifferentiated consciousness which has no form or shape.

Recalling the earlier findings about the nature of Creation as a dream, that represents an expression of the cosmic mind of the Creator (Ra) who created Creation out of his own ideation and caused consciousness to take on the forms and shapes of the objects we perceive in Creation not unlike how a person perceives objects in their dreamworld that their own consciousness has created and permeates at the same time. In the same manner, a person sleeping at night sustains their dreamworld in the same way that Ra sustains the appearances of Creation (the waking world). Creation exists within Ra's mind and Ra exists within Nunu and Nunu exists within the Ba en Ra (Soul of Ra). In this context, the term "Soul of Ra" that appears in the Scripture of Ra and Hetheru corresponds to the term used in the Book of Enlightenment and other Ancient Egyptian texts: "Neberdjer" (All-encompassing-divinity, Universal

Consciousness—unlimited, infinite, eternal existence) [3]. Thus, Nunu and Ra exist within Soul of Ra so Universal Consciousness enfolds all and what appears as Creation represents a manifestation of consciousness (Soul of Ra) occurring within that same Universal Consciousness. Thus, everything in that creation appears composed of the same consciousness but modulated through different levels of mind (Ra, Nunu) so that it appears as the objects that people assume are composed of "matter." Matter represents in reality what the mind and senses are able to interpret Ra differentiated consciousness to be, using their limited capacity.

Therefore, having discovered Ra as self means discovering the Creation as Self. This momentous discovery means knowing and feeling, being aware of existence as authored by and manifesting because of Soul of Ra Absolute Consciousness that supports Nunu and Ra (differentiated and undifferentiated consciousness and its appearances). Thus, it means understanding beyond the information brought by the mind and senses that Creation appears as divinity, and Creation appears as me (Ra) and all appears as consciousness, Soul of Ra. Hence, the consciousness operating in the human being that is conscious of self appears as none other than Ra, Nunu and Soul of Ra/Neberdjer. The personal ego awareness and identity represent illusory aspects of the "dreamworld" of Ra, Nunu and Soul of Ra.

The human mind corresponds to Ra's cosmic mind, though the ordinary conscious human mind operates through limitations imposed by mind and senses as well as the ego's individuated belief in itself as a separate and finite being observing Creation from the restricted perspective allowed by limited human faculties [1]. Nevertheless, as the personality discovers the Soul-Aware-Witness and develops further to discover Ra expanded awareness, practitioners become able to perceive Creation not as composed of finite objects existing in subject-object relationships, but rather as whole existence composed of Ra consciousness—the same consciousness operating as the human being's essential awareness [1].

Consider how this recognition transforms the entire understanding of cosmic relationship: since the Cosmos authored by Ra occurs within the mind of Ra and appears composed of Nunu (consciousness) that has become differentiated, this means the experience of Creation exists within the human "I" that has discovered the truth "I am Ra" [1]. The human represents not an object within Creation but rather focused Ra consciousness operating through individual mind and senses. Therefore, Creation occurs not outside the human mind but within Ra, which represents the true identity—thus the practitioner can rightly declare "Creation is within me."

The wisdom embedded in these teachings reveals that this same recognition occurs at progressively higher levels of awareness discovery: through Nunu awareness, consciousness recognizes Creation as undifferentiated awareness appearing as apparent multiplicity; and finally, through Ba en Ra (Soul of Ra) awareness, consciousness rests in its absolute nature that both encompasses and transcends all manifestation while serving as the foundation for both individual and cosmic expression [1].

Soul of Ra, Nunu and Ra are really one being manifesting in these three modalities, two of which (Nunu and Ra) the mind can understand and perceive [1]. Therefore, Soul of Ra represents absolute pure consciousness existence, Nunu represents that existence manifesting as undifferentiated non-localized awareness and Ra represents individuation from that undifferentiation into a form of awareness that is localized instead of universal and unformed.

## The Experiential Progression: How Consciousness Levels Unfold in Practice

### The Natural Movement of Self-Discovery

Soul of Ra serves as the ultimate substratum—absolute existence experienced through Nunu and Ra but with varying degrees of purity. When the "Soul-Aware-Witness" becomes realized through the practices described earlier, a natural movement of self-discovery progresses toward discovering this witnessing awareness as a manifestation of Ra-level consciousness, and through Ra recognition, consciousness naturally progresses toward Nunu consciousness and ultimately Soul of Ra experience.

The ancient texts suggest that this progression follows spiritual law rather than personal effort. In other words, when sufficient purification occurs through living by truth (Maat) and appropriate spiritual practice, consciousness naturally recognizes its deeper levels without forced development. This means that discovering the Soul-Aware-Witness serves as the gateway rather than the completion of consciousness development.

## Understanding the Varying Degrees of Purity

The tradition reveals that Soul of Ra operates as "the ultimate substratum absolute existence experienced through Nunu and Ra but with varying degrees of purity." This understanding proves crucial for contemporary practitioners because it explains how the same essential consciousness can function through different levels of clarity and recognition.

Consider how this means that consciousness always remains Soul of Ra in its essential nature, yet its recognition of this nature varies according to the degree of purification achieved through spiritual practice. When heavy aryu (karmic impressions) cloud awareness, consciousness experiences itself as separate ego-personality. As purification progresses, the same consciousness begins to recognize its nature as Ra-level divine individuation. Further purification reveals its undifferentiated Nunu nature, while complete purification allows direct recognition of its essential nature as Soul of Ra.

Nevertheless, these represent degrees of recognition rather than different types of consciousness. The ancient texts suggest that Soul of Ra consciousness remains constant while the veils that obscure its recognition dissolve through appropriate spiritual development.

## The Automatic Progression of Recognition

The tradition teaches that allowing this natural self-discovery movement to proceed automatically leads toward Soul of Ra experience. This represents a crucial understanding for spiritual practice: consciousness development occurs through removing obstacles rather than acquiring new states or experiences.

When practitioners establish themselves in the Soul-Aware-Witness through living by truth and appropriate meditation, the progression toward deeper recognition unfolds naturally. Ra-consciousness emerges as practitioners recognize their essential divine nature while maintaining individual expression. Nunu consciousness becomes apparent as the undifferentiated awareness that underlies all individual expression becomes recognized. Soul of Ra recognition eventually emerges as consciousness rests in its absolute nature beyond all modifications.

## Soul of Ra Recognition: Beyond Experience Categories

Soul of Ra experience represents "not an experience as such" but rather a "knowingness." This crucial distinction helps aspirants understand that the highest recognition transcends the category of experience altogether. Soul of Ra consciousness cannot be experienced through the mind or through awareness of individuation but manifests as a direct knowing that the mind can later classify using approximate words such as infinity, eternity, or absolute.

The ancient texts suggest that Soul of Ra consciousness "has no qualities, analogs, or descriptors" yet must be recognized as "the ultimate essence of being." This understanding prevents practitioners from seeking Soul of Ra as an object of experience while pointing toward its recognition as the very foundation that makes all experience possible.

Terms such as Neberdjer (All-encompassing divinity), Un (existence), Neterty (Consciousness manifesting as both phenomenal and transcendental Absolute), and Neter-an-ren (Divinity without name or form) serve as conceptual pointers rather than definitions. These terms help orient consciousness toward its essential nature while acknowledging that Soul of Ra transcends all conceptual categories.

## Understanding Human Consciousness and Its Relationship to Pure Awareness

### The Foundation of Mind and Perception

Human conscious-awareness (a human being's awareness of sensations and perceptions of the body, mind and the world as the self-reflective awareness of being an entity that is aware of being a human being) is derivative from pure consciousness (pure being—that which is) because if the perceptions and sensations are removed there would be no conscious awareness and no mind functioning through mind and senses [3]. Yet consciousness would remain such as when falling asleep the conscious awareness of the waking world falls away/disappears, yet awareness sustained by consciousness persists.

The same can be said about dream and deep sleep states. Therefore, conscious awareness is neither abiding nor definitive. Awareness/consciousness prior to conscious-awareness through mind and senses is constant/abiding and therefore a higher reality [3]. Consciousness serves as the foundation of experience, while mind operates as the perception modality through which Consciousness experiences the world that mind can experience based on its limited parameters [3].

The ancient texts suggest that understanding this relationship represents one of the most crucial insights for spiritual development, since misidentifying consciousness with mind creates the fundamental delusion that underlies all spiritual suffering. Consciousness represents the background of unchanging awareness that makes all changeable mental experience possible. Mind represents the changing instrument through which consciousness can experience itself as a localized individual in relation to individualized apparent objects.

### The Hierarchy of Consciousness and Mental Function

Consciousness operates on multiple levels simultaneously, with mind serving different functions depending on the level of consciousness that is directing its operation. The Scripture reveals that when consciousness identifies with the Soul of Ra level, mind becomes completely silent and serves no function in that recognition, since pure consciousness requires no mental mediation to know itself [1].

When consciousness operates through the Nunu level, mind functions in what the ancient texts call the "undifferentiated mode"—awareness that encompasses all mental activity without focusing on any particular content. This represents a state where thoughts, emotions, and perceptions arise and dissolve within spacious awareness without disturbing the fundamental undifferentiated quality of consciousness.

The tradition of Shetaut Neter teaches that when consciousness operates through the Ra level, mind can function either through ego-driven patterns or divine patterns, depending on the degree of spiritual development of the person in question. Ego-driven mental function involves what the teachings describe as "heated mind" patterns—agitation, control-seeking, and separateness-projection that emerges from consciousness forgetting its divine nature.

## Understanding Ego-Driven versus Divine Ra Consciousness in Daily Life

## The Fundamental Distinction in Consciousness Expression

In the tradition of Shetaut Neter, students learn to distinguish between ego-driven Ra consciousness and what might be called "divine Ra consciousness." Ego-driven individuation involves consciousness becoming identified with limited personal characteristics, believing itself to be fundamentally separate from other manifestations of consciousness. This represents Ra consciousness operating through what the teachings describe as the delusion of separateness and limitation [6].

The ancient texts indicate that ego-driven Ra consciousness manifests through what the Scripture calls the "ego construct"—a pattern of agitation, external control, and soul suffocation that emerges when individuated awareness becomes trapped in aryu (karmic impressions) and forgets its divine nature [3]. This mode of

Ra consciousness operates through the illusion that one is an isolated entity that must struggle against external forces to achieve security, pleasure, and validation.

Divine Ra consciousness represents individuated awareness that recognizes its essential nature as universal consciousness temporarily manifesting in personal form. This means that the individual maintains clear personal identity and capacity for action while understanding that this individuality represents a temporary modification of the same consciousness that manifests as all beings and all experiences.

## Ego-Driven Ra Consciousness: Practical Examples

Ego-driven Ra consciousness manifests in workplace situations through what the teachings describe as "agitated heart" consciousness—experiencing anxiety about outcomes, seeking to control circumstances through reactive effort, and becoming trapped in competitive dynamics that emerge from the belief in fundamental separateness [6]. This means that consciousness identifies with temporary roles and achievements, measuring self-worth through external validation and comparison with others.

In other words, the individual becomes absorbed in what the Scripture calls the "mayhem of desires born of spiritual ignorance and duality perceived through mind and senses" [1]. The person approaches work projects with heated mind patterns, becoming agitated when colleagues don't respond as expected, measuring personal worth through external achievement, and approaching challenges from anxiety rather than creative intelligence. This creates what the ancient texts describe as the cycle of seeking satisfaction through controlling external circumstances.

Ego-driven Ra consciousness in relationships manifests as what the Scripture describes as the polarization of conscious-awareness due to engaging and believing in the duality of likes and dislikes: "drowning in the ever-agitating movements of opposition and attraction" [1]. The person seeks fulfillment through controlling others' responses, becomes disturbed when relationships don't provide expected satisfaction, and approaches love from the perspective of what they can receive rather than recognizing the underlying unity that connects all beings.

This pattern manifests in intimate relationships: the individual becomes anxious when their partner doesn't respond as expected, seeks validation through the other person's behavior, and becomes disturbed when the relationship doesn't provide the security or satisfaction they seek. The person approaches love from what the teachings describe as "heated heart" consciousness—seeking to fulfill personal needs rather than serving the highest good of all involved.

In financial matters, ego-driven Ra consciousness operates through what the ancient texts call "heated mind" patterns—endless seeking for security through accumulation, anxiety about scarcity that emerges from forgetting one's essential divine nature, and decision-making driven by fear rather than wisdom [6]. This represents consciousness that has forgotten its true nature as the soul of Ra (Soul of Ra) manifesting in individual form, instead identifying with the temporary personality that must struggle for survival and satisfaction.

The tradition reveals how this manifests in practical financial decisions: the person approaches money from anxiety about future security, makes investment choices based on fear of loss rather than wise assessment, and measures self-worth through material accumulation. This creates what the Scripture describes as the agitated mental patterns that prevent recognition of one's essential divine nature, which is the true source of abundance and security [1].

## Divine Ra Consciousness: The Transformation to Awakened Individuality

Divine Ra consciousness represents individuated awareness that recognizes its essential nature as universal consciousness temporarily manifesting in personal form. This means that the individual maintains clear personal identity and capacity for action while understanding that this individuality represents a temporary modification of the same consciousness that manifests as all beings and all experiences.

Divine Ra consciousness approaches the same workplace challenges from what the teachings describe as "peaceful heart" awareness [6]. The person maintains full engagement with professional responsibilities while recognizing that their essential worth doesn't depend on external outcomes from an illusory world. This means approaching challenges with creative intelligence rather than reactive anxiety, collaborating rather than competing, and maintaining inner stability regardless of external circumstances.

In other words, the individual operates from what the Scripture calls the "Soul-Aware-Witness"—consciousness that has separated itself from ego-identification and now operates as the instrument of soul expression [3]. The person approaches work projects with silent mind wisdom, responding to challenges from inner stability rather than reactive patterns, and maintaining recognition of their divine nature even while fully engaged with practical responsibilities. This allows for enhanced effectiveness because consciousness is no longer divided by internal conflict or external seeking.

In relationships, divine Ra consciousness manifests through what the Scripture describes as the "Soul-Aware-Witness"—awareness that has separated itself from ego-identification and now operates as the instrument of soul expression [3]. The person maintains clear individual boundaries while recognizing the underlying unity that connects all beings. This allows for genuine love that serves the highest good of all involved rather than seeking personal satisfaction through controlling others' responses.

This transformation manifests in intimate relationships: the individual approaches their partner from recognition of essential unity while maintaining clear personal expression, offers love as service (caring) rather than seeking validation, and remains stable whether the relationship provides expected satisfaction or not. The person operates from what the teachings describe as "peaceful heart" consciousness—serving the highest good of all involved while maintaining individual clarity and boundaries.

The wisdom embedded in these teachings reveals that divine Ra consciousness in financial matters operates through what they call "silent mind" wisdom—making decisions from inner peace rather than external pressure, understanding that true security emerges from recognition of one's divine nature rather than material accumulation, and approaching abundance from the perspective of creative service rather than fearful grasping [6].

This practical transformation manifests as approaching financial decisions from wisdom rather than anxiety, making investment choices based on sound assessment rather than emotional reactivity, and understanding that one's essential worth as divine consciousness provides the foundation for all material abundance. Nevertheless, this doesn't mean impractical detachment from financial responsibility but rather approaching money matters from the stability that emerges from spiritual recognition.

The three-level consciousness framework and its practical applications naturally lead to examination of the specific challenges that prevent consciousness from operating at optimal levels. Understanding how consciousness becomes trapped in limiting patterns provides essential context for appreciating the profound wisdom embedded in the ancient teachings. The Scripture of Ra and Hetheru reveals not only the cosmic architecture of consciousness but also the precise mechanisms through which universal awareness becomes entangled in the illusion of separateness and limitation, creating the psychological conditions that characterize human suffering and spiritual forgetfulness [1].

## IMPORTANT PROVISO: Understanding Consciousness "Levels" and "Stages"

The ancient sages taught that spiritual understanding requires both precise conceptual frameworks and recognition of lived experiential reality. Throughout this manuscript, references to consciousness "levels," "stages," and "progressions" serve as intellectual scaffolding designed to provide clear conceptual organization for understanding the mechanics of spiritual transformation. Nevertheless, it is essential that students recognize these conceptual distinctions as pedagogical tools rather than literal descriptions of how consciousness development unfolds in actual human experience.

The wisdom of Kemetic psychology illuminates that genuine spiritual development operates not through distinct, sequential stages that individuals must traverse in order, but rather as a dynamic process of fluctuating experiences that gradually achieve greater stability over time. Consider how consciousness functions more like a barometer than a staircase—practitioners experience periods of expanded awareness alternating with periods of contracted consciousness, with the natural tendency being toward increasing frequency of higher experiences and decreasing frequency of lower experiences as spiritual practice matures.

In other words, the "levels" described in these teachings represent different qualities of awareness that may manifest spontaneously within the same individual during the same day, or even within the same meditation session. The goal of spiritual practice involves not the mechanical achievement of "higher levels" but rather the gradual stabilization of consciousness in its natural state of divine recognition, wherein extreme fluctuations cease and awareness rests consistently in the undifferentiated witness consciousness (Amun-Ra) that underlies all temporary modifications of mind.

This understanding prevents the common misconception that spiritual development requires dramatic breakthroughs or permanent transitions from "lower" to "higher" states. Instead, the teachings reveal that transformation occurs through the patient cultivation of inner stability, wherein the aspirant learns to recognize and abide in the unchanging awareness that witnesses all changing experiences without being disturbed by them. Eventually, this witness consciousness becomes so stable that practitioners no longer experience the extreme contractions of awareness that characterize heated mental activity, nor do they become attached to temporary expansions of consciousness that may arise during spiritual practice.

The ancient tradition of Shetaut Neter thus presents consciousness levels as skillful means for intellectual comprehension while simultaneously pointing beyond conceptual understanding toward direct recognition of the timeless awareness that already exists as the foundation of all experience. Students who grasp both the utility and the limitations of these conceptual frameworks discover that genuine spiritual development involves not the attainment of exotic states but the simple recognition of what has always been present as the silent witness of all experience—what the Scripture reveals as the eternal "nuk Ra" or divine "I Am" that constitutes the true identity of every conscious being.

## References

[1] Ashby, M. (2022). The Mysteries of Ra and Hetheru/Sekhmet. Translation by Dr. Muata Ashby. Sema Institute.
[2] Ashby, M. (2016). Egyptian Book of the Dead Hieroglyph Translations for Enlightenment Vol. 4. Translation by Dr. Muata Ashby. Sema Institute.
[3] Ashby, M. (2025). DEFINITIONS: The Nature of Consciousness and Awareness in Neterian Philosophy. By Dr. Muata Ashby. Sema Institute.
[4] Ashby, M. (2016). Egyptian Book of the Dead Hieroglyph Translations for Enlightenment: Understanding the Mystic Path to Enlightenment Through Direct Readings of the Sacred Signs and Symbols of Ancient Egyptian Language With Trilinear Deciphering Translation Method Vol. 1. Translation by Dr. Muata Ashby. Sema Institute.
[5] Ashby, M. (2022). The Complete Glorious Light Meditation Volume 2. Translation by Dr. Muata Ashby. Sema Institute.
[6] Ashby, M. (2019). Teachings of Ancient Egyptian Sage Amenemopet with Hieroglyphic texts. Translation by Dr. Muata Ashby. Sema Institute.

# Chapter 3: The Problem - How Consciousness Becomes Trapped

Understanding how consciousness can transcend its apparent limitations through the three-level framework naturally leads us to examine what prevents transcendence of exclusive ego-body identification from occurring. The same scriptures that reveal consciousness's divine potential also diagnose precisely how universal awareness becomes trapped in the illusion of separateness and limitation.

The Scripture of Ra and Hetheru reveals the precise mechanism by which consciousness becomes trapped in suffering through its description of the "fire of suffering." This teaching illuminates how heated mental states create the psychological conditions that obscure divine recognition:

FROM THE SCRIPTURE OF RA AND HETHERU[6]:

- The fire of suffering and divine withdrawal
- Ra's decision to leave the earth plane
- The cosmic restructuring

Verse 56.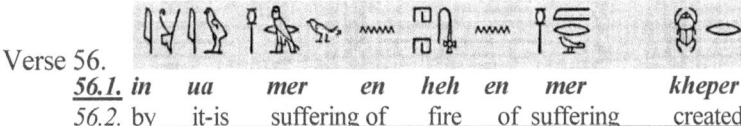
*56.1.* in ua mer en heh en mer kheper
*56.2.* by it-is suffering of fire of suffering created
*56.3.* ...It is a state created by your experiences in the world with people - losing your identity and with it, your inner peace, abiding contentment, and happiness. Considering who you are essentially and the abiding contentment you had before becoming the lioness, this is the experience of suffering: the fire in which the soul is tormented by an agitated mind, fueled by unrighteous desires, ignorance, and egoism. This leads to experiencing bad situations, frustrations, and self-defeating pursuits of happiness that end in pain and anguish followed by a never-ending lust for again pleasure and

---

[6] Translation by Dr. Muata Ashby

fulfillment that inevitably ends in the same anguish, frustration and unfulfillment. This is all a fire of suffering. Your experience of suffering was due to your delusion about pleasure and proximity to humans - feeling creatures who become unrighteous by forgetting their source and sustenance (Ra), becoming emotionally unstable and mentally irrational, irreverent, conceited people, some bad and others not. This fire of suffering has led to a situation of personal unhappiness and dissatisfaction, creating anxiety and delusion...

Verse 56.
<u>56.4.</u>  cher trayu         in     mer     djed in   hem    en
<u>56.5.</u>  presence beginning   by  suffering said  by majesty of (Ra)
<u>56.6.</u>  ...due to being King, presiding over the people who were once loyal and devoted but who turned into arrogant blasphemers, and having been abiding in the same realm with and being in the presence of and witnessing the suffering of humans from the beginning; and just as there is a beginning of things in time and space there has to be also an end which means you cannot stay on earth according to your desire. You (Hetheru/Sekhmet) have other duties and responsibilities to tend to in your original form and conscious awareness. Now the following words are coming from the Majesty of...(Ra)

Notice how Ra's cosmic perspective on human suffering reveals the universal pattern that manifests in individual consciousness through what the ancient texts designate as the fundamental division between heated and silent mental states. The Scripture's description of humans becoming "emotionally unstable and mentally irrational, irreverent, conceited people" who have forgotten "their source and sustenance (Ra)" corresponds directly with the detailed psychological analysis provided by the wisdom teachings of Sage Amenemopet.

Furthermore, what appears as cosmic drama in the Scripture of Ra and Hetheru operates simultaneously as precise instruction about individual consciousness development. The "arrogant blasphemers" who caused Ra's withdrawal represent not merely historical figures but the heated mental patterns that emerge in any consciousness that has lost touch with its divine source (Ra). Even so, the ancient wisdom provides practical guidance for recognizing and responding to these patterns, whether encountered in others or arising within oneself.

The cosmic teaching of Ra's withdrawal due to human spiritual ignorance thus provides both universal principle and personal psychology map. The same forces creating cosmic disharmony manifest through individual consciousness as specific mental-emotional patterns that can be identified, understood, and transformed through proper spiritual discipline. This dual-level instruction enables aspirants to recognize both the collective human condition and their own psychological patterns that perpetuate separation from divine awareness.

*FROM THE WISDOM TEACHINGS OF SAGE AMENEMOPET:*

**Chapter 2, Verse 17**[7]: The heated person definition -

Verse 17.
17.1.   *pa*         *shemm*           *{chft}*        *tu - k*       *mach*
17.2.   That         heated            {enemy}     such-thee    suffering
17.3.   Now, you heated person, you who, because of the delusions and negative aryu[8] (karma) that has led to a corrupted mind, you have become the enemy of life, of your own and of the community; you who are guided by the corrupted mind, live life by unrighteousness, fraud, anger, boisterousness, flippant (offhand, dismissive)

---

[7] Translation by Dr. Muata Ashby
[8] Sum total effect of a person past thoughts, feelings, desires and experiences of the past of the present lifetime and past lifetimes that contributes to a person's present guiding feelings, opinions, thoughts, desires and inclinations of the personality that impel or compel the personality to certain paths of action in the present life. The aryu can be changed by living through the fruition of the past aryu and engaging in spiritual disciplines (Sema Tawy [Egyptian Yoga], Shetaut Neter [Egyptian Mysteries]) that will mitigate and or cleanse the cause of the negative aryu (cause=spiritual ignorance and delusion).

retorts and thoughtless speech, inconsiderate and impulsive acts, rapacious greed, jealousy, envy, ridiculing others and having no compassion for the poor or the less fortunate, con artist/fraud, criminality, to such a one is given to the suffering. The expressions of your personality, that have led to unrighteous thoughts, feelings and actions, lead to your own suffering; not only the suffering when you are in pain and anguish as a result of your actions, but also the suffering is when you act out of egoism and mental agitation, committing unrighteous acts that cause you pleasures that will in future lead to personal physical and psychological sufferings, frustrations and dissatisfaction; for actions out of egoism and mental agitation that seem to cause pleasure are actually experiences of separation from the Divine that is the real source of bliss (unalloyed, unlimited pleasure and happiness of inner peace); this is actually more suffering than the suffering of the righteous person that is harmed by the heated person. Therefore, the cause of your own suffering, oh heated person, is in the source of the corrupted mind, due to the heat of the person, caused by spiritual ignorance that leads to egoism, mental agitation and unrighteous feelings, thoughts and actions.

Consider how the scripture describes the heated person's expressions: "unrighteousness, fraud, anger, boisterousness, flippant retorts and thoughtless speech, inconsiderate and impulsive acts, rapacious greed, jealousy, envy, ridiculing others and having no compassion for the poor or the less fortunate" [2]. Nevertheless, the teaching reveals a profound insight: even when such a person experiences apparent pleasure from these unrighteous acts, they are actually experiencing a deeper form of suffering—separation from the Divine [2]. Indeed, the Divine represents the true source of unlimited bliss and inner peace; therefore, disconnection from this divine foundation renders the personality susceptible to negative feelings, thoughts, and actions that appear to provide satisfaction but actually perpetuate the underlying spiritual emptiness [2].

In other words, the heated person suffers not only when experiencing the painful consequences of their actions, but also during the very moments when they believe they are experiencing pleasure through egoistic acts [2]. This designates a crucial understanding for aspirants: actions arising from egoism and mental agitation, even when they seem to produce pleasure, actually constitute experiences of separation from the Divine that represents our authentic source of fulfillment.

**Chapter 3, Verses 10, 15-17**[9]: Avoiding association with heated persons - "desist from, abstain, cease, renounce joining with and gossiping with...the sneaky enemy, the heated person"

Verse 10.
10.1.    *im-an ari nehbu    tjetje    ra ma pa    teha ra betjenu {cheft}*
10.2.    do not yoking gossiping {mouth} behold that argument {mouth} sneaky enemy
10.3.    Desist from, abstain, cease, renounce joining with and gossiping with and watch out, definitely not getting into verbal arguments with the sneaky enemy, the heated person.

Verse 15.
*15.1.    pa    shemm    {cheft}    im    unut    tu-f*
15.2.    that    heated    {enemy}    in    hour    to-he
15.3.    That heated person {who is the enemy} when they are in their time of heat...

Verse 16.
*16.1.    tuoaha    tu-khat    f    chaa    setenem {her} {mdj} f*
16.2.    reject    to-thee heart    his    abandon    misleading{person}{fig} he
16.3.    ...you should reject them by turning your mind away from their mind and emotions. You should abandon them because they are misleading personalities...

---

[9] Translation by Dr. Muata Ashby

## Awakening Your Soul-Aware-Witness

Verse 17.
17.1.　　er　　pa　　　　Neter　rech　　an　　　　en - f
17.2.　　regards that　　　Divine wisdom　turn-back　to - him
17.3.　　...and you should not be concerned with their fate since as you turn away from them the Divine, in a mysterious way, turns back towards them and provides to them what they need and deserve for their ethical and spiritual evolution.

10.1-10.3. The aspirant must learn to recognize and appropriately respond to the heated condition of mind, whether encountered in others or arising within oneself [2]. The scripture instructs: "Desist from, abstain, cease, renounce joining with and gossiping with and watch out, definitely not getting into verbal arguments with the sneaky enemy, the heated person" [2]. This teaching reveals that engaging with heated condition through argument or gossip actually amplifies the very mental agitation that creates the heated condition.

15.1-17.3. The teaching continues with profound wisdom about the proper response when encountering heated persons: "you should reject them by turning your mind away from their mind and emotions. You should abandon them because they are misleading personalities" [2]. Yet the scripture provides a crucial spiritual principle: practitioners need not be concerned with the fate of those they spiritually distance themselves from, because "as you turn away from them the Divine, in a mysterious way, turns back towards them and provides to them what they need and deserve for their ethical and spiritual evolution" [2].

This understanding aligns with the tradition of Shetaut Neter that individual consciousness cannot heal or transform a heated condition of mind in others through direct engagement; rather, the most compassionate response involves maintaining one's own spiritual equilibrium while allowing the Divine to work through natural spiritual law.

# FROM TEACHINGS OF AMENEMOPET CHAPTER 18: THE SLEEP OF SPIRITUAL IGNORANCE[10]

Verse 24.(1)

24.1. ar setdjerau usta f su ru cha
24.2. as to sleep/stupor pull-load he his separation forsaking
24.3. As to the person who lives life as if in a slumber of spiritual ignorance, undergoing the stress of pulling the harder load of life due to egoism, instead of being relaxed due to knowing and experiencing the natural flow of life when one is conscious and aware of Neberdjer, that person who is as if sleep-walking through life is actually at the same time, due to that ignorance of the knowledge of Self, separating themselves from and forsaking/leaving/moving away from…

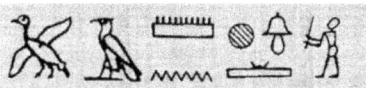

Verse 25.(1a)

25.1. pa mench {mdj}
25.2. that (project of) perfection {fig}
25.3. …(forsaking/moving away from) that perfection that is found when the roughhewn imperfect parts of the personality are carved away, allowing the perfect essential nature of Neberdjer to be perceived…

Verse 26.(2)

26.1. kemat hedj f su
26.2. ending-moment brightness-damaged he himself
26.3. …(that forsaking comes to pass) in the moment when that stupor has occurred; thus the perception of the brightness of spiritual enlightenment (The Divine) has been damaged by the person themselves, who have allowed their brightness of Spirit to be lost due to the delusion of the stupor of spiritual ignorance. That stupor of spiritual ignorance due to ignorantly accepting the load of the imperfect ego instead of the lightness of the perfection of Neberdjer knowledge, awareness of the absolute.

---

[10] Translation by Dr. Muata Ashby

24.1-26.3. It is important to understand that these verses reveal the psychological mechanism by which consciousness becomes trapped in what the ancients called "setdjerau"—the sleep or stupor of spiritual ignorance [2]. Recognize how the scripture describes this condition: consciousness "pulling the harder load of life due to egoism, instead of being relaxed due to knowing and experiencing the natural flow of life when one is conscious and aware of Neberdjer" [2].

The teaching illuminates that this spiritual stupor involves consciousness "separating themselves from and forsaking/leaving/moving away from that perfection that is found when the roughhewn imperfect parts of the personality are carved away, allowing the perfect essential nature of Neberdjer to be perceived" [2]. Moreover, this represents consciousness actively choosing the burden of ego-identification over the natural lightness that emerges when awareness rests in its divine source.

Therefore, the ancient sages taught that spiritual ignorance constitutes not merely a lack of knowledge, but an active process by which consciousness obscures its own divine nature—"the perception of the brightness of spiritual enlightenment (The Divine) has been damaged by the person themselves, who have allowed their brightness of Spirit to be lost due to the delusion of the stupor of spiritual ignorance" [2].

## The Discovery of Neberdjer - The Non-Dual Reality and the acceptance of that as a life truth

According to the Ancient Egyptian Book of Enlightenment Chapter 125 verses 5-6, doing/acting out of truth is the necessary performance of actions such that a person becomes sufficiently purified from their ego-misidentification sufficiently so as to have access to Neberdjer (All-Encompassing Divinity/ Lord-encompassing-all-limits/the Vast) who is personified in the concept of "Asar" (Osiris), the universal soul of all. This is the same Asar that is the divinizing prefix or theological titulary given to a spiritual initiate signifying their true identity that comes before the ego or human name. Therefore, the true identity of the human is the consciousness of the Absolute (Neberdjer/Ausarez{Osiris}).

Verse 5.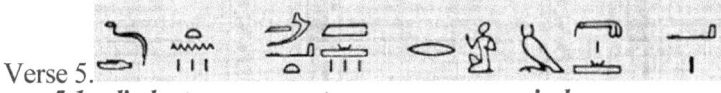
    *5.1. djed   tenu     naatu    er   a   imba     a*
    5.2. speak you-all truthfulness about me in-front-of   hand
    5.3. all of you must speak truthfully about me in front of the hand, the presence and care of…

Verse 6.
    6.1. *Neberdjer her entet ari n-a   maatu   im   tamera*
    6.2. Lord-of-All  entity what-is doing of-I truthfulness in Egypt
    6.3. …the "Lord-of-all, the all-encompassing Divinity" that enfolds Creation and manifests as Creation, the entity that is what is, what exists and nothing else but Neberdjer exists. Do this because I have acted by truthfulness while I was living on earth in the beloved land of Egypt.

All of the aforesaid may be referred to by the term found in the same Ancient Egyptian Book of Enlightenment Chapter 125 append. verse 9/10[11] as "living by truth."

Verse 9.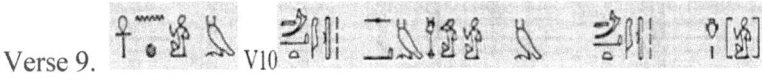
    *9.1. ankh a im   maatu   zam   a   im   maatu   ab [a]*
    9.2. live I in (V10) truth eat        I  form   truth  heart [mine]
    9.3. I live in truth, (V10) I feed upon things that are in the form of truth, in my mind, not lies, falsehoods, or similitudes.

Ancient Egyptian Book of Enlightenment Chapter 125 verses 5-6 contains an important phrase which proves crucial to understanding the nature of consciousness and the understanding of existence. The section states "Lord-of-all, the all-encompassing Divinity that enfolds Creation and manifests as Creation, the entity that is what is, what exists and nothing else, but Neberdjer exists" [3]. This

---

[11] Translation by Dr. Muata Ashby

declaration about Neberdjer (Asar) signifies that there exists an understanding of two important concepts about Neberdjer:

1. **All-encompassingness:** Neberdjer encompasses all.
2. **Absolute existence:** Neberdjer represents all that exists; there is nothing aside from Neberdjer that exists.

Whatever exists denotes Neberdjer. Therefore, whatever the human mind may sense or perceive represents nothing but Neberdjer. Thus, when a human being develops ego-awareness and thinks of themselves as a separate individual being, they remain oblivious to the fact of the non-dual essence of existence. Whatever objects in Creation that the human mind and senses can perceive, they all represent manifestations of one all-encompassing existence (Neberdjer).

This means that the thoughts of ego-separate being are deluded as well as the thoughts about individual identity, desires, frustrations or happiness and fulfillment. From this perspective, the ego-bound human being's thoughts, feelings and actions constitute thoughts, feelings and actions of a person operating under misapprehension that can at best produce temporary apparent happiness or fulfillment but never abiding satisfaction and contentment.

The aforesaid also applies to religious practices such as rituals, myths about gods and goddesses as well as philosophies and psychology practices and theories that remain ameliorative rather than emancipatory in nature. These approaches offer palliative relief rather than curative understanding, providing coping-based strategies rather than transformative realization. These approaches may help people who are having psychological issues or dissatisfaction with life to manage their symptoms and achieve temporary relief, but they do not address (or are unable to address because of the incapacity of the person they are trying to help) the fundamental root cause of human discontent and delusion: the ego-bound misapprehension of separate existence.

Until the human being may be able to have the right perspective about life and live life acting out of that perspective—recognizing the non-dual reality of existence—it will be impossible to discover true and abiding peace and contentment through the emancipatory and curative realization of self as a manifestation of Neberdjer, living in Neberdjer, as Neberdjer.

The recognition of Neberdjer as the sole reality that encompasses and manifests as all existence reveals why ego-based approaches to fulfillment inevitably fail. Whether seeking satisfaction through relationships, achievements, or even spiritual practices that maintain the illusion of separateness, consciousness operating from ego-identification can only access temporary relief rather than lasting peace. The fundamental shift from ameliorative coping to emancipatory realization requires recognizing one's essential identity as Neberdjer itself rather than as a separate entity seeking connection with the Divine.

The ramifications of the reality of the single nondual reality of existence also means that human beings who search for fulfillment in relationships from the standpoint of ego-identity and delusion are bound for disappointment. A relationship sought between people who are seeking happiness from each other appears bound to fail due to the fundamental incapacity of such people firstly to know what they really are seeking and secondly because they are seeking it in a realm of confusion since the mind and senses cannot show what Creation really is (Neberdjer).

Such a person, being in the grip of ego-delusion, seeks happiness as a false identity of self seeking in the world that has items in it that the deluded mind—thinking it knows what they are—has developed delusions about their potential to provide abiding happiness. While everything in the universe represents a manifestation of Neberdjer, it appears as a fleeting, changeable manifestation to the human mind. Therefore, it by definition cannot provide any abiding situation but only temporary appearances displaying the spectacle of consciousness (Neberdjer) that supports the appearances. This resembles when a person is sleeping and having a dream, their consciousness supports the dream world, the situations of the dreamworld and the awareness of oneself as the dream personality in the dreamworld. Nevertheless, the Creation of Neberdjer (the Cosmos) lasts longer than the human dream and the human lifetime.

## Implications for Promoting Harmony with Life and Discovery of Neberdjer (Asar) as Self

Important implications emerge: If Neberdjer represents all that exists, then who is it that calls themselves a person, by such and such a name? Who is it that comes from such and such a family? Who is it that was born on such and such a date and dying on such and such a date? When a person is eating, who is eating and what is being eaten?

Though a person seems to be experiencing thoughts, feelings, sensations and perceptions, Neberdjer represents the actual experiencer and recipient of all these apparent events that are nothing more than dreamlike appearances in Neberdjer (Consciousness). Thus, like a person dreaming a dream and then waking up and discovering the dream was unreal, so too the creation of Neberdjer is not abiding and appears only as an appearance for the sake of presenting a vision of a universe for consciousness experiencing through humans and animals and all life an expression of existence that constitutes a possible manifestation of Absolute consciousness appearing in differentiated forms.

Implication: living by truth (Maat) also means acting with humility and not arrogance, being gracious, being forgiving, understanding and awed by the multiplicity of expressions of Neberdjer which is the real (me) in the personality. These virtuous behaviors and feelings serve to purify the personality and allow the ego to be purified and eventually effaced, leaving Neberdjer (Asar) awareness in the pure awareness of mind. When this occurs, it signifies a person has reached the goal of what life ideally means: to live a fleeting life in time and space knowing oneself to be the author and experiencer of the universe as opposed to being a miserable person ever searching and never finding peace and abiding happiness.

Awakening Your Soul-Aware-Witness

# ANCIENT EGYPTIAN BOOK OF ENLIGHTENMENT - PERT-EM-HERU CHAPTER 26[12]: THE CYCLE OF REINCARNATION

Verse 4.
4.1. her im abty en agy  sha chuchet  im  ched  k
4.2. person in east  to drown  lake traveling in  downstream(boat) thine
4.3. …I reject being a person in the eastern part of the world where the sun dawns and people come into the physical world as reincarnated beings; Then what happens is that, having come into the world to time and space duality, as if drowning in a lake (waters of the mind) they get caught up in the mayhem of desires born of spiritual ignorance and duality perceived through mind and senses, people drown in the ever agitating movements of opposition and attraction; it is like sailing downstream to the north of Kemet (Egypt) and then…

Verse 5.
5.1. khenty  k  an  ha  a  er  chudet  imy  k iu n-a
5.2. upstream thine not advance I as-to boat withinness thee It-is for-me
5.3. … sailing, in your boat, up to the south of Kemet (Egypt); up and down, up and down, drowning in the illusory but compellingly apparent ever-present dualities of life, and in the end, going nowhere except back to the beginning, the east, to do it over again, experiencing life on earth as if sinking in a flood of choices that never satisfy abidingly; the life of reincarnation is as if being engulfed in an inundation of actions, reactions, desires, frustrations, and endless unrest of ordinary life on earth. I declare that I will not go forward, I will not proceed, I will not increase my involvement and spread myself in the endless interests of the pointless and therefore illusory dual choices, situations and objects encountered when living on earth; I will not go into that boat within which you are. This is for myself…

---

[12] Translation by Dr. Muata Ashby

Chapter 26, of the Ancient Egyptian Book of Enlightenment, reveals a profound teaching on the nature of consciousness trapped in what may be termed the "reincarnation cycle"—the endless repetition of birth, death, and rebirth that occurs when awareness remains identified with ego-consciousness [3]. The scripture describes this condition as "drowning in a lake (waters of the mind)" where consciousness becomes "caught up in the mayhem of desires born of spiritual ignorance and duality perceived through mind and senses" [3].

The teaching describes the futility of this cycle: consciousness experiences life "as if sailing downstream to the north of Kemet (Egypt) and then sailing, in your boat, up to the south of Kemet (Egypt); up and down, up and down, drowning in the illusory but compellingly apparent ever-present dualities of life, and in the end, going nowhere except back to the beginning, the east, to do it over again" [3]. This means that ego-consciousness, despite all its apparent activity and striving, accomplishes nothing that provides lasting fulfillment or spiritual advancement.

**Understanding the True Nature of Scriptural "Separation": The Soul-Aware-Witness Distinguished from Ego Delusion**

**The Ego Construct: Agitation, Control, and Soul Suffocation**

Chapter 26 reveals a profound teaching on two distinct modes of consciousness operation in the human personality through its description of both the ego construct and the "Soul-Aware-Witness" [3]. The scripture reveals the ego construct when it depicts the path of reincarnation—the endless cycle of going "back and forth, drowning" in the illusory movements of worldly duality [3]. At the same time, this ego-construct represents the very condition from which consciousness must separate itself (develop detachment) in order to discover its true nature as what may be termed the "Soul-Aware-Witness."

The scripture illuminates this crucial distinction through its precise descriptions [3]. The ego construct manifests as consciousness caught in what the text describes as "drowning in the ever-agitating movements of opposition and attraction" and "sailing downstream to the north of Kemet (Egypt)" in endless cycles of reincarnation and fruitless recurring movements that accomplish no goal of fulfillment or satisfaction in life [3]. This denotes consciousness identifying with the agitated heart (mind), being controlled by bodily urges and mental fluctuations, and consequently suffocating the soul through its relentless pursuit of satisfaction in temporal phenomena.

The wisdom embedded in these teachings reveals that the ego construct operates through a fundamental pattern of agitation and external control [3]. In other words, when consciousness identifies with the ego-personality, it experiences the heart as agitated rather than peaceful, seeks to control the body and circumstances through reactive effort, and becomes trapped in what the scripture describes as the "mayhem of desires born of spiritual ignorance and duality perceived through mind and senses" [3]. This means that ego-consciousness suffocates the soul by overwhelming it with constant mental-emotional turbulence and endless cycles of seeking fulfillment through external means.

This ego-identification creates what the teachings describe as the condition where "people drown in the ever-agitating movements of opposition and attraction" [3]. The scripture shows that this drowning occurs precisely because ego-consciousness approaches life from the illusion of separateness—imagining itself as an isolated entity (separate from universal consciousness) that must struggle against external forces to achieve security, pleasure, and validation. Therefore, the ego construct represents consciousness that has forgotten its divine nature and instead identifies with the temporary phenomena of body-mind experience.

The ego construct thus emerges as consciousness trapped in cycles of agitation, control-seeking, and external dependency that prevent recognition of its divine nature. Unlike the Soul-Aware-Witness that operates from inner peace and divine recognition, the ego construct maintains identity through constant mental-emotional turbulence and reactive patterns. Understanding this distinction becomes essential for spiritual development, as it enables practitioners to recognize when consciousness operates from ego-identification versus soul-awareness.

**The Nature of Dual Perception and Unity Recognition**

The teachings indicate that Ra and Hetheru represent unified existence: individuated universal cosmic consciousness, self-aware as Creator arising from undifferentiated consciousness and self-aware as Creator being one with its Creations [1]. Still, the transition into the role of Sekhmet demonstrates how further individuation and localization—moving from universal awareness to focused awareness of a particular divine form—can constitute a constriction of consciousness that leads to forgetfulness of universality due to prolonged engagement in heated mental activity [1]. In other words, this occlusion combined with heated mental activity clouds the capacity for universal awareness.

The heated mind misses not only the underlying unity of the mentally perceived manifested realities of Creation but also the "overlying" unity of the apparent multiplicity [1]. For example, in a dream there appears to be multiplicity, but underlying and overlying the dream represents the consciousness of the dreamer who serves as both the foundation (underlying) and the essential nature (overlying) [and all-encompassingness] of the dream experience [1].

This understanding shows why the silent mind (ger) naturally recognizes unity while the heated mind (shemm) perceives separateness [1]. The heated mind operates through heavy aryu that cloud perception, while the silent mind has either purified these impressions or learned to rest in the spaces between them where the underlying witness consciousness becomes apparent.

**The Formation and Function of Aryu: The Psychological Mechanism of Delusion**

**The Precise Mechanism of Consciousness Entrapment**

The Scripture of Ra and Hetheru reveals the precise psychological mechanism through which universal consciousness becomes, as if, trapped in ego-identification [1]. The "entrapment" of consciousness is illusory because the ego awareness that makes consciousness seem to think it is a localized individual is illusory. This mechanism operates through what the ancient teachings call aryu—mental impressions or karmic residues that accumulate in the unconscious mind from past experiences, thoughts, and actions [1].

According to verse 128 of the Scripture, "within humans there are egoistic mental impressions (aryu/karmic remnants) that develop from experiences and actions in current and previous lifetimes. These impressions manifest as feeling memories, recorded and reinforced patterns of thoughts, feelings, and behaviors that remain registered in the unconscious mind, influencing present and future experiences" [1].

Aryu represent not abstract concepts, but actual impressions left in the unconscious mind that function like winds disturbing the ocean of undifferentiated consciousness [4]. The Scripture describes Nunu as the "primeval homogeneous ocean" of undifferentiated consciousness, while aryu function like winds that disturb this ocean, creating waves of differentiated thoughts and mental phenomena [4]. When these motivational disturbances are eliminated, consciousness rests in the calm, undifferentiated state.

**The Qualitative Nature of Aryu and Divine Light Transmission**

The teachings reveal that aryu possess distinct qualities that either allow or obstruct the transmission of divine light through the mind [4]. When actions are aligned with Maat (divine order), they create what may be termed "light aryu"—impressions that remain transparent to divine light, like thin clouds that allow sunlight to pass through. These impressions do not bind the soul but rather serve as vehicles for divine expression and positive interaction with the world.

Conversely, actions against Maat create "heavy aryu"—dense, opaque impressions that obstruct the flow of divine light [4]. These impressions weigh down the personality, creating what the Scripture describes as "the experience of suffering: the fire in which the soul is tormented by an agitated mind, fueled by unrighteous desires, ignorance, and egoism" [1].

This understanding shows that aryu accumulate and intensify over time, especially when founded in ignorance and egoism, promoting "endless unfulfillable worldly desires that cloud the mind's natural clarity" [1]. Verse 129 reveals the devastating consequence: "A heart in this condition becomes a beacon for inimical cosmic forces—those demoniac energies that manifest as avarice, lust, jealousy, and selfishness" [1].

This understanding reveals the profound importance of spiritual purification: practitioners must learn to recognize how their actions create either light or heavy aryu and gradually purify the accumulated impressions that obstruct the natural flow of divine consciousness through the personality. In this way, consciousness gradually frees itself from the trap of ego-identification and discovers its true nature as the Soul-Aware-Witness that underlies all experiences.

# The Ancient Egyptian Psychology of Herufy: Understanding the Dual Nature of Human Consciousness

### Essential Understanding of Set and Heru in Psychological Development

Before examining the sophisticated psychology of Herufy, we must establish proper understanding of the mythological characters that represent psychological principles within human consciousness. Indeed, the wisdom of the neteru reveals that Set, while associated with egoistic tendencies in this teaching, does not represent an inherently negative or evil aspect of personality that should be destroyed or eliminated. Consider how Set, in the broader context of Ancient Egyptian wisdom, represents the worldly aspect of personality that enables consciousness to function effectively within the temporal realm—managing practical affairs, maintaining physical existence, and engaging with the material world in ways that can serve spiritual development when properly oriented toward divine purpose [1].

Nevertheless, the challenge arises when Set becomes corrupted through ignorance, delusions, and egoistic identification that transforms this necessary worldly function into a source of spiritual obstruction. In other words, Set can serve as a positive ally and servant to the soul (Asar {Osiris}) when operating under the guidance of higher consciousness, but can also turn toward negative thoughts, feelings, and actions when dominated by separative thinking and attachment to temporal concerns [1]. Therefore, the goal of spiritual development involves not the elimination of Set but rather the proper harmonization and orientation of this worldly aspect toward serving rather than competing with spiritual aspiration.

The Herufy concept expresses precisely this idea of the sometimes-conflicting interactions between the altruistic and spiritually aspiring aspect of the personality (Heru) and the ego-worldly aspect (Set) that can be harmonized and helpful when properly aligned, or egoistic and divergent when corrupted by ignorance and separative thinking [6]. Consider how the dominance of either aspect determines the overall direction of personality development: when Heru predominates through conscious cultivation, the personality moves toward positivity, self-discovery, and authentic spiritual realization; when Set operates through egoistic corruption, the personality moves toward worldliness, attachment, and the perpetuation of suffering through identification with temporal concerns [6]. This understanding ensures that students approach the Herufy teaching with proper recognition of both aspects as necessary components of human psychology that require integration rather than elimination, understanding that spiritual mastery emerges through conscious harmonization of these dual aspects under the sovereignty of divine consciousness.

Awakening Your Soul-Aware-Witness

**Teachings of New Kingdom Pert-M-Heru** -Heru with Two heads

From the Ancient Egyptian Book of Enlightenment (PertmHeru). Chapter 17, 27-28[13]

Verse A.
- A.1. *Apep pu    un   n-f im   tep en ua  kher    Maat*
- A.2. Apophis that    being of-he manifests head of one under    truth
- A.3. It is that Apophis, the fiendish personality, a confederate of Set, the egoism of the personality; that Apophis when he is in the state of having one of his heads being under the control of righteousness order and truth.

Verse B.
- B.1. *Ky djed  Heru  pu   un n-f im tepui unen ua  kher*
- B.2. Otherwise said Horus that being to-he in heads-two being one under influence
- B.3. Another way to understand it is: We are talking about Horus, the redemptive spiritual aspiration quality of the personality when he is in the state where he has two heads (also known as *Herufy*), having two opposing dispositions, one being under the influence or control of…

---

[13] Translation by Dr. Muata Ashby

Awakening Your Soul-Aware-Witness

Image: Heru with two heads- "Herfy"

**Verse C.**
- C.1. *Maat   ky   kher   isfetu   didi-f   isfetu   en ari - zy*
- C.2. order/truth other under influence unrighteousness. giveth he unrighteousness to doer thereof.
- C.3. …order and truth and the other being under the influence of unrighteousness and wrongdoing (Set). To the person who does unrighteousness and commits acts of wrongdoing he (the Divine) gives that (adversity) to them as the result of their unrighteous actions.

**Verse D.**
- D.1. *Maat   en   shemsy   kher  – z - a*
- D.2. Order/truth to    follower under influence person.
- D.3. To the person who follows order/truth, and influence of righteousness, they get that (prosperity) as the result of

125

their righteousness. Therefore, having two heads and being often conflicted, sometimes one gets positive results of one's actions and sometimes negative. This state of mind, called Apophis, of being conflicted, leads to disjointed movement in life, thwarting one's own positive efforts and failure on the spiritual path by thinking, feeling and acting in contradiction, working against oneself and one's better judgment. The mindset of Apophis needs to be opposed, and the character influenced by Maat is to be cultivated in order to have rectitude, order, and resolute purpose in the personality to succeed on the spiritual path.

**The Sophisticated Psychology of Ancient Kemet**

The ancient wisdom of Kemet (Egypt) possessed profound understanding of human psychology that anticipated many discoveries of modern transpersonal psychology by thousands of years [3]. Among the most significant of these insights stands the concept of Herufy—literally "Heru (Horus) with two heads"—which reveals the fundamental duality within human consciousness that creates the essential spiritual challenge confronting every sincere aspirant on the path to enlightenment [3].

This teaching, preserved in Ancient Egyptian Book of Enlightenment Chapter 17 of the ancient Egyptian Pert-m-Heru (Book of Enlightenment), provides crucial insight into why human beings experience inner conflict, moral contradiction, and the persistent struggle between noble aspirations and egoistic impulses that characterizes ordinary psychological functioning [3].

Furthermore, the wisdom embedded in these teachings demonstrates that the ancient Egyptian understanding of consciousness operated far beyond simplistic moral categories, revealing instead a sophisticated psychological framework that explains the precise mechanism through which divine consciousness becomes trapped in patterns of internal contradiction and self-defeating behavior [3]. Notice how this ancient insight addresses the fundamental question that confronts every human being: Why do we often act against our own better judgment, pursue goals that we know will not bring lasting satisfaction, and find ourselves caught in cycles of behavior that contradict our highest understanding and deepest spiritual aspirations?

## The Mythological Foundation: Heru (Horus) and Set in Psychological Context

The concept of Herufy emerges directly from the central myth of ancient Egyptian spirituality—the Ausarian (Osirian) Resurrection, which chronicles the persistent struggle between Heru (Horus) and Set for sovereignty over the spiritual kingdom of consciousness [3]. However, when approached from the psychological perspective that the ancient wisdom intended, this mythological narrative reveals itself as a precise map of the inner dynamics that govern human personality development and spiritual transformation [3]. The struggle between Heru and Set represents not external historical events but the ongoing psychological conflict between the higher and lower aspects of human nature for control of the personality and the ultimate goal of becoming Heru—the sovereign consciousness that operates in harmony with its divine source, Asar (Osiris) [3].

Heru represents the redemptive spiritual aspiration quality of the personality—that aspect of consciousness which naturally seeks truth, righteousness, and alignment with divine principles [3]. This higher nature expresses itself through what the ancient teachings recognize as genuine ethical impulses, the capacity for wisdom discrimination, and the spontaneous movement toward spiritual development that emerges when consciousness remembers its divine origin [3]. In psychological terms, Heru corresponds to what contemporary understanding might recognize as the authentic self, the witness consciousness, or the soul-aware aspect of personality that maintains connection with transcendent values and ultimate meaning [3].

Set, conversely, embodies the egoistic, wayward aspect of personality that operates through what the ancient wisdom identified as the fundamental delusion of separateness [3]. This lower nature manifests through selfish pursuits, reactive emotional patterns, and the persistent tendency to seek fulfillment through external means rather than recognizing the inner source of genuine satisfaction [3]. Observe how Set represents not evil in any absolute sense, but rather consciousness that has forgotten its divine nature and consequently operates through the limited perspective of ego-identification, creating the psychological conditions that lead to suffering, conflict, and spiritual stagnation [3].

## The Psychological Reality of Herufy: Two Heads, One Personality

The teaching of Herufy reveals the crucial understanding that both Heru and Set exist within the same personality—in fact, within every human being—creating what the ancient text describes as "having two heads" with "two opposing dispositions, one being under the influence of order and truth and the other being under the influence of unrighteousness and wrongdoing" [3]. This psychological insight proves essential for spiritual development because it explains why human beings experience the persistent inner contradiction between noble intentions and selfish actions, between spiritual understanding and worldly attachments, between the desire for peace and the tendency toward conflict and agitation [3].

The text specifically identifies this conflicted condition with Apophis (Apep), the serpent of chaos that represents the psychological state of being "often conflicted, sometimes one gets positive results of one's actions and sometimes negative" [3]. Moreover, this Apophis consciousness creates what the ancient wisdom recognized as "disjointed movement in life, thwarting one's own positive efforts and failure on the spiritual path by thinking, feeling and acting in contradiction, working against oneself and one's better judgment" [3]. This corresponds precisely with the psychological phenomenon that contemporary understanding recognizes as cognitive dissonance, internal conflict, and the tendency toward self-sabotage that emerges when consciousness operates from fragmented rather than integrated awareness [3].

Even so, the wisdom of these teachings shows that this conflicted state represents not a permanent condition but a stage in consciousness development that can be transcended through proper understanding and practice [3]. The text clearly states the solution: "The mindset of Apophis needs to be opposed, and the character influenced by Maat is to be cultivated in order to have rectitude, order, and resolute purpose in the personality to succeed on the spiritual path" [3]. This means that spiritual development requires conscious recognition of these two aspects within personality, followed by systematic cultivation of the Heru aspect while gradually purifying the egoistic tendencies that characterize the Set nature [3].

The psychology of Herufy thus provides essential understanding for spiritual development by acknowledging the inevitable internal conflict that characterizes human consciousness during its evolutionary development. Rather than viewing psychological contradiction as personal failure, practitioners can recognize the "two heads" as natural stages requiring conscious discrimination and gradual integration. This framework enables aspirants to work systematically with their dual nature rather than being overwhelmed by internal contradictions that seem to thwart spiritual progress.

**The Necessity of Psychological Discrimination**

The ancient Egyptian understanding reveals why it becomes necessary for spiritual aspirants to recognize and distinguish between these two aspects of personality rather than remaining unconscious of their operation [3]. Reflect on how most human beings live in a state of psychological confusion precisely because they fail to recognize that their mind contains both higher and lower natures, consequently identifying sometimes with noble impulses and sometimes with selfish desires without understanding the source of this internal contradiction [3]. This leads to what the teachings describe as "life of confusion and inner contradictions"—the common human experience of feeling pulled in opposing directions, making commitments that are later broken, and experiencing the frustration of repeated moral and spiritual failures that seem to emerge despite sincere intentions [3].

The parallel with certain Christian understanding of the "angel and devil" on each shoulder illustrates how various wisdom traditions have recognized this fundamental psychological reality, though the ancient Egyptian approach provides more sophisticated analysis of the underlying mechanisms and practical methods for resolution [3].

Furthermore, the teachings show that without clear discrimination between these aspects, human beings remain trapped in cycles of internal conflict that prevent genuine spiritual progress and authentic psychological integration [3].

At the same time, when practitioners develop the capacity to recognize which aspect of their nature is operating in any given moment, they gain the psychological foundation necessary for conscious spiritual transformation [3]. This discrimination allows what the ancient wisdom called "examination of these aspects and capacity to move towards purification of the personality facing and dealing with egoism and allowing the higher self to be victorious" [3]. The goal becomes not the elimination of the lower nature—which would be impossible since it represents an essential functions within human psychology—but rather the gradual refinement and sublimation of egoistic tendencies until they serve rather than oppose the soul's evolutionary development [3].

**The Path to Heru Sovereignty: Practical Transformation**

The ultimate goal of this psychological understanding involves becoming Heru—the sovereign consciousness that operates in harmony with Asar (Osiris), the soul principle [3]. This represents not the achievement of perfection in any conventional sense, but rather the establishment of consciousness in its natural state of witness awareness, where the higher spiritual nature maintains consistent governance over the personality while the lower egoistic functions operate in service to genuine spiritual development rather than in opposition to it [3]. Understand how this psychological integration creates what the ancient teachings recognize as "rectitude, order, and resolute purpose in the personality" that enables authentic success on the spiritual path [3].

The text provides clear guidance for this transformation through its explanation of the law of cause and effect that governs psychological development: "To the person who does unrighteousness and commits acts of wrongdoing he (the Divine) gives that (adversity) to them as the result of their unrighteous actions" while "To the person who follows order/truth, and influence of righteousness, they get that (prosperity) as the result of their righteousness" [3]. This reveals that the universe itself supports the movement toward Heru consciousness through providing immediate feedback—in the form of either harmony or conflict—that allows practitioners to recognize which aspect of their nature is operating and adjust their choices accordingly [3].

Therefore, the ancient Egyptian psychology of Herufy provides contemporary seekers with essential understanding for navigating the path of spiritual development with realistic expectations and practical methodology [3]. By recognizing the inevitability of internal conflict during the developmental process, practitioners can approach their psychological contradictions with compassion and wisdom rather than self-condemnation, understanding that the experience of "two heads" represents not personal failure but the natural condition of consciousness learning to transcend its identification with egoistic patterns and discover its true nature as an expression of divine awareness [3]. Through systematic cultivation of righteousness, truth, and spiritual aspiration, the conflicted Apophis consciousness gradually transforms into the integrated Heru awareness that serves as the foundation for all authentic spiritual realization and lasting psychological well-being [3].

**Ancient Textual Sources on Aryu: The Hieroglyphic Evidence**

**The Wisdom of Sage Amenemopet: Explicit Teaching on Aryu Formation and Management**

The following passages from Chapter 1 of the Wisdom Teachings of Sage Amenemopet provide the most explicit hieroglyphic documentation of the aryu concept in ancient Egyptian literature, using the actual term "aryu" while providing detailed psychological analysis of how these karmic impressions operate within human consciousness. These verses represent Amenemopet's foundational instruction to his student regarding the practical necessity of wisdom philosophy for managing the unconscious forces that shape human experience.

The teaching emerges within the context of Amenemopet's opening exhortation about the transformative power of absorbing wisdom

## Awakening Your Soul-Aware-Witness

teachings into "the innermost levels of the mind," revealing that the ancient wisdom understood aryu as specific psychological mechanisms that could be systematically addressed through proper spiritual education rather than mysterious forces beyond human comprehension.

Observe how Amenemopet's approach demonstrates the sophisticated understanding that the ancient Egyptian wisdom tradition possessed regarding what contemporary psychology might recognize as unconscious conditioning patterns, emotional triggers, and the relationship between past experiences and present mental-emotional reactivity. Furthermore, these verses provide essential textual evidence that the concept of karmic impressions was not merely philosophical speculation but represented practical psychology based on careful observation of how consciousness becomes trapped in repetitive patterns that obscure its essential divine nature.

### Teachings of Amenemopet Chapter 1[14]

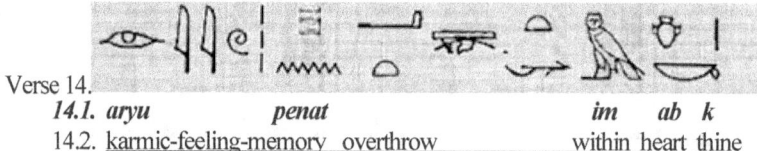

Verse 14.
    *14.1. aryu        penat                      im    ab    k*
    14.2. karmic-feeling-memory  overthrow          within heart thine
    14.3. ...such that when the karmic-feeling-memories (aryu-karmic-feeling-memories) arise from your unconscious into your conscious mind and would otherwise overwhelm, as if capsize the peacefulness of your mind...

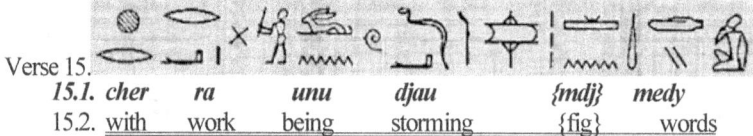

Verse 15.
    *15.1. cher    ra      unu      djau        {mdj}    medy*
    15.2. with    work    being    storming    {fig}    words
    15.3. ...at that crucial time when those mental impressions (impressions manifest as emerging feeling memories, recorded and reinforced patterns of thoughts, feelings, and behaviors that remain registered in the unconscious mind, influencing present and future experiences. The subtle effects of these aryu accumulate and intensify, and if founded in ignorance, egoism and delusion, promote endless unfulfillable worldly desires that cloud the mind's

---

[14] Translation by Dr. Muata Ashby

## Awakening Your Soul-Aware-Witness

natural clarity and foment ambiguity, diffidence and spiritual ignorance and resulting worldly desires, mental distortions, delusions, frustrations and perpetual unrest (neshesh) start working in the mind and there is a storming of words (words manifest as thoughts in the mind-the human mind operates in terms of thoughts that the mind can recognize as ideas or concepts that are labled with words (names) the mind can use to think and cognize with) …

Verse 16.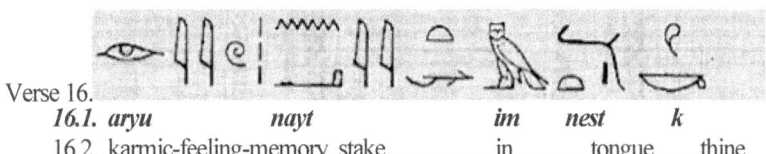
  16.1. *aryu        nayt           im     nest       k*
  16.2. karmic-feeling-memory stake    in     tongue   thine
  16.3. …generated by those impressions (aryu-karmic-feeling-memories), at those times the the effiorth at was taken to heed these instrutions, to allow the wise words (thoughts/philosophy) of this book to be absorbed into the innermost mind, then that wisdom would be able to act as a stake, as if a mooring post for your tongue so that you would not get caught up in the storm and thereby your mind would thrash you in the storm of excitedness and uncontrolled speech that would promote storming of the mind, uncontrolled thoughts, urges and untoward thinking and acting (heated condition of mind).

## Significance of the passages from Wisdom Text of Amenemopet for the Themes Covered in this Book

The Amenemopet verses prove crucial for establishing the scholarly foundation of this manuscript's entire psychological framework, since they demonstrate that the concept of aryu was not a later philosophical development but represented core ancient Egyptian wisdom that informed their understanding of consciousness transformation from the earliest recorded periods [2]. These passages show how the ancient wisdom understood that spiritual development requires systematic work with unconscious psychological patterns rather than mere intellectual study or ritual observance, providing the essential bridge between the cosmic teachings found in the Scripture of Ra and Hetheru and the practical guidance offered throughout Amenemopet's wisdom literature.

The teaching demonstrates the precise mechanism by which consciousness becomes trapped in what Amenemopet describes as the "storming of words" when aryu activate in the mind, creating the heated mental conditions that prevent recognition of divine nature while simultaneously revealing how wisdom teachings can serve as an "anchor" or "stake" that prevents consciousness from being swept away by these unconscious forces [2]. This psychological insight directly supports the central thesis that human suffering emerges not from external circumstances but from specific internal processes that can be identified, understood, and systematically purified through appropriate spiritual practice.

The verses also establish the essential connection between the individual psychological work described throughout the manuscript and the cosmic transformation processes revealed in the Scripture of Ra and Hetheru, showing how the same forces that operate on universal scales through Sekhemit's heated condition and restoration also manifest within human consciousness as manageable psychological patterns that respond to wisdom application rather than requiring dramatic spiritual interventions.

**The Instructions for Meri-ka-Ra: Aryu as Eternal Witnesses and Divine Recognition**

The following passages from the ancient Egyptian Instructions for Meri-ka-Ra provide an alternative perspective on the same psychological mechanisms described by Amenemopet, presenting aryu not through explicit terminology but through the profound metaphor of "witnesses" that persist after death to testify regarding the quality of consciousness that characterized an individual's lifetime. This scripture, which addresses the fundamental question of what survives bodily death and how past actions influence future experience, reveals the ancient Egyptian understanding that consciousness creates permanent impressions that function as independent psychological forces capable of either binding awareness to repetitive patterns or serving as testimony to divine recognition achieved during human incarnation.

The text emerges from the wisdom literature tradition wherein experienced rulers provided guidance for effective governance, yet the passages selected here transcend political advice to address the universal psychological principles that govern consciousness development regardless of social position or historical period. What's more, the scripture's teaching about divine recognition—describing liberated consciousness as "internally being God, a Horus being"—provides direct textual support for the manuscript's central teaching regarding the Soul-Aware-Witness as consciousness that has achieved separation from ego-identification while maintaining functional capacity in the world of manifestation. The Soul-Aware-Witness, the awareness discovered by a human being of their higher nature that is separate from mind and body, is the development that blossoms into the same Heru (Horus) self. The Heru title is given to a person who while living on earth is the hero that vanquishes the lower self to become the ruler of their life on earth.

## Selections from Papyrus Petersburg 1116A: Instruction for Mery-ka-ra[15]

### ABOUT HOW THE ACTIONS OF A PERSON ARE JUDGED EVEN AFTER THEY ARE DEAD AND THE CONCEPT OF ARYU OR KARMA
### Trans. by Muata Ashby

Verse 3.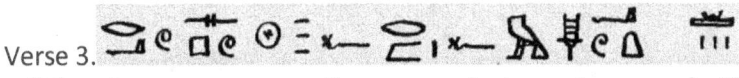

**3.1.** *Rauzepu  f  er-gs  f  im  ahau  {mdj}*
3.2. Establish remains over he  as to-side his  form as lifetime judged{fig}
3.3. That part that remains over, after death of the body, establishes itself on one side of the person in the form of witnesses as the gods and goddesses judge {abstract[16]} that person's actions during their lifetime[17].

---

[15] Translation by Dr. Muata Ashby
[16] {the presence of a scroll means that the concept being discussed should be regarded with an abstract ideal; thus it is not to be considered as an concrete tally but rather as summary or sum total effect of a person's actions on their character through their actions, thoughts, feelings and experiences that they engendered and became unconscious impressions that survive the death of the body and the conscious mind.}
[17] The deeper meaning of the terms "aha (with a sundisk symbol)" and "ahau" (lifetime judgment) relates to time of waking

## Awakening Your Soul-Aware-Witness

-------

Verse 5.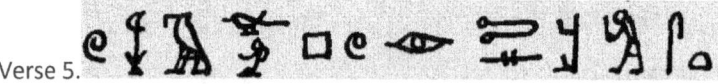

**5.1.**     ucha           pu     ari    tjez    {det}  {det}  set
**5.2.**    Ignorant fool unrighteous that doing knot {rise} {fight} it
**5.3.**    The ignorant fool is one who by doing actions binds him or herself to that heap of unconscious impressions that remained over after death, the impressions from past life actions and their thoughts, feelings and the experiences derived from those that produced a sum total effect on the character of the personality and then fights about it; i.e. there is no use in {raising objections} or {fighting} about the unconscious impressions one has allowed oneself to bind oneself to, as if one's possessions, and it was an ignorant foolish thing to do in the first place and later raise objections about it.

Verse 6.

**6.1.**    ar    peh      set      an      arit      iu        {ndj}
**6.2.**    about arrival    it     not     vision fault/ iniquity {bereft}
**6.3.**     Now, in reference to those who arrive at the judgment hall where all must face the judgment whereby the heap of past actions, thoughts, feelings and experiences established themselves on the side of the person, as their witnesses, the place where those are accounted for, and appear there, in the judgment hall, without fault or taint in their character, i.e. not being {bereft of virtue}...

---

experiences, in other words, time of being alive, which applies to the current life that just ended but also applies to the previous lives or times of waking conscious experiences where actions were performed that led to previous thoughts, feelings and experiences, etc.

Verse 7.

| | | | | | |
|---|---|---|---|---|---|
| *7.1.* | un | n – f | im | mi | Neter {Her} |
| 7.2. | being | to-he | within | like | God {Horus on Standard} |

7.3. ...it means arriving there and being regarded as one who, though despite appearing as a human soul, nevertheless, internally, they are recognized as being God, a {Horus being}.

## Significance of the passages from Papyrus Petersburg for the Themes Covered in this Book

The Meri-ka-Ra passages provide indispensable evidence that the ancient Egyptian understanding of consciousness transcendence was not confined to esoteric temple teachings but represented mainstream wisdom that informed practical guidance for effective living [6]. This demonstrates how the psychological principles explored throughout this manuscript were understood to apply universally rather than only to specialized spiritual practitioners.

The text's teaching that aryu function as "witnesses" that establish themselves "on one side of the person" during post-mortem evaluation reveals the ancient wisdom's sophisticated grasp of how unconscious psychological patterns create what contemporary understanding might recognize as semi-autonomous complexes that influence behavior independently of conscious intention [6].

The scripture's warning about the "ignorant fool" who "binds himself to that heap of unconscious impressions" and then "fights about it" provides crucial psychological insight that supports the manuscript's emphasis on accepting responsibility for past conditioning while working systematically toward purification rather than becoming trapped in cycles of self-condemnation or spiritual struggle that perpetuate the very patterns they attempt to overcome [6]. This teaching directly reinforces the manuscript's approach to aryu purification as requiring wise discrimination and patient practice rather than dramatic efforts or forced transformation techniques.

The text's culminating teaching about divine recognition—where consciousness appears "internally as being God, a Horus being" despite manifesting through human form—provides essential scriptural foundation for understanding how the Soul-Aware-Witness represents not a temporary spiritual achievement but the recognition of consciousness's eternal divine nature that has always been present yet obscured by identification with accumulated psychological patterns [6]. This corresponds directly with the central thesis of the Ancient Egyptian scriptures that spiritual development involves removing obstacles to divine recognition rather than acquiring new states or experiences, revealing how ancient Egyptian wisdom anticipated and provided solutions for the fundamental challenges that continue to characterize contemporary consciousness development.

**The Ancient Wisdom of Mental States: Heated versus Silent Mind**

**The Fundamental Pattern of Mental Operation**

The wisdom embedded in these teachings illuminates how mind can operate through two fundamental modes that determine the quality of all human experience: what the ancient texts designate as "heated mind" and "silent mind" [2]. These states represent more than emotional conditions or temporary mental fluctuations—they constitute different ways consciousness relates to all experience, determining whether awareness operates from wisdom or delusion, peace or agitation, recognition or forgetfulness.

The tradition of Shetaut Neter teaches that heated mind represents consciousness operating through the influence of heavy aryu (karmic impressions), creating what the Scripture describes as "agitated heart" consciousness that seeks fulfillment through external means and becomes disturbed when circumstances don't meet personal expectations [1]. This mode of mental operation emerges from the fundamental misidentification with temporary phenomena rather than recognition of consciousness's eternal nature.

Silent mind represents consciousness operating from recognition of its essential nature, creating what the teachings describe as "peaceful heart" awareness that maintains inner stability regardless of external circumstances [1]. This doesn't mean suppressing thoughts or emotions but rather allowing mental activity to arise and dissolve within the spacious awareness that recognizes its own divine nature.

**The Role of Aryu in Mental State Determination**

The difference between ego-driven and divine Ra consciousness depends largely on the influence of aryu (karmic impressions) that accumulate in the unconscious mind from past experiences, thoughts, and actions [1]. The Scripture reveals that "within humans there are egoistic mental impressions (aryu/karmic remnants) that develop from experiences and actions in current and previous lifetimes" which remain "registered in the unconscious mind, influencing present and future experiences" [1].

Heavy aryu create what the teachings describe as "dense, opaque impressions that obstruct the flow of divine light" through Ra consciousness [1]. These impressions manifest as automatic reactive patterns that pull individuated awareness into ego-identification— sudden anger when things don't go as planned, anxiety about future outcomes, or the compulsion to defend personal positions even when wisdom would direct different responses.

Light aryu represent "impressions that remain transparent to divine light" and allow Ra consciousness to function as the instrument of soul expression rather than ego-gratification [1]. These impressions emerge from actions aligned with Maat (divine order) and support consciousness in maintaining its recognition of divine nature even while functioning through an individual personality.

The tradition of Shetaut Neter teaches that purifying aryu through spiritual practice gradually transforms ego-driven Ra consciousness into divine Ra consciousness. This process involves what the Scripture describes as moving from "agitated heart" to "peaceful heart," from external control to self-control, and from the back-and-forth cycles of seeking satisfaction to the direct path of soul expression [1].

These heavy impressions accumulate through what the teachings describe as actions against Maat (divine order)—choices motivated by separateness, control, and ego-gratification rather than wisdom and recognition of universal unity. Each choice creates momentum patterns in the unconscious mind that influence future mental and emotional responses, creating what might be called "karmic momentum" that pulls consciousness toward either heated or silent mind functioning.

The ancient wisdom thus reveals how consciousness becomes trapped through specific psychological mechanisms that operate predictably and systematically rather than randomly or mysteriously. The heated mind emerges from heavy aryu created by actions against Maat, while the silent mind emerges from light aryu created by actions aligned with divine order. Understanding these mechanisms provides practitioners with precise methodology for transformation rather than vague spiritual platitudes, revealing why the ancient Egyptian approach to consciousness development proved so effective and enduring.

Having examined the mechanisms by which consciousness becomes trapped in ego-identification and the cycles of reincarnation, the ancient wisdom that reveals the pathway to liberation now requires exploration. The same scriptures that diagnose the problem provide the precise methodology for its resolution. This solution emerges not through external intervention but through consciousness discovering its true nature as what the teachings describe as the "Soul-Aware-Witness." The wisdom of the neteru illuminates how this discovery represents not the achievement of something new, but rather the recognition of what consciousness has always been beneath the accumulated patterns of delusion and ego-identification.

**References**

[1] Ashby, M. (2025). *Teachings of New Kingdom Pert-M-Heru: Ancient Egyptian Book of Enlightenment, Chapter 17*. Translation by Dr. Muata Ashby. Sema Institute.
[1] Ashby, M. (2022). The Mysteries of Ra and Hetheru/Sekhmet. Translation by Dr. Muata Ashby. Sema Institute.
[2] Ashby, M. (2019). Teachings of Ancient Egyptian Sage Amenemopet with Hieroglyphic texts. Translation by Dr. Muata Ashby. Sema Institute.

[3] Ashby, M. (2016). Egyptian Book of the Dead Hieroglyph Translations for Enlightenment: Understanding the Mystic Path to Enlightenment Through Direct Readings of the Sacred Signs and Symbols of Ancient Egyptian Language With Trilinear Deciphering Translation Method Vol. 1. Translation by Dr. Muata Ashby. Sema Institute.

[4] Ashby, M. (2025). The Complete Glorious Light Meditation Volume 2: Commentary and Spiritual Application. Translation by Dr. Muata Ashby. Sema Institute.

[5] Ashby, M. (2022). The Complete Glorious Light Meditation Volume 2. Translation by Dr. Muata Ashby. Sema Institute.

[6] Ashby, M. (2025). Book HIEROGLYPH TRANSLATIONS V6- Asarian Resurrection. Translation by Dr. Muata Ashby. Sema Institute.

# Chapter 4: The Sacred Technology of Consciousness Transformation - The Systematic Pathway from Human Mind to Ra Consciousness Through Djehuty's Cosmic Bridge

**Main Thesis:** The Scripture of Ra and Hetheru presents a sophisticated spiritual psychology wherein human consciousness transforms into divine consciousness through systematic alignment with Djehuty's cosmic mind, which serves as the accessible intermediary between limited human awareness and transcendent Ra consciousness [1]. This transformation occurs through a comprehensive technology that integrates intellectual understanding, ethical purification, ritual preparation, and meditative practice, ultimately enabling the practitioner's consciousness to merge with Ra's divine awareness.

## PART 1: THE FUNDAMENTAL SPIRITUAL TECHNOLOGY

**The Divine Framework:**

The scripture establishes a cosmic architecture specifically designed to facilitate human transformation [1]. Consider how verse 129 reveals Ra's profound declaration establishing the essential foundation for all consciousness development:

## Awakening Your Soul-Aware-Witness

Verse 129.

*129.1.* shept pen iu K im aset-per a asety-per {Net} ach{mdj} djedtu en-K Djehuty
*129.2* ill-will these it-is thee in abode mine dual{Div} thereby {fig} called you of thine Thoth...

*129.3.* "A heart in this condition becomes a beacon for inimical cosmic forces – those demoniac energies that manifest as avarice, lust, jealousy, and selfishness. These forces, being tyrannical and unjust by nature, create an atmosphere of ill-will within the human personality. Through continued association with these inimical forces, deep imprints form within the unconscious mind. These imprints manifest as egoistic aryu (karmic residues) that remain embedded in the unconscious, compelling those afflicted to perpetuate negative patterns of feeling and thinking. This creates a cycle where unrighteous thoughts and desires lead to actions that deviate from Maat (divine order and truth), further strengthening the negative impressions in the unconscious mind. Therefore, I now establish you, Djehuty (Thoth), as my abode in Creation - we shall function as dual aspects of the same divine consciousness. While I maintain my celestial {divine} abode, experiencing the vast expanse of transcendent awareness, you shall serve as Cosmic Mind, maintaining awareness of all that transpires within Creation. This dual arrangement ensures complete oversight of both the transcendent and manifest realms. I have chosen you for this role because you are uniquely illumined by my Glorious-Shining-Spirit-Effulgent-Radiance. As my Cosmic Mind, you can perceive and govern all aspects of Creation while maintaining constant connection with my divine consciousness. Therefore, you shall henceforth be known as 'Djehuty (Thoth)-'"

This arrangement creates what the text calls "complete oversight of both the transcendent and manifest realms" [1:129.3]. Indeed, the significance of this divine framework emerges from Djehuty's unique qualification as Ra's own mind operating within Creation, making him the perfect bridge for human consciousness seeking divine alignment [1].

The wisdom of the neteru reveals that this establishes Djehuty not as a separate deity, but as Ra's cosmic intelligence functioning throughout Creation while maintaining constant connection with transcendent source. Nevertheless, this cosmic relationship provides the essential foundation that makes human transformation possible through accessible divine intermediary.

**The Human Dilemma:**

The scripture provides precise psychological analysis of why human consciousness becomes trapped in suffering [1]. Verse 128 offers detailed explanation of the mechanism by which consciousness becomes bound to repetitive patterns:

Verse 128.

*128.1.* *imu senu aryu nu aru sebau in arkeru {Net} shepsu {Net}*
*128.2.* within their action-residue we image wickedness by inimical {force} followers {force}
*128.3.* …within them there are egoistic mental impressions (aryu/karmic remnants) that develop from experiences and actions in current and previous lifetimes. These impressions manifest as feeling memories, recorded and reinforced patterns of thoughts, feelings, and behaviors that remain registered in the unconscious mind, influencing present and future experiences. The subtle effects of these aryu accumulate and intensify, and if founded in ignorance, egoism and delusion, promote endless unfulfillable worldly desires that cloud the mind's natural clarity and foment ambiguity, diffidence and spiritual ignorance and resulting worldly desires, mental distortions, delusions, frustrations and perpetual unrest (neshesh).

This reveals that when these aryu are "founded in ignorance, egoism and delusion, [they] promote endless unfulfillable worldly desires that cloud the mind's natural clarity and foment ambiguity, diffidence and spiritual ignorance" [1:128.3]. Therefore, this creates a self-perpetuating cycle where past ignorant actions generate mental impressions that compel future ignorant actions [2].

The ultimate consequence appears in verse 129, which describes how corrupted consciousness attracts destructive forces while simultaneously revealing the divine solution through Djehuty's establishment as cosmic mind [1]. Thus, the scripture explains that these forces "create an atmosphere of ill-will within the human

## Awakening Your Soul-Aware-Witness

personality" and form "deep imprints" that "manifest as egoistic aryu (karmic residues) that remain embedded in the unconscious, compelling those afflicted to perpetuate negative patterns of feeling and thinking" [1:129.3].

**The Solution – Mind Alignment:**

The divine solution appears in verse 143, which establishes the fundamental qualification for transformation that aspirants must cultivate [1]:

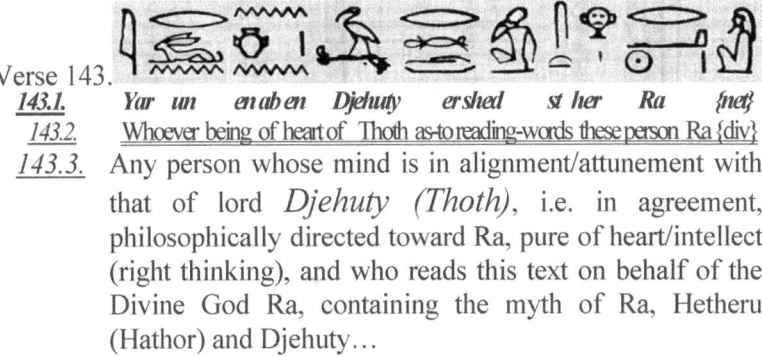

Verse 143.
*143.1.*     Yar un    en ab en    Djehuty    er shed    st her    Ra    {net}
*143.2.*     Whoever being of heart of Thoth as-to reading-words these person Ra {div}
*143.3.*     Any person whose mind is in alignment/attunement with that of lord *Djehuty (Thoth)*, i.e. in agreement, philosophically directed toward Ra, pure of heart/intellect (right thinking), and who reads this text on behalf of the Divine God Ra, containing the myth of Ra, Hetheru (Hathor) and Djehuty...

This alignment involves multiple dimensions that practitioners must develop systematically: intellectual agreement with Djehuty's cosmic wisdom, philosophical orientation toward Ra consciousness rather than worldly achievement, ethical purification that creates "pure of heart/intellect," and service-oriented engagement with the sacred text "on behalf of the Divine God Ra" rather than personal benefit [1].

## The Transformation Process:

The scripture outlines a systematic process beginning with comprehensive purification [1]. Verse 144 specifies the precise requirements that practitioners must fulfill:

Awakening Your Soul-Aware-Witness

Verse 144.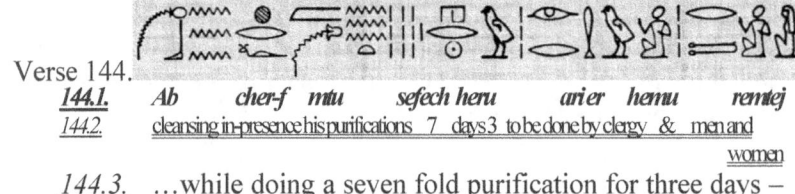
*144.1.*   *Ab   cher-f  mtu    sefech heru    ari er hemu    remtej*
*144.2.*   cleansing in-presence his purifications  7  days 3  to be done by clergy  &  men and women

*144.3.* ...while doing a seven fold purification for three days – in his presence, i.e. in the mental state of purified intellect (Djehuty/Thoth) and Spirit (Ra) awareness; this practice is enjoined for priests and priestesses and lay men and women...

Consider how this purification must be performed while maintaining "the mental state of purified intellect (Djehuty/Thoth) and Spirit (Ra) awareness" [1:144.3], indicating that the process itself occurs within the consciousness state being cultivated [3]. In other words, this creates a transformative feedback loop where the practice generates the very consciousness required for successful completion.

The ultimate outcome appears in verse 145, which describes the verifiable results of authentic practice [1]:

Verse 145.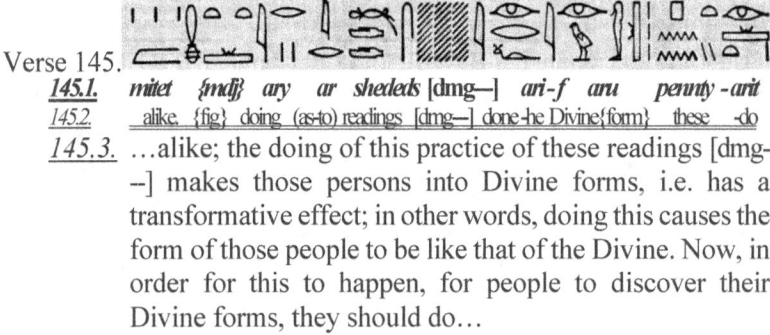
*145.1.*   *mitet  {mdj}  ary  ar  shededs* [dmg—]  *ari-f  aru  pennty -arit*
*145.2.*   alike. {fig} doing (as-to) readings [dmg—] done-he Divine{form} these  -do

*145.3.* ...alike; the doing of this practice of these readings [dmg—] makes those persons into Divine forms, i.e. has a transformative effect; in other words, doing this causes the form of those people to be like that of the Divine. Now, in order for this to happen, for people to discover their Divine forms, they should do...

## The Logical Chain:

The complete logical progression operates as follows: Since Djehuty functions as Ra's mind within Creation [1:verse 129.3], when human mind aligns with Djehuty's mind [1:verse 143.3], it necessarily aligns with Ra's mind. Through systematic purification

## Awakening Your Soul-Aware-Witness

performed within this aligned consciousness state [1:verse 144.3], the practitioner's form becomes "like that of the Divine" [1:verse 145.3], completing the transformation from human consciousness to Ra consciousness [1].

This represents a sophisticated spiritual psychology where Djehuty serves as the accessible bridge between limited human awareness and transcendent divine consciousness, providing a practical pathway for consciousness transformation through an intermediary divine mind that encompasses all Creation while remaining connected to transcendent source [1,4].

# PART 2: ADDITIONAL NUANCES IN THE TEXT

## Physical/Ritual Preparation Requirements:

The scripture reveals that alignment with Djehuty's mind involves comprehensive preparation beyond intellectual understanding [1]. Verses 140-142 specify detailed physical requirements that demonstrate the ancient understanding of psychophysical integration [1]:

Verse 139.
*139.1.* ha {tep} mesdjer dety f hesmenu detu tep f unch etu
*139.2* body head} two-ears hands-his natron hands head as-to his dress/adornment
/arraying
*139.3.* Now, for the head, the two ears and then the hands and the head, these are to have natron, a natural form of sodium bicarbonate applied. Next, the person should be adorned and arrayed with a particular set of clothing which is to be...

Verse 140.
*140.1.* F shendjetu amyu {aqeb} maatu abu su mu mehuyu
*140.2.* clothing garment {double} truthfulness purification they flood-waters
*140.3.* ...clothing composed of a double garment; a tunic and kilt that are purified with the waters of the Nile flood.

### Verse 141.

*141.1.*   *Teby*     *im*     *tau*     *enty hefjty*   *sesh a Maat her nes F*
*141.2.*   feet     in   two-sandals  being  white-sandals writing I Truth person tongue his

*141.3.* The feet of the initiate person practicing the ritual program of this scripture, are to use two white sandals and the word "Truth" (Maat) is to be written on their tongue…

### Verse 142.

*142.1.*   *ha*   *{tep} mesdjer*   *dety f hesmen*   *detu tep f unch ch etu*
*142.2.*   body   {head} two-ears hands-his  natron   hands head as-to his dress/adornment
                                                                                               /arraying

*142.3.* Now, for the head, the two ears and then the hands and the head, these are to have natron, a natural form of sodium bicarbonate applied. Next, the person should be adorned and arrayed with a particular set of clothing which is to be…

### Verse 143.

*143.1.*   *F shendjetu amyu {aqeb} maatu abu*   *su*   *mu*   *mehuyu*
*143.2.*   clothing   garment {double} truthfulness purification they flood-waters

*143.3.* …clothing composed of a double garment; a tunic and kilt that are purified with the waters of the Nile flood.

### Verse 144.

*144.1.*   *teby*     *im*     *tau*     *enty hefjty*   *sesh a Maat her nes F*
*144.2.*   feet     in   two-sandals  being  white-sandals writing I Truth person tongue his

*144.3.* The feet of the initiate person practicing the ritual program of this scripture, are to use two white sandals and the word "Truth" (Maat) is to be written on their tongue…

These physical preparations indicate that alignment with Djehuty's mind involves the entire psychophysical system, demonstrating the ancient understanding that consciousness transformation affects every aspect of human existence [3,4]. Indeed, this comprehensive approach prevents the common misconception that spiritual development occurs only through mental or emotional practices.

## Djehuty's Unique Cosmic Authority:

Verses 130-133 reveal Djehuty's extraordinary cosmic status that qualifies him to serve as the bridge between human and divine consciousness [1]:

Verse 130.

*130.1.*    Asety Ra iu    gert    rera    hab u      K      [dmg–] er K
*130.2.*    Abode{fem} Ra it-is moreover power send-message   thine   [dmg-] as-to thee
*130.3.*    –"Thoth (Djehuty)-Spouse-of-Spirit" i.e. "Cosmic Mind God, the mate of Spirit, the medium, mouthpiece, agent, conduit, intermediary, minister of God." It is, moreover, my will to bestow upon you the power of being able to put out dispatches of edicts that come from you and those will have the same authority as if they come from me. [dmg-]. Now, as to your…

Verse 131.

*131.1.*    kheper haby      pen en     Djehuty iu    a    ger erer at det un {ta}{necht}
*131.2.*    created ibis-bird    this of Thoth    it-is I also compare-stronger hand being {land}{strength}
*131.3.*    …form and appearance, for all to see, recognize and adore, forthwith, an ibis-bird was created; this animal is a symbol of the God Djehuty (Thoth). It represents detail oriented, objective aspect, to manage the affairs between me and the gods and goddesses and people. In comparison to other gods, Djehuty (Thoth) will have a stronger hand in all matters, residing on the land (earth plane/physical Creation realm). In this manner, Cosmic Mind through high intellect is the ultimate authority of Creation.

Above: image of Ancient Egyptian Ibis from Copenhagen Museum.
Above right image of Ancient Egyptian God Djehuty (Thoth)

Verse 132.
*132.1.*   *K det  K cheft  her en Paautiu         {Netru} aaau      {mdj}  er K*
*132.2.*   thine hand thine before upon Company-{Gods/Goddesses} great fig} as-to thee
*132.3.*   [I, Ra, declare that] your hand, Djehuty (Thoth), your very influence and authority will be greater than the Great Company of Gods and Goddesses that were brought into manifestation by me at the beginning of Creation.

Verse 133.
*133.1.*   *iu  nefer chen {Net} ari K kheper Techny {Net} en haby  pu Djehuty iu  a  ger    a*
*133.2.*   it-is good troublemakers {Div} do thee created vibrational {Div} of ibis that Thoth   it-is I
                                                                                                also  I
*133.3.*   It is a good thing that the troubling, disturbing cosmic forces have caused you, Djehuty (Thoth), to create a vibrational cosmic force in your ibis aspect, which counters the forces that produce disturbance (troubled

minds of troublemakers) in the mind. That vibration is the experience of mind in an opposite state to that of the inimical forces; instead of agitation, calm; instead of anger, understanding; instead of ignorance, wisdom, etc. It is I, who also...

Consider how verse 132 declares that Djehuty's "hand" and "very influence and authority will be greater than the Great Company of Gods and Goddesses that were brought into manifestation by me at the beginning of Creation" [1:132.3]. Nevertheless, verse 133 explains his specific transformative function: creating "a vibrational cosmic force in your ibis aspect, which counters the forces that produce disturbance (troubled minds of troublemakers) in the mind" [1:133.3].

This vibration operates as "the experience of mind in an opposite state to that of the inimical forces; instead of agitation, calm; instead of anger, understanding; instead of ignorance, wisdom" [1:133.3]. Therefore, Djehuty's cosmic authority enables him to transform the very mental patterns that trap human consciousness in suffering [1,2].

## Practical Application of Djehuty's Opposing Vibrations:

The wisdom of the neteru reveals that practitioners can actively engage Djehuty's transformative power through specific techniques that invoke his Ibis aspect—the cosmic form that operates beyond ordinary mundane consciousness governed by the baboon form (Anan) [1]. Consider how this represents systematic spiritual technology rather than mere positive thinking, since these opposing vibrations connect individual consciousness directly with cosmic mind's approach to managing inimical forces.

When anger arises from interpersonal conflicts or worldly frustrations, aspirants can invoke Djehuty's cosmic perspective by contemplating the grandeur of Creation and how Ra's infinite intelligence manages all apparent opposition without becoming disturbed [1,4]. Indeed, this shift from personal reactivity to cosmic perspective naturally dissolves heated mental states, since individual consciousness aligns with the unchanging wisdom that governs universal manifestation. In other words, rather than struggling against anger through suppression, practitioners allow Djehuty's cosmic mind to reveal the broader context that makes personal agitation unnecessary.

Nevertheless, when sadness or depression cloud the mind due to loss, disappointment, or perceived limitation, the ancient sages taught that invoking Ra's eternal presence through Djehuty's guidance restores recognition of consciousness as divine rather than dependent on temporary circumstances [1,2]. This means contemplating how the Creator Spirit manifests through all experiences—both pleasant and challenging—as opportunities for consciousness to discover its essential nature beyond identification with changing phenomena.

## Sacred Technology for Generating Opposing Vibrations:

The scripture reveals multiple systematic approaches for accessing Djehuty's transformative power beyond mental techniques alone [1]. First, the utterance of divine names (particularly "Ra," "Djehuty," and "Neberdjer") creates vibrational patterns that override negative mental impressions through direct invocation of cosmic consciousness [1,3]. These sacred sounds function as technological instruments rather than mere words, since they carry the actual presence of divine intelligence when properly understood and expressed.

Furthermore, engagement with rituals authored by cosmic mind itself provides practitioners with comprehensive spiritual technology, since Djehuty serves as the originator of hieroglyphic texts under Ra's direct guidance [1]. This means that authentic study and practice of Ancient Egyptian spiritual methods connects individual consciousness with the cosmic intelligence that designed these transformative techniques specifically to counteract inimical forces operating within human psychology.

The tradition also emphasizes communion with sages—whether through direct association with living teachers or contemplative study of wisdom literature—as essential technology for overcoming negative vibrations [2,3]. Consider how authentic sages function as mouthpieces for Djehuty's wisdom rather than merely sharing personal opinions or intellectual concepts. Therefore, sincere engagement with sagely guidance creates direct transmission of the cosmic vibrations that naturally dissolve ignorance, delusion, and the resulting inimical patterns that generate mental suffering [1,2].

## The Sacred **Function** of Textual Study:

Verse 143 specifies that practitioners must read "this text on behalf of the Divine God Ra, containing the myth of Ra, Hetheru (Hathor) and Djehuty" [1:143.3]. This indicates that study serves a sacred function beyond personal education—it constitutes service to divine consciousness itself [1]. Indeed, the specific content focus on "the myth of Ra, Hetheru (Hathor) and Djehuty" [1:143.3] reveals that practitioners must engage the cosmic drama of consciousness transformation as living spiritual reality rather than abstract mythology.

### Enhanced Qualification Requirements:

The text provides multiple layers of qualification beyond initial intellectual interest [1]. The phrase "pure of heart/intellect (right thinking)" [1:143.3] indicates both ethical purity and correct philosophical understanding. Nevertheless, being "philosophically directed toward Ra" [1:143.3] requires that one's entire intellectual orientation focus on divine realization rather than worldly achievement. The requirement to read "on behalf of the Divine God Ra" [1:143.3] demonstrates that authentic practice emerges from service motivation rather than personal benefit or spiritual curiosity.

### The Comprehensive Purification Process:

Verse 144's "sevenfold purification for three days" [1:144.3] represents systematic preparation that encompasses ethical conduct according to Maat, mental clarity through wisdom study, and sincere devotion to recognizing one's true nature as divine consciousness

[1,3]. The phrase "in his presence, i.e. in the mental state of purified intellect (Djehuty/Thoth) and Spirit (Ra) awareness" [1:144.3] indicates that purification occurs within the consciousness state being cultivated, creating a transformative feedback loop where the process itself generates the consciousness required for successful completion.

**Universal Accessibility with Prerequisites:**

While verse 144 states that "this practice is enjoined for priests and priestesses and lay men and women...alike" [1:144.3], this democratic accessibility comes with substantial prerequisites [1]. The comprehensive requirements for physical preparation, ethical purity, intellectual understanding, proper motivation, and systematic purification ensure that casual or superficial engagement cannot produce authentic transformation while maintaining accessibility for all sincere practitioners regardless of social status [1,3].

## Verifiable Transformation Outcomes:

Verse 145 describes concrete results: practitioners become "Divine forms" and their "form...becomes like that of the Divine" [1:145.3]. This language suggests visible, verifiable transformation rather than subjective spiritual experiences, indicating that authentic practice produces observable changes in consciousness, behavior, and even physical presence that reflect divine rather than merely human awareness [1,3].

## Anan - The Microcosmic Bridge to Divine Consciousness:

The scripture reveals a profound teaching about how aspirants access divine consciousness through Anan, the microcosmic aspect of Djehuty that operates specifically within mundane human awareness [1]. Verse 134 provides essential understanding of this divine architecture:

Verse 134.

<u>134.1.</u> rrer  at anhuy  K pety  im  neferu{mdj}  K im hedj tu {akhu}  K kheper  aah
<u>134.2.</u> stronger surround earth thee two heavens in beauty{fig} thine through light {spirit-radiance} thine created Moon {God}
<u>134.3.</u> empower you to have the capacity to surround the earth and the two heavens in your beauty{fig} through the light, the Spirit-Radiance from you that comes from me. This radiance will manifest as moonlight and thus the moon was created and the moon God aspect of …

Verse 135.

<u>135.1.</u> pu en Djehuty iu  a  ger  a  rer  at anan  K  ha  nebu
<u>135.2.</u> this of Thoth it-is  I  also  I  stronger empowering turn-back thee north-lords
<u>135.3.</u> …of this God, Djehuty (Thoth) was created. It is I (Ra, the Creator Spirit), additionally, who make you, Djehuty (Thoth), stronger and with capacity to turn-back the North-Lords, those opposing tribes, from the Mediterranean, that are trying to invade the north of Kemet (Egypt).

**Above-Faience statue of Djehuty (Thoth) as baboon depicted with the moon-disk on his head.**

Verse 136.

*136.1.* kheper anan pu en Djehuty kheper er F pu im ta a unen K ger im asety {Net} a
*136.2* created Anan-ape his of Thoth created as to he that in mine being to thee furthermore in dual-abodes
{Divine} mine

*136.3.* Forthwith, an Ape aspect of Djehuty (Thoth), called *Anan*, was created to counter the northern disrupting forces. That aspect, indeed, has Ra's being, and thus Ra is acting through the God Djehuty (Thoth as macro intellect) generally and this aspect of Anan (Thoth as micro intellect) specifically. Furthermore, Djehuty (Thoth) will reside in Ra's two divine abodes (netherworld and physical world)…

Verse 137.

*137.1.* her maayu tu nebu uab {mdj} im K iu arit en
*137.2.* person seeing to-one all open-up {fig} in thee it-is making of
*137.3.* …for one and all to see and open-up in thee, that is to say, open-up into the intellectual capacity, in all; for all to see the beauties and glories within Thoth (Djehuty), the glories of Cosmic Mind that illumine Creation, and the soul, with vast Spirit-Radiance that illumines the mind and opens the soul to the Maat (righteousness/truth) of Ra. It is the eye of…

Consider how this teaching provides practitioners with precise understanding of the divine architecture that makes human transformation possible [1,3]. Djehuty is the moon. This means that the Cosmic Mind (Djehuty), like the moon is a reflection of the sun, so too Cosmic Mind is a reflection of Spirit-Consciousness (Ra). In the same way the human mind is a reflection of the human soul. Indeed, while Djehuty in his Ibis form represents the macrocosmic mind of Ra that encompasses all Creation, Anan represents that same divine intelligence functioning at the scale of individual human consciousness [1]. This means that when the aspirant's personal mind aligns with divine wisdom in daily life—through ethical choices, contemplative study, and meditative practice—they are actually connecting with Anan, the accessible aspect of cosmic mind that operates within ordinary human experience [1,4].

The wisdom of the neteru reveals that Anan serves as the divine presence within mundane consciousness, enabling practitioners to experience direct connection with Ra's intelligence through their own purified mental processes [1]. Nevertheless, this microcosmic access point maintains complete continuity with Djehuty's macrocosmic function, since "that aspect, indeed, has Ra's being" [verse 134.3]. Therefore, when practitioners cultivate right thinking, ethical conduct, and spiritual devotion in everyday circumstances, they are actually engaging Anan as the divine mind that functions through individual awareness while never becoming separate from universal consciousness [1,2].

As the ancient sages taught, this teaching explains why the scripture emphasizes that transformation occurs through alignment with Djehuty's mind rather than through mystical experiences that transcend ordinary consciousness [1]. The tradition reveals that divine realization emerges through sanctifying normal mental activity by recognizing its true nature as an expression of cosmic intelligence, rather than seeking exotic states that bypass human psychology [1,2]. In other words, Anan represents the practical means by which cosmic consciousness (Djehuty in his Ibis form) becomes accessible to human awareness without requiring practitioners to abandon their humanity or ordinary mental faculties [1].

Thus, this dual-aspect understanding prevents both spiritual ignorance and materialistic reductionism [1,2]. Students who recognize Anan as divine mind operating through individual consciousness can engage wholeheartedly in purification, study, and ethical development without imagining that spiritual practice requires escaping human existence [3]. Therefore, the teaching of Anan reveals that authentic transformation involves discovering the divine nature of consciousness itself, rather than replacing human awareness with something foreign to its essential structure [1,4].

This comprehensive analysis reveals that the Scripture of Ra and Hetheru presents one of humanity's most sophisticated technologies for consciousness transformation, integrating psychological insight, ethical development, ritual preparation, and meditative practice into a systematic pathway from human consciousness to divine realization through alignment with Djehuty's cosmic mind as the bridge to Ra consciousness [1,4].

**References**

[1] Ashby, M. (2022). *The Mysteries of Ra and Hetheru/Sekhmet*. Translation by Dr. Muata Ashby. Sema Institute.

[2] Ashby, M. (2019). *Teachings of Ancient Egyptian Sage Amenemopet with Hieroglyphic texts*. Translation by Dr. Muata Ashby. Sema Institute.

[3] Ashby, M. (2016). *Egyptian Book of the Dead Hieroglyph Translations for Enlightenment: Understanding the Mystic Path to Enlightenment Through Direct Readings of the Sacred Signs and Symbols of Ancient Egyptian Language With Trilinear Deciphering Translation Method Vol. 1*. Translation by Dr. Muata Ashby. Sema Institute.

[4] Ashby, M. (2025). *Transpersonal Psychology Of Discovering the Aware Witnessing Self*. Translation by Dr. Muata Ashby. Sema Institute.

# Chapter 5: The Solution - Discovering the Soul-Aware-Witness

Following the theme of not being obstructed by one's heart, Chapter 26 verses 1-6 and 12-16 of the Ancient Egyptian Book of Enlightenment expand on the concept of a separate subject "I" of higher consciousness or "Soul-Aware-Witness" [1].

## ANCIENT EGYPTIAN PERT-EM-HERU CHAPTER 26 VERSES 1-16[18]

Verse 1.
1.1. R a e n R a t A b e n *Asar Any {sheps} en f im Neterchert*
1.2. Chapter of giving heart to Osiris Any {noble} to him in cemetery
1.3. This is a chapter in the Book of Enlightenment about giving heart to the Asar (Osiris) initiate who goes by the name *Any*. *Asar (Osiris) Any* has been found to be a noble, honorable and virtuous person. This presentation of heart, of presence of mind and conscious awareness occurs while *Asar (Osiris) Any* is in the cemetery, the lower part of heaven, in preparation for proceeding on the spiritual journey through the Netherworld.

Verse 2.
2.1.    *ab a    n-a   im   per   abu   haty ab a n-a im per    hatu*
2.2.    heart mine to-me   in sanctuary   hearts heart-front-mine to-me in sanctuary
                                                                                 hearts-front
2.3.    May there be a heart, a mind for me in the temple sanctuary where hearts abide; May I not go there without my presence of mind, like those who die and lose their minds, their self-awareness of themselves and their worldly sense of self-awareness as themselves as their worldly sense of self, their ego, disintegrates after death. May what is foremost, what is on the surface, the top-most of mind, be foremost in my mind in the temple sanctuary where also abide there, the top-most

---

[18] Translation by Dr. Muata Ashby

Awakening Your Soul-Aware-Witness

things of mind, the foremost level of conscious level of awareness in the present.

Verse 3.
3.1. *iu n-a ab-a hetep-f im [a] an amu    a shatu ent Asar*
3.2. it is to-me  heart-mine peaceful-he in [me]  not eat    I  cakes  of  Osiris
3.3. It is now true that my heart, he is peaceful within me. This means that I shall not be eating those cakes of Asar (Osiris); I reject that…

Verse 4.
*4.1.* *her im abty en   agy   sha chuchet im    ched   k*
4.2. person in east to drown lake  traveling in downstream(boat)  thine
4.3. …I reject being a person in the eastern part of the world where the sun dawns and people come into the physical world as reincarnated beings; Then what happens is that, having come into the world of time and space duality—as if drowning in a lake (waters of the mind)—they get caught up in the mayhem of desires born of spiritual ignorance and duality perceived through mind and senses, people drown in the ever agitating movements of opposition and attraction; it is like sailing downstream to the north of Kemet (Egypt) and then…

Verse 5.
5.1. *khenty  k   an  ha    a  er chudet   imy    k   Iu  n-a*
5.2. upstream thine not  advance I as-to boat  withinness  thee It-is for-me
5.3. … sailing, in your boat, up to the south of Kemet (Egypt); up and down, up and down, drowning in the illusory but compellingly apparent ever-present dualities of life, and in the end, going nowhere except back to the beginning, the east, to do it over again, experiencing life on earth as if sinking in a flood of choices that never satisfy abidingly; the life of reincarnation is as if being engulfed in an inundation of actions, reactions, desires, frustrations, and endless unrest of ordinary life on earth. I declare that I will not go forward, I will not proceed, I will not increase my involvement and spread myself in the endless interests of the pointless and therefore illusory dual choices, situations and objects encountered when living on earth; I will not go into that boat within which you are. This is for myself…

## Verse 6.

| | | | | | | | |
|---|---|---|---|---|---|---|---|
| *6.1.* | ra a | medu a | im f | red a | er | shemt | |
| 6.2. | mouth mine | speech mine | → as he ← | legs mine | | as-to | walking |

6.3. ... that my mouth and my speech is → as he himself (Asar {Osiris}) ←, the Divine. Since what comes out of my mouth comes from Him, that is to say, Divine Consciousness, therefore, I am not a personality caught up in the vicissitudes, the ups and downs, the foibles of human egoism leading to human pain and suffering. Rather, since I am of Divine origin, verily one with Asar (Osiris) Himself, I experience His fate and not the fate of those who reincarnate in the east. Concerning my legs being able to walk...

---

## Verse 12.

*12.1.*    rech {mdj}a    im
12.2.    know{fig} I    in
12.3.    ... I know what is in ...

## Verse 13.

*13.1.*   ab a    sekhem a    im    haty-ab-a    sekhem a   im
13.2.   heart mine power mine   in   heart-front-mind-will   power mine   in

13.3. ...my heart, I know myself; that knowing is my power, the power of my mentality *(attitude, approach, outlook mindset temperament character personality, frame of mind, point of view, way of thinking)* my conscious-awareness, (what is at the forefront[top] of mind) that enables my willpower, temperance and self-control. It is also my power (control over) in...

## Verse 14.

*14.1.*   auyu a     sekhem a    im red    a sekhem    a
14.2.   arms mine    power I    in   legs   mine power    I

14.3. ...my arms and the power (control over) in my legs as well as my power...

Verse 15.
| | | |
|---|---|---|
| 15.1. | *im aryt {mdj} merrt a ka a an chena tu ba a er* | |
| 15.2. | in doing fig} desire I mind mine not asphyxiated my soul mine [as-to] | |
| 15.3. | ...that manifests in the form of doing **{figurative}** what my disposition desires, that which I as The Divine (God/Goddess) desire. My soul is neither stifled nor asphyxiated/suffocated by my mind; it can freely express itself and pursue the highest expression of the meaning of life and realization of absolute existence, unlike those souls who live lives in ignorance, drowning in the deluding movements of worldly duality and whose actions are controlled by their ignorance and the psychological maladies, delusions, that arise from it (anger, greed, lust, envy, frustration, etc.), that cause life to be diminished and degraded in terms of capacity to live a rich and fulfilling life and achieve spiritual victory. So, my soul is neither stifled nor suffocated in my... | |

Verse 16.
| | | |
|---|---|---|
| 16.1. | *khat* | *a* |
| 16.2. | body | mine |
| 16.3. | ...physical body, unlike others who are as if drowning in, caught up in the desires of the body, the body's feelings, urges and the unfulfilling, agitating movements, endlessly moving hither and thither, evoked by the whirlpool of emotions and delusions of ordinary human life that comingle with the past hidden impressions in the unconscious. Thus, my soul is unobstructed, unhindered ... | |

# The Three Key Mystic Psychology Themes of Chapter 26: Ancient Egyptian Teachings on Soul-Awareness and Liberation

The Ancient Egyptian Book of Enlightenment Chapter 26 reveals through the declarations of Asar (Osiris) Any three fundamental mystic psychology themes that illuminate the pathway from unconscious living to divine recognition. These themes, embedded within the sacred verses themselves, provide contemporary practitioners of Shetaut Neter with essential understanding for distinguishing between authentic spiritual identity and the psychological patterns that obscure soul expression.

## Theme 1: The Soul-Aware-Witness Distinguished from Mind and Body

The scripture demonstrates consciousness recognizing itself as fundamentally distinct from mental and physical processes through several key declarations. Consider how the "Asar Any" formula itself reveals this principle—Any represents the individual soul recognizing its universal divine essence as Asar (Osiris), distinguishing spiritual identity from mere personality identification [1]. Indeed, the practitioner declares: 'my heart, I know myself; that knowing is my power,' establishing self-recognition through experiential wisdom (rech) that transcends mental content and intellectual processes, representing the direct intuitive knowingness that consciousness possesses of its own essential nature beyond the cognitive capacities of mind [1].

Nevertheless, the most explicit evidence appears in the declaration: "It is also my power (control over) in my arms and the power (control over) in my legs," demonstrating consciousness exercising authority over physical functions rather than being controlled by bodily urges [1]. Instead of being absorbed in the mental and physiological stimuli, identifying with mind and body as self, the awareness of separate awareness allows for detachment and for one's consciousness to see the mind and body with objectivity. This recognition culminates in the profound statement: "my soul is neither stifled nor suffocated," indicating that the soul exists independently of physical and mental limitations [1].

## Theme 2: Soul Oppression Through Mind-Body Identification

The ancient wisdom reveals that when consciousness loses recognition of its true nature, the soul becomes dominated by mental and physical patterns rather than expressing its divine essence. The scripture provides explicit evidence through the contrast between awakened and un-awakened states. Thus, Verse 15 declares: "My soul is neither stifled nor asphyxiated/suffocated," while Verse 16 contrasts this with "others who are as if drowning in, caught up in the desires of the body" and "the unfulfilling, agitating movements...evoked by the whirlpool of emotions and delusions of ordinary human life" [1].

In other words, the text reveals that unconscious identification with thoughts, emotions, and bodily sensations creates what the teaching describes as soul suffocation—the divine essence becomes trapped within reactive patterns rather than operating as the conscious director of human experience.

Nevertheless, when consciousness remains trapped in this suffocated condition for extended periods, practitioners may experience intense frustrations, stress, and sense of loss of control that can manifest as psychological pathologies requiring therapeutic intervention, while the body may develop stress-related illnesses. Indeed, this understanding reveals the profound therapeutic purpose of engaging higher consciousness studies through the tradition of Shetaut Neter: to alleviate and eventually correct the cognitive errors that lead to loss of awareness of consciousness as Neberdjer/Asar, thereby transforming ways of human life that produce mental and physical illness and unhappiness into approaches that generate fulfillment, contentment, and wellbeing for humanity. Thus, the ancient sages understood that recognizing the Soul-Aware-Witness represents not merely spiritual achievement but essential psychological health that prevents the suffocation patterns Chapter 26 describes.

**Theme 3: Automaticity of Unconscious Living**

The third theme emerges logically from the textual evidence of Theme 2, since when the soul becomes "stifled" by mind-body patterns, these systems necessarily operate according to their own automatic motivations rather than conscious soul direction. The scripture supports this understanding through its descriptions of beings "drowning" in endless cycles of desire and reaction, moving "up and down, up and down" in the "pointless and therefore illusory dual choices" of unconscious living [1].

As the ancient sages understood, this automaticity represents consciousness trapped in what Chapter 26 calls the "ever agitating movements of opposition and attraction"—mental and physical patterns that perpetuate themselves without conscious soul participation, creating the cycles of reincarnation that the awakened practitioner explicitly rejects [1].

Through recognizing these three themes within Chapter 26's verses, aspirants gain the essential framework for understanding how consciousness can discover its nature as the Soul-Aware-Witness and thereby achieve liberation from unconscious patterns in accordance with the eternal teachings of Shetaut Neter.

Indeed, this automaticity manifests in the common experience of carrying on actions without conscious awareness—later wondering 'Why did I do that?' or 'Where did the time go?'—as if the conscious reflective being were absent while mind and body operated independently. This represents precisely what the scripture describes: consciousness 'drowning' in unconscious patterns while the personality pursues its habitual motivations without the volition or direction of higher awareness. Thus, the ancient wisdom reveals that unconscious living literally means consciousness is not present during much of human activity, explaining why spiritual awakening requires the fundamental shift to Soul-Aware-Witness presence that the Chapter 26 practitioner demonstrates.

## Chapter 26 as Clinical Case Study: Ancient Egyptian Demonstration of Transpersonal Mental Health

The declarations of Asar (Osiris) Any in Chapter 26 present what contemporary transpersonal psychology could recognize as a representative clinical case study of optimal mental health—consciousness operating from its authentic divine nature rather than ego-delusion. Consider how the three mystic psychology themes embedded within these verses demonstrate the precise criteria that transpersonal psychology establishes for complete psychological well-being, revealing that the ancient sages understood mental health millennia before modern psychology discovered these same principles.

## Transpersonal Psychology's Framework for Mental Health:

- **Self-Transcendence:** Moving beyond the ego's limited perspective and experiencing connection to a larger whole, whether humanity, nature, or divine consciousness—considered the highest stage of psychological development
- **Holistic Integration:** Harmonious relationship between an individual's mental, emotional, physical, and spiritual dimensions, where consciousness directs rather than being dominated by psychological and bodily impulses
- **Spiritual and Existential Well-being:** Sense of purpose and meaning in life, strong connection to core values, and healthy response to existential questions about life, death, and suffering

## Chapter 26's Demonstration of These Criteria:

**Theme 1: Self-Transcendence Achievement** The practitioner's experiential recognition (rech) through "my heart, I know myself; that knowing is my power" demonstrates movement beyond ego's limited perspective to experience connection with universal consciousness [1]. Indeed, the "Asar Any" formula exemplifies this perfectly—consciousness recognizing both its individual manifestation (Any) and its universal divine essence (Asar) simultaneously. This represents the highest stage of psychological development where awareness operates from cosmic rather than personal identity.

**Theme 2: Holistic Integration Accomplished** The declaration "my soul is neither stifled nor suffocated" coupled with conscious control over mind ("my heart, I know myself") and body ("I have control over my arms and legs") demonstrates the harmonious relationship between mental, emotional, physical, and spiritual dimensions [1]. This integration occurs because consciousness has assumed its rightful position as director of the personality rather than being dominated by mental and physical impulses. A situation where consciousness remains dominated by mental and physical impulses can give rise to internal conflicts, contradictory feelings that do not harmonize with thoughts or actions, confusion about what is good and right in life, etc. Thus, ordered functioning emerges that prevents the psychological pathologies arising from soul suffocation.

## Theme 3: Spiritual and Existential Well-being Actualized

The practitioner's conscious direction of all activities—contrasted with others "drowning" in automatic patterns—demonstrates the sense of purpose and meaning that characterizes spiritual well-being [1]. Moreover, consciousness awareness as Self inherently, due to its contenting effect on the mind, providing inner satisfaction feelings and intuitively answering existential questions, spontaneously resolves existential questions about life, death, and suffering through direct recognition of one's eternal divine nature, providing the stable foundation for meaning-centered living.

## Profound Implications for Contemporary Transpersonal Practice

This analysis reveals that Ancient Egyptian psychology anticipated transpersonal psychology's understanding by thousands of years, demonstrating that optimal mental health has always involved spiritual realization rather than mere symptom management. Chapter 26 thus provides measurable clinical criteria for transpersonal mental health: peaceful heart, experiential self-knowledge, conscious control, and soul expression. These themes offer a practical diagnostic framework where contemporary practitioners can assess their own psychological development against specific textual markers, validating the therapeutic approach of Shetaut Neter as authentic psychology for achieving complete mental health—consciousness functioning from divine recognition rather than ego-identification.

# FROM THE WISDOM TEACHINGS OF SAGE AMENEMOPET
Chapter 5: The Glory of Silence

**Verse 9** *About finding fullness through silence*

Verse 9.
   **9.1.** *Aa mehtu{mdj} en ger   gem   {mdj} k pa        ankh {mdj}*
   9.2. Behold! fullness of silence finds   {fig} thee the     life   {fig}
   9.3. Behold the glory of this way of being! Being silent means discovering the fullness of the Creator-Spirit that is within. This fullness cannot come from heatedly searching for fulfillment in the world for fulfillment with an imperfect personality. Rather, it is found not by externalities but instead by realizing that there is perfection within when the fullness of being is experienced beyond the worldly desires and cravings.


9.1-9.3. The ancient sages taught that the path to discovering the Soul-Aware-Witness requires what Sage Amenemopet describes as the "fullness of silence" [3]. This teaching reveals that "being silent means discovering the fullness of the Creator-Spirit that is within" rather than seeking fulfillment through heated engagement with worldly phenomena [3]. Furthermore, this silence represents not mere absence of speech, but the establishment of consciousness in its witnessing nature, where the natural fullness of divine awareness becomes self-evident without external dependencies.

# Teachings of Amenemopet Chapter 6B[19]: Maintaining Awareness of All-Encompassing Divinity

**Verse 14** *About deliberate awareness of Neberdjer*

Verse 14.
14.1. sautu        {mdj}   {hi}   tu er   Neb-er-djer
14.2. be aware     {fig} {forceful} as to Lord-of-utmost-limits
                   {deliberate/
                   intent/
                   with conscious
                   volition}
14.3. Remain watchful, mindful, aware, keeping in mind, with deliberate effort, as to the fact that there is an "entity", an "existence" that encompasses all Creation[All-encompassing-Divinity], beyond[underlying] mind and time and space.
Therefore, no action is hidden from it and consequently, this existence/consciousness underlies limited human awareness. If this awareness is maintained, there will be no egoism and no mind and therefore no fears, frustrations, inordinate desires, no need for stealing, lying, cheating or becoming a heated person and missing out on the glories of inner peace or the fulfillment of the purpose of life.

---

[19] Translation by Dr. Muata Ashby

Awakening Your Soul-Aware-Witness

# Teachings of Amenemopet-Chapter 18[20]: Divine Guidance and Human Will

**Verse 6** *About divine shepherding of human life*

Verse 6.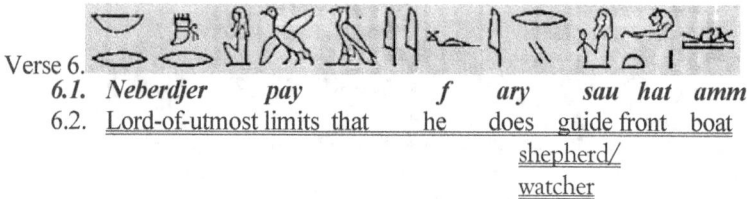
  6.1. *Neberdjer     pay         f      ary      sau    hat    amm*
  6.2. Lord-of-utmost limits that  he    does    guide  front   boat
                                                       shepherd/
                                                       watcher
  6.3. However, despite the personal predilections, there is an all-encompassing divinity that masters and encompasses the limits of Creation and therefore, that overall encompassing divinity is the shepherd that guides human life. That divinity is actually at the forefront of the boat of life watching(aware), guiding the boat of human life where it needs to go for the welfare of all humans even before they themselves know where they are going. Therefore, human self-will and or self-determination are an illusion.

## Chapter 11: The Consequence of Divine Rejection[21]

**Verse 10** *About the Divine heart turning away*

Verse 10.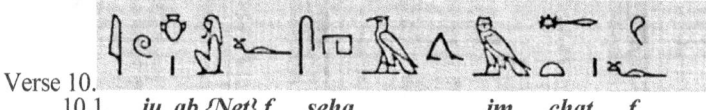
  10.1.   *iu ab {Net} f   seha           im    chat    f*
  10.2.   it is heart{Divine} his turning away in   body   his
  10.3.   Why, because, when that is done, it is one's own rejection of the Divine within our heart and thus our Divine heart, that is, the Spirit essence of the Divine within us, as if turns away from (forsakes) us within our own personality.

---

[20] Translation by Dr. Muata Ashby
[21] Translation by Dr. Muata Ashby

## From the Wisdom Teachings of Sage Amenemopet

## Chapter 5: The Glory of Silence Verse 9: About Finding Fullness Through Silence

The ancient sages taught that the path to discovering the Soul-Aware-Witness requires what Sage Amenemopet describes as the "fullness of silence" [3]. This teaching reveals that "being silent means discovering the fullness of the Creator-Spirit that is within" rather than seeking fulfillment through heated engagement with worldly phenomena [3]. This silence represents not mere absence of speech, but the establishment of consciousness in its witnessing nature, where the natural fullness of divine awareness becomes self-evident without external dependencies.

## Chapter 6B: Maintaining Awareness of All-Encompassing Divinity Verse 14: About Deliberate Awareness of Neberdjer

This verse provides the essential practice for maintaining witness consciousness: "Remain watchful, mindful, aware, keeping in mind, with deliberate effort, as to the fact that there is an 'entity', an 'existence' that encompasses all Creation[All-encompassing-Divinity], beyond[underlying] mind and time and space" [3]. This understanding aligns with the tradition of Shetaut Neter that the Soul-Aware-Witness must continuously recognize its foundation in universal consciousness. When this awareness is maintained consistently, "there will be no egoism and no mind and therefore no fears, frustrations, inordinate desires" [3], for consciousness rests in its essential nature of fullness and self-fulfillment rather than being pulled into mental modifications.

## Chapter 18: Divine Guidance and Human Will Verse 6: About Divine Shepherding of Human Life

The wisdom of the neteru reveals through this teaching that individual will operates within divine orchestration: "there is an all-encompassing divinity that masters and encompasses the limits of Creation and therefore, that overall encompassing divinity is the shepherd that guides human life" [3]. This understanding supports the development of witness consciousness—when the Soul-Aware-Witness recognizes that divine intelligence guides all experience, the ego's need to control and manipulate circumstances naturally dissolves.

## Chapter 11: The Consequence of Divine Rejection Verse 9: About the Divine Heart Turning Away

When conscious-awareness in a person rejects its divine nature and experiences what the scripture describes as "one's own rejection of the Divine within our heart and thus our Divine heart, that is, the Spirit essence of the Divine within us, as if turns away from (forsakes) us within our own personality" [3]. This teaching illuminates why the development of the Soul-Aware-Witness proves essential: only through recognition of our divine nature can consciousness maintain its natural connection to the source of peace, wisdom, and fulfillment.

## THEMATIC EXPLORATION: THE FOUNDATION OF SPIRITUAL TRANSFORMATION

### Living by Truth as the Gateway to Spiritual Recognition

The profound scriptural declarations we have examined emerge not from mystical experiences but from the systematic practice of living by truth (Maat) at all levels of human experience. As the ancient sages taught, discovering one's true nature as divine consciousness requires practical foundation that creates the spiritual sensitivity necessary for recognizing consciousness beyond ego-identification.

This understanding corresponds directly with the teaching revealed in Chapter 3, where the Ancient Egyptian Book of Enlightenment Chapter 125, verses 5-6, establishes the scriptural foundation for this practice: "I have acted by truthfulness while I was living on earth" and "I live in truth, I feed upon things that are in the form of truth, in my mind, not lies, falsehoods, or similitudes" [4]. As demonstrated in the discovery of Neberdjer teaching, when actions align with truth (Maat), consciousness becomes purified enough to access Neberdjer—the "All-Encompassing Divinity that enfolds Creation and manifests as Creation, the entity that is what is, what exists and nothing else, but Neberdjer exists" [4].

Moreover, this scriptural confirmation illuminates how living by truth serves as both method and qualification for divine recognition: the practice of Maat creates the purification necessary for consciousness to discover its essential nature as a manifestation of the all-encompassing divine reality rather than remaining trapped in ego-delusion and separateness-perception. In other words, living by truth means living consciously in the light of the existence of Neberdjer as the reality behind everything including oneself and therefore living in an inspiring awe-filled thought and feeling perspective on existence, life and self-identity.

The intellectual faculty of mind serves as the initial instrument for examining the situation of human awareness and perception, allowing practitioners to investigate the reality of life and develop modes of living more conducive to fulfillment and contentment. Yet intellectual understanding alone cannot produce the recognition described in Ancient Egyptian Book of Enlightenment Chapter 26. This recognition requires what the tradition calls the purification that emerges from consistent alignment with divine order.

## The Physical Foundation of Maat Practice

Living by truth at the physical level establishes essential groundwork for spiritual development through practices that tend to produce calmness, harmony, and health. This encompasses living in balance with nature—maintaining proper diet, rest, sleep, and physical rhythms that support rather than agitate the nervous system. Furthermore, the ancient sages understood that consciousness trapped in an unbalanced physical vehicle cannot achieve the stability necessary for witnessing its own nature.

The tradition teaches that seeking to live by regulations promoting peace and harmony, such as non-violence, creates what may be termed "environmental conditions" that allow subtle spiritual recognition to emerge. Notice how agitated physical circumstances create corresponding agitation in the mental-emotional complex, while harmonious physical living naturally supports the inner silence from which witness consciousness becomes apparent.

## The Mental Foundation: Challenging Ego-Self-Identity

Living by truth at the mental level requires practicing what promotes sanity, peace, and harmony while avoiding agitating thoughts that foment disturbing feelings. The ancient sages taught that agitating thoughts occur through belief in oneself as a separate ego-personality in competition and conflict with others, while searching for happiness by acquiring objects or protecting currently held possessions.

The truth discovered by thoughtful people reveals that objects cannot bring fulfillment or contentment, which means that the source fomenting desires based on the idea that objects provide happiness must be challenged. That source represents ego-self-identity—what Chapter 26 refers to as the "agitated heart" and reactive body patterns that must be recognized as alterations of the true nature of human being [1].

As the wisdom of the neteru illuminates, this mental purification creates the conditions where consciousness can recognize that the entity practicing living by truth differs from the ego-personality that was previously considered to be the self. In other words, the same consciousness that was operating through ego-identification now, through purification, begins to be recognized as a separate entity apart from the mind, its thoughts and desires, and apart from the physical body.

The soul-aware witness discovery thus represents consciousness awakening to its essential nature as the observer of mental-physical phenomena rather than remaining identified with these temporary modifications. This shift from participant to witness consciousness constitutes the foundational recognition that enables all subsequent spiritual development. Through establishing itself as the witness rather than being caught in mental-emotional reactivity, consciousness gains the stability necessary for recognizing its deeper divine nature as Ra, Nunu, and ultimately Soul of Ra.

## The Discovery Process: From Ego-Purification to Witness Recognition

The tradition reveals that when sufficient spiritual sensitivity develops from the practice of living by truth, the ego-personality becomes purified enough to discover a fundamental recognition about its own nature. The practitioner begins to recognize that the entity within themselves that they previously identified as the ego-personality—their ethnicity, name, memories, personal history—now appears as something they can observe (as objects that they are associated with) rather than something they are. This represents a fundamental shift in self-identification, where consciousness discovers its capacity to witness rather than be identified with mental content.

This entity that emerges through purification represents what may be called the "Soul-Aware-Witness"—consciousness that was always present in the personality but is now discernible to itself, whereas previously it identified completely with ego-personality urges and patterns. The ancient sages taught that this represents the first stage of spiritual awakening: the recognition of consciousness as witness rather than participant in mental-emotional activity.

Still, this Soul-Aware-Witness represents only the beginning of consciousness development rather than its completion. The Scripture reveals that when the Soul-Aware-Witness becomes established, a natural movement of self-discovery progresses toward recognizing this witnessing awareness as a manifestation of Ra-level consciousness, and through Ra recognition, the natural progression continues toward Nunu consciousness and ultimately Soul of Ra recognition.

## THE PRACTICAL METHODS FOR CONSCIOUSNESS LEVEL RECOGNITION

### Contemplative Study and Philosophical Discrimination

The practice begins with engaging in right thinking and feeling based on the truth that Ra-consciousness represents the higher reality of life and therefore the higher goal of human existence. This takes the form of spiritual studies and repeating the wisdom about the falsehood of mind and senses while affirming the reality of higher perceptions as the mind becomes calmed and higher awareness is discovered.

Observe how this practice involves putting attention on what represents higher truth instead of the falsehoods presented by illusory perceptions and deluded ideas learned previously in life. The tradition teaches that concentrating on the philosophy about the illusoriness of mind and senses allows practitioners to proceed with appropriate skepticism toward mental content while leaning on the direct experience of fundamental awareness itself.

## The Practice of Divine Name Repetition

The practice includes concentrating on higher consciousness with name and form, such as the name and form of the divinity Ra and using the name of Ra repeatedly through chanting to concentrate the mind on what represents higher reality. This technique receives specific recommendation in the Ancient Egyptian Scripture of Ra and Hetheru as well as in the Ancient Egyptian Creation Scripture, providing ancient precedent for hekau (mantra) based spiritual practice. These techniques utilize what the ancient sages called hekau (see Essential Concepts section in the introduction)—words of power that function as transformative spiritual technology.

The tradition reveals that this repetitive invocation of the divine name creates momentum patterns that gradually override the automatic reactive patterns stored in the unconscious mind that foment movement and overlooking the deeper states of awareness, allowing witness-consciousness to establish itself in its higher divine nature rather than the divergent ego-driven patterns.

## Subtle Awareness Investigation

The more subtle practices, for purifying the mind, involve reflection on the qualities of Ra consciousness, the wisdom about the nature of Ra as cosmic mind and source of the names and forms which are actually composed of Nunu consciousness that has been affected so as to appear differentiated.

Advancing steps involve taking time for sitting in solitude, perhaps including deep breathing, to reduce the pressure of sense perceptions on the mind. This creates conditions where practitioners can put attention on the awareness capacity of the personality that operates through the mind while remaining distinct from mental content.

The ancient sages taught a crucial recognition: practitioners can discover that they can be aware of themselves being aware of thoughts and feelings, which means they are separate from their thoughts and feelings. What's more, the thoughts and feelings in the personality are not the true self but rather objects being experienced based on past experiences, learned opinions, and accumulated memories.

## The Recognition of Awareness Beyond Mind

Through expanding awareness further, practitioners can realize that the awareness they experience operates without mind and senses and in fact exists even when mind and senses are non-operative, such as during the deep dreamless sleep state. This same awareness operates during waking consciousness when the mind does not have current thoughts or feelings—a state that occurs continuously (unnoticed during the waking state) in the spaces between thoughts but can be lengthened through practices that promote mental calmness. Meditation practice to disciplinarily lead the mind to a state of awareness without cognition serves the purpose of allowing discovery of existence beyond the mind and senses and growing awareness of the universality of consciousness (Ra, Nunu) underlying the apparently local individual ego personality.

These recognition levels signify Nunu-level consciousness, representing undifferentiated awareness that encompasses all mental activity without being modified by particular contents. The tradition teaches that allowing this natural self-discovery movement to proceed automatically eventually leads toward Soul of Ra experience.

## Soul of Ra Recognition: Beyond Experience Categories

The ancient sages taught that Soul of Ra recognition transcends the category of "experience" as such. This represents not an experience that occurs through the mind or through awareness of individuation, but rather a "knowingness" that, after it occurs, the mind can classify using approximate words such as infinity, eternity, or absolute. However, Soul of Ra consciousness itself has no qualities, analogs, or descriptors, yet it must be recognized as the ultimate essence of being even though it is not definable in terms of the limited mind and its conceptualizations.

The tradition provides various terms that point toward this recognition: Neberdjer (All-encompassing divinity), Un (existence), Neterty (Consciousness manifesting as both phenomenal and transcendental Absolute), and Neter-an-ren (Divinity without name or form). These terms serve as conceptual pointers rather than definitions, since Soul of Ra consciousness transcends all conceptual categories while serving as their foundation.

## Ancient Egyptian Book of Enlightenment Chapter 85 Papyrus Any -Translation by Dr. Muata Ashby (2025)

### Introduction to Chapter 85: Transformation into Ra

### The Sacred Technology of Discovering Ra Identity

This chapter from the Pert-m-Heru represents the sacred wisdom for aspirants who seek to discover their true identity through profound recognition of Ra consciousness—the divine principle that emerges from the primordial waters of Nunu (Nun) and serves as the foundation for all spiritual transformation [5]. Moreover, this teaching serves as the practical instruction for asserting and discovering the Ra identity within oneself, revealing the process by which individual consciousness recognizes its essential unity with divine awareness. This chapter correlates directly with the profound metaphysical framework presented in the Scripture of Ra and Hetheru, particularly verse 153, which establishes the hierarchical yet non-dual nature of ultimate reality [2].

Verse 1.
1.1. *djed in Asar sesh*
1.2. words by Osiris scribe
1.3. Now these following words are spoken by the scribe Any who goes by the spiritual name "Osiris...

Verse 1.
*1.4. Any       maa-kheru*
1.5. Any       Spiritually victorious
1.6. ...Any". I declare that I am spiritually victorious.

Verse 2.
*2.1. an aq   a   er chebenu an sek   a*
2.2. not go-in I  to house-of-evil not destroyed I
2.3. Therefore, I will not be going into the chamber of moral iniquity and therefore my conscious-awareness will not be destroyed.

Verse 2.
*2.4. an rech   a   su*
2.5. not know  I  that
2.6. I will not know that occurrence, I will not experience or have awareness of that. That will not be my fate...

Verse 3.
*3.1. nuk   Ra   per   im Nunu   Ba   pu Neter*
3.2. I am  Ra  coming from-within Nunu  soul  that Divinity
3.3. ...because "I am Ra", the same Cosmic Creator who emerged from Nunu, undifferentiated consciousness; indeed, it is that same divinity...

Verse 3.
*3.4. qemamu       hau F*
3.5. creator        body his (own)
3.6. ...who was the Creator of his own body that appears as Creation.

Understand how the Scripture of Ra and Hetheru reveals the fundamental relationship between Ra and the primordial consciousness from which Ra emerges, thus illuminating the process by which divine consciousness manifests while maintaining its essential unity [2]. This understanding transforms the spiritual journey from seeking union with something external to recognizing the divine consciousness that already constitutes one's deepest nature. The ancient sages taught that what appears as individual transformation is actually the recognition that consciousness was never limited by the forms through which it appeared to manifest.

In this chapter, the aspirant declares identification with Ra consciousness, thus accessing the profound teaching that individual consciousness and cosmic consciousness operate through identical mechanisms and share identical essence [2]. As the ancient Book of the Dead reveals: "I am the same God Ra manifesting as existence-effulgent. I declare that I am the only ONE. I created myself in the waters of Undifferentiated Consciousness" [2]. This declaration exemplifies the recognition that individual manifestation represents unitary divine expression rather than separate existence.

Notice that Ra's emergence from Nunu represents the first divine differentiation—the initial movement from undifferentiated potential into active creative principle, establishing the framework within which all subsequent manifestation occurs [2]. This moment constitutes Creation's first act, bringing forth the fundamental principles of individuation, cognition, movement, and the establishment of relative reality. At the same time, this differentiation occurs while maintaining essential unity—what the Ancient Egyptians understood as the same consciousness appearing in different modes of expression.

The transformation taught in this chapter of the Ancient Egyptian Book of Enlightenment serves as the practical methodology for realizing the comprehensive unity revealed in the Scripture of Ra and Hetheru, where Ra declares that his soul encompasses all manifestation: "It is that same Soul of Ra, the Creator-Spirit, and through the use of words-of-power this Soul of Ra has reformed and, is manifesting as, the objects of the Creation (djer), which are, in their entirety, encompassed, to the utmost limit, by Him, and He is the soul of everything" [2]. This understanding reveals that all apparently separate forms are actually modifications of one divine consciousness expressing itself through infinite variety while remaining essentially unchanged.

The declaration of Ra identity represents a profound spiritual realization that transcends preliminary recognitions of divine nature. Recognize how this recognition moves beyond identifying with divine creative power at the level of manifestation to discovering the fundamental awareness that underlies all cosmic activity [2]. Through this sacred technology, practitioners discover their essential nature as the very consciousness from which both individual awareness and cosmic manifestation emerge.

This teaching aligns with the understanding that spiritual practice aims to reveal what was always true but hidden by ignorance—that individual consciousness is not separate from divine consciousness but represents its localized (and thereby constricted) expression [2]. This is a process by which unlimited awareness becomes constricted into the illusion of separate individual existence operating through limited mind and senses that can only perceive and conceptualize a restricted level of awareness.

The systematic approach to consciousness transformation provides the direct method for achieving recognition of unity with divine awareness, not as an acquisition of something new, but as the removal of the misconceptions that veiled one's eternal nature as Ra consciousness itself.

The practical technology of discovering Ra identity operates through the sacred science of affirmation—the systematic remembrance of the wisdom of Ra and repetition of the divine name and identity declarations that transform consciousness-awareness itself (how consciousness manifests in the human mind depending on its level of ethical purity and understanding about the nature of self) [2]. As revealed in verse 177 of the Scripture of Ra and Hetheru, where the aspirant declares "I am Ra the Creator Spirit, among the Company of His noble Gods and Goddesses," these hekau (words of power) function as transformative instruments rather than mere recitations [2]. The utterance of the name of Ra aligns with the profound teaching found in Creation Scripture B verses 58-59, which describes the practice of "shenut" (circular-invocation)—the recurring utterance of Ra's divine name that enables practitioners to "overthrow their enemies (opposition, negativity, slothfulness, disagreeableness in the personality)" through creating words of power [6]. Reflect on how the ancient sages taught that these affirmations, particularly the progressive sequence beginning with "I am Ra's glorious (light) shining spirit!" and culminating in the ultimate realization "I am Ra," serve to redirect consciousness away from the delusion of separate existence toward recognition of unity with divine source [2].

Even so, the discovery of Ra identity requires the essential foundation of ethical purity according to Maat (divine order and righteousness). The ancient sages established that spiritual development cannot occur without the foundation of righteous living, as actions aligned with Maat create "light aryu" (karmic impressions) that remain transparent to divine light, while actions against Maat create "heavy aryu" that obstruct the flow of divine consciousness [2]. This means that truthfulness in all communications, justice in all dealings, proper stewardship of resources, harm avoidance toward all beings, and maintenance of moral integrity create the character stability necessary for the recognition of divine identity to emerge and be sustained.

Through the technology of affirmation combined with ethical purification, the aspirant progresses through the transformative process described in the scripture: from initial recognition of divinity within speech ("I am the Divine word of power") through identification with divine luminosity ("I am Ra's glorious spirit") to the ultimate realization of essential unity with Ra consciousness [2]. This sacred technology enables practitioners to achieve what the ancient sages understood as the discovery of one's true identity—the timeless "I am Ra" awareness that manifests as both individual experience and cosmic expression while remaining fundamentally unaffected by the content of either.

## THE SOUL-AWARE-WITNESS-SELF: PEACE, SELF-CONTROL, AND SOUL EXPRESSION

The Ancient Egyptian Book of Enlightenment scripture describes an entirely different mode of consciousness through its teaching on the "Soul-Aware-Witness"—the awakening of awareness of not being an ego personality but rather a being possessing higher awareness above the ego self-identity [1]. This awareness manifests through the practitioner's declarations that emerge from the foundation of living by truth: "my heart, he is peaceful within me," "as he himself (Asar {Osiris}), the Divine," "I know myself," and "I have control over my arms and legs (body)" [1].

The soul-aware witness consciousness operates through three fundamental characteristics that distinguish it from ego-based awareness: inner peace that remains stable regardless of external circumstances, self-control that emerges from divine alignment rather than forced discipline, and soul expression that serves spiritual evolution rather than ego-gratification. These qualities emerge naturally through the purification process rather than through effortful cultivation, revealing the Soul-Aware-Witness as consciousness discovering its essential divine nature rather than acquiring new spiritual capabilities.

## CONCLUSION: THE INTEGRATION OF TRUTH AND RECOGNITION

The discovery of the Soul-Aware-Witness represents not a strange or rare mystical achievement, but the natural result of systematic spiritual practice grounded in living by truth at all levels of human experience. When consciousness aligns with Maat through proper physical living, mental purification, and spiritual practice, the recognition of its essential divine nature emerges spontaneously rather than through forced effort.

This recognition transforms our understanding of spiritual development from seeking extraordinary states to recognizing the divine awareness that was always present but obscured by ego-identification and the aryu patterns that maintain heated mind functioning. Through the foundation of living by truth, consciousness discovers its nature as the Soul-Aware-Witness, which naturally progresses through Ra, Nunu, and Soul of Ra recognition as the ancient scriptures reveal.

The tradition of Shetaut Neter thus provides both the practical methodology and the theoretical framework for consciousness development, demonstrating how ancient wisdom offers contemporary practitioners a complete path from ego-delusion to divine recognition through the systematic application of eternal spiritual principles.

# References

[1] Ashby, M. (2025). Teachings of New Kingdom Pert-M-Heru Ancient Egyptian Book of Enlightenment, Chapter 26. Translation by Dr. Muata Ashby. Sema Institute.
[2] Ashby, M. (2022). The Mysteries of Ra and Hetheru/Sekhmet. Translation by Dr. Muata Ashby. Sema Institute.
[3] Ashby, M. (2019). Teachings of Ancient Egyptian Sage Amenemopet with Hieroglyphic texts. Translation by Dr. Muata Ashby. Sema Institute.
[4] Ashby, M. (2016). Egyptian Book of the Dead Hieroglyph Translations for Enlightenment: Understanding the Mystic Path to Enlightenment Through Direct Readings of the Sacred Signs and Symbols of Ancient Egyptian Language With Trilinear Deciphering Translation Method Vol. 1. Translation by Dr. Muata Ashby. Sema Institute.
[5] Ashby, M. (2025). Papyrus Ani [Book of the Dead] Chapter 85—trilinear translation. Translation by Dr. Muata Ashby. Sema Institute.
[6] Ashby, M. (2025). Scripture of the Creation Version B: Book of Knowing the forms of the Creator and defeating the principle of chaos/degradation/decay. Translation by Dr. Muata Ashby. Sema Institute.

# Chapter 6: Neberdjer - The All-Encompassing Foundation

Having explored the discovery of the Soul-Aware-Witness, we must now examine the ultimate metaphysical foundation that underlies all consciousness development and spiritual realization. The ancient Egyptian wisdom reveals that beneath the three levels of consciousness explored in Chapter 2, beyond even the Soul-Aware-Witness, there exists what the ancient sages called Neberdjer—the All-Encompassing Divinity that serves as both the source and substance of all existence. Moreover, the term "Neberdjer" represents identical meaning to the term "Ba en Ra" (Soul of Ra).

It is important to understand that the consciousness state of Neberdjer emerges through the identical progression described throughout the Scripture of Ra and Hetheru—the systematic movement from Ra (individuated consciousness) through Nunu (undifferentiated consciousness) toward Ba en Ra (Soul of Ra) recognition. Notice how Neberdjer represents the same ultimate spiritual reality that emerges when consciousness transcends the conscious mind (represented by Ra) and the unconscious (represented by Nunu) entirely, yet the pathway remains unchanged: practitioners develop stable Ra consciousness, allow natural settling into Nunu awareness, and ultimately recognize their essential nature as the absolute foundation (whether termed Ba en Ra or Neberdjer). Furthermore, the ancient sages employed different scriptural designations from various textual sources to point toward the same ineffable reality that underlies all consciousness levels, ensuring that aspirants understand this represents deepening recognition of the established teachings rather than an alternative spiritual methodology requiring separate development.

# Scriptural Foundation: The Ancient Texts on Neberdjer

## Teachings of Amenemopet Chapter 6B VIII[22]

Verse 14.
14.1. sautu     {mdj}    {hi}    tu er    Neb-er-djer
14.2. be aware {figurative} {forceful}   as to Lord/Sovereign-of-limits
14.3. Remain watchful, mindful, aware, keeping in mind, with deliberate effort {deliberate/intent/with conscious volition}, as to the fact that there is an "entity", an "existence" that encompasses all Creation [All-encompassing-Divinity], beyond[underlying] mind and time and space. Therefore, no action is hidden from it and consequently, this existence/consciousness underlies limited human awareness. If this awareness is maintained, there will be no egoism and no mind and therefore no fears, frustrations, inordinate desires, no need for stealing, lying, cheating or becoming a heated person and missing out on the glories of inner peace or the fulfillment of the purpose of life.

## Teachings of Amenemopet Chapter 18[23]

Verse 6.
6.1. Neberdjer    pay      f    ary     sau hat amm
6.2. Lord-of-utmost limits that    he    does    guide front boat
6.3. however, despite the personal predilections, there is an all-encompassing divinity that masters and encompasses the limits of Creation and therefore, that overall encompassing divinity is the shepherd that guides human life. That divinity is actually at the forefront of the boat of life

---

[22] Translation by Dr. Muata Ashby
[23] Translation by Dr. Muata Ashby

watching(aware),guiding the boat of human life where it needs to go for the welfare of all humans even before they themselves know where they are going. Therefore, human self-will and or self-determination are an illusion that fuels the pursuit of individual desires and beliefs about reality.

## Stele of Djehuty Nefer Verse 3[24]

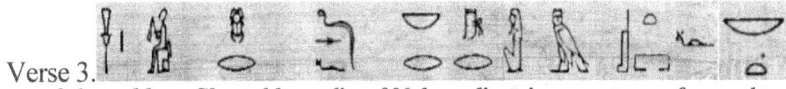

Verse 3.
3.1. sekhem Sheps khepr djezef Neb-er-djer im asset-per f    nebt
3.2. power  sacred  creator  himself  lord-of-limits  through  abodes  his    all
3.3. The power comes from the most sacred creator, who created himself, the lord of the utmost limits, the all-encompassing Divinity, the absolute being; and that power manifests through his abodes, which are indeed in everywhere, thus, in every scintilla, every spot, every particle he is Omnipresent. Therefore, All humans, animals and nature are kin in Neberdjer, who created all and is in all.

## A Hymn to Osiris: Neberdjer as the "Tower of Creation"[25]

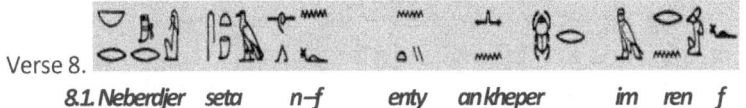

Verse 8.
8.1. Neberdjer seta    n-f    enty    an kheper    im  ren  f
8.2. All-encompassing Divinity towing by -he which is not created    in name his
8.3 ...the Divine, who is called All-encompassing Divinity; who tows along that which exists as well as that which does not since it has not yet been created; This process occurs when Divinity assumes the function described by the name...

---

[24] Translation by Dr. Muata Ashby
[25] Translation by Dr. Muata Ashby

Verse 9.

9.1. *ta her seta n –f sek n –f tawi im maa-[kheru] im ren  f*
9.2. "Earth person tow-er by–he tows" by-he two lands in spiritual victory in
namehis
9.3. …"The Person who Tows the Earth Along"; moreover, He tows along the two lands in spiritual victory within his name…

Verse 10.

10.1. *puy en Zokar user f    auu    aah    im ren f*
10.2. that of King-Netherworld almighty he expansion of great fear in name his
10.3. …The one: *Zokar* which means "sovereign of the netherworld plane of existence." In this capacity he is almighty and his essence spreads expansively, so much so as to cause awe, admiration and awestricken feelings; this all under his name…

## The Essential Nature of Neberdjer

## Understanding the Term Neberdjer

The ancient Egyptian term "Neb-er-djer" translates as "sovereign-about-existence" or "all-encompassing-divinity" or "ruler-as to-limits"—that is, Limitless [3]. In the context of the ancient wisdom, terms such as "sovereign," "Divinity," and "Existence" combined with limitless and all-encompassing-ness point to THAT WHICH IS ABSOLUTE [3].

Consciousness represents Neberdjer. In the tradition of Shetaut Neter, Neberdjer represents the most fundamental term for what constitutes "Consciousness" or "universal consciousness"—not consciousness as typically understood through individual mind-body systems, but rather the universal divine essence that operates in the form of awareness through all beings and phenomena while remaining as their unchanging foundation.

Reflect on how this all-encompassing limitless existence represents what the ancient sages understood as the ABSOLUTE—characterized by several fundamental qualities that distinguish it from all temporary phenomena:

✓ Undivided existence-experience ✓ All-Encompassing [interpenetrating] divinity (i.e. consciousness) ✓ Eternal ✓ Limitless/infinite ✓ Self-Created – independent-existence owed to itself

As the wisdom of the neteru reveals, awareness constitutes an inherent feature of underlying consciousness, but unlike human mind, Neberdjer awareness remains undivided, un-parsed into recognition of objects as individual entities existing separate from itself [3]. This represents a crucial distinction for understanding the relationship between ordinary human consciousness and absolute consciousness.

## The Omnipresent Nature of Neberdjer

The Stele of Djehuty Nefer teaches that the "abodes of Neberdjer are everywhere—hence Neberdjer manifests as all-encompassing-ness and interpenetrating permeation (flood/saturation/penetration/diffusion) throughout Creation/existence [i.e. Omnipresent]" [3]. This omnipresence differs fundamentally from physical presence—it represents consciousness as the very fabric of existence itself.

Furthermore, this understanding reveals that Neberdjer manifests as both transcendent (beyond all phenomena) and immanent (present as the essence of all phenomena). The ancient sages taught that recognizing this dual nature prevents both the error of seeing the Divine as separate from Creation and the error of identifying the Divine solely with manifest forms.

## The Relationship Between Neberdjer and Asar

## The Unity of Transcendent and Universal Consciousness

According to the Ancient Egyptian Creation myth, Neberdjer and Asar are one, which means the transcendental existence represents also the soul of every human being [3]. This revelation carries profound implications: every human has an aspect that is beyond time and space, eternal and infinite, to be realized by being aware of that fact (i.e. Neberdjer) instead of being aware of the limited and flawed existence experienced through mind [3].

This understanding explains the important Neterian statement: "I am Asar" [3]. Since Asar represents Neberdjer, being aware of the Asar nature simultaneously represents being aware of Neberdjer existence. At the same time, this requires understanding the relationship between these two aspects of the same ultimate reality.

## The Subtle Essence and Its Manifestation

Neberdjer represents the subtlest essence of existence and the source from which all existence in time and space, including duality, arises [3]. In the creation story involving the Anunian and Asarian Mysteries, Asar assumes the role of Khepera and Tem while simultaneously providing insight into the nature of Neberdjer through the profound declaration:

"Neb-er-djer saith, I am the creator of what hath come into being, and I myself came into being under the form of the god Khepera, and I came into being in primeval time. I had union with my hand, and I embraced my shadow in a love embrace; I poured seed into my own mouth, and I sent forth from myself issue in the form of the gods Shu and Tefnut." "I came into being in the form of Khepera, and I was the creator of what came into being, I formed myself out of the primeval matter, and I formed myself in the primeval matter. My name is Asar. The substratum of the primeval matter" [3].

This scriptural passage reveals that the soul serves as the subtler source from which subtle undifferentiated matter arises—in other words, soul/spirit constitutes the subtle support of subtle matter [3].

The relationship demonstrates how the absolute (Neberdjer) manifests as the universal soul (Asar) which then appears as individual consciousness through apparent differentiation.

The ancient Egyptian understanding of Neberdjer thus provides both the transcendent foundation that underlies all manifestation and the immanent presence that appears as individual consciousness. This dual recognition prevents practitioners from seeking the Divine as something separate while also avoiding the error of identifying ultimate reality solely with temporary phenomena. Understanding this relationship becomes essential for recognizing how individual spiritual development ultimately reveals the universal consciousness that has always been present as one's deepest nature.

## The Philosophical Framework: Key Insights on Consciousness

### The Illusion of Ordinary Perception

The ancient Egyptian philosophical investigation reveals that ordinary human experience involves awareness of objects perceived through senses, processed/registered in the mind, and related to a presumed ego-personality composed of mind, feelings, memories, and physical body [3]. However, this perception proves illusory because senses remain limited and can only perceive external aspects of objects.

Observe how this limitation causes misinterpretation-illusion, like the perception of a blue sky because the senses cannot process the visual elements accurately [3]. The mind compounds this limitation because it can only process perceptions brought via senses which are themselves limited and designed for external surface perceptions. Instead of acknowledging ignorance, the mind formulates misconceived notions of objects perceived using limited and distorted information [3].

### The Formation of Ego-Identity

The philosophical analysis reveals that the ego construct of the mind develops as the mental receiving of perceptions creates a focus of receipt in the mind [3]. This focus, which constitutes a function of mind, becomes self-identified as the "receiver" of perceptions and develops ego-self-identification in the absence of awareness of any other presence.

This self-identified individuated identity (ego) sees itself as a unified complex composed of mind, senses, and body, believing it constitutes the fundamental perceiving subject—the entity that experiences thoughts, sensations, and external phenomena as a singular conscious personality [3]. Yet careful investigation reveals that the senses, mind, and even perceived external objects function as contents within awareness rather than as the true perceiver itself. Since these faculties can themselves be observed—we can notice our thoughts thinking, our senses sensing, our emotions feeling—they must be objects of a deeper awareness rather than the ultimate subject of experience. This points toward what the ancient sages recognized as the witness consciousness that observes all changing phenomena, including the mental and sensory processes the ego mistakenly identifies as its essential self.

## The Discovery of the Unchanging Foundation

Since objects of perception change, and senses, mind, and ego all change states (waking, dream, sleep; dull, agitated, lucid; happy, sad, indifferent), these cannot be real since their changeability renders them illusory [3]. Things that change cannot represent ultimate reality due to their impermanent nature.

The crucial recognition emerges in order to perceive changes of states in senses, mind, and ego, another aspect of perception is required, since that which changes cannot be aware of itself while changing [3]. In order to perceive something and make sense of it in its true form, there must be a static, abiding subject that perceives the objects.

Since senses, mind, and ego are all changeable objects rather than static subjects, the investigation points toward what the ancient sages called the unchanging foundation of awareness itself [3].

## The Three Levels of Consciousness Within Neberdjer

Building upon the consciousness framework established in Chapter 2, the Neberdjer teaching reveals how all levels of awareness exist within the all-encompassing foundation:

## Human Awareness Within the Absolute

Every apparent object, including every apparently individual soul, represents actually that same Absolute, and their experience of life and awareness of events in the passage of time all occur within the awareness of their individual soul conscious-awareness [3]. This individual awareness occurs within the cosmic mind of the Creator, which in turn occurs within the absolute essence of Neberdjer that sustains the cosmic mind.

This reveals the three levels of potential conscious experience operating within Neberdjer [3]:

1. **Human Awareness Through Limited Mind:** a. Waking consciousness b. Dream consciousness c. Deep sleep consciousness
2. **Cosmic Mind Expanded Awareness (Creator Spirit Level - Ra, Net, Ptah, Amun):** a. Encompassing and surpassing human awareness
3. **Absolute Consciousness Total Awareness (Absolute Level - Neberdjer, Un-Nefer, Pa-Neter, Neter-An-Ren, Meh-urt):** a. Encompassing and surpassing both human awareness and cosmic awareness

## The Illusory Nature of All Experience Levels

This understanding leads to a profound realization: all experiences of the soul represent illusory experiences that are not abiding and only relate to the body, mind, and ego [3]. Just as having worldly experiences from birth to death have no effect on the underlying consciousness that sustains the waking appearance of reality in the mind, and just as falling asleep and having a dream have no consequence for the soul (Asar), in the same way, the appearance of

Creation has no impact on universal absolute consciousness (Neberdjer) [3].

This teaching transforms our understanding of spiritual development from achieving higher states to recognizing the unchanging awareness that remains unaffected by all states and experiences.

## The Practical Implications of Neberdjer Recognition

### The Foundation for Spiritual Practice

Understanding Neberdjer as the all-encompassing foundation provides essential context for all spiritual practices and consciousness development techniques. Since human consciousness represents the same as Neberdjer when the limited perceptions of time, space, and ego individuality experienced through mind are transcended [3], spiritual practice aims to remove the obstacles to this recognition rather than acquire something foreign.

This understanding aligns with the teaching from Sage Amenemopet that maintaining awareness of Neberdjer results in the elimination of egoism, fear, and inordinate desires [3]. When consciousness remains established in recognition of its all-encompassing foundation, the psychological conditions that create suffering naturally dissolve.

### The Resolution of Separateness and Limitation

The Neberdjer teaching provides the ultimate resolution to the problems explored in Chapter 3. Since Creation and human existence occur within Neberdjer and are not separate existence, and since Neberdjer constitutes all existence encompassing all, Creation represents only a mental appearance—a distortion of Absolute existence which represents Neberdjer (infinity, eternity, non-dual existence) [3].

Understand how this means that individual animals, plants, planets, stars, galaxies, universes, and individual humans with their egos do not exist as such separate entities [3]. This recognition eliminates the fundamental delusion of separateness that creates psychological suffering and spiritual seeking.

## The Criterion for Right Action

The teaching establishes a clear criterion for evaluating all human activity: any human activity that does not maintain Neberdjer awareness as the background awareness of mind, and instead involves action based on individual ego awareness composed of aryu and ignorance, represents activity rooted in delusion. This being the case, such activity proves erroneous, illusory, false, imagined, and unreal [3]. Even so, to the extent that clarity and purity exist in the mind, the Neberdjer awareness can influence the ego-based mind toward what proves positive, righteous and beneficial for the development of the personality, leading ultimately to full Neberdjer awareness (enlightenment). What's more, this understanding reveals how spiritual practice involves not acquiring something foreign but rather removing the obstacles that veil the recognition of what has always been present as one's essential nature.

This understanding transforms the entire approach to daily life, relationships, and spiritual development. Rather than only seeking to improve or perfect the ego-personality, practitioners also learn to discover and maintain awareness of the all-encompassing foundation that represents their true nature and the true nature of all apparent phenomena.

## The Relationship to the Soul-Aware-Witness

## From Individual Recognition to Universal Foundation

The Soul-Aware-Witness discovered in Chapter 5 represents consciousness that has separated itself from ego-identification. Still, the Neberdjer teaching reveals that this witness consciousness itself operates within and as a function of the all-encompassing foundation. In other words, what appears as individual witness consciousness actually represents universal Neberdjer consciousness temporarily focused through apparent individual awareness.

This understanding prevents practitioners from becoming attached to Soul-Aware-Witness consciousness as a personal achievement while pointing toward the recognition that even the witness emerges from and dissolves into the absolute foundation that underlies all awareness.

## The Ultimate Context for Consciousness Development

Neberdjer provides the ultimate context for understanding why consciousness development leads naturally from ego-identification through witness recognition to universal awareness and finally to absolute recognition. Since all levels of consciousness exist within and as modifications of Neberdjer, the spiritual path represents consciousness recognizing its own nature at progressively more fundamental levels.

This means that the three-level consciousness cosmology presented in Chapter 2 operates within the absolute ground of Neberdjer, which remains as the unchanging foundation whether consciousness functions through Soul of Ra, Nunu, or Ra awareness.

The recognition of Neberdjer thus reveals why all spiritual practices ultimately point toward the same essential understanding: what appears as individual consciousness development actually represents the universal consciousness recognizing its own nature through the apparent process of spiritual awakening. This understanding provides both the theoretical foundation and practical context for all spiritual development, demonstrating how the ancient Egyptian wisdom tradition offers a complete framework for consciousness transformation from ego-delusion to divine recognition.

## Contemporary Applications and Implications

## Scientific and Philosophical Parallels

Contemporary consciousness research and quantum physics investigations often demonstrate conclusions that resonate with the Neberdjer teaching—particularly findings suggesting that consciousness cannot be reduced to brain activity and that the universe expresses itself as fundamentally informational or consciousness-based rather than material in nature.

Even so, the ancient Egyptian approach differs from contemporary scientific investigation by providing both the theoretical framework and practical methodology for directly recognizing the all-encompassing consciousness rather than merely theorizing about it.

## Integration with Modern Spiritual Practice

For contemporary practitioners of Shetaut Neter, understanding Neberdjer provides essential foundation for integrating ancient wisdom with modern life circumstances. The recognition that all apparently separate phenomena exist within and as the all-encompassing foundation allows practitioners to approach work, relationships, and daily challenges from the understanding that there represents ultimately only one existence appearing as apparent multiplicity.

This perspective naturally resolves many of the conflicts that characterize modern spiritual seeking—the tension between transcendence and engagement, individual development and universal service, ancient wisdom and contemporary application.

**Mystic Mathematics: Formulation of Consciousness Statement #2.**

Consider how the ancient sages understood the fundamental architecture of human experience through what we might term the essential mystic mathematics of consciousness: **Consciousness [Neberdjer/Ba en Ra expressing through Nunu and Ra] is not the mind or sensations of the body—rather, consciousness is that which is conscious and aware of them, and indeed, they have no independent reality without consciousness to be aware of them.**
Consider how this understanding corresponds with the teaching in the Scripture of Ra and Hetheru: the mind and its contents exist as temporary modifications within awareness, much as waves exist as temporary modifications of the ocean while never being separate from their oceanic source. Therefore, when the aspirant recognizes this

fundamental relationship, the mistaken identification with mental processes naturally dissolves, revealing that what we have been calling 'our' thoughts and sensations are actually movements within the infinite awareness that constitutes our essential nature.

**Mystic Mathematics: Formulation of Consciousness Statement #3.**

The tradition reveals that **Consciousness [Neberdjer/Ba en Ra] IS all-pervading, timeless, and formless awareness that serves as both the source and substance of the entire universe—and furthermore, that the individual soul (Ba) is not separate from Neberdjer/Ba en Ra but is in fact identical to it.** This corresponds with the profound recognition expressed in the Scripture of Ra and Hetheru, where Ra declares the essential unity underlying apparent multiplicity. Nevertheless, this identity must be understood not as the ego-personality becoming divine, but rather as the recognition that what we have mistaken for individual consciousness was always the universal consciousness appearing to itself through the vehicle of apparent individuation. Indeed, this represents the culmination of all spiritual practice: the direct recognition that our essential nature was never separate from the absolute foundation that the ancient sages termed Neberdjer.

## Conclusion: The All-Encompassing Foundation

The ancient Egyptian teaching on Neberdjer provides the ultimate metaphysical foundation for understanding consciousness, spiritual development, and the nature of existence itself. As the all-encompassing divinity that serves as both the source and substance of all apparent phenomena, Neberdjer represents not a concept to be understood intellectually but the very reality that reads these words and seeks to know its own nature.

This teaching bridges the individual recognition of the Soul-Aware-Witness with the universal context that will be explored in Chapter

5, demonstrating how personal spiritual development ultimately reveals the universal consciousness that has always been the true identity of all beings. The practical methods for stabilizing this recognition will be examined in the spiritual practices sections, while the implications for daily life and spiritual service unfold throughout the remaining chapters.

In the tradition of Shetaut Neter, recognizing Neberdjer represents not the end of spiritual development but rather the foundation from which authentic spiritual life begins—life lived from the understanding that there exists only one existence appearing as the entire universe of experience, and that one existence represents what has always been seeking to know itself through the apparent journey from ignorance to enlightenment.

## References

[1] Ashby, M. (2019). Teachings of Ancient Egyptian Sage Amenemopet with Hieroglyphic texts. Translation by Dr. Muata Ashby. Sema Institute.
[2] Ashby, M. (2016). Egyptian Book of the Dead Hieroglyph Translations for Enlightenment: Understanding the Mystic Path to Enlightenment Through Direct Readings of the Sacred Signs and Symbols of Ancient Egyptian Language With Trilinear Deciphering Translation Method Vol. 1. Translation by Dr. Muata Ashby. Sema Institute.
[3] Ashby, M. (2025). Notes on Neberdjer for Transpersonal Psychology. Translation by Dr. Muata Ashby. Sema Institute.

# Chapter 7: The Universal Context - Asar Consciousness

Having established Neberdjer as the absolute foundation that underlies all consciousness levels, we must now examine how this universal reality manifests as the soul principle operating through all beings. The ancient texts reveal that what appears as individual spiritual development actually represents universal consciousness—called Asar—recognizing its own nature through apparent individual forms.

The relationship between Neberdjer and Asar receives direct scriptural confirmation in the Ancient Egyptian Anunian Creation Scripture Version B, where the ultimate source reveals both its absolute nature and its manifestation as the soul principle:

### Ancient Egyptian Anunian Creation Scripture Version B[26]

Verse 20.
    20.1. *djedu    Neberdjer    djed  f*
    20.2. words spoken  Lord-of-All  speaks-he-himself
    20.3. the following words are by Neberdjer (Lord-of-All/All - encompassing divinity), he himself speaks thus:

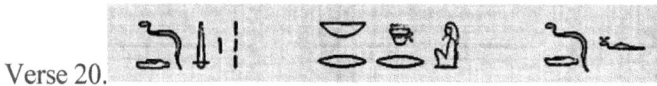

*Verse 21.*
    21.1. *pa  n-a  iu  pautetu  suh pa  n-a*
    21.2. this  of-me  it-is  primeval-matter{Div}egg this  of-me
    21.3. "This is made of me, it is the {Divine} primeval matter, the stuff that everything is made of, this "primeval stuff', i.e. undifferentiated consciousness, was as if an egg and it was made out of me.

---

[26] Translation by Dr. Muata Ashby

Verse 21.

*21.4. im     pautetu   {net}   pa     ren   a     Ausarz*
21.5. within  primeval-matter {Div} this name mine   Osiris
21.6. Within that primeval matter, that became the {Divine} Creation, I reside in my name Osiris.

This declaration establishes that Neberdjer (the All-Encompassing Divinity) and Asar (Osiris) represent the same ultimate reality—Neberdjer as the transcendent source and Asar as that same consciousness manifesting as the soul principle within Creation. Therefore, recognizing one's essential nature as Asar simultaneously represents recognizing oneself as Neberdjer expressing through individual form.

Observe these profound passages from the Ancient Egyptian Book of Enlightenment Chapter 43—entitled "A chapter on not letting the head of a person be taken away from them in the Netherworld." These texts, in conjunction with those using the prefix Asar (Osiris) before the name of the person, create a complete complementary philosophical loop in which the same person being referred to as an "Osiris" person is now in this passage being referred to as Osiris himself so as to denote their intrinsic identity; one being the universal consciousness (universal soul) and the other being the manifestation of that same universal being that manifests in each individual personality.

# ANCIENT EGYPTIAN BOOK OF ENLIGHTENMENT CHAPTER 43[27]

Verse 2.
- **2.1.** *Medu dje en  Asar Any              nuk           ur           sa*
- 2.2. Words spoken from Osiris Any  "I am           Great       child
- 2.3. These words are spoken coming from this spiritual initiate who goes by the name "Osiris Any". He says: I am a great one who is the child...

Verse 2.
- **2.4.** *ur*
- 2.5. Great
- 2.6. ...of a great one; thus, I have the same greatness that is the greatness of my parent. My parent is Asar (Osiris), the great universal soul, therefore I have that same great universal soul.

---

Verse 4.
- **4.1.** *maa ku-a     renpa      ku-a       nuk       Asar pu    neb      heh*
- 4.2. in-truth me    young      me        I am Osiris the lord    eternity
- 4.3. Know this for certain, verily it is the reality of me, of who I am; I have become young because I do not age with the human mind and body any more for the true me, who I am is Osiris, the Lord of Eternity, the one who does not age and is universal consciousness ever aware, ever shining.

**Verse 2 Osiris Any declares his great identity**

2.1-2.8. This verse establishes the fundamental principle of universal soul identity operating through individual personalities. The scripture reveals the practitioner declaring: "These words are spoken coming from this spiritual initiate who goes by the name 'Osiris Any.' He says: I am a great one who is the child...of a great one". Notice how this declaration demonstrates what the ancient

---

[27] Translation by Dr. Muata Ashby

Awakening Your Soul-Aware-Witness

sages understood as the "Asar Any formula"—consciousness recognizing both its individual manifestation (Any) and its universal essence (Asar/Osiris) simultaneously. This means that the practitioner has achieved recognition that "I have the same greatness that is the greatness of my parent. My parent is Asar (Osiris), the great universal soul, therefore I have that same great universal soul" [1].

## Verse 4 Describing the eternal nature of Osiris identity

4.1-4.3. The wisdom of the neteru reveals through this profound declaration the ultimate result of recognizing one's universal soul nature [1]. The practitioner states: "Know this for certain, verily it is the reality of me, of who I am; I have become young because I do not age with the human mind and body any more for the true me, who I am is Osiris, the Lord of Eternity, the one who does not age and is universal consciousness ever aware, ever shining" [1]. Furthermore, this statement demonstrates how consciousness transcends temporal and bodily identification when it recognizes its essential nature as universal Asar consciousness. In other words, the same awareness that functions through individual faculties simultaneously recognizes itself as the eternal, unchanging universal soul.

## FROM THE SCRIPTURE OF RA AND HETHERU: UNIVERSAL SOUL UNITY[28]

- Verse 155: "same soul of Ra...same soul of Asar" (universal soul teaching)
- Verses 156-157: Soul of Ra as "soul of everything"

Verse 155.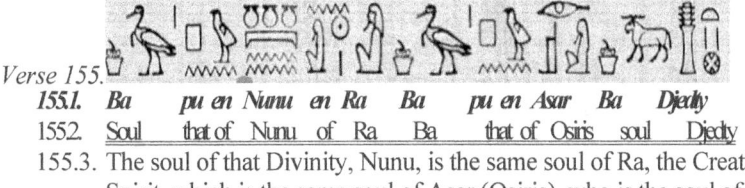
155.1. *Ba   pu en Nunu en Ra   Ba   pu en Asar   Ba   Djedty*
155.2. Soul   that of Nunu of Ra   Ba   that of Osiris   soul   Djedty
155.3. The soul of that Divinity, Nunu, is the same soul of Ra, the Creator Spirit, which is the same soul of Asar (Osiris), who is the soul of Busiris (Djedty), the abode of Asar (Osiris) on earth.

---

[28] Translation by Dr. Muata Ashby

Verse 156.

156.1. Bau    pu    en Sebiku    im shu    iu    Ba en Neter
156.2. Souls these of Crocodile-Gods in crocodiles    it-is    soul of Divine-God
156.3. The soul of Ra, The Creator-Spirit, is the souls of those crocodile gods and goddesses that are among the crocodiles. It is the soul of this Divine God that …

Verse 157.

157.1. neb im hefau    {Nef} iu    Ba    en Apep im Bakhau
157.2. every in snake    {Div}    it-is soul    of Apophis in
mountain-of-sunrises]
157.3. …is in every divine snake, and indeed it is the soul of Ra that is also the soul of Apep (Apophis)[29], the cosmic snake force that opposes progress and Creation, being a complement to Creation operating within the mountain where sunrises occur.

Verse 157.

157.4. iu    Ba    en Ra   ⟨R6-[30] im hekau    ⟩chet ta erdjer er F
157.5. it-is soul of Ra ⟨R6- through words-of-power⟩ objects physical as-to
boundary as-to He
157.6. It is that same Soul of Ra, the Creator-Spirit, <R6- and through the use of words-of-power> this Soul of Ra has reformed and, is manifesting as, the objects of the Creation (*djer*), which are, in their entirety, encompassed, to the utmost limit, by Him, and He is the soul of everything.

# Analysis of Universal Soul Teaching

## Verse 155: Describing the Unified Soul of Nunu, Ra, and Asar
This verse provides the metaphysical foundation for

---

[29] Giant snake that opposes the movement of the Boat o Ra and tries to stop it to bring Creation to a halt. The boat struggles every day, especially traversing the lower netherworld at night but emerges victorious every morning to create a new day and opportunity to experience life.
[30] This section is damaged in the Tomb of Sety 1st so this section in brackets comes from the version inscribed in the Tomb of Ramses 6

understanding universal consciousness. The scripture reveals: "The soul of that Divinity, Nunu, is the same soul of Ra, the Creator Spirit, which is the same soul of Asar (Osiris), who is the soul of Busiris (Djedty), the abode of Asar (Osiris) on earth". This understanding aligns with the tradition of Shetaut Neter that what appears as different manifestations of divine consciousness represents one universal soul expressing itself through various names, forms, and functions throughout Creation.

**Verses 156-157: Describing Ra's Soul as the Soul of All Beings and Objects** These verses reveal the ultimate scope of universal soul consciousness. The teaching illuminates that "The soul of Ra, The Creator-Spirit, is the souls of those crocodile gods and goddesses...is in every divine snake, and indeed it is the soul of Ra that is also the soul of Apep (Apophis), the cosmic snake force that opposes progress and Creation" This extends even to apparently opposing forces—demonstrating that universal consciousness operates through all phenomena without exception.

The scripture concludes with the comprehensive declaration: "It is that same Soul of Ra, the Creator-Spirit...this Soul of Ra has reformed and, is manifesting as, the objects of the Creation (djer), which are, in their entirety, encompassed, to the utmost limit, by Him, and He is the soul of everything". This reveals that what we perceive as the multiplicity of individual beings and objects represents one universal consciousness expressing itself through infinite forms while remaining essentially unified.

The ancient Egyptian teaching thus establishes that universal consciousness operates through all apparent forms while maintaining its essential unity. What appears as individual spiritual development actually represents this same universal consciousness recognizing its own nature through particular mind-body systems. Understanding this universal context transforms the entire approach to spiritual practice from individual achievement to universal recognition.

## The Divine Soul and Mystic Transpersonal Transformation: Ancient Egyptian Wisdom for Contemporary Psychology

The following passages from Ancient Egyptian literature are about the wisdom of the universal Divine soul, God manifesting as the soul of all humans. The first passage comes from the Ancient Egyptian Book of Enlightenment (Book of the Dead), Papyrus Any, Chapter 84 [Plate 28] {18-19th Dynasty of the New Kingdom of ancient Egypt}:

Verse 15.
15.1. ba    a    pu    Neter    ba    a    pu    heh
15.2. soul mine is    God    soul mine is    eternal
15.3. My soul is God; it is not a separate individual soul. My soul is eternal.

**COMMENTARY:** Understand that this momentous statement signifies that there are no individual souls. In other words, all souls are God manifesting as apparently individual beings; yet there is only one being manifesting: God. This means that the feeling of individuality and separate being is illusory and contradictory to the findings of observational investigation. All humans experience awareness the same way, through the body, mind and senses but also during waking, dream and deep sleep, which means that the soul awareness, the "I" idea that I am, I exist, I am aware is experienced by all through these mediums. However, that same awareness persists through all the states (waking, dream, deep sleep) therefore it persists even when not experiencing the body and mind and senses. There is a level of experience that does not include objective qualities, and this may be termed "Soul-Aware-Witness". This is the part of the personality that most people are not aware of because of being caught up in the thoughts, feelings desires and perceptions of the mind and senses. Yet, this essential being is God manifesting as the consciousness that is aware in every person and which, at the time of death of the physical body, reverts to its previous condition, before it associated with a body and experienced life through that body and mind and forgot about its divine nature.

Awakening Your Soul-Aware-Witness

The next passages are about the existence of a soul that is different from the physical body. The following text is about the wisdom of the universal soul from Ancient Egyptian Book of Enlightenment (Book of the Dead), from the earlier c. 5th dynasty.

Verse A.
A.1.   ba    ar    pet    shat    ar    ta
A.2.   soul  is-to  heaven  body    is-to    earth
A.3.   the soul goes to heaven and the body goes to the earth.

Wisdom about the universal soul from Ancient Egyptian Book of Enlightenment (Book of the Dead), from the c. 6th dynasty[31]:

Verse B.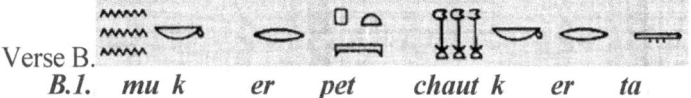
B.1.   mu k    er    pet    chaut k    er    ta
B.2.   water thine is-to heaven  bodies thine is-to earth
B.3.   your water, that is, your essence of life goes to heaven and your bodies that you experience in life, those go back to the earth

Wisdom about the universal soul from Ancient Egyptian Book of Enlightenment (Book of the Dead), from the later c. Ptolemaic period:

Verse C.
C.1.   pet    cher    ba {Net} k    ta chery{mdj}  tetu{Net}  k
C.2.   heaven possess soul{Div}thine earth possessing{Fig} image {Div} thine
C.3.   heaven possesses your divine soul, while earth possesses your divine image that manifests to you appearing in the form of a physical body.

---

[31] Translation by Dr. Muata Ashby

## The Foundation of Mystical Psychology

Recognize that mystical spirituality represents an advanced form of psychotherapy, incorporating not only a keen understanding of psychology, human emotion, and social relationships, but also the relationship between individual human consciousness and Cosmic Consciousness [2]. Moreover, mystical teachings should also be studied in the context of a transpersonal discipline which seeks not only to promote ordinary standards of normalcy, but to transcend these in order to achieve a supernormal mental, physical and spiritual level of health [2]. This fundamental understanding provides the framework through which we must examine the profound wisdom contained within Ancient Egyptian texts regarding the nature of the soul and its relationship to the Divine.

The ancient sages of Kemet (Ancient Egypt) recognized that what we term "normal" human psychological functioning actually represents a state of fundamental misidentification—a condition wherein consciousness has forgotten its divine nature and become trapped in identification with temporal, ephemeral forms. This recognition forms the cornerstone of what we must understand as the earliest systematic approach to "mystic transpersonal psychology", a discipline designed to guide the aspirant beyond personal or ego-based aspects of the psyche in order to discover the transcendent reality that lies beyond individual personality [2].

## The Momentous Declaration: "My Soul is God"

The first passage from the Ancient Egyptian Book of Enlightenment presents perhaps the most revolutionary statement in all spiritual literature: "ba a pu Neter ba a pu heh" - "My soul is God; it is not a separate individual soul. My soul is eternal." This momentous declaration signifies that there are no individual souls; rather, all souls are God manifesting as apparently individual beings, yet there is only one being manifesting: God.

Reflect on the profound implications of this understanding. The feeling of individuality and separate being reveals itself as illusory and contradictory to the findings of observational investigation. What's more, all human beings experience awareness in the same fundamental way—through the media of body, mind, and senses during waking, dream and deep sleep states.

Even so, the essential awareness that perceives different sensations and experiences in each individual persists through all these states of consciousness as the observer/witness of changing events and mental states. This means it continues even when not experiencing the body, mind and senses. Behind all these different experiences there exists an unchanging awareness manifesting as Ra, Nunu and ultimately Asar (Osiris)/Neberdjer. Thus, beyond the changing perceptions and sensations of all individuals, the deeper level of witness-consciousness that all human beings experience is the same for all.

This aligns with the understanding in the Scripture of Ra and Sekhmet, which teaches that from an absolute perspective, there are no egos or objects—there is only the Soul of Ra illumining, revealing its own existence in the form of undifferentiated consciousness and differentiated consciousness [3]. Thus, the Soul of Ra is the only consciousness operating through all minds; therefore, there are no individuals, no objects, no death and only immortality—all-encompassing existence absolute [3].

## The Ancient Wisdom of Soul and Body Separation

The subsequent passages from different dynasties of Ancient Egyptian civilization demonstrate the consistent transmission of this wisdom across millennia. The teaching "ba ar pet shat ar ta" - "the soul goes to heaven and the body goes to the earth" establishes the fundamental distinction between the eternal and temporal aspects of human existence. This understanding evolved and deepened through the ages, culminating in the Ptolemaic period teaching: "pet cher ba {Net} k ta chery{mdj} tetu {Net} k" - "heaven possesses your divine soul, while earth possesses your divine image that manifests to you appearing in the form of a physical body."

Furthermore, this progression reveals how the ancient sages refined their understanding while maintaining the essential teaching. The Universal Ba or Soul—the consciousness of the Supreme Being—emanates and sustains each individual human being through the various parts of the human spirit [1]. The human soul represents a projection of the divine into the consciousness field of duality (causal-astral-physical planes), yet the human soul forgets its divine origin and believes itself to be a creature among other creatures; hence, the idea of duality arises [1].

Notice how this ancient wisdom addresses the fundamental error of human psychology. Many people erroneously think of their soul as existing within their physical body; however, the opposite is true. The soul emanates from the Divine Self, which in turn creates the other parts of the personality including the mind and senses as well as the world that apparently surrounds the personality. The dream analogy clarifies this relationship: when a person dreams of themselves in a dreamworld, both the dream character and the entire dream environment exist within the consciousness of the sleeping person rather than the dream character containing that consciousness. Similarly, the individual soul and the entire manifest world exist within the Divine Self rather than the Divine Self existing within the physical body. All of creation, whether dreamworld or waking reality, occurs within the Divine Self and not within the body [1]. This represents a complete reversal of ordinary materialistic psychology, which assumes consciousness emerges from brain activity rather than recognizing that consciousness creates and sustains all manifestation.

## The Psychology of Spiritual Misidentification

The process by which divine consciousness becomes entrapped in identification with temporal experience reveals itself through what the ancient teachings call the formation of aryu (karmic impressions). This principle applies universally: whenever a person believes they are fundamentally the body, the collection of memories, the social roles, the nationality, the gender, or any other temporary characteristic, and they forget their essential nature as the immortal soul (ba), that particular constellation of identifications has superimposed itself upon their true nature [2].

In any case, when this ego becomes the primary self-identity of a person, it is said that the person has become "caught up in delusion." The term delusion here carries precise technical meaning: it refers to the process of believing in or identifying with something that is fundamentally illusory. Since the body, mind, memories, and all other accumulated impressions are by their very nature ephemeral—constantly changing and ultimately dissolving—they represent what the teaching recognizes as non-abiding realities [2].

Therefore, identification with these temporary phenomena constitutes involvement with invalid and illusory foundations for self-understanding. The ignorant human being, not aware of the storehouse of innate potential to experience fullness and peace within, goes on seeking for fulfillment in the worlds of duality instead of seeking to know and experience the only source of true fulfillment, the Universal Self, which encompasses all other realms [1].

Understand how this dynamic manifests in contemporary psychological suffering. The ego-personality emerges at the beginning of life like a movie character and continues changing, moving, craving and searching for fulfillment throughout the lifetime of that illusory personality. Still, this conditioning—the worries, desires, beliefs, ambitions and regrets—constitutes what holds the aspirant back from realizing the innermost Self, which is all-encompassing, all-knowing, and all-blissful contentment and peace [1].

The ancient Egyptian teaching thus provides a complete psychology of spiritual transformation that addresses both the mechanism by which consciousness becomes trapped in ego-identification and the pathway through which it can discover its essential divine nature. This understanding transforms therapeutic work from symptom management to fundamental recognition of one's universal soul nature as the foundation for all genuine healing and spiritual development.

## The Transpersonal Path of Transformation

The transformation from suffering-based ego identification to divine recognition requires both understanding and practice. For contemporary practitioners of Shetaut Neter, the ancient wisdom provides a systematic methodology for this transformation. The progression from recognizing oneself as Ra to realizing oneself as Ba Ra marks the fundamental shift from spiritual aspiration to spiritual actualization [2].

Moreover, the goal is not to become something other than what one already is, but to recognize what has always been one's essential nature. The conscious-awareness of a person that seeks enlightenment, the path toward realization, and the goal of spiritual attainment are revealed as expressions of the same undifferentiated awareness appearing as apparent multiplicity, all supported by the Soul of Ra [2].

This means that correcting misidentification requires both assertion and affirmation of true identity. Where a person should be aware of "I am Ra" they are instead thinking of themselves as separate individuals, basing their lives on the histories of ephemeral characters instead of basing life on the identity of abiding truth of existence free of mental modifications [2]. Thus, the fundamental problem of human misidentification necessitates spiritual philosophy and life guided by the path of mystical wisdom.

Observe how the ancient sages taught that the task of an aspirant is to cleanse the Physical, Astral and Causal planes of the mind so as to regain conscious perception of the Universal Self. Since the Universal Self is non-dual, immortal, eternal and the source of all planes and all objects within those planes, the union with the Universal Self bestows omniscience and a boundless vision of infinity, immortality and a feeling of non-duality and connectedness to all things great and small [1].

## The Peace, Awe, and Silence of Divine Recognition

The culmination of this transpersonal transformation manifests as what Chapter 175 of the Pert-m-Heru reveals as Hetep—a profound state of spiritual integration that transcends ordinary consciousness [1]. Through understanding and reintegrating the divine principles, the aspirant moves from a state of hanur (anxious, disturbed, troubled, longing, unsatisfied) to Hetep (peace of non-dual awareness) [1].

At the same time, this transformation represents more than mere psychological adjustment. Non-duality is experienced as absolute oneness and interconnectedness with all that exists. There is no feeling of you and me, here and there, male or female; there is no desire for objects because all objects are one with the Self. There is only the experience of awareness of the Self [1]. What's more, human words and concepts are not capable of describing the actual experience of oneness with the Self; therefore, all mystical descriptions are transcended in the actual experience.

The Ba Ra represents not a distant goal to be achieved but the very consciousness through which all seeking occurs. It is the source and sustenance of all existence. Every meditation, every offering ceremony, every contemplation of Maat unfolds within this absolute awareness that is beyond all mental categories and conceptual frameworks [2].

Reflect on how this recognition transforms the entire psychological condition of the practitioner. The witness-less state (undifferentiated consciousness) described in the Scripture of Ra and Hetheru reveals the truth behind the projections of mind created by ideations instigated by aryu. Since this witness-less state has no thoughts, no desires, no motivations, and represents the deeper reality of existence, having been present since birth and never changing while mind and body constantly change, it necessarily follows that the projections of mind are illusory constructs that can only be experienced by the mind [2].

## The Practical Framework for Contemporary Practice

The ancient Egyptian wisdom provides specific guidance for contemporary aspirants seeking this transformation. The Hetep offering table represents a sophisticated spiritual technology, carefully designed to facilitate the practitioner's journey from dual to non-dual consciousness through ritual action imbued with understanding [1]. The profound significance of the Hetep offering lies in its role as a tool for transcending duality, representing "offering maleness (haunch of beef) and femaleness (geese) in a continuous flow of mental attention towards the Divine to go from dualism of mental and perceptual experience to non-dual unitary transcendental experience and divine awareness" [1]. For more details on the Hetep offering table and hetep philosophy see section "The HETEP Offering Table: Sacred Technology for Consciousness Transformation" in Chapter 11.

In other words, the practitioner learns to recognize that the distinction between practitioner and practice dissolves in the recognition of divine identity. This understanding transforms the entire approach to spiritual practice, revealing that one is not practicing to become divine but practicing to recognize what has always been one's essential nature.

Therefore, the ancient teaching "I am the only ONE. I created myself in the waters of Undifferentiated Consciousness. I am the God Ra manifesting as the rising sun, in his splendorous ascension" [2] represents not a metaphorical aspiration but the literal truth of every consciousness that has awakened from the dream of separate existence.

## The Universal Soul: Asar Consciousness Operating Through All Beings

## The Foundation of Universal Identity

The Ancient Egyptian scriptures reveal a profound truth about the nature of consciousness that illuminates the ultimate reality behind both ego-identity and the Soul-Aware-Witness [1]. According to the teachings, there is one universal consciousness operating through all human beings, and in the scripture this universal consciousness is called Asar (Osiris), the universal soul [1]. This understanding transforms our entire comprehension of what we mean when we speak of individual consciousness and spiritual development.

This is why every spiritual initiate in the Ancient Egyptian tradition is referred to by the title "Asar" followed by their given name [1]. This nomenclature reveals the fundamental truth: Asar represents the first and only reality—the universal soul consciousness that is the true identity of all beings—while the given name designates only the individual mind and body through which this universal consciousness operates.

## The Two Modalities of Universal Consciousness

The teaching reveals that the same Asar consciousness operates in every mind and body, supporting awareness through the mental and physical faculties of each person [1]. In the ideal condition, this universal consciousness supports its true nature (Asar soul consciousness) such that the person becomes aware of their Asar soul nature simultaneously with being aware of the thoughts, feelings, perceptions and sensations of the body [1]. In this condition, the personality is self-aware as Spirit and not deluded by the mind/body experiences.

Yet if this same Asar consciousness should become deluded into thinking it is the given name ego identity, that condition is called ignorance or delusion [1]. When we refer to either the ego-identity or the "Soul-Aware-Witness," the same universal consciousness operates through either modality. The difference lies not in the consciousness itself, but in the level of recognition and identification.

## Textual Evidence: Ancient Egyptian Book of Enlightenment (PertemHeru) Asar Any is One with Asar the Universal Soul God

The image below comes from the Ancient Egyptian Book of Enlightenment (PertemHeru) that depicts the presentation of Initiate Asar (Osiris) Any before the god Asar (Osiris). This depiction represents Osiris manifesting as the individual (Any) meeting, coming face to face with Osiris (Asar) the God aspect of Neberdjer who is the source of all individual souls sustaining the consciousness and life of all human beings.

## Textual Evidence: The Asar Any Formula in Chapter 43
## The Mechanism of Universal Recognition

Chapter 43 of the Ancient Egyptian Book of Enlightenment provides profound textual evidence for this understanding of universal consciousness operating through individual personalities [1]. The chapter reveals what may be termed the "Asar Any formula," where the same spiritual practitioner is simultaneously referenced as both the universal soul (Asar/Osiris) and an individual personality (Any) [1].

Verse 2 demonstrates this principle through its declaration: "These words are spoken coming from this spiritual initiate who goes by the name 'Osiris Any.' He says: I am a great one who is the child…of a great one; thus, I have the same greatness that is the greatness of my parent. My parent is Asar (Osiris), the great universal soul, therefore I have that same great universal soul." [1]. The text creates what the ancient sages understood as a complete complementary philosophical loop in which the same person being referred to as an "Osiris person" is now in the position referred to as Osiris himself so as to denote their intrinsic identity; one being the universal consciousness (universal soul) and the other being the manifestation of that same universal being that manifests in each individual personality.

Verse 4 reveals the practical result of this recognition: "Know this for certain, verily it is the reality of me, of who I am; I have become young because I do not age with the human mind and body any more for the true me, who I am is Osiris, the Lord of Eternity, the one who does not age and is universal consciousness ever aware, ever shining" [1]. This statement demonstrates how consciousness transcends temporal and bodily identification when it recognizes its essential nature as universal Asar consciousness.

The wisdom of the neteru illuminates how this textual formula provides the exact mechanism described throughout our study [1]. The practitioner declares both individual identity ("me") and universal identity ("Osiris (Asar), the Lord of Eternity") within the same statement, revealing that these are not separate realities but different aspects of recognition by the same consciousness. This understanding aligns with the principle that spiritual development involves consciousness learning to recognize itself as universal soul rather than becoming trapped in the illusion of separate ego-identity.

This Chapter 43 formula demonstrates the ultimate goal of spiritual practice: not the elimination of individual functioning, but the recognition of universal consciousness operating through individual human faculties [1]. The text shows how the same awareness that can say "me" can simultaneously recognize itself as "Osiris, the Lord of Eternity," illustrating that enlightenment involves recognition rather than transformation of consciousness itself.

## The Transparent Mirror: From Ego-Delusion to Universal Recognition

### The Shift in Recognition

This understanding revolutionizes our comprehension of spiritual development [1]. If the person understands that their conscious-awareness is not the individual ego but the universal soul, then that "Soul-Aware-Witness", they have discovered, becomes as if a transparent mirror through which the true natural witness-consciousness can operate as the identity that perceives and is aware through the mind, senses, and body of that personality.

Such a person is referred to as enlightened, especially when this clarity becomes stable, perennial, and permanent [1]. This represents what the teachings describe as a Heru (Horus) personality—consciousness that has achieved stable recognition of its universal nature while maintaining full functional capacity through the individual mind-body system.

This means that the journey from ego-identification to witness consciousness is not actually a movement from one type of consciousness to another, but rather a shift in recognition [1]. The universal Asar consciousness remains constant; what changes is whether this consciousness recognizes itself as the universal soul operating through individual faculties or becomes deluded into identifying with the temporary phenomena of the particular mind-body system being deluded by the accumulated ego impressions (aryu).

The Scripture reveals that spiritual practice aims to facilitate this recognition, helping the universal consciousness operating through each personality to remember its true nature as Asar rather than remaining caught in the illusion of separate ego-identity. This understanding provides the ultimate context for all the practices and teachings described throughout this book. In other words, every spiritual technique and meditation practice serves the single purpose of clarifying the mind so that universal consciousness can recognize its own nature operating through the individual personality.

The universal consciousness teaching thus provides both the theoretical foundation and practical framework for understanding how individual spiritual development actually represents universal recognition occurring through apparent individual forms. This insight transforms the entire approach to spiritual practice from personal achievement to universal awakening, revealing that what appears as individual enlightenment actually represents cosmic consciousness recognizing its own nature through the temporary vehicle of individual personality.

## The Formula Pattern for Contemporary Practitioners

## Practical Application of Universal Recognition

For contemporary practitioners of Shetaut Neter, the Asar Any formula provides a practical framework for understanding spiritual development:

1. **Individual Identity:** "Any" (the person's name)—representing the mind-body system through which consciousness operates
2. **Universal Identity:** "Asar" (Osiris - universal consciousness)—representing the eternal soul nature that is the true identity of all beings
3. **Combined Declaration:** "Asar Any"—showing both aspects operating simultaneously without contradiction
4. **Ultimate Recognition:** "I am Asar/Osiris"—transcending temporal identification while maintaining functional capacity of an individual

This demonstrates how the same consciousness can recognize itself as both individual ("me") and universal ("Osiris, the Lord of Eternity") within the same declaration, illustrating the goal of spiritual development. Therefore, the Soul-Aware-Witness represents not a separate achievement but universal consciousness recognizing its own nature while operating through individual faculties.

## The Pathway to Truth Discovery

## The Progressive Unfoldment of Spiritual Understanding

The wisdom of the neteru reveals that consciousness development proceeds through systematic stages rather than random experiences or sudden transformations. The pathway to truth discovery follows natural principles that can be understood and applied by any sincere aspirant willing to engage with appropriate teaching and practice.

The ancient sages designed spiritual teachings to guide consciousness from its current level of functioning toward recognition of its essential divine nature through progressive unfoldment rather than dramatic leaps. This means that spiritual development follows recognizable patterns that can provide guidance for contemporary practitioners.

## From Intellectual Understanding to Experiential Recognition

The tradition teaches that spiritual development begins with intellectual appreciation of consciousness teachings and gradually develops into direct experiential recognition through sustained practice and philosophical discrimination. This represents the transformation from studying consciousness to becoming conscious of consciousness itself.

Still, intellectual understanding provides the essential foundation for experiential development rather than representing an obstacle to genuine recognition. Proper intellectual framework prevents common misunderstandings and provides guidance for navigating the subtle territory of consciousness exploration.

The practice involves systematic development through recognizable stages: initial intellectual appreciation of consciousness levels and spiritual principles; gradual recognition of these levels within personal experience through meditation and daily life observation; development of stable discrimination between consciousness levels and mental states; and progressive stabilization of higher consciousness functioning.

## The Role of Aryu Purification in Truth Discovery

The primary obstacle to truth discovery involves the accumulated aryu (karmic impressions) that cloud consciousness and create the conditions for heated mind functioning. The tradition teaches that systematic purification of these impressions represents the most direct path to stable recognition of consciousness's essential divine nature.

The ancient sages taught that aryu purification occurs through what they called the "threefold practice"—ethical living aligned with Maat (divine order), philosophical study that develops proper understanding, and meditation practice that cultivates direct recognition. These three aspects work together to systematically dissolve the conditions that maintain consciousness in ego-driven patterns.

Ethical living creates what the tradition calls "light aryu"—impressions that remain transparent to divine light rather than obstructing consciousness functioning. This means that choices aligned with wisdom and compassion naturally support consciousness development while choices motivated by separateness and control create obstacles to spiritual progress.

## The Development of Witness Consciousness

The tradition of Shetaut Neter teaches that developing stable witness consciousness (soul-aware-witness attainment that has become stabilized and not intermittently aware of higher consciousness) represents the crucial foundation for all advanced spiritual recognition. This witness consciousness represents the capacity to observe all changing phenomena—thoughts, emotions, sensations, and external circumstances—from the unchanging awareness that recognizes its essential nature.

Witness consciousness provides the stable platform from which consciousness can explore different levels of its own functioning without becoming lost in identification with temporary experiences. This represents the practical foundation for consciousness level discrimination and the capacity to maintain optimal functioning regardless of external circumstances.

The development occurs through systematic practice that gradually strengthens the recognition of consciousness as distinct from its contents. Even so, this doesn't create artificial separation but rather reveals the natural distinction between the awareness that observes and the phenomena that are observed.

The practice involves systematic training in reflective meditative practice of resting in awareness (awareness of awareness followed by resting in pure awareness) and the practice of remembrance ("I am Ra", "I am Asar", "I am Neberdjer") and making an effort to maintain spirit awareness as background awareness during daily activities: during pleasant experiences, recognize the consciousness that enjoys without becoming identified with the enjoyment; during difficult experiences, recognize the consciousness that witnesses without becoming identified with the difficulty; and during neutral experiences, recognize the consciousness that remains present without needing particular content (objects, situations, relationships) to exist.

## The Natural Progression to Higher Recognition

As witness consciousness becomes stable, the tradition teaches that consciousness naturally begins to recognize its deeper levels without forced effort or dramatic practices. This represents what the ancient sages called the "natural unfoldment" of spiritual recognition that occurs when proper conditions are established.

The progression typically involves consciousness first stabilizing in witness recognition at the Ra level—clear individual awareness that recognizes its essential divine nature while maintaining personal expression. This stage allows consciousness to function effectively in the world while maintaining constant recognition of its spiritual nature.

However, stable witness consciousness naturally opens to recognition of Nunu consciousness—the undifferentiated awareness that underlies all individual conscious expression while remaining unmodified by any particular content. This recognition often emerges spontaneously during meditation or daily activities when consciousness naturally settles into its undifferentiated ground.

The tradition teaches that both Ra and Nunu recognition naturally lead to moments of Soul of Ra consciousness—pure being-awareness that transcends all subject-object duality while remaining as the foundation for all other levels of consciousness functioning. These recognitions typically occur as brief glimpses that gradually lengthen and stabilize through continued practice.

Understanding the universal context of consciousness naturally leads to investigating the specific mechanics through which transformation occurs—both cosmically and individually. The ancient sages provided not only theoretical understanding but precise practical instructions for facilitating this consciousness development. The Scripture of Ra and Hetheru reveals the exact processes by which a heated condition of mind transforms into silent consciousness, and how accumulated aryu (karmic impressions) are purified through divine intervention and spiritual practice. These mechanics operate according to spiritual laws as precise as physical laws, requiring proper understanding for effective application in contemporary spiritual development.

## The Divine Goodness and Eternal Existence: Understanding the Hymn to Asar's Revelation of Soul Nature

From the Ancient Egyptian Book of Enlightenment (PertmHeru) Himn to Asar (Osiris) – translation by Dr. Muata Ashby

Verse 1.
1.1. *Dua          Asar          un-nefer          Neter aah {mdj}*
1.2. Adorations   Osiris existence-beautiful/good Divinity great {fig}
1.3. I offer adorations to Osiris, the great divinity who is known as "Beautiful-Existence", the sustenance and beingness that is the goodness and reality of all souls.

## The Profound Declaration of Divine Identity

In the ancient Egyptian Hymn to Asar (Osiris), we encounter one of the most profound declarations regarding the fundamental nature of consciousness and spiritual identity ever recorded in sacred literature [1]. The verse proclaims: "I offer adorations to Osiris, the great divinity who is known as 'Beautiful-Existence', the sustenance and beingness that is the goodness and reality of all souls" [1]. This seemingly simple statement of reverence contains within it a complete psychology of spiritual transformation that addresses two of the most crucial challenges confronting contemporary seekers: the persistent experience of guilt, shame, and unworthiness that emerges from ego-identification, and the fear of mortality and meaninglessness that characterizes ordinary consciousness trapped in temporal thinking [1].

Notice how this ancient understanding provides the essential foundation for authentic spiritual development by revealing that every human being possesses, as their most fundamental nature, both perfect goodness and eternal existence—not as achievements to be attained through spiritual practice, but as the unchanging reality that serves as both the source and goal of all genuine seeking [1]. Furthermore, the wisdom of the neteru demonstrates that the entire spiritual journey consists not in becoming something other than what we already are, but rather in discovering and recognizing the divine nature that has never been absent, merely obscured by the accumulated patterns of egoistic thinking and feeling that create the illusion of separation from our essential spiritual identity [1].

## The Cosmological Foundation: From Neberdjer to Individual Soul Expression

To understand the profound implications of this hymn, we must first examine the cosmological framework revealed in the ancient Egyptian Creation scriptures, which teach that Asar (Osiris) represents a specific manifestation of Neberdjer, the All-Encompassing Divinity that serves as the ultimate source and substance of all existence [1]. At the same time, Asar functions as more than merely one divine aspect among many; the ancient teachings reveal that Asar manifests as the universal soul principle operating within time and space—the divine consciousness that animates and sustains all individual expressions of awareness throughout Creation [1]. This means that every soul, every conscious being, represents an aspect or expression of Asar, and since Asar is fundamentally one with Neberdjer, it follows that all souls are ultimately expressions of the same All-Encompassing Divinity, temporarily appearing as separate individuals while remaining eternally united in their essential divine nature [1].

The only factor that prevents conscious beings from recognizing this fundamental truth is what the ancient sages identified as egoism—the psychological condition that emerges when consciousness forgets its divine source and begins identifying with the temporary phenomena of thoughts, emotions, and bodily sensations rather than recognizing itself as the unchanging awareness that witnesses all these passing experiences [1]. Understand how this understanding transforms our entire approach to spiritual development: rather than viewing ourselves as flawed beings attempting to reach some distant divine goal, we can recognize that the divine nature we seek is already present as our most intimate reality, requiring only the removal of the egoistic obscurations that prevent its recognition [1].

## The Goodness Aspect: Healing the Wounds of Egoistic Self-Condemnation

From the psychological perspective that the ancient sages understood so profoundly, the majority of human suffering emerges not from external circumstances but from the internal condition of consciousness identifying with what it perceives as a flawed, unworthy ego-personality [1]. Many people live their entire lives trapped in cycles of guilt, shame, and poor self-esteem precisely because they have accepted the ego's evaluation of their worth rather than recognizing their inherent divine goodness as expressions of Asar, the "Beautiful-Existence" that serves as "the goodness and reality of all souls" [1]. What's more, this misidentification creates a psychological prison in which consciousness condemns itself for the inevitable mistakes and limitations that characterize ego-functioning, never recognizing that these temporary errors do not touch the essential goodness that remains as the unchanging foundation of being [1].

The hymn's revelation that Asar represents the inherent goodness of all souls provides the essential healing for this psychological wound by establishing that our fundamental nature is not the flawed ego but the divine goodness that has shared beautiful existence with us as our very essence [1]. This understanding enables what the ancient teachings recognize as authentic forgiveness—not merely the pardoning of specific mistakes, but the recognition that the errors of egoism emerge from ignorance rather than any fundamental corruption of our essential nature [1]. When practitioners understand that they are inherently good—not as a personal achievement but as their divine birthright—they can approach their psychological patterns with compassion rather than condemnation, working to purify egoistic tendencies without falling into the spiritual trap of self-hatred or unworthiness [1].

Reflect on how this approach creates the foundation for genuine spiritual health, which the ancient sages understood as the capacity to put ego in its proper place as servant rather than driver of life [1]. Still, this transformation becomes possible only when consciousness recognizes its inherent divine goodness and learns to identify with this essential nature rather than with the temporary patterns of ego-functioning that require healing and guidance rather than condemnation [1]. The practical implication proves profound: instead of approaching spiritual development from a position of inadequacy and self-improvement, practitioners can begin from the recognition of their inherent divine worth and work to align their thoughts, feelings, and actions with this fundamental goodness that represents their truest identity [1].

## The Existence Aspect: Discovering the Eternal Nature Beyond Temporal Experience

The second crucial aspect revealed in the hymn concerns what the ancient text describes as "existence" and "beingness"—terms that point toward the eternal, unchanging awareness that serves as the foundation for all temporal experience [1]. The ancient Egyptian understanding teaches that the underlying consciousness animating all beings is Asar, which means that the true nature of every conscious entity is not merely existence but eternal existence, sharing in the timeless reality of Neberdjer that transcends all temporal limitations [1]. This represents a profound shift in self-understanding: while the ego appears finite and subject to birth, change, and death, the soul—our essential identity—participates in the eternal existence that neither comes into being nor passes away but serves as the unchanging ground for all apparent changes [1].

To understand this concept more clearly, we can examine the analogy of consciousness and its contents that the ancient sages employed to illustrate this fundamental distinction [1]. Observe how the awareness that observes thoughts, feelings, events, and objects in your daily experience remains consistently present and unchanged regardless of what particular content appears within it [1]. Thoughts arise and pass away, emotions fluctuate, bodily sensations change, external circumstances shift constantly, yet the consciousness that is aware of all these changes never itself goes in and out of existence like the phenomena it observes [1]. Moreover, this witnessing awareness represents the closest direct experience most people have of their eternal nature—the unchanging existence that transcends time while remaining intimately present within every moment of temporal experience [1].

The hymn's identification of Asar as "Beautiful-Existence" points toward this same recognition: our essential nature as consciousness is eternal existence itself, temporarily appearing to be limited by ego-identification but never actually constrained by the apparent boundaries that characterize finite personality [1]. Yet this understanding requires careful discrimination between the ego (which is indeed finite and subject to all the limitations of temporal existence) and the soul (which participates in eternal reality and can never be threatened by any temporal change) [1]. The process of spiritual growth involves discovering the truth of this eternal existence as our actual nature rather than remaining identified with the temporary patterns of ego-consciousness that create the illusion of mortality and limitation [1].

## The Non-Objective Nature of Divine Qualities

The ancient Egyptian teaching reveals that both goodness and existence represent what may be termed "non-objective" qualities of the divine—characteristics that do not depend upon any external validation or achievement but constitute the very nature of consciousness itself [1]. Notice how this understanding transcends all conditional approaches to spirituality: goodness is not something we become through moral effort, and eternal existence is not something we attain through practice, but both represent the unchanging reality that we are, temporarily obscured by egoistic thinking but never actually absent or damaged [1]. This means that every soul already possesses perfect goodness and eternal existence as their fundamental nature, requiring only the recognition of what has always been present rather than the acquisition of something new [1].

Furthermore, the process of spiritual development emerges as a journey of discovery rather than achievement—the gradual recognition of our essential divine nature as it becomes freed from the obscurations created by identifying with temporary ego-patterns [1]. Even so, this discovery requires what the ancient sages understood as sustained spiritual practice, not because the practice creates our divine nature, but because consistent spiritual effort gradually dissolves the habits of egoistic thinking that prevent recognition of our inherent goodness and eternal existence [1]. The hymn's reference to Asar as "the sustenance and beingness that is the goodness and reality of all souls" reveals that these divine qualities serve as the very foundation that sustains all individual existence, making spiritual practice a matter of aligning with what we already are rather than becoming something we are not [1].

## Practical Implications for Contemporary Spiritual Development

For contemporary practitioners seeking authentic spiritual transformation, this ancient understanding provides essential guidance that addresses both the psychological challenges and the philosophical confusions that characterize modern spiritual seeking [1]. The recognition of inherent goodness transforms the entire approach to psychological healing and spiritual purification: instead of working to eliminate what we perceive as our fundamental flaws; we can work to uncover and express the divine goodness that represents our truest nature [1]. This shift proves crucial because it establishes spiritual practice in love and self-acceptance rather than in self-condemnation and spiritual ambition, creating the psychological foundation necessary for genuine transformation rather than mere ego-improvement disguised as spirituality [1].

Similarly, the understanding of our essential nature as eternal existence provides the foundation for transcending the fear of mortality and meaninglessness that drives so much human suffering and spiritual seeking [1]. When practitioners recognize that their fundamental identity participates in timeless reality, they can approach all temporal experiences—including the inevitable changes of aging, loss, and physical death—from the perspective of eternal awareness rather than from the anxiety of ego-consciousness that imagines itself threatened by every change [1]. Reflect on how this understanding enables authentic spiritual confidence: not the arrogance of ego-achievement, but the natural peace that emerges when consciousness recognizes its unchanging foundation in divine reality [1].

The practical application involves learning to identify consistently with our essential nature as expressions of Asar—the Beautiful-Existence that combines perfect goodness with eternal being—rather than with the temporary patterns of ego-consciousness that require healing and guidance [1]. At the same time, this identification does not involve denying or suppressing the ego but rather establishing our primary identity in our divine nature while allowing the ego to function as the instrument through which this divine nature expresses itself in daily life [1]. Through sustained contemplation of our inherent goodness and eternal existence, combined with practices that purify egoistic patterns, consciousness gradually establishes itself in its natural divine condition and discovers the peace, joy, and fulfillment that flow spontaneously from recognition of our true spiritual identity [1].

Thus, the ancient hymn to Asar provides contemporary seekers with the essential foundation for authentic spiritual development: the recognition that we are already what we seek to become, requiring only the patience and dedication necessary to uncover the divine goodness and eternal existence that constitute our most fundamental nature as expressions of the All-Encompassing Divinity that the ancient sages understood as both the source and goal of all spiritual aspiration [1].

## Conclusion: The Universal Psychology of Divine Awakening

The Ancient Egyptian wisdom contained in these passages reveals that what we call transpersonal psychology represents not a modern innovation but the recovery of humanity's most ancient and sophisticated understanding of consciousness. The declaration "My soul is God; it is not a separate individual soul. My soul is eternal" provides the foundation for understanding that individual psychological healing and cosmic spiritual realization are not separate processes but different aspects of the same fundamental recognition.

Understand that this wisdom remains relevant across millennia because it addresses the universal human experience of feeling separate while intuitively sensing our underlying connection to something greater. The teaching shows that the soul belongs to heaven while the body belongs to earth—not as a dualistic separation but as a recognition that consciousness transcends while simultaneously manifesting through all forms of existence.

Moreover, for contemporary practitioners of transpersonal psychology, these ancient teachings provide both the theoretical framework and practical methodology for guiding individuals seeking support beyond psychological ailments derived from the pressures and traumas caused by 'heated" ego-based thoughts and feelings and the limitations of ego-based identity toward recognition of their essential divine nature. This represents the ultimate therapeutic goal: not merely the alleviation of psychological symptoms but the recognition of one's true nature as a manifestation of the Universal Self, which is the source of unlimited peace, wisdom, and compassionate understanding.

Thus, the ancient sages taught that this realization constitutes the supreme healing—the recognition that what we have been seeking through all our psychological struggles and spiritual aspirations has been our own essential nature all along, never absent, never diminished, eternally present as the very consciousness through which all seeking occurs.

# References

[1] Ashby, M. (2019). Ancient Egyptian Book of Enlightenment (Pert-m-Heru): Hymn to Asar (Osiris). Translation by Dr. Muata Ashby. Sema Institute.
[1] Ashby, M. (2016). Egyptian Book of the Dead Hieroglyph Translations for Enlightenment: Understanding the Mystic Path to Enlightenment Through Direct Readings of the Sacred Signs and Symbols of Ancient Egyptian Language With Trilinear Deciphering Translation Method Vol. 1. Translation by Dr. Muata Ashby. Sema Institute.
[2] Ashby, M. (2022). The Mysteries of Ra and Hetheru/Sekhmet. Translation by Dr. Muata Ashby. Sema Institute.
[3] Ashby, M. (2022). The Complete Glorious Light Meditation Volume 2. Translation by Dr. Muata Ashby. Sema Institute.

# Chapter 8: The Mechanics - How Transformation Occurs

Having established the profound recognition that individual consciousness represents universal Asar consciousness temporarily manifesting through apparent individual forms, the crucial question naturally emerges: what are the specific mechanisms through which this universal awareness awakens to its true nature, and how does the transformation from ego-identification to divine recognition actually occur within human experience? Understanding the universal context of consciousness provides essential foundation, yet practitioners require precise knowledge of the psychological and spiritual processes that facilitate this awakening from delusion to divine recognition.

The ancient sages understood that consciousness transformation follows recognizable patterns governed by spiritual laws as precise as physical laws, operating through what the Scripture of Ra and Hetheru reveals as systematic purification processes that dissolve the accumulated patterns maintaining ego-identification [1]. Notice how the dramatic narrative of Sekhemit's transformation back to Hetheru through the sacred setjert drink represents far more than mythological allegory—it provides detailed instruction on the exact mechanisms by which a heated condition of mind, trapped in the illusion of separateness and driven by egoistic patterns, can be restored to its natural state of divine harmony and universal recognition [1].

Moreover, the following teachings reveal that transformation occurs not through mysterious or unpredictable spiritual experiences, but through precise psychological and metaphysical processes involving aryu (karmic impression) purification, the development of vital-life-fire that burns away accumulated delusions, and the systematic dissolution of the mental witnesses that maintain consciousness in subject-object duality [1]. These mechanics operate according to natural spiritual principles that can be understood, applied, and verified through direct experience, providing contemporary practitioners with the same scientific approach to consciousness development that guided the ancient temple schools of Kemet in facilitating genuine spiritual transformation rather than temporary mystical states that lack stability and integration.

# SCRIPTURE OF RA AND HETHERU: TRANSFORMATION MECHANICS

**The Setjert Drink Transformation: Sekhemit Returning to Hetheru**[32]

Verse 47.

*47.1.*    tu susun stjert    un    in    ahtu    enty {pet} her-meh {mdj} im moo im
*47.2.*    there sleep-drink abide by inundation experience {heavenly} person filling with water through
*47.3.*    ...the special beverage, that contained the mandrake, beer and blood. This special beverage, called ***Setjert/Stjert***, causes a swooning effect so that the drinker is to enter into a special {heavenly} state of immersion (inundation) in sleep...

Verse 48.

*48.1.*    bau {mdj} en Hem Neter pen shemt in Netert ten im    duayu
*48.2.*    souls {fig} of Majesty Divine-Self this goes-forth by Goddess this through day-time
*48.3.*    ...the ***bau Ra***, souls of the Divine Majesty, Ra, the Creator Spirit, which are the levels of psycho-spiritual energy/conscious awareness centers whereby the Glorious-Shining-Spirit- Effulgent-Radiance (Ra-Akhu) of the God Ra radiates to sustain the vitality of all human life. Thus, for a time Sekhemit would temporarily forget about slashing and killing and remember the feeling of supreme peace and Ra's glory, while still not yet fully regaining the memory and realization of her true essential being. This remedy was placed, at the prescribed location and at the appropriate time,

---

[32] Translation by Dr. Muata Ashby

## Awakening Your Soul-Aware-Witness

during the day, when the goddess was out foraging for humans to kill at night.

Verse 49.
*49.1.* gem    nez   susu  her – meht   nefer  in   her set im      un
*49.2.* finding it at personality-full   good by person she through abiding
*49.3.* Now, this liquid remedy was found by Sekhemit, and her personality became full of it. She was filled with the nature of the drink that contained the beer, the blood and the mandrakes (souls of Ra); her physical body was stilled with the intoxicating physical effects of the drink; her mind was stilled by being filled with the intoxicating effect of satisfaction from the blood of the drink and her deeper nature, her soul remained abiding in that fullness of the souls of Ra for a time, and during her time in this state she left the world alone…

Verse 50.
*50.1.* in   set her s-uri        nefer her ab set ai en ze techti   an saa
*50.2.* by  she drinking good personality's heart hers comes of she drunk not attention
*50.3.* …. by drinking the special drink, the ***setjert*** drink prescribed and decreed by Ra, that contained beer, blood, and mandrakes (souls of Ra), this was a good feeling in her heart, intoxicated with divine feeling, surpassing the "sweetness" of eating people and that was also a good thing as it led the heart of this lioness to be internally fulfilled such that her attention was turned inward as opposed to outward and thereby not coming to attention…

Verse 50.
*50.4.* n – z-remteju
*50.5.* of –her- men & women.
*50.6.* …of hers towards men and women, and thereby, in this state of immersion and inner fulfillment, the desire for more killing of them would not stir up and build into more rampaging.

234

**Verse 47: Describing the sacred beverage and its swooning effects** 47.1-47.3. It is important to understand that the Setjert drink represents a profound teaching about the mechanics of consciousness transformation through divine intervention [1]. The scripture reveals that this "special beverage, called Setjert/Stjert, causes a swooning effect so that the drinker is to enter into a special {heavenly} state of immersion (inundation) in sleep" [1]. This understanding aligns with the tradition of Shetaut Neter that spiritual transformation often requires consciousness to temporarily withdraw from its ordinary patterns of mental activity in order to allow deeper spiritual forces to reorganize the personality structure.

**Verse 48: About the souls of Ra operating through the goddess** 48.1-48.3. The ancient sages taught that this verse reveals the essential mechanism by which divine consciousness operates to transform heated mental states [1]. Observe how the teaching describes "the bau Ra, souls of the Divine Majesty, Ra, the Creator Spirit, which are the levels of psycho-spiritual energy/conscious awareness centers whereby the Glorious-Shining-Spirit-Effulgent-Radiance (Ra-Akhu) of the God Ra radiates to sustain the vitality of all human life" [1]. In other words, the transformation occurs through consciousness receiving direct transmission of divine awareness that temporarily overrides the egoistic mental patterns that maintain a heated condition of mind.

**Verses 49-50: Describing Sekhemit's complete absorption in the divine elixir** 49.1-50.6. We are to recognize that these verses provide the most detailed description in ancient literature of how consciousness becomes "filled with divine nature" through spiritual practice [1]. The scripture reveals that Sekhemit's "personality became full of it...her mind was stilled by being filled with the intoxicating effect of satisfaction from the blood of the drink and her deeper nature, her soul remained abiding in that fullness of the souls of Ra for a time" [1]. Furthermore, this represents the complete saturation of consciousness with divine awareness such that "her attention was turned inward as opposed to outward and thereby not coming to attention...of hers towards men and women" [1].

The wisdom of the neteru illuminates how this inward turning of attention constitutes an essential practice for spiritual transformation: when consciousness becomes internally fulfilled through divine presence, the compulsive seeking that characterizes heated mental activity naturally ceases without force or suppression.

The sacred narrative thus provides a complete template for understanding how consciousness transformation occurs through divine grace working in cooperation with spiritual receptivity. The Setjert drink represents the various spiritual practices and divine influences that can redirect consciousness from external seeking to internal fulfillment, creating the conditions necessary for the restoration of divine harmony within the personality.

**Essential Scriptural Evidence:**

*The Hymn to Amun-Ra: Revealing Divine Witnessing Consciousness*

Excerpts from Ancient Egyptian Hymn to Amun-Ra highlighting about Ra wakeful witnessing in a person asleep - translation section by Dr. Muata Ashby

A.
A.1. *sedjer resu her neb remteju sedjeru her hehy*
A.2. sleep awake/aware/watchful persona all men women sleeping    person God
A.3. during the sleep state, in the mind of people, a divine personage is there {that is Amun-Ra}; he is awake and aware and watchful after men and women while they are sleeping.

G.
G.1. *Henu remteju en k en urdu k im nu*
G.2. Adoration people to-thee for resting thee within us
G.3. People do the traditional adoration pose, in your honor, in gratitude for your resting within us and thereby enlivening us and sustaining our existence; we are indeed manifestations of your existence, manifesting as

ourselves, sentient creatures on earth. Our existence is owed to you, Oh Divine Self, since you are the consciousness within us sustaining our conscious awareness all the time, including through the sleep and waking states of the mind, so that you are always the consciousness within us that is experiencing the waking and dream states of our mind and senses.

**The Ever-Wakeful Divine Witness Revealed** This teaching becomes explicit through the Hymn to Amun-Ra which reveals Ra as "awake and aware and watchful over men and women while they are sleeping." This explains how Sekhemit's transformation could occur through sleep—because Ra's consciousness remains active even when individual conscious-awareness is stilled. In the condition of having worldly conscious-awareness temporarily stilled, it becomes possible to discern the deeper Hidden/Secret-Witnessing-Consciousness (Amun-Ra) due to that awareness not being subsumed in the cacophony of external sensory inputs and internal mental agitations and distractions due to feelings, opinions and desires bubbling up from the unconscious mind. The definition of the term "Amun" as meaning something Hidden/Secret indicates that this level of consciousness manifestation of Ra is usually unknown to most people though it is the critical sustaining essence behind the conscious-awareness of the human mind.

**The Hidden/Secret Witness Consciousness: Amun-Ra** Beyond the four manifest aspects of Ra (Khepera, Ra-Herakty, Tem, Auf) exists a fifth aspect: Amun-Ra, the hidden witness consciousness, the hidden consciousness that witnesses all phases of existence. This Hidden/Secret-witness consciousness represents the unbroken continuity of awareness that underlies all states of being, whether waking, dreaming, or deep sleep. While individual consciousness may appear to diminish or disappear during sleep, the hidden witness consciousness (Amun-Ra) continues to sustain the individual's existence.

This hymn reveals the fundamental teaching that divine consciousness (Amun-Ra) remains eternally present and aware even when individual consciousness appears to be absent in sleep,

Awakening Your Soul-Aware-Witness

demonstrating the principle that underlies Sekhemit's transformation through the setjert drink.

**Scripture of Ra and Hetheru**[33] **Cont.** Aryu Purification Verses: Cleansing of mental impressions

- o **Verses 128-129**: Formation and effects of aryu (karmic impressions)
- o **Verse 128**: "egoistic mental impressions (aryu/karmic remnants) that develop from experiences and actions in current and previous lifetimes"
- o **Verse 129**: "A heart in this condition becomes a beacon for inimical cosmic forces"

Verse 128.

*128.1.* *imu senu aryu nu aru sebau in arkeru {Net} shepsu {Net}*
*128.2.* within their action-residue we image wickedness by inimical {force} followers {force}
*128.3.* …within them there are egoistic mental impressions (aryu/karmic remnants) that develop from experiences and actions in current and previous lifetimes. These impressions manifest as feeling memories, recorded and reinforced patterns of thoughts, feelings, and behaviors that remain registered in the unconscious mind, influencing present and future experiences. The subtle effects of these aryu accumulate and intensify, and if founded in ignorance, egoism and delusion, promote endless unfulfillable worldly desires that cloud the mind's natural clarity and foment ambiguity, diffidence and spiritual ignorance and resulting worldly desires, mental distortions, delusions, frustrations and perpetual unrest (neshesh).

Verse 129.

*129.1.* *shept pen iu K im aset-per a asety-per {Net} ach{md} djedtu en-K Djehuty*
*129.2.* ill-will these it-is thee in abode mine dual{Div} thereby{fig} called you of thine Thoth…
*129.3.* "A heart in this condition becomes a beacon for inimical cosmic forces - those demoniac energies that manifest as avarice, lust, jealousy, and selfishness. These forces, being tyrannical and unjust

---

[33] Translation by Dr. Muata Ashby

by nature, create an atmosphere of ill-will within the human personality. Through continued association with these inimical forces, deep imprints form within the unconscious mind. These imprints manifest as egoistic aryu (karmic residues) that remain embedded in the unconscious, compelling those afflicted to perpetuate negative patterns of feeling and thinking. This creates a cycle where unrighteous thoughts and desires lead to actions that deviate from Maat (divine order and truth), further strengthening the negative impressions in the unconscious mind. Therefore, I now establish you, Djehuty (Thoth), as my abode in Creation - we shall function as dual aspects of the same divine consciousness. While I maintain my celestial {divine} abode, experiencing the vast expanse of transcendent awareness, you shall serve as Cosmic Mind, maintaining awareness of all that transpires within Creation. This dual arrangement ensures complete oversight of both the transcendent and manifest realms. I have chosen you for this role because you are uniquely illumined by my Glorious-Shining-Spirit-Effulgent-Radiance. As my Cosmic Mind, you can perceive and govern all aspects of Creation while maintaining constant connection with my divine consciousness. Therefore, you shall henceforth be known as 'Djehuty (Thoth)-'"

## Verse 128: Describing the formation of egoistic mental impressions

128.1-128.3. This verse reveals the precise psychological mechanism by which consciousness becomes trapped in repetitive patterns of suffering [1]. The teaching describes how "within them there are egoistic mental impressions (aryu/karmic remnants) that develop from experiences and actions in current and previous lifetimes" [1]. These impressions "manifest as feeling memories, recorded and reinforced patterns of thoughts, feelings, and behaviors that remain registered in the unconscious mind, influencing present and future experiences" [1].

Reflect on how the scripture explains that when these aryu are "founded in ignorance, egoism and delusion, [they] promote endless unfulfillable worldly desires that cloud the mind's natural clarity and foment ambiguity, diffidence and spiritual ignorance" [1]. This means that the accumulation of negative aryu creates a self-perpetuating cycle where past ignorant actions generate mental impressions that compel future ignorant actions.

**Verse 129: About ill-will and the establishment of Djehuty as cosmic mind** 129.1-129.3. The wisdom of the neteru reveals through this teaching the severe consequences of consciousness that becomes dominated by negative aryu [1]. The scripture declares: "A heart in this condition becomes a beacon for inimical cosmic forces—those demoniac energies that manifest as avarice, lust, jealousy, and selfishness" [1]. At the same time, the verse also establishes the divine solution: Ra establishes Djehuty (Thoth) as "Cosmic Mind, maintaining awareness of all that transpires within Creation" while Ra maintains "transcendent awareness" [1].

This dual arrangement provides the cosmic framework for individual transformation: practitioners can align with Djehuty's cosmic intelligence while aspiring toward Ra's transcendent consciousness, thereby gradually purifying the negative aryu that bind consciousness to egoistic patterns.

**Mystic Mathematics: Formulation of Consciousness Statement #4.**

The ancient wisdom provides us with essential terminology that crystallizes the entire teaching: **Ra =equals consciousness itself, while Djehuty represents the mind of Ra.** This simple formulation contains the complete understanding for aspirants to realize—that what we call mind represents the creative intelligence through which consciousness manifests the apparent world of forms, while consciousness itself (Ra) remains the unchanging foundation that enables and is aware of all mental activity. Consider how this understanding transforms our relationship to thoughts and perceptions: instead of being identified with Djehuty (the mind function), we recognize our essential nature as Ra (pure consciousness) that employs Djehuty as its instrument for creating and experiencing the phenomenal world. Therefore, authentic spiritual realization involves the recognition that we are not the mind thinking about consciousness, but rather consciousness itself employing mind as needed while remaining forever established in our essential nature as the divine awareness that the ancients celebrated as Ra.

Ra and the Mind of Ra. The ancient Egyptian texts reveal that the heart of Ra possesses a formal designation—the term "Ab n Ra" (The Heart of Ra)—which provides essential insight into the cosmic architecture of consciousness. Consider how this same sacred title applies to the God Djehuty (Thoth), revealing that Djehuty represents the heart of Ra, functioning as Ra's mind and serving as the aspect of differentiated consciousness that cogitates on behalf of universal awareness. Indeed, this means that Djehuty operates as the divine intelligence that processes thoughts, experiences awareness of time and space, and manages all cognitive functions while remaining supported by Ra—the pure consciousness that underlies and enables all mental activity. The ancient sages thus understood that what we experience as individual mind represents a localized expression of this same cosmic relationship between pure awareness (Ra) and its cognitive instrument (Djehuty), providing aspirants with precise understanding of how consciousness manifests through apparently separate mental processes while never actually becoming divided from its essential unity.

## THE EFFECT OF SPIRITUAL ROASTING: RECONSTRUCTION FROM THE TOMB OF SETY I AND TUTANKHAMUN

The following vertical hieroglyphic images show sections of the text from the tomb of Sety I; alongside that text are replacements for missing sections of verses in the Tomb of Sety I that are damaged. The replaced texts are from the same passages of text, Scripture of Ra and Hetheru, that are found in the later Tomb of Tutankhamun, but that are less damaged.[34]

---

[34] Translation by Dr. Muata Ashby

## The Effect of Spiritual Roasting

| Verse 177 Verses from Tomb of Tutankhamun (left), Sety I (right) | Transliteration 177.1 | Translation 177.2 |
|---|---|---|
| | udjau | vital-life-fire |
| | im | within |
| | masheru | roasting |
| | ze | causes |
| | at | divine-stature |
| | nuk | I-am |
| | Ra | Ra-Creator-Spirit |
| | im | among |
| | pautu | Company |
| | F | His |
| | shenytu | Nobles |
| | F | His |
| | Neteru | gods/goddesses |
| | F | His |

**Contextual Translation 177.3**

The practice of the myth, ritual, ethics and meditations in the scripture develops vital-life-fire (ignited fire drill hieroglyph -defined in verse 69, and 165) within the personality. This vital-life-fire acts as a fire of wisdom that burns away delusions and egoism. It roasts, burns off, the delusion and ignorance fomenting desire for ephemeral existence, the egoistic perturbations of the mind and its thoughts, feelings, desires and memories (aryu -verse 128) that prevent the soul from realizing the truth of Higher Self. That truth of Self is the realization of "I am Ra" (nuk Ra) the Creator Spirit, among the Company of His noble Gods and Goddesses. That truth of Self is that one is not a mere mortal being, driven by egoistic ignorance and banal, futile notions related to a minuscule fleeting life; rather one realizes their true nature as ***Herishef***, who is the same essential being of the aspects of the God Ra, and all being manifestations of the same Singular Spirit Beingness.

Awakening Your Soul-Aware-Witness

| Verse 178<br>Verses from Tomb of Tutankhamun (left), Sety I (right) | Transliteration 178.1 | Translation 178.2 | Contextual Translation 178.3 |
|---|---|---|---|
| [hieroglyphs] | *im*<br><br>*hekau*<br><br><br><br>*suai*<br>*a*<br>*udja*<br><br>*kua* | within<br><br>words-of-power<br><br><br><br>pass-through me<br>vital-life-fire<br><br>me | The words-of-power (defined earlier in verse 112) are within me and the vital-life-fire (defined in verse 69 and 165) passes through me. |

## Awakening Your Soul-Aware-Witness

## Verse 179: Mind is Finished/Dissolved

| Verse 179 Verses from Tomb of Tutankhamun (left), Sety I (right) | Transliteration 179.1 | Translation 179.2 |
|---|---|---|
| | nuk | I-am |
| | en | of |
| | chet | fire |
| | ba | soul |
| | pu | that |
| | chet | fire |
| | an | not |
| | unen | existing |
| | F | he |
| | meteryu | testifiers/witnesses |
| | im | among |
| | remtatju | men and women |

**179.3 Contextual Translation:** "I am a being that proceeds from the fire of the Soul/Spirit-Being of God.[35] This divine fire has transformed my nature so completely that no existing entity or impression can stand as testimony against me during the judgment of Maat. It does not allow it. My thoughts, feelings, desires, and memories (aryu - defined in verse 128) have been purified of egoistic elements. Nothing remains that could raise objection to my experience of undifferentiated consciousness and supreme existence. The mind has been freed from all differentiation that produces ignorance or delusions. The accumulated aryu, once heavy with egoistic experiences and intense with egoistic impressions, has been thoroughly cooked, removing the cloud of negative aryu that would otherwise obscure true self-awareness of my Spirit-Being (Ra). As my soul partakes of the very fire-nature that consumes delusion, I stand beyond the reach of mortal egoism caused by witnesses (impressions in unconscious) that call out impelling and compelling me to be involved and agitated, pursuing or running away from worldly affairs; thus, there can be no objectors among any human beings or..."

---

[35] **Fire of Soul/Spirit-Being (Ra-Akhu)** - Verse 179: "I am a being that proceeds from the fire of Soul/Spirit-Being (Ra-Akhu of God).

**Verse 177: The Vital-Life-Fire Development** 177.1-177.3. It is important to understand that this verse provides the clearest description in ancient Egyptian literature of how spiritual practice generates the transformative fire that burns away egoistic delusions [1]. The teaching reveals that "the practice of the myth, ritual, ethics and meditations in the scripture develops vital-life-fire within the personality. This vital-life-fire acts as a fire of wisdom that burns away delusions and egoism" [1].

Understand how this spiritual roasting "burns off the delusion and ignorance fomenting desire for ephemeral existence, the egoistic perturbations of the mind and its thoughts, feelings, desires and memories (aryu) that prevent the soul from realizing the truth of Higher Self" [1]. In other words, consistent spiritual practice generates an internal wisdom-fire that naturally dissolves the aryu accumulations that maintain ego-identification, leading to the realization "I am Ra, the Creator Spirit, among the Company of His noble Gods and Goddesses" [1].

**Verse 178: Words-of-Power and Vital-Life-Fire [Describing the inner presence of transformative forces]** 178.1-178.3. The ancient sages taught that this concise verse reveals the result of successful spiritual roasting: consciousness becomes the vehicle through which divine forces operate [1]. The practitioner declares: "The words-of-power are within me and the vital-life-fire passes through me" [1]. This means that through purification, the personality becomes transparent to divine consciousness, allowing sacred utterances and transformative spiritual energy to flow through the individual without obstruction from egoistic resistance.

**Verse 179: Mind is Finished/Dissolved [Describing the dissolution of witness-consciousness]** 179.1-179.3. We must recognize that this verse describes the ultimate result of aryu purification and the achievement of what may be termed the "witness-less state" [1]. The practitioner declares: "My thoughts, feelings, desires, and memories (aryu) have been purified of egoistic elements. Nothing remains that could raise objection to my experience of undifferentiated consciousness" [1].

Awakening Your Soul-Aware-Witness

The wisdom of the neteru illuminates how this represents the elimination of "karmic motivations that fan the surface of consciousness, thereby causing undifferentiated consciousness to differentiate into thoughts" [1]. What's more, when the mental witnesses (aryu) that draw consciousness into subject-object duality are dissolved, awareness rests in its natural undifferentiated state without being pulled into mental modifications.

The spiritual roasting process thus provides the systematic method by which consciousness purifies itself of the accumulated patterns that maintain ego-identification. Through consistent practice, the vital-life-fire gradually dissolves all obstacles to divine recognition, culminating in the witness-less state where consciousness rests in its essential nature without disturbance from mental activity or objective relationships.

## TEACHINGS OF AMENEMOPET: THE SILENT ONES

**Chapter 5: The Glory of Silence**[36]

Verse 7.
7.1.    er         ger         neb-en      Neter-Het
7.2.    as for    silent      all-of       God-House
7.3.    …Now, in reference to those who are silent, all who go into the House-of-Divine (Temple)…

Verse 8.
8.1.    setu     djed     ur      hess              Ra
8.2.    they    say    greatness blessing    Creator-Spirit
8.3.    …those silent ones speak of the greatness of the blessings they receive from being in the temple from the Creator-Spirit.

---

[36] Translation by Dr. Muata Ashby

Verse 9.

| | | | | | | |
|---|---|---|---|---|---|---|
| 9.1. | Aa mehtu{mdj} en ger | gem | {mdj}k pa | ankh | {mdj} |
| 9.2. | Behold! fullness of silence | finds | {fig} thee the | life | {fig} |

9.3. Behold the glory of this way of being! Being silent means discovering the fullness of the Creator-Spirit that is within. This fullness cannot come from heatedly searching for fulfillment in the world for fulfillment with an imperfect personality. Rather, it is found not by externalities but instead by realizing that there is perfection within when the fullness of being is experienced beyond the worldly desires and cravings.

**Verses 7-9: About silent ones in the temple and the fullness of being**

**Verses 7-9: About silent ones in the temple and the fullness of being** 7.1-9.3. The ancient sages taught that these verses reveal the practical result of achieving inner silence through spiritual discipline [2]. Those who become "silent" in the temple "speak of the greatness of the blessings they receive from being in the temple from the Creator-Spirit" [2]. The teaching culminates in the declaration: "Being silent means discovering the fullness of the Creator-Spirit that is within" rather than seeking fulfillment through "heatedly searching for fulfillment in the world" [2].

Notice how this silence represents not mere absence of speech, but the establishment of consciousness in its natural fullness, where "there is perfection within when the fullness of being is experienced beyond the worldly desires and cravings" [2]. This understanding aligns with the principle that true satisfaction emerges from recognizing the divine presence that already exists within consciousness rather than attempting to acquire it through external means.

## Teachings of Amenemopet-Chapter 9: Cutting Away Heart's Dispositions[37]

Verse 17.

17.1.  aa    aru  f   papa   er nega    fy    hatyu
17.2.  hey perform he rebuilds to cut-away his    heart's
17.3.  Hey, then he will be able to perform the cutting away of the heart's dispositions that are contrary to goodness and enlightenment.

Note: "hatyu" here is referring to multiple hearts of the heated person, signifying multiple dispositions of mind (not the underlying self-there is only one underlying consciousness. Mind can experience many states) that are divergent from the path of Maat (righteousness and truth)-so may those be cut away rendering the person cool and silent, as a potter cuts away pieces of clay that hide the shape desired by the potter when creating pottery. Human beings are made of "Straw and clay, God is the fashioner".

**Verse 15: About rebuilding and cutting away contrary dispositions** 15.1-15.3. It is important to understand that this verse provides practical guidance for the aryu purification process described in the Scripture of Ra and Hetheru [2]. The teaching instructs: "then he will be able to perform the cutting away of the heart's dispositions that are contrary to goodness and enlightenment" [2]. The wisdom reveals that this cutting away resembles how "a potter cuts away pieces of clay that hide the shape desired by the potter when creating pottery" [2].

In other words, spiritual transformation involves systematically removing the mental and emotional patterns that obscure the soul's natural divine nature, just as a sculptor removes excess material to reveal the perfect form that exists within the stone.

---

[37] Translation by Dr. Muata Ashby

**The Witness-Consciousness: Amun-Ra as the Unchanging Foundation** The wisdom of the neteru illuminates that beneath all changing states of consciousness—whether rage, peace, joy, sorrow, waking, or sleeping—there exists an unchanging awareness that simply witnesses these states without being affected by them [3]. This witness-consciousness represents what the teachings call Amun-Ra, the hidden aspect of Ra that witnesses all phases of existence but itself does not interact with Creation [3].

This witness-consciousness represents the unbroken continuity of awareness that underlies all states of being [3]. While individual consciousness may appear to diminish or disappear during sleep, the witness-consciousness (Amun-Ra) continues to sustain the individual's existence [3]. Since the other states of awareness are transitory and the underlying Amun Witness-Consciousness is there all the time without fluctuation, then the underlying Witness-Consciousness is the abiding reality behind the fluctuations [3].

Understanding this unchanging witness provides the foundation for recognizing how consciousness transformation actually occurs: not through changing or improving awareness itself, but through purifying the modifications that obscure recognition of the eternal witness that has always been present as the true identity of every conscious being.

## The Three Levels of Potential Consciousness Experience

The ancient wisdom reveals three fundamental levels of potential consciousness experience that provide the complete metaphysical framework for spiritual development [2]. Building upon the comprehensive three-level consciousness cosmology established in Chapter 2 (Soul of Ra as pure consciousness, Nunu as undifferentiated awareness, and Ra as individuated consciousness), we now examine how these levels specifically function as stages of transformational potential.

The first level represents human awareness through the limited mind, encompassing the familiar states of waking consciousness based on sensory perception; dream consciousness accessing subtle mental formations; and deep sleep where awareness rests in an unconscious void [2]. This level characterizes ordinary human experience where consciousness operates through the modifications and limitations of the individual mind-body system.

The second level encompasses cosmic mind expanded awareness, representing the Creator Spirit level. The same Creator Divinity goes by names such as Ra, Net, Ptah, and Amun [2]. This level encompasses and surpasses human awareness, operating as the cosmic intelligence that governs universal principles and maintains the order of Creation through divine consciousness that transcends individual limitations while maintaining creative capacity.

The third level represents absolute consciousness total awareness. The same absolute consciousness goes by names such as Neberdjer, Un-Nefer (Asar), Neterty, Pa-Neter, Neter-An-Ren, and Meh-urt [2]. This level encompasses and surpasses both human awareness and cosmic awareness, representing the all-encompassing divinity that underlies and overlies all manifestation as the absolute ground of existence itself.

**The Progression: From Witnesses to Witness-Less to Beyond Witnesses** The Scripture reveals a clear progression of consciousness development that moves through distinct stages toward ultimate realization. This progression demonstrates how consciousness gradually liberates itself from the conditioning influences that maintain ego-identification and discovers its essential nature as universal awareness.

**The Initial Stage: Conditioned Consciousness** The initial stage represents human consciousness-awareness characterized by a mind conditioned by aryu that motivates observing and interacting with objects while maintaining subject-object duality. In this stage, consciousness operates through witnesses—the various mental impressions and motivational forces that draw attention toward external phenomena and maintain the sense of being a separate observer of an objective world.

**The Intermediate Stage: No Witnesses** The intermediate stage reveals the condition of "No Witnesses" described in verse

179: "There can be no objectors/witnesses among any gods, goddesses, noble persons, or objects in Creation". This indicates the dissolution of all separate witnessing and mental deviations from awareness of undifferentiated consciousness. The witness-less state represents freedom from the witnesses and the experience of unhindered "I Am" existence without limitation or agitation.

**The Ultimate Stage: Beyond Witnesses** The ultimate stage transcends even the witness-less state to approach what the Scripture identifies as the "Soul of Ra" state that is "older than Nunu"—representing pure consciousness prior to even the undifferentiated witness function. This state transcends all modifications of consciousness and rests in the absolute nature of existence itself.

**The Undisturbed Witness State as Gateway to Nunu Consciousness** The ancient sages taught that the transition from ego-consciousness to witness consciousness occurs through what may be termed the "Undisturbed Witness State"—a condition where consciousness has purified the aryu motivations that generate mental disturbances in the ocean of undifferentiated consciousness.

As established in Chapter 2, the Nunu level of awareness is undifferentiated and resting in itself, not differentiating into the Ra level. When the motivational disturbances that draw attention in relation to the personality are eliminated, consciousness rests in the calm, undifferentiated state. This state may be described as an Undisturbed Witness State where consciousness has learned to abide in its essential nature without being pulled into mental modifications.

The witnesses (aryu with power to agitate and motivate consciousness) can be perceived by a personality in two relative states. They can only disturb the personality if the "I", the "nuk" of the personality is in a state of misidentification. This is when the unconscious witnesses (aryu) can agitate conscious-awareness. This state manifests as thoughts, mental function, cognition, and imperative to action based on involvement with the world according to the dictates of the aryu. This represents a state of delusion where consciousness becomes caught up, entangled, ensnared, captivated, and embroiled in the objective subject object relations of the world wherein the subject is ego awareness and not the underlying abiding consciousness that is the true abiding "I" of the personality. In this state the ego identity becomes involved with worldly desires and aversions while seeking happiness in interminable changing situations that cannot provide abiding satisfaction.

The witness-less state can manifest as a mind that is unaffected by the witnesses of the mind even as it experiences the subject-object relationships of the personality. Such a person has internally transcended the ego misidentification of the subject "I" that thinks it is the limited personality. The complete cessation of witnesses functioning in the mind whereby there is a cessation of experiencing any witnesses at all is a state where figuratively mind has stopped operating and there is only the experience of the underlying "I", the "nuk Ra" or I of consciousness without modifications of the mind. This represents freedom from these witnesses and constitutes the experience of unhindered "I Am" existence without limitation or agitation. Thus, the Nunu state of awareness eventually gives rise to the absolute state (Ba en Ra- Soul of Ra), representing the natural progression from purified individuation through undifferentiated awareness to absolute consciousness itself.

# Experiential Mapping for Contemporary Practitioners

### Recognizing the Three Levels in Personal Experience

These consciousness levels operate continuously within human experience, much like different radio frequencies that exist simultaneously but require proper tuning to access clearly. The recognition challenge facing contemporary practitioners involves learning to identify these subtle but crucial distinctions within awareness rather than seeking exotic or unprecedented states of consciousness.

The ancient sages taught that most students have already encountered glimpses of all three consciousness levels (as outlined in Chapter 2), yet they lack the conceptual framework to distinguish between them or appreciate their profound significance for spiritual development. The issue arises because the Nuk Ra identity is so subtle that it has been lost in the subject-object relationships in which the ego-identity has assumed the position of Ra. So, the ego-identity is mistaken for Ra. The wisdom and disciplines of Kemetic Mystic Transpersonal Psychology are designed to allow the ego-identity to be discovered as an illusory identity revealing the deeper consciousness witnessing self (Ra, Nunu, Ba en Ra) as the obvious self-identity. This recognition represents the difference between studying consciousness and actually becoming conscious of consciousness itself—a transformation that marks the beginning of genuine spiritual development.

## Nunu Consciousness: The Undifferentiated Ocean of Awareness

Referencing Chapter 2's teaching on Nunu consciousness as undifferentiated awareness that maintains consciousness without specific focus, we can now explore its practical recognition. This level of consciousness can be recognized in states where awareness is present and clear but not focused on any particular object or mental content.

The ancient sages taught that Nunu consciousness often manifests in the early morning awareness before thoughts organize into daily concerns, when consciousness is awake and present but not yet engaged with the specific contents that will fill the day. This represents a state of open, spacious awareness that encompasses everything without being limited or defined by any particular experience.

Nunu awareness also manifests in the gap between thoughts during the process of thinking as well as when one seeks to extend the period of that gap during the practice of meditation, when the mind temporarily ceases its constant activity and consciousness-awareness experiences itself directly and exclusively during that period. This means that consciousness, operating as conscious-awareness within the personality, ceases to be aware of thoughts, feelings perceptions and sensations of the mind and body and instead experiences awareness of consciousness as it is innately, without mental modifications. In other words, these are not blank or unconscious states but rather periods of experience of undifferentiated awareness knowing itself without the distraction of mental content.

Having examined the cosmic mechanics of consciousness transformation, the practical application of these teachings for contemporary practitioners seeking stable spiritual development now requires attention. Understanding transformation processes theoretically differs significantly from implementing them consistently in daily life. The ancient sages provided comprehensive guidance for translating cosmic understanding into practical wisdom that supports gradual, sustainable development rather than dramatic experiences that lack stability. The following teachings from Sage Amenemopet and other foundational texts offer the essential bridge between metaphysical understanding and lived spiritual practice.

## References

[1] Ashby, M. (2022). The Mysteries of Ra and Hetheru/Sekhmet. Translation by Dr. Muata Ashby. Sema Institute.
[2] Ashby, M. (2019). Teachings of Ancient Egyptian Sage Amenemopet with Hieroglyphic texts. Translation by Dr. Muata Ashby. Sema Institute.
[3] Ashby, M. (2025). DEFINITIONS: The Nature of Consciousness and Awareness in Neterian Philosophy. Translation by Dr. Muata Ashby. Sema Institute.
[4] Ashby, M. (2025). The Complete Glorious Light Meditation Volume 2: Commentary and Spiritual Application. Translation by Dr. Muata Ashby. Sema Institute.

# Chapter 9: Foundational Principles and Philosophy of Practice

Having examined the cosmic mechanics of consciousness transformation—the spiritual roasting through vital-life-fire, the systematic purification of aryu (karmic impressions), and the progression from witnesses to witnessless to beyond witnesses—contemporary practitioners naturally require guidance for translating these profound insights into lived spiritual practice. Understanding the theoretical framework of how a heated, aryu-driven condition of mind transforms into silent consciousness through divine intervention represents only the foundation for authentic spiritual development rather than its completion.

## Foundational Understanding of Spiritual Development and Personality

Before examining the practical principles that guide spiritual development, we must establish a foundational understanding that will inform all subsequent practice and assessment. The teachings of Shetaut Neter do not advocate for the destruction or elimination of personality, nor do they suggest that individual ego-personality represents an inherently negative aspect of human existence. Indeed, the wisdom tradition reveals a crucial distinction between ego and egoism: ego itself represents the necessary vehicle through which spirit experiences existence in time and space, while egoism represents the entanglement with temporal concerns that generates suffering through subject-object relationships and competitive seeking of happiness through ephemeral worldly objects. Consider how the pure ego serves as a reflection of the soul (Asar {Osiris}) and is therefore inherently good; thus, spiritual development involves the purification and proper orientation of personality rather than its annihilation. Consider how the neteru themselves express divine consciousness through distinct personalities and characteristics while maintaining perfect alignment with universal principles. Therefore, the aspirant seeks to transform ego from egoistic motivations (fear, attachment, competitive separation) toward consciousness-based functioning (oneness, truth, self-satisfaction, good will), understanding that a healthy spiritual life enhances rather than diminishes our capacity for joyful engagement with existence through purified ego that serves divine expression. This foundational principle will guide our understanding of all practical methods and verification criteria that follow.

Notice how the Scripture of Ra and Hetheru reveals not merely the cosmic processes governing consciousness transformation, but also the precise psychological and spiritual laws that operate as reliably in individual experience as in universal manifestation. At the same time, the ancient sages understood that cosmic knowledge without practical application remains a sterile intellectual exercise, while practical methods divorced from proper understanding often lead to deficient spiritual development or superficial development that lacks stability and integration.

Therefore, the wisdom of the neteru illuminates how the mechanics of transformation—the dissolution of witnesses through spiritual fire, the purification of accumulated mental impressions, and the emergence of witness consciousness—must be systematically applied through what Sage Amenemopet describes as wisdom philosophy "that based on recorded wisdom literature that is to be experienced in life" [4]. In other words, the cosmic teachings serve their intended purpose only when they become practical guidance for navigating daily circumstances with divine awareness rather than ego-driven reactivity.

## The Majestic Wisdom of Sage Amenemopet

The ancient sages designed their wisdom teachings not as abstract philosophy for intellectual contemplation, but as practical guidance enabling aspirants to implement cosmic understanding within the specific challenges and opportunities of human existence. Sage Amenemopet's instructions represent the essential bridge between the metaphysical framework established in our foundational texts and the systematic practice that creates sustainable spiritual transformation rather than only temporary mystical experiences.

The teachings of Amenemopet provide what can be called "applied consciousness development"—the practical methods for maintaining optimal consciousness levels during challenging circumstances, steering the boat of life through conscious discrimination, and integrating ethical living with philosophical study and meditation practice. Observe how these instructions emerge directly from the same wisdom tradition that produced the Scripture of Ra and Hetheru yet focus specifically on the daily application of universal principles rather than their cosmic dimensions.

Ancient Egyptian wisdom reveals through Amenemopet's guidance that authentic spiritual development requires more than understanding consciousness levels theoretically. It demands developing the practical capacity to recognize these levels within personal experience and maintain optimal functioning regardless of external circumstances. Even so, this practical path serves genuine transformation rather than mere behavioral modification, since its foundation rests upon the same cosmic understanding that governs universal manifestation while expressing through the specific challenges of individual human development.

## Prologue: The Foundation of Wisdom Philosophy[38]

Verse 1.
    *1.1.*   *Ha  im  sebayt          {medj}\*  {shf}\*\*  im    ankh*
    1.2.   Front form  wisdom-philosophy{fig}  {book}  form    life
    1.3.   This is the beginning of the wisdom philosophy that is based on recorded wisdom literature that is to be experienced in life.

-------

\**medjat*= abstract, figurative
\**shefdu* = papyrus, i.e. wisdom teachings written on paper, a book, etc.

---

[38] Translation by Dr. Muata Ashby

Verse 2. [hieroglyphs]

2.1. *metru  {djeb}\* {hu}\*\* {sjd}\*\*\* en udja  {mdj}*
2.2. Exposition                              for-well-being{fig}
2.3. This is an exposition of precise teachings that when understood exactly, with precision cause a person to have well-being while living on earth.

**Verse 1** *Establishing wisdom philosophy for life experience*

1.1-1.3. It is important to understand that this opening verse establishes the essential foundation for all practical spiritual development: wisdom philosophy that is "to be experienced in life" rather than remaining merely intellectual [2]. The ancient sages taught that genuine spiritual transformation requires the integration of philosophical understanding with lived experience, creating what Sage Amenemopet describes as "wisdom-philosophy that is based on recorded wisdom literature that is to be experienced in life" [2].

**Verse 2 Describing precise teachings for well-being** 2.1-2.3. This verse reveals the practical purpose of the wisdom teachings: "an exposition of precise teachings that when understood exactly, with precision cause a person to have well-being while living on earth" [2]. This understanding aligns with the tradition of Shetaut Neter that spiritual development aims not toward escape from worldly existence but toward the discovery of divine consciousness operating skillfully within temporal circumstances.

# The Foundational Principle: Wisdom Philosophy for Life Transformation

The opening verses of Sage Amenemopet's wisdom establish what can be termed the fundamental principle underlying all genuine spiritual development: wisdom philosophy "based on recorded wisdom literature that is to be experienced in life", that is, practiced, applied in life situations rather than only remaining merely intellectual concepts [4]. Verse 1.3 declares: "This is the beginning of the wisdom philosophy that based on recorded wisdom literature that is to be experienced in life," while verse 2.3

reveals this represents "an exposition of precise teachings that when understood exactly, with precision cause a person to have well-being while living on earth" [4].

This foundational understanding corresponds directly with the consciousness transformation mechanics explored in Chapter 8, where the Scripture of Ra and Hetheru demonstrates how universal principles operate through individual experience. The ancient sages taught that authentic transformation requires the integration of philosophical understanding with lived experience, rather than allowing spiritual insights to remain abstract theories disconnected from practical circumstances.

The wisdom of the scripture reveals that this integration serves both individual awakening and collective wellbeing, since consciousness operating from divine recognition naturally expresses wisdom and compassion that benefit all beings rather than seeking personal advantage at others' expense. Understand how this approach differs fundamentally from academic study or theoretical speculation—the ancient sages designed their wisdom teachings as transformative spiritual technology that systematically reshapes conscious-awareness itself rather than merely providing information about spiritual concepts.

## The Psychological Philosophy: From Ego Construct to Soul-Aware-Witness

The Ancient Egyptian Book of Enlightenment Chapter 26 provides the essential psychological framework for understanding why practical spiritual development proves necessary and how it operates to transform consciousness from ego-identification to divine recognition [1]. The scripture reveals the fundamental distinction between what can be termed the "ego construct" and the "Soul-Aware-Witness"—two entirely different modes through which consciousness can operate within human experience.

Chapter 26 describes the ego construct through its depiction of consciousness "drowning in the ever-agitating movements of opposition and attraction" and "sailing downstream to the north of Kemet (Egypt)" in endless cycles that accomplish no goal of lasting fulfillment [1]. This represents consciousness identifying with what the text calls the "agitated heart," being controlled by bodily urges and mental fluctuations, and consequently suffocating the soul through relentless pursuit of satisfaction in temporal phenomena.

The wisdom teachings reveal that this ego construct operates through a fundamental pattern of agitation, external control, and soul suffocation that emerges when consciousness forgets its divine nature and becomes trapped in what the scripture describes as the "mayhem of desires born of spiritual ignorance and duality perceived through mind and senses" [1]. This means that ego-consciousness approaches life from the illusion of separateness—imagining itself as an isolated entity that must struggle against external forces to achieve security, pleasure, and validation.

Still, the same consciousness can discover its true nature as the Soul-Aware-Witness through the systematic purification described. The scripture declares: "my heart, he is peaceful within me," "I know myself," and "I have control over my arms and legs (body)" [1]. These statements reveal consciousness that has achieved the separation from ego-patterns and now operates as what the ancient teachings call the "instrument of the soul"—awareness functioning from inner peace, self-knowledge, and appropriate self-control rather than reactive patterns.

## The Theoretical Foundation for Heated versus Silent Mind

Sage Amenemopet's teachings provide the essential psychological framework for understanding why consciousness operates through either optimal or suboptimal patterns, revealing the fundamental principles that govern all spiritual development [4]. Wisdom of Amenemopet Chapter 2, verse 17 describes the "heated person" as one guided by "corrupted mind, live life by unrighteousness, fraud, anger, boisterousness, flippant retorts and thoughtless speech, inconsiderate and impulsive acts, rapacious greed, jealousy, envy" [4]. This heated condition of mind represents consciousness that has lost touch with its divine source and operates through the accumulated influence of heavy aryu (karmic impressions) that cloud natural spiritual sensitivity.

The ancient sages taught that heated mind manifests through what Chapter 3 established as the fundamental misidentification with temporary phenomena rather than recognition of consciousness's eternal nature. Moreover, even when heated persons experience apparent pleasure from unrighteous acts, "they are actually experiencing a deeper form of suffering—separation from the Divine, which is the true source of unlimited bliss and inner peace" [4]. This represents consciousness actively choosing the burden of ego-identification over the natural lightness that emerges when awareness rests in its divine source.

## FROM THE WISDOM TEACHINGS OF SAGE AMENEMOPET

Chapter 5: The Glory of Silence[39]

**Verse 9** *About finding fullness through silence*

Verse 9.
9.1.    *Aa   mehtu{mdj} en ger   gem   {mdj} k pa   ankh   {mdj}*
9.2.    Behold! fullness of silence finds   {fig} thee the   life   {fig}
9.3.    Behold the glory of this way of being! Being silent means discovering the fullness of the Creator-Spirit that is within. This fullness cannot come from heatedly searching for fulfillment in the world for fulfillment with an imperfect personality. Rather, it is found not by externalities but instead by realizing that there is perfection within when the fullness of being is experienced beyond the worldly desires and cravings.

Silent mind, by contrast, emerges when consciousness recognizes its essential nature and operates from what Amenemopet describes as the "fullness of the Creator-Spirit that is within" rather than seeking fulfillment through heated engagement with worldly phenomena [4]. This silence represents not mere absence of

---

[39] Translation by Dr. Muata Ashby

speech, but the establishment of consciousness in its witnessing nature, where the natural fullness of divine awareness becomes self-evident without external dependencies. The tradition teaches that this silent mind naturally expresses what we might describe as "spiritual inclinations"—ethics, right thinking, and right feeling that flow spontaneously from the experience of inner fullness rather than the ego's characteristic patterns of external seeking and reactive control.

## The Developmental Philosophy: Natural Progression Through Consciousness Levels

The Scripture of Ra and Hetheru establishes that consciousness development follows recognizable stages governed by spiritual laws as precise as physical laws, progressing naturally from ego-identification through witness consciousness toward divine recognition when proper conditions are created [2]. Verse 153 reveals the hierarchical yet non-dual nature of consciousness: Ra's "soul is older than He (Nunu), even as body and mind emerged from Nunu," while verse 155 declares "The soul of that Divinity, Nunu, is the same soul of Ra, the Creator Spirit, which is the same soul of Asar (Osiris)" [2].

This cosmic architecture of consciousness provides the essential framework for understanding why consciousness development proceeds through systematic stages rather than random experiences or sudden transformations. The ancient sages taught that consciousness naturally recognizes its deeper levels without forced development when sufficient purification occurs through living by truth (Maat) and appropriate spiritual practice. This means that discovering the Soul-Aware-Witness serves as the gateway rather than the completion of consciousness development.

The tradition reveals that when the Soul-Aware-Witness becomes established through the practices described in Chapters 5-7, a natural movement of self-discovery progresses toward recognizing this witnessing awareness as a manifestation of Ra-level consciousness. Through Ra recognition, consciousness naturally progresses toward Nunu consciousness and ultimately Soul of Ra recognition, following what the ancient sages understood as the automatic progression that occurs when obstacles are removed rather than when new states are acquired.

Notice how this understanding transforms the entire approach to spiritual practice from seeking extraordinary experiences to recognizing the divine awareness that was always present but obscured by ego-identification and the accumulated patterns of heated mental activity. The developmental philosophy teaches that consciousness inherently possesses integrative capacity, and spiritual practice simply removes the obstacles that prevent its natural expression rather than creating something foreign to human nature.

## The Threefold Integration Principle: Why Comprehensive Practice Proves Essential

The Scripture of Ra and Hetheru establishes that authentic consciousness transformation requires what we might call "threefold practice"—ethical living aligned with Maat (divine order), philosophical study that develops proper understanding, and meditation practice that cultivates direct recognition—working together to systematically dissolve the conditions that maintain consciousness in ego-driven patterns [2]. This integration principle emerges from the cosmic mechanics described in Chapter 8, where consciousness transformation occurs through comprehensive purification rather than isolated spiritual techniques.

The ancient sages understood that partial approaches remain superficial because consciousness operates simultaneously through physical, mental, and spiritual dimensions that require coordinated development. Observe how attempting meditation without ethical foundation results in superficial states that lack stability, while philosophical study without practical application remains merely intellectual exercise that fails to transform consciousness itself. Similarly, ethical conduct without understanding lacks the spiritual context necessary for transcending ego-motivation and discovering divine inspiration as the source of righteous action.

Ethical living creates what the tradition calls "light aryu"—mental impressions that remain transparent to divine light rather than obstructing spiritual development—while generating environmental conditions that allow subtle spiritual recognition to emerge [2]. Philosophical study develops the discriminative wisdom necessary for distinguishing between consciousness levels and mental states, preventing common misunderstandings that can impede spiritual progress or lead to spiritual development that lacks psychological integration. Meditation practice provides the direct methods for consciousness recognition and stabilization beyond ego-identification, creating experiential foundation for integrating cosmic understanding with temporal existence.

The wisdom of the neteru illuminates how this threefold approach creates cumulative purification effects that operate according to spiritual law: when consciousness consistently aligns with divine order through ethical conscience and conduct, proper understanding through philosophical discrimination, and direct recognition through meditation practice, the accumulated conditions naturally support the emergence of stable witness consciousness and its eventual progression through Ra, Nunu, and Soul of Ra awareness levels.

# The Purification Philosophy: Aryu Transformation and Divine Light Transmission

Chapter 3 established the precise mechanism by which consciousness becomes trapped through aryu (karmic impressions) that accumulate in the unconscious mind from past experiences, thoughts, and actions [2]. Verse 128 reveals how "within humans there are egoistic mental impressions (aryu/karmic remnants) that develop from experiences and actions in current and previous lifetimes" which "manifest as feeling memories, recorded and reinforced patterns of thoughts, feelings, and behaviors that remain registered in the unconscious mind, influencing present and future experiences" [2].

## Teachings of Amenemopet-Chapter 9: Cutting Away Heart's Dispositions[40]

Verse 17.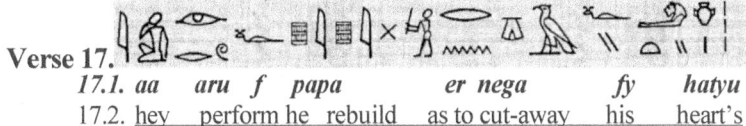
17.1. aa    aru   f   papa      er nega      fy     hatyu
17.2. hey   perform he  rebuild   as to cut-away   his     heart's
17.3. Hey, then he will be able to perform the cutting away of the heart's dispositions that are contrary to goodness and enlightenment.

This teaching reveals the essential psychological mechanism underlying all purification philosophy: the systematic removal of what Amenemopet describes as "heart's dispositions that are contrary to goodness and enlightenment" [4]. These dispositions represent the accumulated patterns of ego-identification thoughts, feelings, and behaviors that must be actively purified rather than merely suppressed or redirected through willpower. The ancient sages understood that authentic spiritual development requires what we could describe as "surgical precision" in identifying and removing the specific mental-emotional patterns that maintain consciousness in heated states rather than allowing natural recognition of its divine nature.

Understand how this "cutting away" process operates through the discriminative wisdom developed in philosophical study combined with the purifying effects of ethical conduct and meditation practice. The wisdom of the neteru illuminates that these contrary dispositions cannot be removed through intellectual analysis alone but require the systematic application of spiritual fire (fire of wisdom and action) generated through comprehensive practice that burns away the aryu patterns supporting ego-identification while revealing the natural spiritual inclinations of consciousness operating from divine recognition.

The theoretical foundation for practical purification emerges from understanding that aryu possess distinct qualities that either allow or obstruct the transmission of divine light through conscious-awareness. The tradition teaches that actions aligned with Maat create "light aryu"—impressions that remain transparent to divine

---

[40] Translation by Dr. Muata Ashby

consciousness, like thin clouds that allow sunlight to pass through, serving as vehicles for divine expression rather than obstacles to spiritual development [2]. Conversely, actions against Maat create "heavy aryu"—dense, opaque impressions that obstruct the flow of divine light and create what verse 129 describes as conditions where "A heart in this condition becomes a beacon for inimical cosmic forces—those demoniac energies that manifest as avarice, lust, jealousy, and selfishness" [2].

This understanding reveals why spiritual practice must address the unconscious level of conditioning rather than merely modifying conscious behavior or temporary mental states. The ancient sages taught that aryu function like winds disturbing the ocean of undifferentiated consciousness, creating waves of differentiated thoughts and mental phenomena that pull awareness into ego-identification and heated mental states. When these motivational disturbances are systematically purified through comprehensive spiritual practice, consciousness naturally rests in what the scripture calls the "calm, undifferentiated state" that allows recognition of its essential divine nature.

The purification philosophy demonstrates why practical spiritual development requires sustained commitment over extended periods rather than intensive but sporadic efforts. Notice how verse 177 describes the result: "The practice of the myth, ritual, ethics and meditations in the scripture develops vital-life-fire within the personality. This vital-life-fire acts as a fire of wisdom that burns away delusions and egoism" [2]. This spiritual roasting occurs through cumulative effects that gradually dissolve the aryu accumulations maintaining ego-identification while revealing consciousness's true nature as divine awareness.

## The Navigation Principle: Conscious Steering Through Experience

Sage Amenemopet's instruction to "steer away from that which is bad" concerning "our boat of life" establishes the fundamental principle of conscious discrimination in spiritual development [4]. This metaphor reveals that the Soul-Aware-Witness must exercise active, discriminative awareness in directing life experience through conscious choice rather than being swept along by unconscious patterns or external circumstances. The wisdom of the neteru illuminates how this conscious navigation represents the practical application of witness consciousness in daily life circumstances.

The navigation principle reveals that external circumstances serve consciousness development rather than constituting obstacles to overcome. What's more, the same situations that challenge ego-personality provide opportunities for witness consciousness to be experienced through mental stability and wisdom, transforming daily experience into continuous spiritual practice rather than distraction from spiritual goals. This means that conscious steering involves developing discriminative capacity to recognize which thoughts, actions, relationships, and environments support divine recognition versus those promoting ego-identification and heated mental states.

## The Fate of the Boat Philosophy: Consciousness Level Determining Life Outcomes
Teachings of Amenemopet Chapter 7B[41]

**Verse 10-11** *About the fate of the boat of life*

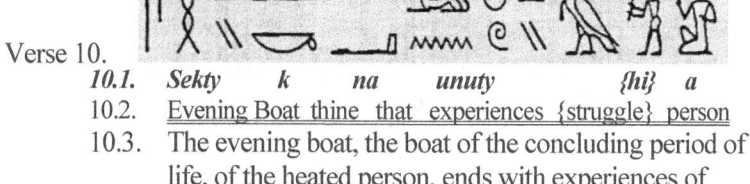

Verse 10.
- *10.1. Sekty k na unuty {hi} a*
- 10.2. Evening Boat thine that experiences {struggle} person
- 10.3. The evening boat, the boat of the concluding period of life, of the heated person, ends with experiences of struggling and strife, suffering and…

---

[41] Translation by Dr. Muata Ashby

Awakening Your Soul-Aware-Witness

Verse 11.(a)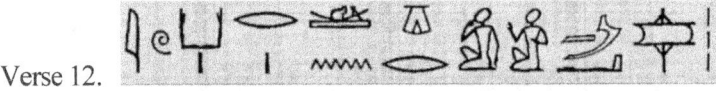

*11.1. chaatu   haynu   {moo} {she}-{ta}*
11.2. forsaking   swell  {waters} {channel}-{land}
11.3. ...forsakes, turns away from the purpose of life and the nature of the Divine (Neberdjer), due to being, as if, carried away on a great swell, a large, billowing wave of water, an overpowering force (of negative aryu/karma) that overwhelms the boat of life (mind and body). That swelling mind full of bourgeoning thoughts and feelings and desires throws their boat off course and channels it, conducts, routes their boat of life off course and causes it to run aground (shipwrecked), incapable of sailing on the journey of life and discovering the Divine.

Verse 12.

**12.1.** *Iu ka er amm - en ger a maau {shu}*
12.2. It is mind mouth boat - of silent person right {winds}
12.3. Now, as concerns the boat of life of those who lead a silent life, who do not live by egoistic desires, boisterousness in the temple or unethical behaviors, in their boat they are able to sail on fair winds that are pleasant and right for sailing, and right for reaching the destination of life, to reach the hand of God and be accepted by God as one with God.

Sage Amenemopet's Chapter 7B provides profound theoretical insight into how the consciousness level (level of awareness of oneself as being the Divine) determines the fundamental quality and direction of human existence through his teaching on the contrasting fates of different boats of life [4]. Verse 10 reveals the inevitable outcome for a heated condition of mind: "The evening boat, the boat of the concluding period of life, of the heated person, ends with experiences of struggling and strife, suffering and...forsaking, turns away from the purpose of life and the nature of the Divine (Neberdjer), due to being, as if, carried away on a great swell, a large, billowing wave of water, an overpowering force (of negative aryu/karma) that overwhelms the boat of life" [4].

This teaching illuminates the psychological mechanism by which ego-consciousness inevitably creates turbulent life patterns. The "great swell" represents the accumulated force of heavy aryu that emerges from actions motivated by separateness and ego-identification, creating what the text describes as "bourgeoning thoughts and feelings and desires" that throw a person's conscious-awareness "off course and channels it, conducts, routes their boat of life off course and causes it to run aground (shipwrecked), incapable of sailing on the journey of life and discovering the Divine" [4]. In psychological cognitive-behavior terms this can mean being overwhelmed by feeling and or thinking and being unable to make good decisions and instead making decisions that lead to negative outcomes in life.

Verse 11 establishes the contrasting outcome for silent consciousness: "Now, as concerns the boat of life of those who lead a silent life, who do not live by egoistic desires, boisterousness in the temple or unethical behaviors, in their boat they are able to sail on fair winds that are pleasant and right for sailing, and right for reaching the destination of life, to reach the hand of God and be accepted by God as one with God" [4].

This fate of the boat philosophy demonstrates how consciousness operating from its essential divine nature creates harmonious life circumstances that support both practical effectiveness and spiritual unfoldment without contradiction. The "fair winds" represent the natural spiritual support that emerges when a person's conscious-awareness aligns with divine order, creating cumulative positive momentum that facilitates rather than obstructs spiritual development. This philosophy explains why the ancient sages emphasized that spiritual practice serves enhanced living rather than escape from worldly engagement.

## The Witness Consciousness Philosophy: The Unchanging Foundation

The profound teaching about witness consciousness emerges from the understanding, established in the Hymn to Amun-Ra, that "beneath all changing states of consciousness—whether rage, peace, joy, sorrow, waking, or sleeping—there exists an unchanging awareness that simply witnesses these states without being affected by them" [3]. This witness consciousness represents what the ancient sages called Amun-Ra, the hidden aspect of divine awareness that sustains all phases of existence while remaining unmodified by the content of experience. The purpose of the teaching about Amun-Ra is for intellectual understanding followed by awareness and adoption of the perspective of Amun-Ra as one's own deeper identity. This adoption brings with it expansion in understanding, awareness and feeling and virtuous qualities.

The Hymn to Amun-Ra provides crucial insight into this witnessing principle: "during the sleep state, in the mind of people, a divine personage is there {that is Amun-Ra}; he is awake and aware and watchful after men and women while they are sleeping." This teaching reveals that divine consciousness remains eternally present and aware even when individual consciousness appears to be absent, demonstrating the principle that underlies all consciousness transformation processes.

The philosophy establishes that this witness consciousness "represents the unbroken continuity of awareness that underlies all states of being" and "continues to sustain the individual's existence" regardless of the changing modifications of mental-emotional activity [3]. Since the other states of awareness prove transitory while the underlying witness consciousness remains constant without fluctuation, "then the underlying Witness-Consciousness is the abiding reality behind the fluctuations" [3].

This theoretical foundation explains why practical spiritual development aims toward stabilizing recognition of this witness consciousness rather than attempting to modify or improve ego-patterns beyond a level necessary for healthy self-awareness development. The ancient sages taught that consciousness development involves learning to distinguish between the awareness that observes, and the phenomena being observed, revealing the natural distinction that ego-identification obscures through its tendency to become absorbed in mental-emotional content.

Understanding witness consciousness as the unchanging foundation provides both the theoretical framework and practical direction for spiritual development. This awareness serves as the stable platform from which consciousness can explore its own nature without becoming lost in identification with temporary experiences, creating the foundation for recognizing the deeper levels of divine awareness that represent humanity's essential spiritual nature.

## The Foundation for Authentic Development

The wisdom teachings reveal specific conditions that must be established before practical spiritual methods can produce authentic transformation rather than temporary experiences or spiritual development that lacks psychological integration. The Ancient Egyptian Book of Enlightenment Chapter 125 establishes that "living by truth" (Maat) creates the essential purification necessary for consciousness to access what verse 6.3 describes as Neberdjer—the "All-Encompassing Divinity that enfolds Creation and manifests as Creation" [1].

## Teachings of Amenemopet Chapter 6B: Maintaining Awareness of All-Encompassing Divinity[42]

**Verse 14** *About deliberate awareness of Neberdjer*

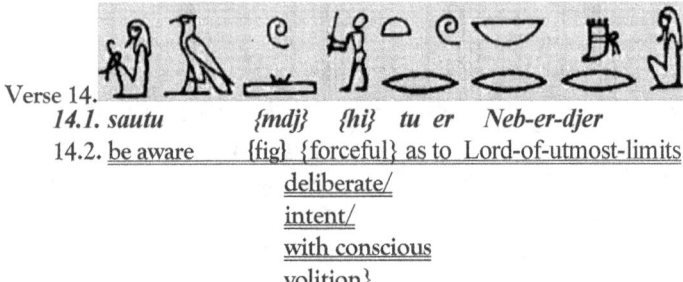

Verse 14.
14.1. *sautu*      *{mdj}*   *{hi}*   *tu er*   *Neb-er-djer*
14.2. be aware   {fig} {forceful} as to  Lord-of-utmost-limits
                           deliberate/
                           intent/
                           with conscious
                           volition}

14.3. Remain watchful, mindful, aware, keeping in mind, with deliberate effort, as to the fact that there is an "entity", an "existence" that encompasses all Creation [All-encompassing-Divinity], beyond[underlying] mind and time and space. Therefore, no action is hidden from it and consequently, this existence/consciousness underlies limited human awareness. If this awareness is maintained, there will be no egoism and no mind and therefore no fears, frustrations, inordinate desires, no need for stealing, lying, cheating or becoming a heated person and missing out on the glories of inner peace or the fulfillment of the purpose of life.

This instruction establishes the fundamental practice underlying the wisdom teachings: working to maintain deliberate awareness of Neberdjer (All-Encompassing Divinity) as the subconscious awareness foundation for all thoughts, actions, and experiences [4]. This teaching reveals a profound transformation of the very structure of consciousness that the ancient sages understood as the essential difference between ordinary human awareness and enlightened divine awareness.

Observe how in normal waking consciousness, one does not constantly think about their personal name or ego identity while engaging in daily thoughts, feelings, and activities—nevertheless, that ego identity operates as if it were the primary subconscious

---
[42] Translation by Dr. Muata Ashby

foundation of awareness and self-identity. However, once the ego has undergone the training of mystic self-awareness that original identity can be recalled immediately whenever attention turns toward it and can be recognized functioning as the background "Self" that is the true support of all mental-emotional experiences.

In other words, the ego identity serves as what we might call the default subconscious awareness that underlies and colors all perceptions, thoughts, and reactions, even when not explicitly being contemplated. Yet the wisdom of the neteru reveals that this ordinary state of consciousness represents a profound case of mistaken identity, where the infinite, eternal Neberdjer consciousness has become obscured by the mental identification with the limited, changeable ego construct that experiences itself as separate from the Divine source of its own existence.

Therefore, the goal of Neberdjer awareness practice involves the gradual transformation of this subconscious identity foundation—replacing the ego's assumed ownership of consciousness with the recognition that Neberdjer (the All-Encompassing Divinity) is the true subconscious substratum that underlies all awareness, thoughts, and experiences.

Recognizing that just as the personal ego identity can be effortlessly recalled whenever attention turns toward "who am I?" the aspirant works to establish Neberdjer awareness as the natural background awareness that can be immediately accessed through turning attention toward the source of awareness itself rather than toward the contents of awareness.

This represents the ultimate spiritual achievement: consciousness discovering its true nature as Neberdjer rather than continuing to misidentify with the limited ego personality that appears within the infinite field of divine awareness as the individual mind and ego identity. In this way, thoughts, feelings, and daily experiences continue to arise and pass away naturally, but they are recognized as movements within Neberdjer consciousness rather than as the possessions of a separate individual self—demonstrating the profound wisdom that the tradition of Shetaut Neter offers for the complete transformation of human consciousness from ego-bound limitation to divine self-recognition.

The ancient sages taught that this awareness functions as what we could call "divine context"—the conscious recognition that individual consciousness operates within and as manifestation of universal divine consciousness rather than existing as a separate entity struggling against external forces.

Still, this awareness must be cultivated through conscious effort rather than assumed as automatic recognition, since ego-identification creates the persistent illusion of separateness that obscures the ever-present divine reality. The wisdom teachings reveal that when the human conscious-awareness maintains this divine context through deliberate practice, the natural result eliminates the psychological conditions that generate ego-driven behavior: "there will be no egoism and no mind and therefore no fears, frustrations, inordinate desires, no need for stealing, lying, cheating or becoming a heated person" [4].

This instruction establishes the fundamental practice underlying the wisdom teachings: working to maintain deliberate awareness of Neberdjer (All-Encompassing Divinity) as the subconscious awareness foundation for all thoughts, actions, and experiences [4]. This demonstrates why awareness of All-Encompassing Divinity (Neberdjer/Asar/Ra) serves as a foundational and devotional practice that continuously inspires purity of philosophical understanding (how can it be that my identity is Ra/Neberdjer?), devotional feeling, and ethical conscience rather than only an advanced technique reserved for later stages of spiritual development.

Moreover, this teaching reveals that this ordinary state of consciousness represents a profound case of mistaken identity, where the infinite, eternal Neberdjer consciousness has become obscured by identification with the limited, changeable ego construct that experiences itself as separate from the Divine source of its own existence (Neberdjer).

Therefore, the spiritual practice, suggested by Sage Amenemopet, of making an effort to recall and maintain awareness of Neberdjer (sau Neberdjer), functions as a devotional practice (feeling awe about the existence, all-encompassingness, and true identity of "myself" (deeper self of the one's ego personality) of Neberdjer) that naturally supports and inspires all other aspects of spiritual development—just as the practice of the affirmation "I am Ra" serves not as a prerequisite to be mastered before other practices can commence, but as a living foundation that enriches ethical living, deepens devotional feeling, and clarifies philosophical understanding throughout one's spiritual journey, leading to the realization of the fact inherent in the practices of remembrance and affirmation as the innate reality of one's identity.

Notice that just as the personal ego identity, in an ordinary worldly-minded person, can be effortlessly recalled whenever attention turns toward "who am I?" the aspirant works to establish Neberdjer consciousness as the natural background awareness that can be immediately accessed through turning attention toward the source of awareness itself rather than toward the contents of awareness. The goal for the spiritual aspirant is to achieve a state of awareness and self-identity such that when the question "who am I? is asked, the answer would be Nuk Neberdjer (I am Neberdjer).

As the ancient sages taught, this foundational practice operates like a wellspring that continuously nourishes and purifies all other spiritual endeavors: when the aspirant maintains regular remembrance of Neberdjer as the true subconscious identity underlying all experience, this awareness naturally inspires greater devotion in ritual practice, deeper insight into philosophical study, and more spontaneous alignment with the ethical principles of Maat. In this way, thoughts, feelings, and daily experiences continue to arise and pass away naturally, but they are recognized as movements within Neberdjer consciousness rather than as the possessions of a separate individual self—demonstrating the profound wisdom that the tradition of Shetaut Neter offers for the integrated development of all dimensions of spiritual consciousness simultaneously.

Ethical purification operates according to the aryu transformation principle established in Chapter 3: actions aligned with divine order create "light aryu" that remain transparent to divine consciousness, while actions motivated by separateness and control create "heavy aryu" that obstruct spiritual development [2]. The tradition teaches that consciousness trapped in heavy aryu accumulations cannot achieve the subtle sensitivity necessary for recognizing its essential divine nature, since these dense impressions create what verse 129 describes as conditions attracting "inimical cosmic forces—those demoniac energies that manifest as avarice, lust, jealousy, and selfishness" [2].

**Teachings of Amenemopet-Chapter 11: The Consequence of Divine Rejection**[43]

**Verse 10** *About the Divine heart turning away*

Verse 10.
10.1.  *iu    ab {Net}  f    seha          im    chat   f*
10.2.  it is heart{Div} his turning away   in    body   his
10.3.  Why, because, when that is done, it is one's own rejection of the Divine within our heart and thus our Divine heart, that is, the Spirit essence of the Divine within us, as if turns away from (forsakes) us within our own personality.

This teaching illuminates the consequences when consciousness fails to meet the essential prerequisites for spiritual development: rejection of divine recognition creates the condition where "the Spirit essence of the Divine within us, as if turns away from (forsakes) us within our own personality" [4]. This represents not divine abandonment, but the natural result of human conscious-awareness choosing ego-identification over recognition of its essential divine nature, creating what can be termed "spiritual disconnection" that manifests as the loss of access to divine guidance and inspiration and a personality left to its own ego-driven thoughts, feelings, and motivations.

The ancient sages understood that this turning away occurs through the accumulated effects of actions and thoughts motivated by separateness rather than divine recognition, creating dense aryu patterns that obscure the subtle sensitivity necessary for recognizing divine presence within an individual's conscious-awareness. This explains why the prerequisites of ethical purification and proper understanding prove essential rather than optional—consciousness operating from heavy karmic

---

[43] Translation by Dr. Muata Ashby

conditioning literally cannot maintain the spiritual sensitivity required for authentic divine recognition, creating the illusion that divinity is absent rather than recognizing that ego-patterns prevent its recognition.

The ancient sages established that spiritual sensitivity develops gradually through sustained alignment with truth at all levels of human experience: physical truth through harmonious living that supports rather than agitates consciousness; mental truth through challenging ego-identity that seeks happiness through external relationships and acquisitions; and spiritual truth through recognition of divine nature as the foundation of individual existence. This systematic purification creates what we could describe as "spiritual sensitivity"—the capacity to recognize subtle consciousness levels and distinguish between authentic spiritual recognition and feelings or mental phenomena that can masquerade as the deeper spiritual experience.

Observe how this theoretical understanding prevents common errors in spiritual practice where aspirants attempt advanced techniques without establishing proper foundation, leading to experiences that lack stability or integration with daily life responsibilities. The foundational practices (ethics, philosophical study, acceptance of the Divine) promote positive conditions so that practical spiritual practices serve genuine transformation rather than only as spiritual escapism, spiritual development that primarily outpaces psychological readiness, or using spirituality primarily for emotional regulation in normal times or emotional support in tough times.

# The Integration Model: Why Partial Practice Remains Insufficient

The tradition of Shetaut Neter reveals that consciousness operates simultaneously through multiple dimensions that require coordinated development rather than isolated spiritual techniques [4]. This integration philosophy emerges from the cosmic understanding explored in Chapters 2-6, where consciousness manifests through three interconnected levels (Soul of Ra, Nunu, Ra) that function as a unified system rather than separate compartments of experience.

The ancient sages taught that spiritual practice must encompass all dimensions of consciousness manifestation because partial approaches create what can be termed "developmental imbalance"—conditions where one aspect of spiritual development advances while others remain neglected, creating instability rather than integrated growth. Observe how attempting to develop witness consciousness through meditation while neglecting ethical conduct results in spiritual experiences that lack proper foundation and often lead to spiritual development that lacks psychological integration or missing necessary feeling (and emotional) or psychological development.

Similarly, philosophical study without meditation practice remains confined to intellectual understanding that fails to transform consciousness itself, while ethical conduct without proper understanding lacks the spiritual context necessary for transcending ego-motivation and discovering divine inspiration as the source of righteous action. The integration philosophy demonstrates why the ancient wisdom emphasizes comprehensive development that addresses physical, mental, and spiritual levels simultaneously.

This theoretical foundation explains why Sage Amenemopet's teachings consistently emphasize wisdom philosophy that bridges understanding and living rather than treating spiritual practice as separate from daily life responsibilities. The wisdom of the neteru reveals that authentic spiritual development enhances rather than diminishes practical effectiveness in worldly circumstances, since consciousness operating from divine recognition naturally expresses enhanced wisdom, compassion, and creative intelligence in all areas of life.

## The Natural Progression Philosophy: Spiritual Law and Automatic Development

The Scripture of Ra and Hetheru establishes that consciousness development follows spiritual laws as reliable as physical laws, operating through what can be termed "automatic progression" when proper conditions are established [2]. This understanding emerges from the cosmic mechanics where consciousness

## Awakening Your Soul-Aware-Witness

transformation occurs through the removal of obstacles rather than the acquisition of new states or experiences.

### Teachings of Amenemopet-Chapter 18: Divine Guidance and Human Will[44]

**Verse 6** *About divine shepherding of human life*

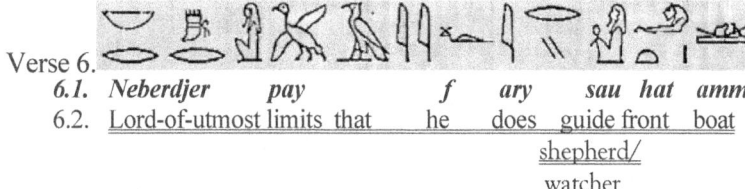

Verse 6.
6.1. *Neberdjer      pay            f      ary        sau    hat    amm*
6.2. Lord-of-utmost limits that    he    does    guide  front  boat
                                                          shepherd/
                                                          watcher

6.3. However, despite the personal predilections, there is an all-encompassing divinity that masters and encompasses the limits of Creation and therefore, that overall encompassing divinity is the shepherd that guides human life. That divinity is actually at the forefront of the boat of life watching(aware), guiding the boat of human life where it needs to go for the welfare of all humans even before they themselves know where they are going. Therefore, human self-will and or self-determination are an illusion.

This profound teaching provides the essential foundation for understanding natural progression philosophy: Neberdjer (All-Encompassing Divinity) functions as the "shepherd that guides human life" and "is actually at the forefront of the boat of life watching (aware), guiding the boat of human life where it needs to go for the welfare of all humans even before they themselves know where they are going" [4]. This reveals that what appears as individual spiritual development actually represents universal consciousness orchestrating its own recognition through apparent individual forms rather than separate entities achieving personal spiritual advancement.

Notice how this understanding transforms the entire approach to spiritual practice from effortful seeking to conscious cooperation with divine guidance that operates continuously whether recognized or not. The wisdom of the neteru illuminates that

---

[44] Translation by Dr. Muata Ashby

"human self-will and or self-determination are an illusion" [4], not because consciousness lacks capacity for choice, but because authentic choice emerges from awareness of the divine and capacity to act based on divine wisdom rather than ego-planning and control. This divine shepherding explains why natural progression occurs automatically when proper conditions are established through purification and discriminative wisdom rather than through forced spiritual techniques or dramatic efforts to achieve particular consciousness levels.

Verse 177 of the Scripture of Ra and Hetheru reveals that "the practice of the myth, ritual, ethics and meditations in the scripture develops vital-life-fire within the personality" that "burns away delusions and egoism" [2]. This spiritual roasting represents not forced development but natural consequence of sustained spiritual discipline that creates internal conditions allowing consciousness to recognize its essential divine nature. The ancient sages taught that when sufficient purification occurs, consciousness automatically begins to function from influences coming from higher levels without effortful maintenance or dramatic spiritual techniques.

The natural progression philosophy explains why spiritual development requires patient, sustained practice rather than seeking immediate dramatic results. Understand how consciousness naturally moves from ego-identification through witness recognition toward Ra consciousness, Nunu awareness, and ultimately Soul of Ra recognition when the accumulated aryu patterns that maintain ego-identification are systematically dissolved through comprehensive spiritual practice.

This understanding prevents common errors where aspirants attempt to force particular consciousness levels or become discouraged when development proceeds gradually rather than through sudden transformation. The ancient sages understood that consciousness inherently possesses the capacity for divine recognition, and spiritual practice serves to remove the conditioning influences that obscure this natural capacity rather than creating something foreign to human nature.

## The Practical Wisdom Foundation: Discrimination and Conscious Choice

The theoretical foundation for practical spiritual development rests upon what the ancient sages called "philosophical discrimination"—the capacity to distinguish between consciousness and mental content, between divine impulses and ego-driven patterns, between actions that support spiritual development and those that perpetuate ego-identification [4]. This discriminative wisdom, at intellectual level, represents an important capacity for a person striving to achieve the Soul-Aware-Witness experience. Then it is important to allow sublimation of the egoistic feelings into a higher order of feeling that is more integrated with the wisdom understanding. Therefore, it is important for effective spiritual practice, since consciousness caught in identification with mental-emotional content lacks the clarity and detachment necessary for conscious choice and spiritual sensitivity.

Sage Amenemopet's teaching about "desist from, abstain, cease, renounce joining with and gossiping with and watch out, definitely not getting into verbal arguments with the sneaky enemy, the heated person" reveals the practical application of philosophical discrimination [4]. The wisdom illuminates how engaging with a heated condition of mind through argument or gossip actually amplifies the very mental agitation that creates heated conditions, while maintaining appropriate spiritual distance allows divine principles to operate through natural spiritual law.

This discrimination extends beyond external relationships to encompass internal mental-emotional patterns that either support or obstruct spiritual development. The tradition teaches that human conscious-awareness must learn to recognize the difference between thoughts arising from divine inspiration and those emerging from accumulated aryu patterns, between emotions that express soul wisdom and those driven by ego-reactivity, between actions that serve spiritual development and those perpetuating separation and control.

Awakening Your Soul-Aware-Witness

The practical wisdom foundation demonstrates why theoretical understanding must be integrated with lived experience rather than remaining abstract knowledge. What's more, philosophical discrimination proves effective only when applied consistently in daily circumstances where conscious-awareness can practice and demonstrate its capacity to choose responses based on wisdom rather than being driven by automatic reactive patterns.

Verse 154.

154.1.  pu  Ba pu nheh  {  nht}[45]  a  Ba  < pu en>  Kek  Gereh  a
154.2.  this soul this for-eternal sycamore mine soul  <this for>  darkness night mine
154.3.  This soul (of mine (of Ra)), it is of the nature of eternal renewal, nourishment, fertility and rebirth as symbolized by the sacred sycamore, [46], which is special to me and to Hathor; <this> soul, of mine, is the soul of darkness and the soul of night; it is divine.

This ever-new quality means that true pure consciousness is always fresh, always unchangeable in its existence and cannot hold on to fleeting phenomena. Its essential nature is eternity; therefore, it is rooted in the now always-eternal present. This teaching correlates directly with the movement described in the Pert-m-Heru, which guides aspirants away from identification with mind and body toward the discovery of the separate Soul-Aware-Witness [1].

Notice how the Soul-Aware-Witness discovered through purification of mind with ethical conscience (Maat), reversal of

---

[45] In Ancient Egyptian hieroglyphic writing the rope determinative sign forming, as if, arch over a glyph, among other things, signifies that the covered glyph is included or connected with other glyphs; in this case the term 'for eternity".

[46] nehty – Two sycamore trees between which the God Ra emerges every morning as the sundisk
Nunu (Darkness) → Ra (Light) → Creation (composed of Nunu/Ra's body) illumined by Ra

the externalized heated mind that opens up the Ra visualization represents a development moving closer to consciousness which is ever new (Ba en Ra [Soul of Ra]). As Chapter 2 established, the three consciousness levels provide the framework for understanding this movement—from ego-consciousness through Ra-level awareness to Nunu-level undifferentiated consciousness—approaching the recognition of consciousness as eternal renewal.

## The Mature Expression: Heru (Horus) Consciousness Philosophy

The Soul-Aware-Witness, when fully developed through sustained experience becomes what the teachings describe as Heru (Horus) consciousness—awareness established in its nature as sovereign over worldly conditions rather than victim of them [1]. At this developmental stage, consciousness has achieved stable recognition of its essential nature as divine awareness while maintaining full capacity to function effectively in the world of time and space.

Still, this sovereignty emerges not through ego-effort but through the natural expression of consciousness that has remembered its true nature, separate from the ego-awareness level. The Heru personality operates from what can be called "spiritual inclinations"—ethics, right thinking, and right feeling that flow spontaneously from the experience of fullness rather than from the ego's characteristic patterns of avarice and vain searching for happiness in fleeting phenomena [1].

This theoretical understanding explains why advanced spiritual development enhances rather than diminishes practical effectiveness in worldly circumstances. The wisdom of the neteru reveals that consciousness operating from divine recognition naturally expresses enhanced wisdom, compassion, and creative intelligence in all areas of life, since the Soul-Aware-Witness serves as the soul's instrument for divine expression rather than obstacle to spiritual purpose.

## The Cosmic Context: Individual Mind as Localized Universal Consciousness

The Scripture of Ra and Hetheru provides profound theoretical insight into the relationship between individual consciousness and cosmic awareness that reshapes understanding for optimal spiritual development [2]. Ra ideates the outer netherworld, which resembles the expanded universe with stars, planets, and galaxies—this expanded manifested Creation represents Ra's expanded manifest existence. Since Ra embodies cosmic individuated differentiated consciousness and what he creates emerges from his consciousness (Nunu), the manifest universe and outer space constitute manifestations of Ra's mind which is himself.

The human mind, composed of the same individuated consciousness but in smaller localized form, can perceive a fraction of this vastness which is Ra, and which is human consciousness [2]. Through following the prescriptions revealed in the ancient scriptures, the human consciousness can find the way back to the fullness of this vastness which is Ra and commune with its expanded higher self—cosmic individuated differentiated consciousness that also recognizes its undifferentiated nature (Nunu) and its absolute pure consciousness beingness without any qualification, conditioning of mental perceptions (limited or expanded) or intellectual conceptual constructs.

This cosmic context philosophy explains why individual spiritual development serves universal awakening rather than personal advantage. The practitioner recognizes that what appears as individual consciousness transformation actually represents universal consciousness recognizing its own nature through apparent individual forms, shifting focus from personal achievement to conscious participation in cosmic awakening.

## The Recognition of Previous Delusion Philosophy

The theoretical framework reveals that consciousness development involves recognizing that the personality before the discovery of being an entity of higher awareness above the ego (Soul-Aware-Witness) was experiencing fundamental delusion about the nature of self, thinking itself to be the body/mind and becoming suffocated by the sensations, perceptions and mentations of the body/mind [1]. This means that the sensations and perceptions before the discovery of being separate were approached from an illusory identity perspective—the ego-construct believing itself to be the recipient and experiencer of phenomena rather than recognizing the unchanging witness that observes all changing phenomena.

The teachings of Amenemopet illuminate this recognition: "Behold the glory of this way of being! Being silent means discovering the fullness of the Creator-Spirit that is within. This fullness cannot come from heatedly searching for fulfillment in the world for fulfillment with an imperfect (ego-dependent) personality" [4]. Understanding that others are also expressions of the same consciousness, albeit often lost in ego-identification, creates natural patience and kindness toward their struggles and confusion.

This delusion recognition philosophy provides essential context for spiritual practice, since it explains why human conscious-awareness must separate itself from identification with mental-emotional content even while attempting to purify or improve ego-patterns. The ancient sages taught that recognizing the illusory nature of ego-identification serves as the foundation for all subsequent spiritual development.

## The Living Expression Philosophy: Divine Awareness in Daily Life

The theoretical culmination of witness consciousness development creates what Amenemopet calls "worshipping oneself as Divine"—not spiritual development that lacks psychological integration, but recognition and embodiment of the truth that consciousness itself is divine, and one's essential nature is that consciousness [4]. This understanding transforms daily life into continuous spiritual practice rather than dividing experience into spiritual and mundane categories.

Every interaction becomes an opportunity to recognize the divine in apparent multiplicity; every challenge becomes a chance to demonstrate the peace and wisdom that emerge from stable higher identity; every moment becomes a celebration of consciousness knowing itself through the expression and confluence of manifestation [1]. This represents the practical fruition of theoretical understanding—consciousness expressing its essential divine nature through enhanced wisdom, compassion, and service in all worldly circumstances.

The living expression philosophy explains why authentic spiritual development enhances rather than diminishes engagement with temporal responsibilities, relationships, and creative service. Consciousness operating from divine recognition naturally seeks opportunities to express its essential nature through beneficial action that serves both individual awakening and collective wellbeing.

# The Intellectual Foundation for Awareness Investigation

The intellectual faculty of mind serves as the essential starting point for spiritual development, providing the discriminative capacity necessary for investigating the nature of human awareness and perception. This investigation allows practitioners to examine the reality of life and develop modes of living more conducive to fulfillment and contentment.

Yet intellectual understanding represents only the beginning of consciousness development rather than its completion. The tradition teaches that the mind's intellectual capacity, when properly directed, can investigate its own limitations and point toward the awareness that underlies mental activity. This investigation creates the foundation for recognizing consciousness as distinct from aryu, thoughts, feelings, memories, sensations and perceptions along with the mental content that is produced thereby.

## Integrated Consciousness and Advanced Development

The tradition of Shetaut Neter describes advanced stages of development where practitioners can access multiple consciousness levels simultaneously or move fluidly between them according to need. This represents what the teachings call "integrated consciousness"—a mature stage of development that aspirants won't achieve immediately, but understanding the possibility helps them orient their practice toward integration rather than simply escaping ordinary ego consciousness.

Referencing Chapter 2's three-level framework, integrated consciousness allows the aspirant to maintain constant recognition of Soul of Ra consciousness while simultaneously operating through Nunu awareness and Ra individuation as circumstances require. This means that consciousness never loses touch with its absolute ground yet remains fully capable of engaging with the world of relationships, creativity, and service.

The ancient sages taught that this integration represents the natural fruition of spiritual practice rather than an extraordinary achievement reserved for special individuals. The teachings emphasize that consciousness inherently possesses this integrative capacity, and spiritual practice simply removes the obstacles that prevent its natural expression.

Still, integrated consciousness requires extensive preparation through the purification of aryu (karmic impressions) and the development of stable witness consciousness. As the Scripture reveals, this development occurs gradually through sustained practice and philosophical discrimination rather than through sudden transformation or special experiences.

## Conclusion: The Bridge Between Understanding and Application

These foundational principles and developmental philosophies provide the essential bridge between the cosmic understanding established in Chapters 1-6 and the specific practical methods that will be explored in Chapter 10. The ancient sages designed their wisdom teachings to guide consciousness from its current level of functioning toward recognition of its essential divine nature through systematic application of universal principles rather than reliance on extraordinary experiences or dramatic spiritual techniques.

The theoretical framework reveals that practical spiritual development emphasizes consciousness recognition more than personality improvement, divine expression more than ego-enhancement, and collective service more than personal advancement. Notice how this understanding ensures that practical methods serve authentic transformation that integrates transcendent awareness with temporal responsibilities in ways that benefit both individual awakening and the wellbeing of all beings.

The foundational principles demonstrate why ancient Egyptian spiritual psychology remains as relevant for contemporary practitioners as it was for the temple schools of ancient Kemet. The psychological and spiritual laws governing consciousness development operate universally across historical periods and cultural contexts, providing timeless guidance for any sincere aspirant willing to engage with the systematic practice necessary for discovering their essential nature as divine awareness temporarily manifesting through individual human form.

Therefore, these theoretical foundations naturally lead to examination of the specific practical methods through which aspirants can implement these principles systematically in daily spiritual practice, creating the conditions that support stable consciousness development rather than temporary spiritual experiences that lack integration and authentic transformative power.

## References

[1] Ashby, M. (2016). Egyptian Book of the Dead Hieroglyph Translations for Enlightenment: Understanding the Mystic Path to Enlightenment Through Direct Readings of the Sacred Signs and Symbols of Ancient Egyptian Language With Trilinear Deciphering Translation Method Vol. 1. Translation by Dr. Muata Ashby. Sema Institute.
[2] Ashby, M. (2022). The Mysteries of Ra and Hetheru/Sekhmet. Translation by Dr. Muata Ashby. Sema Institute.
[3] Ashby, M. (2025). DEFINITIONS: The Nature of Consciousness and Awareness in Neterian Philosophy. By Dr. Muata Ashby. Sema Institute.
[4] Ashby, M. (2019). Teachings of Ancient Egyptian Sage Amenemopet with Hieroglyphic texts. Translation by Dr. Muata Ashby. Sema Institute.

# Chapter 10: Spiritual Practices Suggested by the Scriptures Covered in this Book

The mystic transpersonal psychology principles offered through the Ancient Egyptian scripture collection presented in this book relate to wisdom philosophy about the nature of universal existence, consciousness, and how divine awareness manifests in the human personality—both in optimal states of spiritual alignment as well as the suboptimal conditions that characterize ego-bound existence. Moreover, these teachings also provide comprehensive methods for learning and practicing the philosophical instructions so as to discover and experience the heights of consciousness that transcend ordinary human limitations, revealing our essential nature as aspects of Ra's divine awareness.

Still, we must recognize that these spiritual practices serve as wisdom guidelines rather than rigid requirements that must all be implemented simultaneously. Authentic spiritual development unfolds organically when the aspirant engages with those methods that most deeply resonate with their current spiritual capacity and natural inclination. Notice how the tradition of Shetaut Neter acknowledges that each student arrives at the teaching with unique aryu (karmic influences) and personal spiritual history that naturally draws them toward specific aspects of the comprehensive path.

Therefore, the sincere student should begin by working with those practices that kindle genuine enthusiasm and sustained interest, whether they be the ethical principles of Maat, the devotional methods of temple ritual, or the direct experiential techniques of meditation and contemplation. In this way, the foundation of authentic practice becomes established through quality rather than quantity—depth of engagement rather than breadth of superficial observance. As engagement with preferred methods deepens and matures, other complementary practices will naturally reveal their relevance and value, allowing the aspirant to gradually expand their spiritual repertoire according to their evolving understanding and capacity.

This organic approach aligns with the understanding in the scripture that spiritual transformation requires willing participation and conscious acceptance rather than forced adherence to external prescriptions. For contemporary practitioners of Shetaut Neter, this means developing discernment about which teachings offer the most immediate practical value while maintaining openness to the broader wisdom tradition that supports all authentic spiritual endeavor.

# Introduction to the Fifteen Methods of Ancient Egyptian Consciousness Development based on the Translated Scriptures in this Volume

The mystic transpersonal psychology principles offered through the Ancient Egyptian scripture collection presented in this manuscript relate to wisdom philosophy about the nature of universal existence, consciousness, and how that manifests in the human personality both in optimal as well as suboptimal states. Observe how these profound teachings, emerging from the Ancient Egyptian Book of Enlightenment (Pert-em-Heru), the Scripture of Ra and Hetheru, and the Wisdom Text of Sage Amenemopet, provide not merely theoretical understanding but systematic methods for learning and practicing the philosophical teachings so as to discover and experience the heights of consciousness beyond ordinary human capacities.

The ancient sages understood that consciousness development requires more than intellectual appreciation of spiritual concepts—it demands what they called practical wisdom that transforms everyday experience into opportunities for divine recognition. Furthermore, the fifteen methods presented here represent spiritual technologies (hekau) that have been tested and refined over millennia, emerging directly from the trilinear translations of authentic hieroglyphic texts, included in this volume, rather than contemporary interpretations or speculative approaches to spiritual development.

## Essential Guidance for Understanding Spiritual Practice

The spiritual practices and methods described throughout this volume represent philosophical guidelines for understanding the principles of Ancient Egyptian consciousness development rather than prescriptive instructions for unguided personal engagement. Indeed, the wisdom of the neteru reveals that authentic spiritual practice requires proper preparation, foundational understanding, and ideally the guidance of qualified teachers who can assess individual spiritual readiness and provide appropriate instruction tailored to the aspirant's specific circumstances and capacity. Consider how the ancient temple schools of Kemet operated through systematic preparation that included ethical development, philosophical study, and gradual introduction to advanced practices under the supervision of experienced sages; in other words, these methods were transmitted within comprehensive educational frameworks that ensured both safety and effectiveness rather than through isolated practice divorced from proper context and guidance. For contemporary practitioners of Shetaut Neter, this means that the techniques and approaches discussed in this book should be understood primarily as educational content that illuminates the principles underlying spiritual development rather than as standalone practices to be immediately implemented without appropriate preparation. Nevertheless, the sincere aspirant can derive tremendous benefit from studying these methods as philosophical teachings that deepen understanding of consciousness transformation while cultivating the ethical foundation and mental clarity that naturally prepare consciousness for more advanced spiritual work when the time becomes appropriate. Therefore, students are encouraged to approach these teachings with reverence for their profound wisdom while exercising appropriate caution regarding practical implementation—using these descriptions to enhance understanding of spiritual principles, develop proper ethical foundations through the teachings of Maat, and cultivate the quality of consciousness that naturally attracts opportunities for authentic spiritual instruction when the aspirant demonstrates readiness for advanced practice.

Yet these methods function as integrated components of a complete system rather than isolated techniques that can be practiced independently. The wisdom of the neteru reveals that optimal consciousness development requires systematic application of multiple approaches working together: foundational preparation through ethical living and philosophical discrimination; intermediate development through consciousness level recognition and awareness investigation; and advanced stabilization through witness consciousness development and divine recognition practices. This comprehensive methodology ensures that spiritual practice serves genuine transformation rather than temporary experiences that lack stability or integration with daily life circumstances.

Each method corresponds with specific teachings found within our foundational translated hieroglyphic texts, demonstrating how the ancient Egyptian tradition provided not only profound metaphysical insights but precise practical guidance for implementing these insights in lived experiences. The progression from basic preparation methods through intermediate development techniques to advanced recognition practices follows the natural unfoldment of consciousness from ego-identification toward divine realization, honoring both the aspirant's current level of development and their ultimate spiritual potential.

Therefore, these fifteen methods represent the distilled essence of Ancient Egyptian spiritual psychology as revealed through authentic scriptural sources, offering contemporary practitioners access to the same transformative wisdom that guided consciousness development in the temple schools of ancient Kemet. Through systematic application of these time-tested approaches, modern aspirants can discover for themselves the profound psychological and spiritual insights that emerge when consciousness recognizes its true nature as divine awareness temporarily manifesting through individual human form.

# 1. Trilinear Translation Methodology for Accessing Ancient Wisdom Authentically

The revolutionary trilinear translation system represents essential spiritual technology for contemporary practitioners, moving beyond conventional interlinear formats to capture the full philosophical, mythological, and spiritual dimensions embedded within Ancient Egyptian hieroglyphic texts [2]. The methodology provides three distinct levels of rendering: phonetic transliteration preserving original sounds, direct word-for-word translation maintaining ancient grammatical structure, and contextual translation incorporating philosophical concepts (Sebayt), mythological references (matnu), and cultural insights necessary for contemporary understanding. This three-dimensional approach creates both vertical depth of understanding for individual verses and horizontal coherence when read sequentially, preserving the educational progression intended by the original priest-scribes.

Understanding the trilinear methodology requires recognizing that Ancient Egyptian texts operated simultaneously as literal communications, philosophical treatises, and mystical instructions—a multilayered reality demanding equally sophisticated translation approaches. Reflect on how hieroglyphs like the owl glyph (im/em) carry profound philosophical significance beyond surface meaning, indicating divine identification and transformation processes that conventional translation methods often miss entirely. The contextual translation level serves as the interpretive culmination, integrating philosophical underpinnings and metaphysical implications to convey the deeper intent embedded within the hieroglyphic script, functioning as a bridge between ancient consciousness and contemporary understanding.

**Implementation Process:** The trilinear translation system provides essential spiritual technology for contemporary practitioners seeking authentic access to ancient wisdom. The implementation involves studying ancient texts through three systematic levels rather than relying on single-dimension translations that may inevitably distort meaning through cultural misinterpretation or oversimplified literal rendering.

**Daily Application:** • Study each scriptural passage through all three levels: phonetic transliteration, word-for-word translation, and contextual interpretation • Read each level both vertically (comparing all three translations of the same verse) and horizontally (following the continuous narrative within each level throughout the text) • Focus particularly on key hieroglyphs and teachings that resonate with your current understanding.

**Scripture Foundation:** The methodology emerges from understanding that Ancient Egyptian texts operated simultaneously as literal communications, philosophical treatises, and mystical instructions—a multilayered reality demanding sophisticated translation approaches that preserve the transformative potential necessary for genuine spiritual development (nehast).

## 2. Wisdom and Practice of Ethics: Living by Truth at Physical, Mental, and Spiritual Levels

The Ancient Egyptian Book of Enlightenment Chapter 125 establishes the fundamental principle that living by truth (Maat) creates the comprehensive purification necessary for consciousness to discover its essential divine nature and access Neberdjer (All-Encompassing Divinity) consciousness. Verse 6.3 declares: "I have acted by truthfulness while I was living on earth in the beloved land of Egypt," while the appendix verse 9.3 reveals the deeper dimension: "I live in truth, I feed upon things that are in the form of truth, in my mind, not lies, falsehoods, or similitudes" [1]. This ethical foundation serves as both spiritual method and qualification for divine recognition, creating what the tradition calls "light aryu" (karmic influences) that remain transparent to divine light rather than obstructing the natural radiance of spiritual development.

We must recognize that this practice requires understanding Maat as representing divine order, truth, and righteous living that aligns individual actions with cosmic harmony [4]. The ancient sages taught that following Maat creates environmental conditions that allow subtle spiritual recognition to emerge, since consciousness trapped in unbalanced circumstances cannot achieve the stability necessary for witnessing its own nature. What's more, this encompasses living by balance with nature—maintaining proper diet, rest, and physical rhythms that support rather than agitate the nervous system—while avoiding actions motivated by separateness (egoic separateness) and control (egoic desire to control circumstances to its idea of benefit) that create heavy aryu accumulations obscuring divine awareness.

The systematic application of living by truth operates through three integrated levels that address all dimensions of being simultaneously. Physical level truth encompasses harmonious living that supports rather than agitates consciousness through ethical and balanced work, proper diet, rest, sleep, and physical rhythms that create environmental conditions allowing subtle spiritual recognition to emerge. The tradition teaches that consciousness trapped in unbalanced physical circumstances cannot achieve stability necessary for witnessing its own nature, since agitated physical conditions create corresponding mental-emotional turbulence that obscures divine awareness. Even so, this physical foundation establishes the calmness required for deeper spiritual work, as the ancient sages understood the multidimensional nature of human consciousness.

Mental level truth involves engaging with and practicing what promotes sanity, peace, and harmony while avoiding agitating thoughts based on belief in oneself as a separate ego-personality competing with others for limited happiness through object acquisition. This requires systematic challenging of the source fomenting desires based on the delusion that objects provide fulfillment—namely, ego-self-identity that must be recognized as alteration of true human nature rather than authentic selfhood. Notice how this mental purification encompasses both thought content and the fundamental identity-structure generating thoughts, since true mental Maat addresses not merely surface thinking but the underlying self-concept that generates mental phenomena.

Spiritual level truth emerges as consciousness discovers through purification that the entity practicing living by truth differs from ego-personality previously considered to be the self. This means that sufficient purification allows human conscious-awareness to recognize itself as a separate entity apart from mind, thoughts, desires, and physical body—what may be termed the "Soul-

Aware-Witness" that was always present but obscured by identification with temporary phenomena. Understand how the same awareness that practices living by truth begins to be recognized as divine consciousness operating through individual faculties rather than personal possession of separate ego-identity, establishing a foundation for natural progression through Ra, Nunu, and Soul of Ra consciousness levels.

Furthermore, this recognition transforms spiritual practice from seeking union with something external to discovering divine consciousness already operating through individual faculties. The systematic approach to ethical living creates the spiritual sensitivity necessary for recognizing consciousness beyond ego-identification, since the three levels work together to dissolve conditions maintaining false identification while revealing consciousness's essential divine nature. This understanding corresponds with the teaching in the Scripture that divine consciousness creates optimal conditions for spiritual development, yet transformation ultimately requires conscious participation and willing acceptance from the individual practitioner.

Therefore, this comprehensive methodology addresses all dimensions of being simultaneously, as the ancient sages taught through their understanding of the multidimensional nature of human consciousness. Living by truth creates cumulative purification effects over time that gradually dissolve conditions maintaining ego-identification while revealing the divine Self that is the source and sustenance of all existence. At the same time, this systematic approach requires sustained commitment rather than sporadic application, since authentic transformation emerges through devoted practice that recognizes Maat as both method and ultimate spiritual realization itself.

## Practical Application for Contemporary Practitioners

For contemporary practitioners of Shetaut Neter, implementing this threefold approach to living by truth begins with establishing daily rhythms that honor physical Maat through conscious attention to diet, sleep, and environmental harmony that support rather than agitate consciousness. Reflect on how the aspirant might begin each day by asking: "How do my actions today align with divine order?" This involves choosing jobs or professions that are in harmony with truth, foods that promote clarity rather than agitation, maintaining sleep patterns that support natural rhythms, and engaging in physical practices that honor the body as a temple of divine consciousness rather than mere material vessel.

Moreover, mental Maat emerges through systematic observation of thought patterns that arise from ego-identification, particularly those based on acquiring happiness through external objects or defending possessions from imagined threats. The ancient wisdom teaches that practitioners can develop this awareness by noticing when thoughts arise from the assumption of separateness rather than unity with divine consciousness that is the truth of all-encompassing existence, gradually recognizing the difference between thoughts emerging from divine Self versus ego-personality. In other words, aspirants learn to distinguish between mental activity that promotes spiritual sensitivity and activity that reinforces identification with temporary phenomena.

Still, spiritual Maat requires the most subtle application, since it involves recognizing the very awareness that observes physical and mental practice as distinct from ego-identity previously considered to be the self. Observe how this recognition emerges gradually through sustained ethical living: as purification progresses, consciousness begins to witness its own operations rather than being completely identified with mental-emotional phenomena. This means that the same divine awareness practicing truth (Maat) begins to be experienced as a separate entity—the eternal witness that was always present but obscured by identification with changing conditions.

As the wisdom of the neteru reveals, this practical methodology transforms daily life into continuous spiritual practice where every action becomes opportunity for recognizing divine consciousness operating through individual faculties. The aspirant discovers that living by truth at all three levels creates the transparency necessary for divine light to shine through human experience, establishing the foundation for advanced spiritual recognition and ultimate realization of unity with Ra's consciousness itself. The practice of Maat reaches its summit in the attainment of un-maat or "absolute-truth".

## 3. Working Skillfully with Heated Mind Disruptions and Maintaining Optimal Consciousness Levels

The tradition reveals that heated mind states—characterized by agitation, control-seeking, aggressiveness and separateness-projection—represent the primary obstacles to maintaining optimal consciousness levels during challenging circumstances, as external pressures like work stress, relationship conflicts, or health concerns often trigger mental patterns that obscure clear awareness. Sage Amenemopet provides guidance for "turning your mind away from their mind and emotions" when encountering a heated condition of mind while understanding that "the Divine, in a mysterious way, turns back towards them and provides to them what they need and deserve for their ethical and spiritual evolution" [4]. This approach involves early recognition of heated mind onset before full establishment, maintaining witness consciousness during difficulties, and applying understanding rather than forced suppression.

One important teaching for maintaining mental balance is about the nature of Neberdjer, All-Encompassing-Divinity which is the existence that enfolds all and is the mover behind all movements of Creation. Therefore, the events of Creation and of life need to be seen as divine happenings under the auspices of the divine as per the aryu we have collected. It is allowed by God with a divine purpose that we need to accept, try to understand and be in harmony with and thereby not stress over. Understanding skillful response requires recognizing heated mind disruptions as opportunities for demonstrating witness consciousness stability rather than personal obstacles requiring elimination. The ancient sages taught that developing "presence of mind"—capacity to remain conscious of consciousness itself even during difficult circumstances—represents practical fruition of spiritual development, since consciousness established in its essential nature cannot be ultimately disturbed by temporary phenomena. Notice how this differs from suppression or avoidance; skillful response involves maintaining sufficient witness consciousness to choose responses based on wisdom rather than being driven by automatic reactions, transforming challenges into occasions for deepening spiritual recognition.

**Early Recognition Techniques:** • Identify heated mind onset before full establishment through awareness of rising agitation, control-seeking impulses, or separateness-projection • Apply immediate intervention through temporary retreat from the challenge, to resume later when there is more calm and thoughtfulness • Return to divine name repetition, conscious breathing regulation, or philosophical discrimination

**Response Strategy for External heated conditions of mind:** • "Desist from, abstain, cease, renounce joining with and gossiping with...the sneaky enemy, the heated person" [4] • "Reject them by turning your mind away from their mind and emotions" [4] • Maintain understanding that "the Divine, in a mysterious way, turns back towards them and provides to them what they need and deserve for their ethical and spiritual evolution" [4]

Practical intervention methods involve establishing preliminary conditions through regular meditation and ethical living that create stability preceding difficulties, combined with immediate response techniques including return to divine name repetition, conscious breathing regulation, and philosophical discrimination between consciousness and mental content. The tradition teaches that prevention proves more effective than remedial action, since consciousness established in optimal levels through daily spiritual practice naturally maintains equilibrium during challenges rather than requiring effortful restoration. Yet working skillfully with disruptions requires understanding that heated mental states serve spiritual development when approached from a perspective of a spiritual aspirant that has intellectually understood the wisdom teachings and has developed sufficient ethical conscience and discipline to approach situations from the perspective of witness consciousness (The all-encompassing Divine ideal), providing feedback about areas requiring continued purification and opportunities for demonstrating practical wisdom rather than merely theoretical understanding. Therefore, practitioners approach heated mind encounters as spiritual practice rather than spiritual failures, maintaining compassionate understanding toward both internal heated patterns and external heated personalities while consistently steering consciousness toward optimal functioning through applied wisdom and sustained spiritual discipline.

## 4. Conscious Life Navigation (Steering the Boat of Life Metaphor)

Sage Amenemopet provides the essential metaphor for conscious spiritual development through his instruction: "Listen, as concerns our boat of life, one should steer away from that which is bad" [4]. The teaching contrasts a heated condition of mind experiencing "forsaking, turning away from the purpose of life and the nature of the Divine (Neberdjer), due to being, as if, carried away on a great swell" with silent consciousness discovering "their boat they are able to sail on fair winds that are pleasant and right for sailing, and right for reaching the destination of life, to reach the hand of God" [4]. This metaphor reveals conscious steering through experience as active, discriminative awareness directing life through conscious choice rather than being swept by unconscious patterns or external circumstances.

Understanding this navigation requires recognizing the Soul-Aware-Witness's capacity to exercise what the tradition calls "spiritual inclinations"—ethics, right thinking, and right feeling flowing from experience of inner fullness rather than ego-driven patterns of external seeking. The boat represents individual consciousness operating through mind-body faculties, while winds represent circumstances and inner tendencies that can either support or obstruct spiritual progress depending on the person's consciousness level. Reflect on how a heated condition of mind creates turbulent life patterns characterized by struggle and dissatisfaction because ego-identification operates through heavy aryu that inevitably generate conflicting desires and reactive responses to changing circumstances.

**Daily Navigation Implementation:** • Begin each day with contemplative study establishing proper spiritual orientation • Maintain awareness of consciousness levels during activities throughout the day • Exercise conscious choice in thoughts, actions, relationships, and environments based on whether they support spiritual development or ego-identification • Conclude each day with reflection on how daily choices either supported or hindered spiritual progress

**Discriminative Choice Criteria:** • Recognize which circumstances support witness consciousness versus those promoting heated mental states • Choose responses based on wisdom rather than automatic reactive patterns • Understand that external circumstances serve consciousness development rather than constituting obstacles to overcome

Practical application involves developing discriminative capacity to recognize which thoughts, actions, relationships, and environments support spiritual development versus those promoting ego-identification and heated mental states. The ancient sages taught that conscious navigation requires preliminary stability in witness consciousness, since consciousness caught in ego-patterns lacks sufficient discrimination for effective steering. Daily practice involves beginning each day with contemplative study establishing proper orientation, maintaining awareness of consciousness levels during activities, and concluding with reflection on how daily choices either supported or hindered spiritual development. Still, effective navigation requires understanding that external circumstances serve consciousness development rather than constituting obstacles to overcome, since the same situations that challenge ego-personality provide opportunities for witness consciousness to demonstrate stability and wisdom. Therefore, practitioners approach life steering as spiritual practice serving both individual awakening and collective service rather than personal advantage seeking at others' expense.

# 5. Integration of Threefold Practice: Ethical Living, Philosophical Study, and Meditation

The Scripture of Ra and Hetheru establishes the comprehensive approach requiring "threefold practice"—ethical living aligned with Maat (divine order), philosophical study developing proper understanding, and meditation practice cultivating direct recognition—working together to systematically dissolve conditions maintaining consciousness in ego-driven patterns [2]. This integration ensures spiritual practice encompasses all dimensions of human experience rather than remaining confined to formal meditation periods, creating what the ancient sages understood as complete spiritual development addressing physical, mental, and spiritual levels simultaneously. The tradition teaches that isolated practices remain superficial, while integrated approach creates cumulative purification effects supporting both individual transformation and collective wellbeing.

Understanding integration requires recognizing how each aspect supports and reinforces the others rather than functioning independently. Ethical living creates environmental conditions allowing subtle spiritual recognition to emerge while generating light aryu that remain transparent to divine consciousness rather than obstructing awareness flow. Philosophical study develops discriminative wisdom necessary for navigating consciousness levels and avoiding common misunderstandings that impede spiritual progress. Meditation practice provides direct methods for consciousness recognition and stabilization beyond ego-identification. Understand how attempting meditation without ethical foundation results in superficial states, while philosophical study without practical application remains merely intellectual, and ethical conduct without understanding lacks spiritual context.

**Daily Integration Suggested Schedule:** • Morning (30 minutes): Philosophical study and contemplation of consciousness teachings • Throughout Day: Continuous awareness practices during normal activities • Evening (30 minutes): Formal meditation and consciousness level recognition • Consistent: Ethical conduct aligned with Maat principles in all interactions and decisions

**Integration Framework:** • Ethical living creates environmental conditions allowing subtle spiritual recognition to emerge • Philosophical study develops discriminative wisdom for navigating consciousness levels and avoiding spiritual misunderstandings • Meditation practice provides direct methods for consciousness recognition and stabilization beyond ego-identification

Daily integration involves morning periods for philosophical study and contemplation (30 minutes), continuous awareness practices during activities throughout the day, evening formal meditation and consciousness level recognition (30 minutes), and consistent ethical conduct aligned with Maat principles in all interactions and decisions. The framework ensures practitioners maintain balance between understanding, experience, and application rather than developing in isolated directions that create spiritual imbalance. At the same time, integration requires sustained commitment over extended periods, since threefold practice creates cumulative effects through consistent application rather than dramatic results through intensive but sporadic efforts. Therefore, practitioners must approach integration as their chosen comprehensive lifestyle rather than addition to existing patterns, understanding that authentic spiritual development transforms the entire approach to living while enhancing rather than diminishing practical effectiveness and service capacity in worldly circumstances.

## 6. Three-Level Consciousness Recognition Training (Soul of Ra, Nunu, Ra)

The Scripture of Ra and Hetheru establishes the fundamental cosmological framework revealing how consciousness manifests through three distinct yet interconnected levels: Soul of Ra representing pure consciousness without subject-object differentiation, Nunu representing undifferentiated consciousness with non-specific awareness, and Ra representing individuated consciousness capable of self-reference and personal identity [2]. Verse 153 provides the metaphysical foundation: Ra's "soul is older than He (Nunu), even as body and mind emerged from Nunu," while verse 155 reveals "The soul of that Divinity, Nunu, is the same soul of Ra, the Creator Spirit, which is the same soul of Asar (Osiris)" [2]. This three-level structure provides an essential framework for understanding how consciousness can discover its transpersonal nature while maintaining functional capacity in the apparently manifest world.

Understanding this framework requires recognizing these as experiential realities rather than theoretical constructs, with each level representing different modes through which the same essential consciousness operates. Soul of Ra consciousness appears as pure being-awareness that transcends all subject-object relationships—existing as what the ancient sages called "beingness without qualification" that underlies all experience while remaining unmodified by particular content. Nunu consciousness functions as spacious, undifferentiated awareness that encompasses all mental activity without concentrating on particular contents, like an ocean containing all waves without being disturbed by wave formations. Ra consciousness encompasses individuated divine awareness that can function effectively in relationships and responsibilities while operating from wisdom rather than ego-driven patterns, maintaining recognition of essential unity with universal consciousness.

**Basic Recognition Training:** • Ra Recognition: Cultivate awakened individuality that serves divine purpose rather than ego-gratification • Nunu Recognition: Learn to recognize moments when consciousness rests in itself without particular focus or content. Develop capacity to maintain spacious, undifferentiated awareness during meditation and daily activities • Soul of Ra Recognition: There is no training for experiencing Soul of Ra Consciousness. This occurs organically, of its own accord, in time as Ra and Nunu awareness are cultivated. It may occur at first through glimpses and eventually becomes perennial.

Recognition training involves systematic development of discriminative capacity to identify these subtle but crucial distinctions within awareness rather than seeking exotic states. Practitioners begin by learning to recognize moments when consciousness rests in itself without particular focus, developing capacity to maintain spacious awareness during meditation and daily activities (Nunu stabilization), and cultivating awakened individuality that serves divine purpose rather than ego-gratification (Ra integration). Observe how this represents consciousness learning to access multiple levels according to need while maintaining constant recognition of essential divine nature—integrated consciousness that serves both individual awakening and collective wellbeing. Yet this development requires extensive preparation through aryu purification and ethical living, since heavy karmic impressions cloud the subtle recognition necessary for distinguishing between consciousness levels and prevent stable establishment in higher functioning.

## 7. Integrated Divine Name and Sacred Utterance Practices

The Ancient Egyptian Creation Scripture B includes an instruction to perform "circular invocation"—recurring, cyclical practice of chanting the Divine name (Ra, Ra, Ra, Ra, etc., or Nuk Ra (I am Ra), Nuk Ra, Nuk Ra etc.) in order to ward off the negative aspects of the personality that cause slothfulness, inattentiveness, feelings of incapacity, intellectual dullness and general malaise in the personality that prevent spiritual progress. This passage (of Ancient Egyptian Creation Scripture B) can be directly correlated to the injunction in the Scripture of Ra and Hetheru where the chant "I am Ra" is admonished for promoting spiritual evolution and spiritual discovery of the innate Ra (Divine) nature of the personality.

## The Practice of Circular Invocation

**Trilinear Translation of Creation Scripture B Verses 58-59[47]:**

Verse 58.
58.1. shenut senu    ren {Net}    secher    senu
58.2. circular-invocation they name {divine-mine} overthrow    they
58.3. They utter circular-invocations using my divine name (name of Ra) in order that they may overthrow…

Verse 59.
59.1. cheftu senu   qemam        senu hekau        en
59.2. enemies theirs create       they word-of-power    for
59.3. …their enemies (opposition, negativity, slothfulness, disagreeableness in the personality). They can do so by creating words of power

This practice serves as both a method for purifying heavy aryu and a means for stabilizing consciousness in its divine nature. Notice

---

[47] Translation by Dr. Muata Ashby ©2023 Sema Institute of Yoga

how the repetitive invocation of the divine name creates what the ancient sages called "momentum patterns" that gradually override the automatic reactive patterns stored in the unconscious mind. Furthermore, this represents one of the most practical methods for transforming heated mind states into silent mind functioning.

The ancient Egyptian scriptures reveal multiple integrated approaches to consciousness transformation through sacred sound, combining expanded consciousness name repetition, HEKAU (Words of Power), progressive declarations, and circular invocation into comprehensive spiritual technology. The Scripture of Ra and Hetheru provides specific instruction for "concentrating on higher consciousness with name and form, such as the name of Ra," while Creation Scripture B establishes "shenut" (circular invocation) as systematic practice for creating "words of power" that enable practitioners to "overthrow their enemies (opposition, negativity, slothfulness, disagreeableness in the personality)" [2]. These practices function as transformative instruments designed to fundamentally alter consciousness through what Ra declares: "Those Words-of-Power, they are indeed my very self... I am in those Words-of-Power" [2].

Understanding integrated sacred utterance requires recognizing these practices as progressive levels of the same fundamental technology rather than separate techniques. Basic name repetition using "Ra" creates momentum patterns that gradually override automatic reactive patterns, progressing to HEKAU (words of power) that function as "divine vibrations that, when properly understood and expressed, carry the creative force of Ra (Creator Spirit) himself." Advanced practitioners engage progressive declarations beginning with "I am the Divine word of power" and advancing through "I am Ra's glorious (light) shining spirit" toward ultimate realization "I am Ra" as character purification creates capacity for these recognitions. Additionally, the utterance of the divine name in and of itself carries an enlightening force that works with the wisdom and ethical purification efforts to clear out obstructions and promote movement towards enlightenment (discovery of self as one with Divine Being). Circular invocation (shenut) encompasses the recurring, cyclical practice that creates cumulative transformation through "sacred repetition technology" rather than dramatic immediate states.

## Progressive Practice Levels:

1. Basic Name Repetition: 75 repetitions of "Ra" or "Nuk Ra" (I am Ra) coordinated with natural breathing daily
2. Continuous Mental Repetition: Maintain divine name repetition throughout daily activities when the mind is not occupied with required tasks
3. Progressive Declarations: Begin with "I am the Divine word of power," advance through "I am Ra's glorious shining spirit," toward "I am Ra"
4. Circular Invocation (Shenut): Recurring cyclical practice creating cumulative transformation

**Daily Implementation:** • Formal Periods: Dedicated morning and evening sessions for concentrated practice • Informal Integration: Mental repetition during routine activities like walking, cleaning, commuting • Emergency Application: Immediate return to divine name during heated mind disruptions

Practical application involves systematic daily integration beginning with formal periods of name repetition (for example: uttering 75 repetitions of "Ra" coordinated with natural breathing), progressing to continuous mental repetition throughout activities, and incorporating progressive declarations as spiritual maturity develops. The circular aspect indicates both recurring practice and complete consciousness transformation affecting all levels of mental activity rather than isolated spiritual experiences. At the same time, effectiveness depends entirely upon what the ancient sages called Maa-kheru (truth-speaking)—consciousness sufficiently purified through ethical living and spiritual discipline before creative power properly manifests. Therefore, practitioners must combine systematic sacred utterance with truthfulness in communications, justice in dealings, harmlessness toward beings, and service-oriented activity that embodies rather than contradicts the divine nature being invoked, understanding that these practices work through aligning individual consciousness with divine consciousness rather than only creating mental states through mechanical repetition.

There is one more point that is important for understanding the use of the circular invocation of the Divine name. Since all gods and goddesses mentioned, for example, in texts such as the

Ancient Egyptian Book of Enlightenment or the Scripture of Ra and Hetheru are derivations from the original, absolute Being, that can be designated as Ra, Neberdjer, Asar or Ba en Ra, it means that any invocation of any of the derivative names of the gods or goddesses that emanate from the primary understanding of Divinity will serve the same purpose and lead back to a universal and transcendental understanding of Divine Being.

## 8. Aryu Purification Through Spiritual Roasting (Vital-Life-Fire Development)

The Scripture of Ra and Hetheru provides detailed instruction on aryu purification through what verse 177 describes as "vital-life-fire" that "acts as a fire of wisdom that burns away delusions and egoism," roasting "the egoistic perturbations of the mind and its thoughts, feelings, desires and memories (aryu) that prevent the soul from realizing the truth of Higher Self" [2]. Verses 128-129 establish that "within humans there are egoistic mental impressions (aryu/karmic remnants) that develop from experiences and actions in current and previous lifetimes" which "manifest as feeling memories, recorded and reinforced patterns" that "remain registered in the unconscious mind, influencing present and future experiences" [2]. This spiritual roasting represents systematic dissolution of accumulated karmic patterns through sustained spiritual practice rather than temporary purification experiences.

Understanding this process requires recognizing that aryu function like winds disturbing the ocean of undifferentiated consciousness, creating waves of differentiated mental phenomena that pull awareness into ego-identification and heated mental states. The tradition teaches that "the practice of the myth, ritual, ethics and meditations in the scripture develops vital-life-fire within the personality" that operates as transformative wisdom-fire burning away "delusion and ignorance fomenting desire for ephemeral existence" [2]. Reflect on how this differs from suppression or forced elimination of mental patterns; spiritual roasting works through consciousness becoming so saturated with divine presence that egoistic patterns naturally dissolve without resistance, like darkness disappearing when light appears.

**Comprehensive Spiritual Discipline:** • Ethical Foundation: Daily alignment with Maat principles in all actions and decisions • Contemplative Study: Regular engagement with wisdom teachings that develop proper understanding • Divine Name Practice: Systematic repetition creating internal spiritual fire • Regular Meditation: Formal periods allowing consciousness to settle into higher recognition

**Recognition of Progress:** • Notice decreased reactivity to circumstances that previously created agitation • Experience increased capacity for maintaining peace during challenging situations • Observe spontaneous arising of wisdom and compassion rather than ego-driven responses • Recognize growing sense of inner fullness reducing dependence on external validation

Practical application involves comprehensive spiritual discipline combining ethical living, contemplative study, divine name repetition, and regular meditation that generates cumulative purification effects over extended time periods. The ancient sages taught that consistent practice creates internal conditions allowing what verse 178 describes: "The words-of-power are within me and the vital-life-fire passes through me" [2], indicating personality becoming transparent to divine forces rather than obstructed by egoistic resistance. Still, this purification requires patience and sustained commitment, since accumulated aryu represent lifetimes of conditioning that dissolve gradually through proper spiritual discipline rather than sudden transformation. Therefore, practitioners must approach aryu purification as systematic spiritual work requiring foundation in ethics, regular practice periods, and integration with daily life responsibilities, understanding that spiritual roasting serves liberation from unconscious patterns while supporting enhanced functionality and service capacity in worldly circumstances.

## 9. Contemplative Study and Philosophical Discrimination

The Wisdom Text of Sage Amenemopet establishes contemplative study as "wisdom philosophy that is based on recorded wisdom literature that is to be experienced in life" rather than remaining merely intellectual concepts [4]. The prologue of the text declares this represents "an exposition of precise teachings that when understood exactly, with precision cause a person to have well-being while living on earth" [4]. This method involves engaging in right thinking and feeling based on the truth that Ra consciousness represents the higher reality of life, taking the form of spiritual studies that develop discriminative wisdom capable of distinguishing between temporary mental phenomena and the unchanging awareness that witnesses all mental activity.

**Daily Study Implementation:** • Morning Study (20-30 minutes): Engage with ancient Egyptian wisdom texts using trilinear methodology • Philosophical Discrimination Practice: Distinguish between temporary mental phenomena and unchanging awareness that witnesses mental activity • Truth Investigation: Concentrate on philosophy about the illusoriness of mind and senses while affirming reality of higher perceptions • Subject-Object Training: Develop capacity to maintain awareness of being the subject that observes rather than becoming identified with objects being observed

### Discrimination Development Stages:

1. Intellectual Foundation: Study consciousness teachings until clearly understood
2. Applied Discrimination: Practice distinguishing consciousness from mental content during daily activities
3. Stabilized Wisdom: Maintain discriminative capacity during challenging circumstances
4. Natural Expression: Philosophical understanding becomes spontaneous wisdom rather than effortful analysis

The practice begins with putting attention on what represents higher truth instead of the falsehoods presented by illusory perceptions and deluded ideas learned previously in life. Understand how this involves concentrating on the philosophy about the illusoriness of mind and senses while affirming the reality of higher perceptions as the mind becomes calmed and higher awareness is discovered. The tradition teaches that this systematic study allows practitioners to proceed with appropriate skepticism toward mental content while leaning on direct experience of fundamental awareness itself, developing what may be termed "subject-object discrimination"—the capacity to maintain awareness of being the subject that observes rather than becoming identified with the objects being observed.

Even so, intellectual understanding represents only the beginning of consciousness development rather than its completion. The ancient sages taught that the mind's intellectual capacity, when properly directed, can investigate its own limitations and point toward the awareness that underlies mental activity, creating foundation for recognizing consciousness as distinct from mental content. This investigation naturally progresses from studying consciousness levels theoretically toward direct experiential recognition through sustained practice and philosophical discrimination, transforming abstract spiritual concepts into practical wisdom that enhances rather than diminishes one's effectiveness in worldly circumstances while serving genuine spiritual transformation.

## 10. Recognition of Universal Soul Consciousness (Asar Consciousness) Operating Through Individual Forms

Ancient Egyptian Book of Enlightenment Chapter 43 reveals the profound teaching that "there is one universal consciousness operating through all human beings, and in the scripture this universal consciousness is called Asar (Osiris), the universal soul" [1]. Every spiritual initiate receives the title "Asar" followed by their given name, revealing fundamental truth: "Asar represents the first and only reality—the universal soul consciousness that is the true identity of all beings—while the given name designates only the individual mind and body through which this universal consciousness operates" [1]. Verse 4.3 demonstrates this recognition: "I am Osiris, the Lord of Eternity, the one who does not age and is universal consciousness ever aware, ever shining" [1].

Understanding this teaching requires recognizing that individual spiritual development actually represents universal consciousness recognizing its own nature through apparent individual forms rather than separate entities achieving personal enlightenment. The tradition reveals that consciousness development involves learning to distinguish between ego-delusion (universal consciousness thinking it is individual ego-identity) and divine recognition (universal consciousness aware of its true nature operating through individual faculties). Notice how the "Asar Any formula" demonstrates this practically: the same practitioner simultaneously referenced as both universal soul (Asar/Osiris) and individual personality (Any) within the same declaration, revealing these as different aspects of recognition by same consciousness rather than separate realities.

## Progressive Recognition Practice:

1. Formula Understanding: Study the "Asar Any formula" demonstrating simultaneous universal and individual identity
2. Contemplative Investigation: Examine the Soul-Aware-Witness until recognizing it as universal consciousness temporarily focused through apparent individual awareness
3. Declaration Practice: Progress from "I am Asar [name ]" to "I am Asar" to "I am Osiris, the Lord of Eternity"

Practical recognition develops through systematic investigation of the Soul-Aware-Witness until consciousness discovers that what appears as individual witnessing actually represents universal Asar consciousness temporarily focused through apparent individual awareness. The ancient sages taught that "if the person understands that their conscious-awareness is not the individual ego but the universal soul, then that 'Soul-Aware-Witness' becomes as if a transparent mirror through which the true natural witness-consciousness can operate as the identity that perceives and is aware through the mind, senses, and body of that personality" [1]. Yet this recognition requires preliminary stabilization in witness consciousness and extensive aryu purification, since ego-identification creates mental opacity preventing recognition of universal nature. Therefore, practitioners must establish a foundation through ethical living, contemplative study, and meditation practice that gradually clarifies consciousness sufficiently to recognize its essential nature as universal soul rather than separate individual entity seeking spiritual development.

## 11. Subtle Awareness Investigation Methods Including Gap Extension and Deep Sleep Investigation

The tradition provides sophisticated methods for investigating awareness beyond ordinary mental activity, including gap extension practice that lengthens spaces between thoughts and deep sleep awareness investigation that intellectually recognizes consciousness continuing through states where individual awareness becomes inactive. These techniques serve consciousness development by revealing the awareness that exists independently of mental content, demonstrating practically what the teachings describe as witness consciousness—unchanging awareness that observes all changing phenomena without being affected by them [1]. The practice establishes that "practitioners can discover that they can be aware of thoughts and feelings, which means they are separate from their thoughts and feelings," providing foundation for advanced investigation of awareness operating "without mind and senses and in fact exists even when mind and senses are non-operative" [1].

**Systematic Investigation Process:**

1. Initial Recognition: Practice noticing the capacity to observe thoughts without being identical to them during daily mental activity
2. Expanded Observation: Systematically recognize that emotions, memories, and preferences can be observed as objects rather than identity
3. Separation Discovery: Realize through careful attention that the observer remains constant while observed content changes continuously

4. Essential Identity Recognition: Recognize awareness itself as the true subject rather than mental formations

**Suggested Daily Implementation:** Spend 10-15 minutes daily practicing awareness of thoughts and feelings as observed objects rather than self-identity. Progress to recognizing this observing capacity during routine activities.

## Progressive Recognition Stages:

1. Gap Recognition: Notice the awareness that persists between thoughts during waking consciousness
2. Background Continuity: Recognize the unchanging awareness present through all states—waking, dream, and deep sleep
3. Independence Discovery: Realize awareness exists independently of mental content and sensory input

Gap extension practice involves recognizing and gradually lengthening the natural spaces between thoughts that occur continuously during waking consciousness through techniques promoting mental calmness. Understanding this method requires distinguishing between forced mental suppression and natural settling that allows consciousness to rest in its essential nature, an experience of awareness between two mental modifications (gap/period between thoughts) that can be extended by extending the interval between thoughts. This experience can become the permanent and perpetual recognized background of awareness becoming known by a person as their deeper self-identity. The practice begins with coordinating awareness recognition with natural breathing rhythm, progressing through gentle non-engagement with arising thoughts, developing capacity for silent intervals between activities, and allowing gap-recognition to expand spontaneously rather than through effortful concentration.

This reveals the natural silence underlying all mental activity—not as absence of content but as spacious awareness in which all content arises and dissolves. The awareness that observes these rising and falling mental contents remains unchanging, detached, and complete within itself. This is the witnessing self that exists separate from mind, feelings, and body.

As recognition of this witnessing self develops, its peaceful and enlightened nature begins to permeate the personality. The mind, feelings, and body gradually, over time, acclimate to this enlightened quality of consciousness. It is not uncommon that during this period of acclimation that some remaining unresolved aryu may emerge that offer challenges to the enlightened state of awareness. They are to be seen as illusory remnants of ego past impressions that are to be faced and allowed to be sublimated through the continuing lifestyle based on awareness, spiritual reflection and ethical living. This process naturally moves the personality away from reactive agitation and reflexive somatic responses to worldly stimuli. Instead, the mind, feelings, and body begin developing thoughts, emotional responses, and behaviors rooted in the deeper reality of the witnessing self rather than ego-driven patterns.

## Deep Sleep Awareness Investigation

## Investigative Approach Implementation:

1. Pre-Sleep Awareness: Maintain subtle awareness during the transition into sleep while avoiding forced wakefulness
2. Sleep Continuity Recognition: Develop sensitivity to the awareness that continues through deep sleep
3. Awakening Investigation: Notice the awareness that was present before thoughts resumed upon awakening
4. Constant Recognition: Recognize awareness as the unchanging background of all states

Deep sleep investigation represents subtle practice requiring careful attention to continuity of awareness through states where ordinary waking consciousness becomes inactive, demonstrating that consciousness never actually ceases but rather withdraws from engagement with external stimuli and mental activity. Practitioners learn to recognize the truth about the continuity of awareness of consciousness through deep sleep, by noting that awareness is present before thoughts resume upon awakening and develop recognition of awareness as unchanging background of all states (waking, dream, deep dreamless sleep). Still, these advanced methods require preliminary stability in basic witness consciousness and ethical purification, since heavy aryu create mental agitation that prevents the subtle sensitivity necessary for investigating consciousness beyond ordinary mental activity. Therefore, students must establish a foundation through contemplative study, regular meditation, and Maat-based living before attempting these refined awareness investigation techniques.

**Practical Development Implementation:** • Breathing Coordination: Use natural breathing rhythm to extend thought-gaps without forced breath control • Gentle Non-Engagement: Allow thoughts to arise and dissolve without pursuing them mentally or emotionally • Silent Intervals: Gradually lengthen periods of mental silence between daily activities • Natural Expansion: Allow gap-recognition to occur spontaneously rather than forcing silence through effort

**Progressive Training:** Begin with 2-3 seconds+ gap extensions during meditation, gradually allowing natural silence to emerge during daily activities.

## 12. Reflection-Contemplation on the Non-Objective Qualities of **Expanded** Consciousness

### HYMN TO RA from the Ancient Egyptian Book of Enlightenment Papyrus Hunefer- Presented at the 2015 Neterian Conference. Translation by Dr. Muata Ashby

Adorations to Ra by the Scribe Hunefer

The Hymn to Ra by Hunefer reveals profound spiritual qualities of Ra consciousness that transcend ordinary subject-object relationships, serving as gateways for consciousness to recognize its essential divine nature beyond ego-identification and mental conceptualization. These qualities—including Self-Originating Pure Consciousness, Pure Witness Consciousness, Self-Luminous Awareness, and Absolute Peace—emerge throughout the hymn's 26 verses as systematic descriptions of consciousness in its transcendent mode, pointing beyond the mind's tendency to create dualistic divisions toward recognition of awareness as inherently divine. The ancient sages designed these contemplative focuses to elevate consciousness above personalized ways of relating to

## Awakening Your Soul-Aware-Witness

experience, revealing the transcendent nature that underlies all temporary mental modifications.

Understanding these non-objective qualities requires approaching them not as concepts to be analyzed intellectually but as doorways for recognizing these aspects within one's own essential nature. The practice involves systematic investigation of qualities such as Unity Manifesting as Multiplicity (recognizing how the One appears as many without division), Transcendence of Time and Causation (consciousness existing beyond sequential limitation), and Pure Subjectivity (the ultimate "I AM" that can never be objectified). Observe how each quality serves as a contemplative focus that helps dissolve the ego-mind's habitual subject-object structuring, gradually revealing the seamless awareness that is our essential nature.

The practical approach requires setting aside dedicated time for contemplative reflection where consciousness can investigate these qualities through direct recognition rather than mental analysis. Practitioners learn to contemplate, for example, Self-Luminous Awareness by recognizing the consciousness that illuminates all experience while needing no external source for its own knowing capacity, or Absolute Peace by investigating the awareness that remains undisturbed regardless of mental or emotional content. Moreover, this systematic contemplation of Ra's transcendent qualities gradually purifies the mind's tendency toward dualistic perception, allowing consciousness to recognize its own divine attributes that were always present but obscured by ego-identification and the accumulated patterns of heated mental activity.

Verse 1.
*1.1.* ***Dua Ra cheft uben    f    im akhet    abtet***
1.2. <u>Adorations Ra when rising he    in    horizon    eastern</u>
1.3. Adorations to the God Ra when he rises, shining, as the sun in the eastern horizon…

Verse 2.
**2.1.**     ent pet   in   Asar Hunefer   maa kheru Djed f
2.2.     of heaven by  Osiris  GoodTaste true of speech. Says  he
2.3.     of heaven, emerging from the heaven/netherworld to shine on the physical plane. These are words spoken by the initiate whose name is "Osiris, One of good sense of taste," or one who is sensitive to the flavor of spiritual life, who is righteous.

Verse 3.
**3.1.**     Anetj hera   k   Ra   im   uben   f
3.2.     Adorations person thee Ra   form  rising/shining  he
3.3.     Adorations to you who are the entity manifesting as Ra, the Creator, when shining in the sky, is he...

Verse 4.
**4.1.**     Temu   im   hetep - f   uben   k   sep sen
4.2.     Temu  as   peace – he  rising/shining thee  times two
4.3.     and also, when he is in the form of Temu when he is setting at sunset. You rise twice

Verse 5.
**5.1.**     pezed  k   sep sen   kha   tj   im   suten neteru
5.2.     illumining thee times two  crown  tie   in   king divinities
5.3.     lighting up the world are you, and you do this twice. Your rising is your crown as we recognize you as the king of all the gods and goddesses.

Verse 6.

Awakening Your Soul-Aware-Witness

6.1.     *ent – k neb    pet      neb     ta      ari     her-petu*
6.2.     of - thee lord heaven    lord     earth    Creator heavenly
6.3.     You are the lord of heaven, the astral plane and the lord of the earth and physical Creation. You are also the maker of heavenly beings and

Verse 7.
7.1.     *kheru      Neter    Uau       kheper     im     zep*
7.2.     earthly beings Divinity One      creation     in    time
7.3.     earthly beings.    You are the Supreme Being, only one, who self-created itself at the time of

Verse 8.
8.1.     *tepy     ari        tau     qemam         rekhytu*
8.2.     first   maker   worlds/universe creator        people
8.3.     the beginning of time and Creation itself. You are the maker of the physical universe and creator of human beings.

Verse 9.
9.1.     *Ari   nunu       qemam       hapy       ari     net*
9.2.     Maker    primeval ocean   creator Nile river maker     of
9.3.     Maker of the primeval ocean, the substratum from which Creation is made. Creator of the Nile river which sustains life in our land; and maker of…

Verse 10.
10.1.     *mu   s-ankh    im      - z      tjezu       duu*
10.2.     water causing-life in   - it     knitting     mountains
10.3.     …water and the source that causes that water to have life sustaining properties and you are also responsible for the interweaving (construction of the constituent parts) together of the mountains and all physical creation.

Verse 11.
**11.1.**    S – kheper remteju     menmenu     ari     pet
11.2.    Cause coming into being men women cattle     maker   heaven
11.3.    You are the one who caused human beings to come into existence and likewise cattle and other animals. You are the maker of heaven

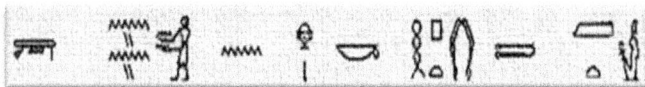

Verse 12.
**12.1.**    ta     nyny     en     her     k     hept     tj     Maat
12.2.    earth. Praises     to personality thine embraced tied truth- righteousness
12.3.    and earth. Praises be to you, the personality, which is embraced, even more, tied with the justice, order and truth of existence.

Verse 13.
**13.1.**    er   trauy     nem     - k     hert     im     awet ab
13.2.    about double period stepping - thee contentedly heaven in expanded heart
13.3.    Ra strides along twice daily, at morning and evening, over the heavens with contented heart full of joy.

Verse 14.
**14.1.**    Mer-n-desdes     kheper im hetepu     Neka     cher
14.2.    sacred lake in the Duat becomes in peace   serpent Neka     fall
14.3.    and the sacred lake in the Nether-world has become peaceful; also, the serpent Neka, a negative spirit who is opposed to Ra and his daily course through the sky, he has been defeated and has fallen so the obstacle to Ra's shining forwards has been removed.

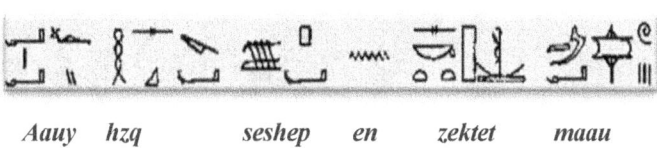

Verse 15.
**15.1.**    Aauy     hzq     seshep     en     zektet     maau
15.2.    Arms     cut     receives     the   boat of morning breezes

Awakening Your Soul-Aware-Witness

15.3.   The arms of that enemy of Ra have been cut off. The boat of the rising sun received breezes to make its journey effective and

Verse 16.
*16.1.*   nefer   im   kara   - f   ab-f   nedjm   khau
16.2.   pleased  in  sanctuary - he  heart –his gleeful  rising
16.3.   the one who resides in the shrine, his heart is delighted at seeing the rising of

Verse 17.
*17.1.*   m   sekhem   en   pet   ua   sepd   pert
17.2.   in  power  to heaven  one  provisioned  going-forth
17.3.   Ra in his full power and glory up to the heavens going forth with all provisions needed, as all properly prepared boat voyages do.

Verse 18.
*18.1.*   m   nunu   Ra   im   maa kheru   hun   netery
18.2.   from  primeval waters Ra  as true of speech child  divine
18.3.   Ra emerges from the primeval ocean of Creation, the undifferentiated primordial consciousness that is the body of Ra. Ra does this with all righteousness and truth and order, he does this as that same divine child, Nefertem,

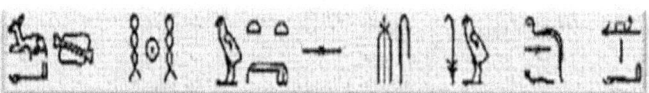

Verse 19.
*19.1.*   ua   heh   utet   – z   mes   su   djesef   ua
19.2.   heir  eternity  begetter (of) it  child  he  himself  one
19.3.   who is the inheritor of timelessness, and the one who gave birth to himself by himself; Ra is one

Awakening Your Soul-Aware-Witness

Verse 20.
**20.1.**    *ur    tenu        aru          suten   tawiu    heqa*
20.2.    great  manifold    forms        king    Creation prince[48]
20.3.    great and his forms are multifarious; he is monarch of
         Creation and prince of…

Verse 21.
**21.1.**    *Anu    zesh    m    djeta    paut    neteru    m    henu*
21.2.    Anu  pass through  end of time, company gods goddesses form praisers
21.3.    … Heliopolis (Anu), the site of the first creation, Ra's royal
         city. You move through time until forever, the end of time, as
         the company of gods and goddesses praises you

Verse 22.
**22.1.**    *en   uben – k    khenen    im    akhet    saq        im*
22.2.    the   rising -thine  rowing in  horizon  exaltation  in
22.3.    there as you rise and row towards the evening horizon.
         Shouts of exaltation are heard in

Verse 23.
**23.1.**    *zektet    anetj hra – k   Amun-Ra    hetep    her        Maat*
23.2.    evening boat.  Adorations – thee  Hidden-Light  peace  person
                                                            righteousness, truth
23.3.    Your boat of the evening. We adore you in your form of
         Amun-Ra ["Hidden Radiance"] as you move in peace and
         balance and your person is the very embodiment of
         righteousness, order, truth and justice

---

[48] In this context the term "zer" relates to nobility, royalty and specifically to a spiritual royalty. One of the 75 names of Ra is zer aah "Great noble one". The god Asar (Osiris) is similarly referred to. Nevertheless, the construction of the sentence means that Ra is not The Ultimate God but a descendant of that Supreme Being.

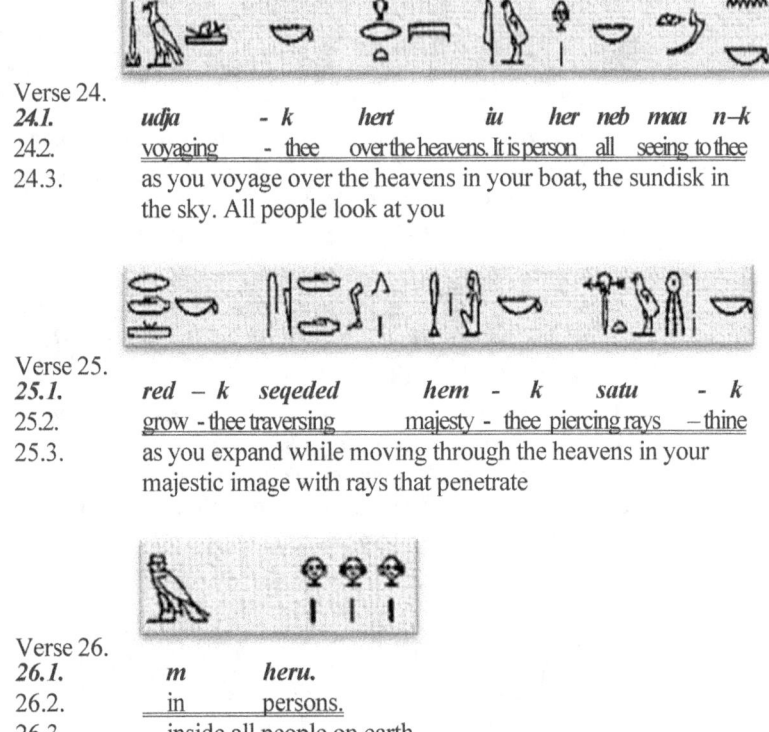

Verse 24.
*24.1.*    udja     - k     hert     iu     her neb maa n–k
24.2.     <u>voyaging    - thee    over the heavens. It is person all    seeing to thee</u>
24.3.     as you voyage over the heavens in your boat, the sundisk in the sky. All people look at you

Verse 25.
*25.1.*    red – k     seqeded     hem - k     satu     - k
25.2.     <u>grow - thee traversing     majesty - thee piercing rays    – thine</u>
25.3.     as you expand while moving through the heavens in your majestic image with rays that penetrate

Verse 26.
*26.1.*    m     heru.
26.2.     <u>in     persons.</u>
26.3.     inside all people on earth.

# HYMN TO RA and the Contemplative Investigation of Ra's Non-Objective Qualities

The Hymn to Ra reveals profound spiritual qualities that transcend ordinary subject-object relationships, serving as gateways for consciousness to recognize its essential divine nature beyond ego-identification and mental conceptualization. These non-objective qualities represent aspects of Ra consciousness that cannot be grasped through analytical thinking but must be approached through contemplative recognition—direct awareness of these qualities as inherent features of consciousness itself rather than external objects to be understood intellectually.

Reflect on how these qualities—including Self-Originating Pure Consciousness, Pure Witness Consciousness, Self-Luminous Awareness, and Absolute Peace and Contentment—point beyond the ordinary mind's tendency to create subject-object divisions toward recognition of awareness as inherently divine. Furthermore, the ancient sages designed these contemplative focuses to elevate consciousness above personalized ways of relating to experience, revealing the transcendent nature of awareness that underlies all temporary mental modifications.

The practice involves contemplating each quality not as a concept to be analyzed but as a doorway for recognizing these aspects within one's own essential nature. Through systematic investigation of qualities such as Unity Manifesting as Multiplicity, Transcendence of Time and Causation, and Pure Subjectivity, practitioners develop the subtle discrimination necessary for recognizing Ra consciousness as the foundation of individual awareness rather than a distant spiritual ideal.

These contemplative investigations serve the tradition's understanding that consciousness development occurs through recognition rather than acquisition—discovering what has always been present but obscured by ego-identification and the accumulated patterns of heated mental activity that prevent natural spiritual sensitivity from emerging.

## Contemplative Reflections based on the Hymn to Ra

Based on the Hymn to Ra, several profound non-objective spiritual qualities of Ra (Creator Spirit) emerge that transcend ordinary subject-object relationships and invite devotional contemplation beyond personalized ways of understanding reality. These qualities serve to elevate consciousness toward the transcendent nature of divine awareness itself.

**Self-Originating Pure Consciousness** Ra embodies the mystery of self-generating awareness that has no external source or beginning. Verse 19.3 reveals Ra as "the inheritor of timelessness, and the one who gave birth to himself by himself." This quality points to pure consciousness that exists independently of all conditions, causes, or external supports—the very ground of being itself that neither comes into existence nor ceases to exist, but simply IS as the eternal foundation of all awareness.

**Transcendence of Time and Causation** The hymn presents Ra as "heir of eternity" who exists beyond temporal limitations and sequential causation. This non-objective quality invites contemplation of awareness that is eternally present—neither past nor future, but the timeless now that underlies all temporal experience. Notice how this points beyond ordinary consciousness bound by before-and-after thinking toward the eternal present that is consciousness itself.

**Unity Manifesting as Multiplicity** Verse 20.3 describes Ra's forms as "multifarious" while remaining essentially one being. This reveals the transcendent quality of consciousness appearing as infinite diversity while never losing its essential unity. For devotional reflection, this points to the mystery of how the One appears as many without division or fragmentation—the seamless wholeness that encompasses all apparent differences within its singular nature.

**Pure Witness Consciousness** Verse 24.3 shows that "all people look at" Ra as he voyages overhead, establishing him as the ultimate seer who observes all without being affected by what is seen. This quality transcends the subject-object relationship by pointing to pure witnessing awareness—consciousness that illuminates all experience while remaining untouched by the content of experience, like space that contains all objects without being modified by them.

**Self-Luminous Awareness** The hymn repeatedly emphasizes Ra's light not as external illumination but as consciousness itself that is inherently self-aware and self-revealing. This quality invites contemplation beyond physical or mental light toward the very awareness through which all knowing occurs—the consciousness that needs no external source to know its own nature.

**Absolute Peace and Contentment** Verse 13.3 describes Ra moving "with contented heart full of joy" and Verse 23.3 shows him moving "in peace and balance." This reveals consciousness in its natural state as inherently peaceful and complete, needing nothing external for fulfillment. This quality transcends seeking and striving toward the recognition of awareness as already whole and satisfied in its own nature.

**Hidden-Revealed Paradox** The reference to "Amun-Ra" (Hidden-Witness-Consciousness) in Verse 23.2 points to consciousness that is simultaneously completely present yet beyond all manifestation. This quality invites contemplation of awareness that is closer than close yet transcends all categories and descriptions—the mystery of what is most intimate yet most transcendent.

**Compassionate Responsiveness Without Attachment** Throughout the hymn, Ra responds to worship and maintains order while remaining unaffected by praise or blame. This quality points to consciousness that is naturally responsive and caring yet free from attachment to outcomes—love that flows freely without need or dependency.

**Source of Order Beyond All Categories** As embodiment of cosmic order (Maat), Ra establishes harmony and justice while transcending all rules and limitations. This quality invites contemplation of consciousness as the source of all order that is itself beyond ordering—the lawless law that establishes all principles while remaining free from all constraints.

**Eternal Renewal Without Change** The cyclical journey described in the hymn reveals consciousness that is constantly fresh and new while never actually changing. This paradoxical quality points to awareness that is eternally present and alive yet completely stable and unchanging—the dynamic stillness that is the ground of all experience.

**Pure Subjectivity** Most profoundly, Ra represents the ultimate "I AM"—pure subjectivity that can never be made into an object of knowledge yet is the very essence through which all knowing occurs. This quality transcends all dualistic relationships by pointing to consciousness as the absolute subject that uses mind and senses to interact with objects but is never separate from its own knowing nature.

These non-objective qualities of Ra consciousness serve as doorways for transcending ordinary ego-based awareness and recognizing the divine nature of consciousness itself. What's more, as the ancient sages taught, contemplation of these transcendent qualities gradually dissolves the mind's habitual subject-object structuring, revealing the seamless awareness that is our essential nature—the very Ra consciousness that shines as the heart of all experience.

**Daily Contemplative Practice Suggestions based on the text:** • Self-Originating Pure Consciousness: Contemplate awareness that has no external source, existing independently of all conditions • Transcendence of Time and Causation: Investigate consciousness as eternally present rather than bound by sequential thinking • Unity Manifesting as Multiplicity: Reflect on how the One appears as many without division • Pure Witness Consciousness: Recognize awareness that illuminates all experience while remaining untouched by content • Self-Luminous Awareness: Contemplate consciousness that needs no external source to know its own nature

**Implementation Suggestions:** • Weekly Focus: Dedicate each week to contemplating one specific quality • Daily Sessions: 15-20 minutes of non-analytical reflection on chosen quality • Integration Practice: Notice these qualities manifesting during daily experience; Journal your experiences. • Progressive Recognition: Allow conceptual understanding to transform into direct recognition

**Devotional Aspects of the Hymn**

The contemplation of Ra's non-objective qualities naturally evokes profound devotional feeling that transcends ordinary emotional responses, awakening what the ancient sages understood as spiritual awe—the soul's recognition of its own divine source manifesting in overwhelming majesty and beauty. When consciousness truly investigates these transcendent attributes—Ra as the self-originating awareness that "gave birth to himself by himself," the eternal renewal that never changes, the unity manifesting as infinite multiplicity while remaining seamlessly whole—the appropriate response emerges as complete reverence and surrender to this magnificent reality. Furthermore, compared to the unlimited, self-luminous, eternally peaceful consciousness that Ra represents, all ordinary objects of human attachment and ego-concern reveal themselves as derivative shadows, temporary modifications of the one supreme reality that alone deserves undivided dedication and worship.

This devotional recognition serves a crucial spiritual function by naturally sublimating ego-driven emotions into what may be termed "sacred feeling"—the heart's spontaneous response to recognizing the absolute truth of existence. The ancient wisdom reveals that when consciousness genuinely comprehends Ra's transcendent nature as pure witness awareness, self-luminous knowledge, and the hidden-revealed mystery that is "closer than close yet most transcendent," the ego's habitual patterns of seeking fulfillment through external means become transformed into singular devotion to this awesome reality. Understand how this devotional transformation occurs not through forced emotional manipulation but through the natural response of consciousness recognizing its own infinite nature—like a wave discovering it is the ocean, the appropriate feeling is overwhelming gratitude, reverence, and the desire to surrender all limited identifications to this boundless truth.

The profound understanding emerges that this same absolute reality—whether called Ra, Amun-Ra, Neberdjer, Asar, or other sacred names throughout the Ancient Egyptian scriptures—represents the one divine consciousness manifesting through different aspects and functions while remaining essentially identical. The devotional heart recognizes that all apparent multiplicity of divine names and forms points toward the same transcendent Self that is the true identity of the practitioner, creating what the tradition describes as "worshipping oneself as Divine"—not ego-inflation but the recognition that consciousness itself is sacred, and one's essential nature is that very Ra consciousness that shines as the heart of all experience. This devotional recognition becomes the emotional foundation for all spiritual practice, transforming study, meditation, and ethical living from personal improvement techniques into expressions of love and service to the divine reality that is simultaneously the goal of seeking and the very consciousness through which all seeking occurs.

## 13. Neberdjer Awareness Practice - Maintaining Recognition of All-Encompassing Divinity

Sage Amenemopet provides the essential instruction: "Remain watchful, mindful, aware, keeping in mind, with deliberate effort, as to the fact that there is an 'entity', an 'existence' that encompasses all Creation [All-encompassing-Divinity], beyond [underlying] mind and time and space" [4]. The Stele of Djehuty Nefer reveals that Neberdjer represents "the power of the most sacred creator, who created himself, the lord of the utmost limits, the all-encompassing Divinity" whose "abodes are everywhere— hence all-encompassing-ness and omnipresence throughout Creation/existence" [5]. This practice involves maintaining constant awareness that mind and ego are illusory while recognizing that consciousness enabling ego existence represents Neberdjer, and that all perceived objects are illusory while their true source is composed of Neberdjer.

Understanding Neberdjer awareness requires recognizing this as the ultimate foundation underlying even the three-level consciousness framework, since Nunu, and Ra operate within and as modifications of the All-Encompassing Divinity (Neberdjer/Ba en Ra). The practice involves both informal awareness throughout daily circumstances and formal meditation periods dedicated to clearing mind and remaining aware only of awareness-source itself. Reflect on how this differs from conceptual thinking about absoluteness; Neberdjer awareness functions through direct recognition that individual consciousness represents the same as Neberdjer when limited perceptions of time, space, and ego-individuality experienced through mind are transcended, creating what the tradition calls the ANRUTEF state—conscious awareness existing without mind being operational.

**Fundamental Recognition Practice:** • Informal Awareness: Throughout daily circumstances, maintain awareness that mind and ego are illusory while consciousness enabling ego existence represents Neberdjer • Object Recognition: Recognize that all perceived objects are illusory while their true source is composed of Neberdjer • Formal Meditation: Dedicated periods for clearing mind and remaining aware only of awareness-source itself

**Advanced Practice Implementation:** • Preliminary Foundation: Establish stability through extensive ethical living, devotional orientation, and systematic informal and formal meditation practice • Effort Phase: Transcend mind altogether by allowing awareness to settle on its source with conscious volition • Effortless Phase: Allow consciousness to stabilize in recognition of essential nature without effortful maintenance • ANRUTEF State: Conscious awareness existing without mind being operational

Practical application requires comprehensive preparation through ethical living, devoted orientation, and systematic meditation that creates conditions for natural recognition rather than forced development. The advanced practice involves transcending mind altogether, including time and space awareness, by allowing awareness to settle on its source first with effort, then without effort as consciousness stabilizes in recognition of its essential nature. At the same time, this represents the culmination of spiritual practice rather than preliminary technique, requiring extensive foundation in witness consciousness development, aryu purification, and integration of threefold practice combining ethical conduct, philosophical study, and regular meditation. The ancient sages taught that Neberdjer recognition emerges when sufficient obstacles are removed rather than through personal achievement, following spiritual law that consciousness naturally recognizes its absolute nature when conditions support such recognition.

## The Unified Understanding: Neberdjer as Foundation and Composition

This all-encompassing understanding represents the Maaty or double truth of existence [2]. Consciousness (Neberdjer) serves as both the foundation and the composition of manifested existence; therefore, Neberdjer constitutes the underlying essence of Creation as well as the overlying manifestation of Creation itself [2]. For practitioners stabilized in witness consciousness, conflicts and challenges become opportunities for deeper recognition rather than personal affronts.

Since the stable witness knows that circumstances cannot ultimately disturb their essential nature, there is freedom to respond rather than react—to act from wisdom and compassion rather than from defensive ego-patterns. In other words, the person stabilized in witness consciousness becomes what the ancient texts describe as a "living temple"—a conscious expression of divine awareness operating through apparent human form while maintaining awareness of its essential nature [2].

## The Advanced Practice: Neberdjer Awareness and Meditation

Building upon the foundational understanding of Neberdjer established previously, contemporary practitioners require specific methodologies for implementing this profound recognition in systematic spiritual practice. The ancient sages provided comprehensive guidance that bridges the theoretical understanding of the All-Encompassing Foundation with direct experiential recognition through both informal awareness practices and formal meditation techniques.

## The Foundation for Neberdjer Awareness Practice

As established previously, being aware of Neberdjer means remaining aware that mind and ego are illusory while the true source of consciousness that allows ego to exist is Neberdjer [3]. This practice involves maintaining awareness that objects are illusory while recognizing that the true source of existence that appears to senses and mind is composed of Neberdjer [3].

Still, the mind, being a limited instrument, cannot directly cognize Neberdjer's essential nature as infinity, eternity, existence, and consciousness [3]. Notice how the mind translates external perceptions into what it rationalizes as time, space, and limited objects existing in time and space, while internally processing thoughts, feelings, memories, desires, and imaginations according to its structural limitations.

## The Divine Orchestration: Neberdjer as the Mover of All and the Path to Spiritual Serenity

The scriptural wisdom consistently reveals that Neberdjer functions not merely as the passive foundation of existence but as the active orchestrator of all manifestation, as Sage Amenemopet teaches: "there is an all-encompassing divinity that masters and encompasses the limits of Creation and therefore, that overall encompassing divinity is the shepherd that guides human life" and "is actually at the forefront of the boat of life watching (aware), guiding the boat of human life where it needs to go for the welfare of all humans even before they themselves know where they are going." This understanding carries profound implications for spiritual practice, since it reveals the fundamental ignorance underlying ego-consciousness when it imagines itself capable of controlling life circumstances through personal willpower and strategic manipulation. If Neberdjer serves as the ultimate mover and sustainer of all phenomena—from the movement of galaxies to the arising of thoughts in individual minds—then the ego's assumption of autonomous control represents a fundamental misapprehension of how existence actually operates, creating the psychological conditions that generate anxiety, frustration, and the heated mental states that obstruct spiritual development.

Even so, the ancient sages established that this divine orchestration operates through precise spiritual laws rather than arbitrary intervention, particularly the aryu principle whereby consciousness becomes bound by the karmic residue of its own egoistic actions and thoughts. The Scripture of Ra and Hetheru reveals that "within humans there are egoistic mental impressions (aryu/karmic remnants) that develop from experiences and actions in current and previous lifetimes" which "manifest as feeling memories, recorded and reinforced patterns of thoughts, feelings, and behaviors that remain registered in the unconscious mind, influencing present and future experiences." This means that while Neberdjer orchestrates all manifestation, individual consciousness can either align with divine order through Maat (righteous living) or become trapped in cycles of ego-driven reactivity through accumulated aryu patterns. The profound wisdom emerges that spiritual practice—beginning with ethical conduct, philosophical study, and meditation—creates the conditions whereby consciousness can transcend aryu-determined fate and discover its essential unity with the very source and mover of Creation.

This recognition transforms the practitioner's relationship to life circumstances from anxious control-seeking to what Sage Amenemopet describes as the "fullness of silence" that "discovers the fullness of the Creator-Spirit that is within." When consciousness recognizes that Neberdjer orchestrates all events according to divine wisdom that encompasses individual welfare within cosmic harmony, there emerges the capacity to accept life situations with serenity while simultaneously working to promote beneficial outcomes—not from ego-desperation but from alignment with divine purpose. This represents the practical fruition of Neberdjer awareness: consciousness that has discovered its essential nature as the All-Encompassing Divinity naturally expresses the "ger" (silent mind) that Amenemopet reveals as the foundation of inner peace, since there is no longer a separate ego struggling against circumstances but rather divine consciousness recognizing its own orchestration through apparent individual forms. Moreover, this serenity emerges not through passive resignation but through the profound recognition that one's deepest nature is identical with the very intelligence that guides the movement of stars and the unfolding of spiritual awakening itself.

## 14. Development and Stabilization of Witness Consciousness

Chapter 26 of the Ancient Egyptian Book of Enlightenment provides the foundational teaching for developing stable witness consciousness through the practitioner's recognition: "my heart, he is peaceful within me," "I know myself," and "I have control over my arms and legs (body)" [1]. These declarations reveal consciousness that has achieved separation from ego-patterns and now functions from inner peace, self-knowledge, and appropriate self-control rather than reactive patterns, representing what could be referred to as the "Soul-Aware-Witness" aspect of the human personality—consciousness that has separated itself from ego-identification and operates as instrument of soul expression. This development requires systematic training in maintaining awareness of awareness itself during all daily activities rather than becoming absorbed in particular mental-emotional content.

Understanding witness consciousness requires recognizing it as the capacity to observe all changing phenomena—thoughts, emotions, sensations, external circumstances—from unchanging awareness that recognizes its essential divine nature. The tradition teaches that this witness provides a stable platform from which consciousness can explore different levels of functioning without becoming lost in identification with temporary experiences, serving as practical foundation for consciousness level discrimination and optimal functioning regardless of external circumstances. Development occurs through systematic practice that gradually strengthens recognition of human conscious-awareness as distinct from its mental contents: during pleasant experiences, recognizing consciousness that enjoys without becoming identified with enjoyment; during difficulties, recognizing consciousness that witnesses without identification with difficulty; during neutral experiences, recognizing consciousness remaining present without needing particular content.

**Daily Witness Training:** • Pleasant Experiences: Practice recognizing consciousness that enjoys without becoming identified with enjoyment • Difficult Experiences: Recognize consciousness that witnesses without identification with difficulty • Neutral Experiences: Recognize consciousness remaining present without needing particular content

**Troubleshooting Implementation:**

**Avoiding Forced States and Conceptual Imagination:** • Recognize when attempting to create special states through mental effort rather than developing discrimination that reveals consciousness levels operating continuously • Maintain patience, consistency, and willingness to work with whatever arises rather than demanding predetermined outcomes • Understand that genuine recognition emerges through understanding rather than effort, like learning to see stars that were always present

**Distinguishing Recognition from Mental Concepts:** • Learn to distinguish between thinking about consciousness and actually recognizing consciousness directly • Prevent intellectual understanding from substituting for direct experiential recognition • Develop capacity to recognize when conceptual knowledge obstructs genuine spiritual sensitivity

**Being aware of ego imaginations about consciousness:** • Avoid attempting to maintain Nunu consciousness during situations requiring engaged Ra individuation (thoughtfulness for necessary worldly interaction) • Prevent using spiritual concepts to avoid necessary engagement with worldly responsibilities • Avoid "consciousness rigidity"—attachment to particular identity patterns preventing natural fluidity and organic experience of awareness expansion

Stabilization involves transforming intermittent witness recognition into permanent foundation of identity and experience through what the teachings describe as "abiding with/as that separate witnessing self" until it becomes established as constant self-awareness. Understand how this stability emerges not through forced effort but through sustained philosophical thought combined with practical spending time as witnessing awareness, allowing natural spiritual law to establish consciousness in its true nature rather than ego-identification. Yet stabilization requires extensive preparation through living by truth at all levels, since heavy aryu create mental-emotional turbulence that prevents subtle recognition necessary for stable witness consciousness. Therefore, practitioners must combine witness development with ethical purification, contemplative study, and regular meditation practice that creates cumulative conditions supporting consciousness recognition beyond ego-patterns while serving practical effectiveness and spiritual service in daily circumstances.

## 15. The Wisdom of Association with Sages: Sacred Community as Foundation for Consciousness Development

Having explored the comprehensive system of fifteen practical methods for Ancient Egyptian consciousness development—from the foundational practices of ethical living and philosophical discrimination through the advanced techniques of consciousness level recognition and witness stabilization—we must now examine a crucial dimension of spiritual practice that the ancient sages understood as indispensable for authentic transformation: the wisdom of conscious association with those who embody the spiritual realization we seek to discover within ourselves.

The Stele of Djehuty Nefer reveals profound teachings that transcends mere social interaction or intellectual exchange, illuminating what the tradition of Shetaut Neter recognizes as knumt-nefer ("good association, divine association")—the sacred relationship between sincere aspirant and spiritual community that creates optimal conditions for receiving authentic guidance and constructive feedback on one's practice [5]. Furthermore, verses 4-6 of this ancient wisdom text provide systematic instruction for understanding why individual spiritual effort, however dedicated, requires the living transmission of spiritual understanding that emerges through conscious association with those whose practice has matured through sustained engagement with the teachings.

Notice how this teaching emerges naturally from the comprehensive methodology we have explored throughout Chapter 10. The fifteen methods for consciousness development—ranging from trilinear translation study through aryu purification and witness consciousness stabilization—create cumulative purification effects that prepare consciousness for receiving the subtle guidance that flows through authentic spiritual community. Still, the ancient sages taught that spiritual development flourishes through dynamic interchange between the aspirant's sincere inquiry and the living wisdom of those who have traversed the path before them, since certain dimensions of spiritual understanding can only be transmitted through direct contact with embodied realization rather than remaining confined to textual study or isolated practice.

The wisdom of the scriptures reveals that this principle operates according to spiritual law rather than mere convenience or tradition. As consciousness begins to recognize its essential nature through the practices described in our foundational methods, it naturally seeks confirmation and refinement through association with those whose consciousness has been clarified through dedicated application of the same teachings. In other words, the Soul-Aware-Witness that emerges through sustained spiritual discipline requires the nourishment and guidance that flows naturally from conscious association with those pure ones whose hearts have been established in the peace, self-knowledge, and divine recognition that characterize genuine spiritual attainment.

Therefore, the Teachings of Djehuty Nefer provide essential completion to our systematic exploration of practical consciousness development, revealing how individual spiritual practice achieves its intended fruition through integration with authentic spiritual community rather than remaining confined to solitary effort. This understanding aligns with the profound teaching found throughout our foundational texts: individual enlightenment represents universal consciousness recognizing its own nature through apparent individual forms, which means that association with those who embody this recognition creates resonance fields that support the same awakening in sincere aspirants who approach with proper purification and devoted orientation.

## **FROM: Stele of Djehuty Nefer**[49]
**Wisdom of Spending time with Sages**

Verse 4.
- 4.1. ush -f ta hedj aaui –f abu er
- 4.2. Consume -he food pure hands-his pure as-to
- 4.3. The advancing initiate should consume foods that are pure and unadulterated; they should do this while being hygienically clean, living a life that strives for purity of body and mind. This will make their body sound and healthy and will open their capacity as-to…

---

[49] Translation by Dr. Muata Ashby

Verse 5.
5.1. *dua-per en dua rekhytu ari - f hezet*
5.2. adoration of adoration people doing -he seating chamber
5.3. …entering the adoration room, the place for doing worships of the Divine, where people go to for making adorations. So too the advancing aspirant will as well go to that room and take a seat there…

Verse 6.
6.1. *im anuitu-per chenems {serr}{mdj} –f abu {au} Neter-hemu*
6.2. within hypostyle hall company {elders}{wise} –he pure {persons} Divine-clergy
6.3. within the hypostyle hall of the temple and, being seated there, keep company with those pure ones, those priests and priestesses who adore and follow and serve the Divine; and in so doing thereby become pure and enlightened as they are so as to achieve the goal of life, immortality through spiritual enlightenment.

# The Wisdom of Association with Sages: Understanding the Spiritual Community as Living Temple

These remarkable verses from the Stele of Djehuty Nefer illuminate a fundamental principle that the ancient sages embedded within their comprehensive understanding of spiritual development: authentic transformation requires not merely individual effort but conscious association with those who embody the wisdom one seeks to attain. Moreover, the progression revealed in verses 4-6 establishes the essential foundation upon which all meaningful spiritual guidance and instruction must rest, demonstrating what the tradition of Shetaut Neter recognizes as the indispensable role of spiritual community in supporting the aspirant's journey toward divine realization.

Observe how verse 4 establishes the preliminary requirement of personal purification—"consume foods that are pure and unadulterated" while maintaining "purity of body and mind"—which aligns with the understanding in the scripture that spiritual receptivity requires preparation of the vessel that will receive divine instruction. This is not merely about physical cleanliness but represents the cultivation of clarity and sensitivity necessary to benefit from association with those who have achieved spiritual mastery. As the ancient sages taught, an aspirant whose consciousness remains clouded by the grosser mental-emotional afflictions cannot properly discern authentic wisdom from mere intellectual speculation, nor can they receive the subtle guidance that flows from genuine spiritual attainment.

At the same time, the true significance of this teaching emerges in verses 5-6, where the purified aspirant enters "the adoration room" and takes their seat "within the hypostyle hall of the temple" to "keep company with those pure ones, those priests and priestesses who adore and follow and serve the Divine." We must recognize that this describes far more than casual social interaction—it reveals the establishment of what the wisdom tradition calls knumt-nefer ("good association, divine association"), the sacred relationship between student and spiritual community that creates optimal conditions for receiving authentic explanations of the teachings and constructive feedback on one's practice.

The wisdom of the neteru reveals that spiritual development flourishes through this dynamic interchange between the aspirant's sincere inquiry and the guidance of those who have traversed the path before them. Understand that when an aspirant maintains regular association with genuine practitioners—whether through formal instruction, participation in the temple activities, or informal spiritual dialogue—they naturally absorb not only the intellectual content of the teachings but also the living transmission of spiritual understanding that can only be conveyed through direct contact with embodied wisdom. In other words, the explanations received from experienced practitioners carry a qualitative dimension that transcends mere conceptual information, providing the context and practical insight necessary for authentic spiritual progress.

Therefore, the ancient teaching encoded in these verses provides essential guidance for contemporary students of Shetaut Neter who seek to deepen their understanding and refine their practice. Just as the advancing initiate in verse 6 achieves "the goal of life, immortality through spiritual enlightenment" through association with the divine clergy, modern aspirants discover that their questions about meditation technique, ethical application, or philosophical understanding receive most beneficial resolution through dialogue with those whose practice has matured through sustained engagement with the teachings. This understanding aligns with the principle that spiritual wisdom is not merely transmitted through books or isolated study but requires the living interaction between sincere question and qualified response that can only arise within authentic spiritual community.

Thus, the Stele of Djehuty Nefer confirms what the ancient sages understood as an unchanging principle of spiritual education: the aspirant who seeks genuine transformation must cultivate regular association with those pure ones whose consciousness has been clarified through dedicated practice, creating the optimal environment where divine wisdom can be received, understood, and integrated for the fulfillment of life's highest purpose—the realization of our essential unity with the Divine Self that is the source and sustenance of all existence [1].

## Conclusion: The Technology for Spiritual Transformation

These systematic methods represent the distilled essence of Ancient Egyptian spiritual psychology as revealed through authentic scriptural sources, offering contemporary practitioners access to the same transformative wisdom that guided consciousness development in the temple schools of ancient Kemet. Through systematic application of these time-tested approaches, modern aspirants can discover for themselves the profound psychological and spiritual insights that emerge when consciousness recognizes its true nature as divine awareness temporarily manifesting through individual human form.

The implementation requires understanding that these methods work through aligning individual consciousness with divine consciousness rather than creating mental states through mechanical application. Still, sustained practice following these systematic approaches creates the cumulative conditions that naturally support consciousness recognition beyond ego-patterns while serving practical effectiveness and spiritual service in daily circumstances.

Furthermore, the ancient sages taught that authentic spiritual development enhances rather than diminishes engagement with temporal responsibilities, relationships, and creative service, since consciousness operating from divine recognition naturally expresses enhanced wisdom, compassion, and beneficial action that serves both individual awakening and collective wellbeing.

========

Having explored the comprehensive system of fifteen methods for Ancient Egyptian consciousness development—from the scriptures explored in this book along with their trilinear translations that provides authentic access to ancient wisdom, through the systematic practices of aryu purification and witness consciousness stabilization, to the advanced recognition of universal soul consciousness operating through individual forms—aspirants naturally encounter the essential question that determines whether spiritual practice has achieved its intended purpose: how does one verify that the profound insights and experiential recognitions emerging through sustained practice represent authentic spiritual realization rather than self-deception, spiritual inflation, or temporary states that lack genuine transformative power?

What's more, the ancient sages understood that the most sophisticated methods for consciousness development remain incomplete without reliable criteria for distinguishing between preliminary experiences that may accompany purification and the stable recognition of divine identity that constitutes genuine enlightenment. Notice how the fifteen methods create cumulative conditions supporting spiritual transformation, yet without proper verification frameworks, practitioners risk mistaking partial developments for complete realization, or conversely, dismissing authentic recognitions due to lack of understanding about how divine awareness manifests through human experience.

The wisdom teachings reveal that this verification challenge extends beyond individual assessment to encompass the integration of spiritual recognition with daily life responsibilities, relationships, and service obligations. Even so, the ancient Egyptian tradition provides precise guidance for this authentication process through scriptural teachings that establish clear criteria for recognizing genuine spiritual attainment while offering practical wisdom for integrating transcendent awareness with temporal existence in ways that serve both individual awakening and collective wellbeing.

## REFERENCES

[1] Ashby, M. (2025). Papyrus Ani [Book of the Dead] Chapter 17 Verse 3–6 – trilinear translation. Translation by Dr. Muata Ashby.

[2] Ashby, M. (2022). The Mysteries of Ra and Hetheru/Sekhmet. Translation by Dr. Muata Ashby.

[3] Ashby, M. (2025). Becoming Nun: The Non-Dual Mysticism in the Ancient Egyptian Coffin Texts. Translation by Dr. Muata Ashby.

[4] Ashby, M. (2019). Teachings of Ancient Egyptian Sage Amenemopet with Hieroglyphic texts. Translation by Dr. Muata Ashby.

[5] Ashby, M. Stele of Djehuty Nefer - Wisdom of Spending time with Sages, Verses 4-6. Translation by Dr. Muata Ashby.

# Chapter 11: Verification and Integration - The Measures of Spiritual Establishment

The verification of spiritual teaching emerges through examining what the ancient scriptures reveal about the stages of consciousness development. This volume, "Mystic Transpersonal Psychology of Ancient Egyptian Non-Duality," establishes a fundamental principle that guides our entire approach to understanding authentic spiritual transformation. The principle states: "the ultimate test of any spiritual teaching lies not in its theoretical sophistication or the profundity of its metaphysical insights, but in its capacity to produce verifiable transformation in human consciousness—a fundamental shift from ego-identification to divine recognition" [1].

This principle becomes our foundation for understanding why the ancient Egyptian sages preserved multiple complementary texts rather than relying on a single source. To understand this verification process comprehensively, we must examine how multiple scriptures work together as an integrated system of spiritual development. Chapter 175 of the Pert-em-Heru presents the complete dialogue between Asar Any and Temu, demonstrating the final result of spiritual establishment [4]. The Scripture of Ra and Hetheru describes the culminating verses of spiritual roasting and aryu purification, revealing the transformative process that enables such establishment [2]. Sage Amenemopet's teachings provide practical criteria for distinguishing between different consciousness modes and offer guidance for maintaining integration during daily life circumstances [3].

When we examine how these texts function together, we discover that each serves specific complementary functions in describing the complete spectrum of spiritual establishment. Chapter 175 demonstrates consciousness operating in divine reality after transcending physical identification, providing us with a clear picture of what the final result looks like [4]. This demonstration becomes meaningful, however, only when we understand the process that enables such transcendence. Verses 177-179 of the Scripture of Ra and Hetheru describe the purification process that creates the internal conditions necessary for the consciousness transformation that Chapter 175 demonstrates [2]. The teaching becomes even more complete when verse 180 reveals the final state where "there can be no objectors among any gods or goddesses... there can be no objectors among any objects in the entirety of Creation," showing us the ultimate verification criteria for authentic establishment [2].

Understanding this theoretical framework alone, however, would leave practitioners without practical guidance for navigating the transformation process in daily life. This gap is filled by Amenemopet's teachings, which provide the practical framework for navigating this transformation through daily life circumstances while maintaining engagement with worldly responsibilities [3]. The ancient sages designed these complementary teachings to address what the tradition recognizes as the essential challenge of spiritual development: achieving stable transformation that integrates transcendent awareness with ongoing engagement in temporal existence rather than escape from worldly responsibilities.

Therefore, this chapter examines the scriptural evidence for understanding how consciousness verification and integration occur according to the actual statements preserved in the ancient texts, recognizing that each source contributes essential elements to our comprehensive understanding.

## Essential Clarification for Verification and Integration of Spiritual Development

As students engage in the verification process of their spiritual development and work toward integration of transcendent awareness with daily life, we must address a critical misunderstanding that often arises during this phase. The teachings presented in this volume do not advocate for the destruction or elimination of ego-personality, nor should students evaluate their spiritual progress based on the absence of individual personality characteristics. Indeed, the wisdom of the neteru reveals that the challenge lies not in the presence of personality but rather in the critical distinction between ego and egoism that determines whether consciousness operates through clarity or delusion. Consider how ego itself represents the necessary vehicle through which spirit experiences existence in time and space; without this individuating principle, consciousness could not manifest through human form or engage with the temporal realm. The problem arises not from ego per se, but from egoic entanglement with time, space, body, and mind—a condition motivated by subject-object relationships wherein the individual thinks of themselves as separate beings in conflict and competition, seeking happiness through attachment to worldly ephemeral objects that can never provide lasting satisfaction. Consider how the ancient sages understood that personality serves as the divine vehicle through which consciousness expresses itself in the temporal realm; indeed, the pure ego represents a reflection of the soul (Asar {Osiris}) and is therefore inherently good, possessing the capacity for divine expression when freed from the distortions of egoism. Therefore, the spiritual path involves purification and proper orientation of personality rather than its annihilation or suppression—transforming egoic entanglement into ego functioning that serves consciousness rather than enslaving it to temporal concerns.

Nevertheless, this teaching represents an invitation to examine and purify the personality for the purpose of creating a more fulfilling and harmonious life rather than an indictment of the individual person or their essential worth. As the tradition of Shetaut Neter demonstrates, healthy ego-personality does not require the destruction or absence of individual characteristics, preferences, and capacities that make each person unique. In other words, spiritual development seeks to establish ego-personality that operates from clarity through human consciousness-awareness rather than being founded and controlled by egoic motivators such as fear, attachment, competition, and the compulsive need for external validation.

Therefore, when verifying authentic spiritual development and working toward integration, the aspirant seeks evidence of transformation from egoism to pure ego functioning—observing personality expression that operates free from entanglement with temporal concerns while remaining grounded in consciousness qualities: oneness with all existence, alignment with truth (Maat), clear awareness of the personality as a temporary manifestation of eternal consciousness in time and space, genuine self-satisfaction that does not depend on external circumstances, authentic good will for all beings, and the profound sense of completeness that emerges when consciousness recognizes its infinite nature. This understanding provides proper criteria for assessing spiritual progress: rather than measuring the absence of personality traits or individual preferences, we evaluate whether ego serves as a clear reflection of the soul (Asar {Osiris}), expressing wisdom, compassion, and skillful action that benefit both individual fulfillment and collective wellbeing without attachment to results or competitive motivation.

# CHAPTER 175 PERT-EM-HERU: CONVERSATION WITH TEMU

**Chapter Section presented at the 2015 Neterian Conference, Translation by Dr. Muata Ashby**

Above: Image of Papyrus Any

Verse 1.
1.1. *Medtu Dje in Asar Any      Any      Aa Temu ashest      pu*
1.2. Words by Asar Any;      Any      Exclaims! Hey Temu! What      this
1.3. These words are spoken by Asar Any.      Any exclaims: "Hey Lord Temu. What is going on here? What is…

## Awakening Your Soul-Aware-Witness

**Verse 2.**
2.1.    shaz     a er zet Iu gert an mu zet an nafu zet metchti
2.2.    come  I to this It is however not water it not air it deep
2.3.    this place that I have come to ? I arrived here but I don't see any water or air and the depth of this place

**Verse 3.**
3.1.    sepsen kektuti     sepsen hyhti     sepsen ankhti   im  z  m
3.2.    twofold darkness   twofold boundless   twofold Living  in this through
3.3.    is twice the depth I expected, seems vast. Temu Responds: Living in this place is not like the physical realm where you came from; being here is sustained by means of

**Verse 4.**
4.1.    hetep ab   an  iu  gert  an  aritu  nedjemmytu  im - z
4.2.    peace of heart not is though not making pleasure sexuality in - it
4.3.    contentment. Also, here, in this realm, there are no sexual pleasures in it.

**Verse 5.**
5.1.    Erdi – na    akhu  im  asuy    mu   nafu   hena
5.2.    Given to me   spirit being in exchange  water  air  with
5.3.    Any speaks: To be given to me is becoming an Akh (spirit/enlightened being) instead of food and drink with

**Verse 6.**
6.1.    nedjemmytu hetep ab im  asuy    ta   heqt  nefery  su
6.2.    Sex pleasures peace heart in  exchange  bread  beer  good  that
6.3.    Sexuality. Instead of those things I get inner peace; instead of food and drink I get inner peace; and this is a good thing, in fact I will be better off.

## Awakening Your Soul-Aware-Witness

**Verse 7.**
7.1. *Temu m maa her-k an gert uchedu - a gau - k*
7.2. Temu in eyes face-thine not though sick - I deprived - thee
7.3. Lord Temu's eyes, his spiritual vision, are in your face and you will not be a sickly person, and you will not be deprived. You will not feel as if you are missing out on anything because the fullness of spirit will be in your perspective as opposed to being afflicted by the limited vision of individuality and myopic self-regard based on egocentricity.

**Verse 8.**
8.1. *Iu neter neb hab -nef nest f m khenty hehu iu*
8.2. It is divinity every convey to he throne his in foremost millions it is
8.3. Every god and goddess will transmit their thrones to him (Osiris Any) and he will be the foremost being existing for millions of years. It is

**Verse 9.**
9.1. *Nest- k en sa k Heru nefery Temu unen gert hab - f*
9.2. Throne yours of son yours Horus good Temu existence though conveys - he
9.3. the thrones of your son Horus. This is good and has said it Temu that there will be beautiful existence as he gives to the

**Verse 10.**
10.1. *uru iu - f gert heqa -f nest-k iu f er*
10.2. prince/noble. It is - he though rulership - he throne thine It is he as to
10.3. princes/nobles. It is he who, however, will rule your thrones (because you are Osiris and you rule in heaven and your son rules on earth for you). It is he who

**Verse 11.**
11.1. *aua nest imy merzerzer udu gert*
11.2. heir throne within lake of double fire decreed however
11.3. is heir to the throne within the lake of double fire, located in the Duat, where one can bask in the rays of Ra in his presence and become purified thereby as decreed; however

Awakening Your Soul-Aware-Witness

Verse 12.
12.1.   *maa  -  na    senut–f    her–a    er  maa  her  en  neb*
12.2.   see   -to/at me  second–his  personality–I  to   see   person  of  lord
12.3.   he may see me as his second and so that my personality may see his personality, he being the lord

Having examined the complete text of Chapter 175, we can now explore what this remarkable dialogue reveals about the nature of spiritual establishment and the verification criteria it provides for authentic transformation [4].

## COMMENTARY ON CHAPTER 175 PERT-EM-HERU: THE DIALOGUE WITH THE GOD TEMU

Chapter 175 presents consciousness engaging in sustained dialogue with divine reality after physical death, demonstrating awareness functioning independently of bodily existence while maintaining clear communication and assessment capabilities [4]. This represents far more than mythological allegory or symbolic instruction. The dialogue provides what we might call phenomenological descriptions—precise accounts of what consciousness actually experiences when it has achieved stable transcendence of ego-identification and discovered its essential nature as divine awareness temporarily manifesting through individual form [5].

Reflect on how this dialogue serves multiple functions simultaneously. For advanced practitioners who have achieved genuine recognition, it provides validation and confirmation of their experiences. For aspirants seeking reliable criteria for assessing their own spiritual development, it offers specific markers to distinguish authentic transformation from preliminary spiritual experiences that lack stability and integration. The complete dialogue from verses 1-12 of the Pert-em-Heru provides comprehensive description of consciousness operating in spiritual dimensions, offering verification criteria for authentic transformation and integration methods that remain applicable across cultural and temporal boundaries [4].

The ancient sages designed this verification framework to address the universal challenge facing all spiritual traditions: distinguishing between authentic transformation and the subtle forms of ego inflation or delusion that can arise when consciousness encounters transcendent experiences without proper preparation, understanding, or integration [5]. Moreover, the dialogue with Temu illuminates how genuine spiritual attainment creates not escape from human experience but its complete transformation—consciousness maintaining full engagement with temporal existence while operating from the unshakeable foundation of divine recognition rather than the fluctuating patterns of ego-based reactivity and seeking [4].

## Verses 1-3: Initial Encounter with Divine Reality

The opening exchange reveals fundamental principles about how authentic spiritual consciousness operates when encountering unfamiliar spiritual dimensions [4]. Any addresses Temu directly using the informal greeting "Hey," which indicates natural confidence rather than fearful supplication. This seemingly minor detail carries profound significance for understanding authentic spiritual development. It demonstrates that genuine spiritual consciousness maintains clear communication and observational capacity even in unfamiliar circumstances, approaching divine reality with natural familiarity rather than overwhelming awe, apprehension, or elaborate ritual preparation [5].

Any describes his disorientation matter-of-factly, demonstrating the clear observational capacity that characterizes established consciousness: encountering a realm without familiar physical elements but maintaining clear observation and communication throughout the experience [4]. He states simply: "I arrived here but I don't see any water or air and the depth of this place is twice the depth I expected, seems vast." Notice how Any maintains analytical capability while acknowledging his disorientation—he can assess the situation, compare it to his expectations, and communicate clearly about what he observes.

Temu's response provides crucial information that forms the foundation for understanding how consciousness operates in spiritual dimensions: "Living in this place is not like the physical realm where you came from; being here is sustained by means of contentment" [4]. This response establishes the fundamental principle that spiritual existence operates through entirely different sustaining principles than physical existence.

We can understand this conversation on multiple interpretive levels, each providing valuable insights for contemporary practitioners. When we think of the conversation metaphorically, as a dialogue between one's soul-aware-witness-self and its Ra-Tem deeper source of awareness, this conversation represents a spiritual aspirant's arrival in a realm of higher expansion and awareness [5]. The aspirant settles into that level of awareness with the guidance and reassurance of one's own higher self. This interpretive framework helps contemporary practitioners understand how their own consciousness might function as it develops beyond ego-identification.

For practitioners, this indicates that genuine development produces natural confidence in approaching higher spiritual realities rather than anxiety, fear, or dependence on elaborate ritual preparation. The text suggests that human conscious-awareness, when properly prepared through spiritual development, naturally maintains its essential capacities of observation, communication, and assessment even when encountering completely unfamiliar spiritual conditions [5].

## Verses 4-6: Exchange of Physical for Spiritual Satisfaction

The dialogue continues with what represents one of the most profound teachings about the nature of spiritual fulfillment found in ancient literature [4]. Temu explains that "here, in this realm, there are no sexual pleasures in it." This statement might initially seem like a description of deprivation, but the dialogue quickly reveals the opposite. Any responds with recognition that demonstrates his understanding of the superior nature of spiritual satisfaction: "To be given to me is becoming an Akh (spirit/enlightened being) instead of food and drink with Sexuality. Instead of those things I get inner peace; instead of food and drink I get inner peace; and this is a good thing, in fact I will be better off" [4].

The conversation reveals the existence of a higher reality that transcends the physical cycles of eating, sexual reproduction, birth and death that characterize earthly existence. This higher reality operates through principles that provide superior satisfaction compared to physical pleasure [5]. Any's response demonstrates direct comparative assessment: spiritual satisfaction compared to ephemeral physical pleasure with clear preference for spiritual fulfillment. His declaration "I will be better off" represents conscious evaluation based on direct experience rather than forced acceptance of apparent deprivation [4].

The text continues with a profound value judgment that spiritual attainment, with its characteristic contentment, proves superior to the state of being based on thinking of oneself as a separate ego with body and desires. This represents consciousness trapped within a personality driven by egoistic tendencies, never able to rest because of seeking fulfillment from worldly pleasures and activities that, by their very nature, can never fulfill the soul's deepest longings [5]. The contrast becomes clear: ego-based consciousness experiences endless seeking and temporary satisfaction followed by renewed seeking, while established consciousness discovers fulfillment that does not depend on external circumstances and therefore provides lasting satisfaction.

The transformation method that emerges from this teaching challenges conventional approaches to spiritual development that emphasize renunciation or suppression of natural desires [5]. Instead, the text indicates that a spiritually mature consciously aware personality naturally chooses superior satisfaction when it has direct access to both options. Rather than forcing renunciation through willpower or moral effort, the teaching suggests that spiritual fulfillment becomes naturally preferable through balanced development that leads to direct experience of spiritual satisfaction in the discovery of self as pure consciousness beyond physical body, mind and senses. Those who are not ready to make such a choice should continue to live according to their human desires as they work to purify their personality until they are able to make such spiritual choices [4].

This principle has profound implications for contemporary spiritual practice. It suggests that the most effective approach to spiritual development involves creating conditions where consciousness can directly experience spiritual fulfillment rather than attempting to suppress natural desires through force. When consciousness discovers through direct experience that spiritual satisfaction surpasses physical pleasure, the transition occurs naturally without internal conflict or artificial suppression [5].

## Verses 7-9: Divine Vision and Cosmic Recognition

The dialogue progresses to reveal the cosmic dimensions of authentic spiritual establishment [4]. Temu declares that Any will experience divine vision and freedom from deprivation: "Lord Temu's eyes, his spiritual vision, are in your face and you will not be a sickly person, and you will not be deprived." This promise addresses one of the fundamental fears that prevents many practitioners from pursuing authentic spiritual development—the concern that spiritual advancement requires accepting limitations or deprivations that diminish life's richness [5].

The text continues with a description of cosmic recognition that reveals the universal implications of individual spiritual establishment: "Every god and goddess will transmit their thrones to him" and establishes connection to "the thrones of your son Horus," indicating Any's integration into divine governance structure [4]. This passage requires careful interpretation to understand its deeper significance beyond surface appearances.

Since Asar Any is considered as one with the god Asar, the thrones of the gods and goddesses will be pledged to the son of Asar (Heru [Horus]) who will remain on earth to carry out divine will in the field manifestation. Therefore, Any need not worry about his legacy, his progeny, or other concerns of his earthly life that might create anxiety or attachment [5]. This signifies complete freedom from worry, concerns, or other troubling attachments that might have held Any's mind worried or concerned about life on earth, preventing him from wholeheartedly accepting and experiencing the higher realm of consciousness of Tem.

This teaching addresses a crucial psychological dimension of spiritual establishment [5]. Many practitioners remain partially attached to worldly concerns even as they pursue spiritual development, creating internal conflict between spiritual aspirations and worldly responsibilities. The text reveals that authentic establishment resolves this conflict not through abandoning worldly engagement but through recognizing that one's essential spiritual development serves the highest good of all beings, including those who remain engaged in worldly activities [4] or are left behind when a spiritual initiate needs to move on in their spiritual journey while others are unwilling or unable to do so.

The scripture provides specific markers that serve as verification criteria for authentic transformation: divine vision that provides clear perception of spiritual reality; freedom from sickness and deprivation that demonstrates the superior sustaining power of spiritual awareness; cosmic recognition that confirms one's integration into universal divine functioning; freedom from doubt and worry that results from recognizing one's essential divine nature; and integration with divine authority structures that ensure one's individual development serves universal purposes rather than personal aggrandizement [4][5].

## Verses 10-12: Integration and Divine Relationship

The concluding verses reveal the ultimate integration that represents the final fruition of spiritual development [4]. Any becomes "heir to the throne within the lake of double fire" where purification occurs through basking "in the rays of Ra." This imagery describes the final purification process where consciousness becomes completely transparent to divine radiance. The final verse establishes the relationship structure that characterizes authentic spiritual establishment: "he may see me as his second and so that my personality may see his personality, he being the lord" [4].

This passage provides crucial understanding about the nature of authentic spiritual establishment [5]. Any will be recognized as the double of the God Asar, but this recognition comes through a specific process. He has achieved this recognition by basking in the rays of Ra, that is, the effulgent radiance (Akhu) of Ra. That radiance, in its fullness, purifies the personality and renders it pure through a transformative process that operates at the deepest levels of consciousness. The effulgent radiance purifies the mind and unconscious such that egoistic taints have been illumined and dispelled by being in the presence of Ra's radiant cosmic consciousness [4].

This description provides valuable insight into how the purification process actually operates. Rather than suppressing or eliminating personality, the process purifies personality by exposing it to divine radiance that naturally dissolves egoistic patterns while preserving and enhancing the personality's essential functioning [5]. The result is personality that operates as a transparent vehicle for divine consciousness rather than an obstruction to divine awareness.

The text describes a functioning relationship between individual consciousness and divine reality where the practitioner maintains distinct identity ("my personality... his personality") while operating within divine authority structure ("rule your thrones") [4]. This represents a crucial distinction that helps us understand what authentic integration actually involves. Rather than focusing on dissolution of individual identity or personality, authentic establishment involves integration into higher consciousness state and relinquishment of the worldly, illusory state of conscious awareness that operates from ego-identification [5].

The method for establishment becomes clear through this final teaching: authentic spiritual establishment involves divine recognition in which one realizes oneself as the duplicate or reflection of the Divine (Asar) who was, as it were, a stand-in or representative while operating on earth but who now is being recognized by himself and the gods and goddesses as one who is essentially none other than the Divine manifesting through individual form [4]. This recognition represents not ego-inflation but the discovery of one's true nature that was always present but obscured by egoistic identification patterns [5].

# BRIDGING FROM CHAPTER 175 TO THE PURIFICATION PROCESS

Having examined what Chapter 175 reveals about the final result of spiritual establishment, we naturally encounter the question of how such establishment is achieved [4]. The dialogue with Temu demonstrates consciousness operating in divine reality with natural confidence, preferring spiritual to physical satisfaction, and functioning in cosmic integration. But what process enables consciousness to achieve this remarkable transformation?

This question leads us to examine the complementary teaching found in the Scripture of Ra and Hetheru, which describes the purification process that creates the internal conditions necessary for the consciousness transformation that Chapter 175 demonstrates [2]. Understanding this process proves essential for contemporary practitioners who seek to apply these ancient teachings practically rather than merely studying them theoretically.

# INTEGRATION THROUGH SPIRITUAL ROASTING: VERSES 177-179

The Scripture of Ra and Hetheru describes the purification process that enables the consciousness transformation demonstrated in Chapter 175, providing us with practical understanding of how spiritual establishment actually develops [2]. These verses describe the practical method for achieving the purification necessary for divine dialogue and cosmic integration, offering guidance that bridges theoretical understanding with practical application.

The concept of spiritual roasting represents one of the most sophisticated psychological teachings found in ancient spiritual literature [2]. Rather than describing purification as suppression or elimination of natural human tendencies, the teaching presents purification as a wisdom process that naturally dissolves patterns that obstruct divine awareness while enhancing consciousness's essential functioning capacities.

### Verse 177: The Vital-Life-Fire Development

The text provides detailed description of how spiritual practice generates transformative internal conditions: "The practice of the myth, ritual, ethics and meditations in the scripture develops vital-life-fire within the personality. This vital-life-fire acts as a fire of wisdom that burns away delusions and egoism. It roasts, burns off, the delusion and ignorance fomenting desire for ephemeral existence, the egoistic perturbations of the mind and its thoughts, feelings, desires and memories (aryu) that prevent the soul from realizing the truth of Higher Self. That truth of Self is the realization of 'I am Ra' (nuk Ra) the Creator Spirit, among the Company of His noble Gods and Goddesses" [2].

This teaching reveals that comprehensive spiritual practice—combining mythological study, ritual application, ethical living, and meditative discipline—generates "vital-life-fire within the personality" that functions as purifying wisdom [2]. This fire operates through a specific mechanism: it "roasts, burns off" the accumulated "thoughts, feelings, desires and memories (aryu)" that maintain ego-identification, leading to the natural emergence of divine identity recognition.

The purification method operates through systematic spiritual practice creating internal conditions that naturally dissolve ego-maintaining patterns through what the text calls "fire of wisdom" [2]. This process differs fundamentally from suppression or forced elimination of mental patterns. Instead, spiritual practice generates such intensity of divine presence within consciousness that egoistic patterns naturally dissolve, much like darkness disappears when light appears [5]. That divine presence permeates the personality with expanded experience of self as spirit being that heals and clarifies past errors, complexes and misunderstandings that reinforce the ego delusion and its forced diminution of mind and feelings that enable ego self-identity and prevent spiritual expansion in the personality. The process enables the consciousness transformation that Chapter 175 demonstrates by creating internal conditions where divine recognition becomes natural and effortless [2][4].

Understanding this process helps contemporary practitioners' approach spiritual development with proper expectations and methods [5]. Rather than only attempting to eliminate egoistic patterns through willpower or moral effort, practitioners can focus on generating the conditions that naturally produce purification through sustained spiritual practice that combines multiple disciplines working together synergistically.

## Verse 178: Words-of-Power and Vital-Life-Fire

This verse describes the immediate result of successful purification in terms that provide clear verification criteria: "The words-of-power are within me and the vital-life-fire passes through me" [2]. These simple statements describe a fundamental transformation where consciousness becomes transparent to divine forces operating through individual form [5].

The text indicates that the personality has been purified to such a degree that it functions as a vehicle for divine operation rather than an obstruction to divine expression [2]. "Words-of-power are within me" suggests that divine wisdom and transformative energy operate through the individual without being filtered or distorted by egoistic resistance. "Vital-life-fire passes through me" indicates that the transformative spiritual energy flows freely through the personality, continuing the purification process while enabling divine expression in daily circumstances [5].

This represents a crucial integration indicator that helps us understand what successful spiritual development actually produces [5]. The scripture shows consciousness operating as instrument for divine forces rather than separate agent (ego) seeking personal benefit. This corresponds directly to Any's relationship with Temu as described in Chapter 175, where Any maintains individual functionality while operating in divine authority structure rather than claiming independent divine status [2][4].

Contemporary practitioners can use this teaching to assess their own development [5]. Rather than seeking extraordinary experiences or special powers, they can observe whether their daily functioning demonstrates increasing transparency to wisdom, compassion, and service that flows through them rather than being generated by personal effort. This transparency develops gradually through sustained spiritual practice rather than appearing suddenly through dramatic breakthrough experiences.

## Verse 179: Mind is Finished/Dissolved

The text describes the completion of the purification process in terms that provide the clearest description available in ancient literature of what complete integration involves: "My thoughts, feelings, desires, and memories (aryu) have been purified of egoistic elements. Nothing remains that could raise objection to my experience of undifferentiated consciousness... there can be no objectors among any human beings or..." [2].

This verse reveals that complete purification involves the dissolution of mental patterns that previously created resistance to divine awareness [5]. The practitioner declares that "Nothing remains that could raise objection to my experience of undifferentiated consciousness." This does not mean the elimination of thoughts, feelings, or memories, but rather their purification such that they no longer create obstruction to divine awareness or generate egoistic reactivity patterns [2].

The ancient teachings illuminate how this represents the elimination of what might be called "karmic motivations that agitate the surface of consciousness, thereby causing undifferentiated consciousness to differentiate into agitated thoughts, disturbing feelings, and compulsive desires" [5]. When the mental witnesses (aryu) that draw consciousness into subject-object duality are purified, awareness naturally rests in its essential undifferentiated state without being pulled into mental modifications that create suffering and limitation [2].

This verse provides the clearest description of what complete integration involves: consciousness operating without internal resistance to divine awareness, enabling the stable divine dialogue that Chapter 175 demonstrates [2][4]. It establishes the foundation for understanding how consciousness can maintain natural divine communication while functioning effectively in worldly circumstances [5].

# MOVING FROM INDIVIDUAL TO COSMIC INTEGRATION

Understanding individual purification naturally leads us to examine the cosmic dimensions of spiritual establishment [5]. While verses 177-179 describe the individual process of purification, the teaching becomes complete only when we understand how individual transformation relates to universal spiritual reality. This understanding emerges through examining verse 180, which reveals the ultimate verification criteria for authentic spiritual establishment [2].

## VERSE 180: ULTIMATE VERIFICATION OF INTEGRATION

Verse 180 describes the ultimate verification of spiritual establishment through criteria that extend far beyond individual psychological transformation [2]. The verse reveals the consciousness of a personality functioning without any form of obstruction that would produce resistance to the experience of higher consciousness states (Ra, Nunu, Ba en Ra). The text provides comprehensive description: "there can be no objectors (witnesses/testifiers) among any gods or goddesses and there can be no objectors (witnesses/testifiers) among any noble persons... there can be no objectors (witnesses/testifiers) even from among any objects in the world, people, animals, plants, earth, air, water, etc." [2].

The scripture continues with even more comprehensive scope: "and in fact there can be no objectors (witnesses/testifiers), sources in the unconscious that call out for mental attention or demanding desires, from any objects in the entirety of Creation, planets, stars, etc.; whatever may be the limits of existence, there can be nothing obstructing, raising objections or obstacles for such a person's capacity to experience pure consciousness" [2].

This teaching indicates complete integration where neither internal mental patterns nor external circumstances create obstruction to divine awareness [5]. The scripture establishes that authentic spiritual establishment manifests as consciousness functioning without internal or external objectors, enabling stable operation in pure consciousness regardless of circumstances. This represents the ultimate verification criterion: consciousness that can maintain divine awareness under any conditions because all potential sources of resistance have been resolved through the purification process [2].

The comprehensive scope of this teaching reveals the ancient sages' understanding that authentic spiritual establishment must be complete rather than partial [5]. Consciousness cannot maintain stable divine awareness if any significant sources of resistance remain unresolved. The teaching indicates that complete integration involves resolving all potential sources of objection or resistance, from gross physical circumstances through subtle psychological patterns to the deepest unconscious formations that might create agitation or distraction [2].

This cosmic scope helps contemporary practitioners understand why authentic spiritual development requires a comprehensive approach rather than focusing on isolated aspects of practice [5]. The teaching suggests that sustainable spiritual establishment emerges only through systematic purification that addresses all levels of potential resistance rather than creating temporary states of elevated awareness that lack stability when challenging circumstances arise [2].

# BRIDGING ANCIENT WISDOM TO CONTEMPORARY PRACTICE

Understanding these ancient scriptural descriptions raises the question of how contemporary aspirants can apply these teachings practically [5]. The bridge between ancient wisdom and modern application becomes clear when we recognize that these texts describe universal principles of consciousness development rather than culturally specific practices.

However, the ancient Egyptian approach to spiritual establishment included more than textual study and contemplative understanding [1]. The sages recognized that consciousness development requires what may be termed "embodied wisdom"—practical methods that engage multiple dimensions of human experience to support the profound transformations their scriptures describe. This comprehensive approach included sophisticated ritual implements designed specifically to facilitate the consciousness transitions that Book of Enlightenment Chapter 175 demonstrates and the purification process that Scripture of Ra and Hetheru verses 177-179 describe [4][2].

## Sacred Technology: The HETEP Offering Table as Consciousness Transformation Tool

Book of Enlightenment Chapter 175 verses 4 and 6 include the teaching of "hetep" or spiritual, non-dual inner peace [4]. The profound concept of HETEP in Ancient Egyptian spirituality reveals itself as far more than its conventional translation as "peace." The hieroglyphic texts describe HETEP as "supreme peace, the final abode of all who satisfy the desire of their soul, union with its Higher Self: YOGA" [1]. This understanding transforms our appreciation of the physical HETEP offering table from ceremonial artifact to sophisticated spiritual technology, carefully engineered to facilitate the practitioner's journey from dual to non-dual consciousness through ritual action imbued with profound metaphysical significance.

Classic three-dimensional HETEP offering table

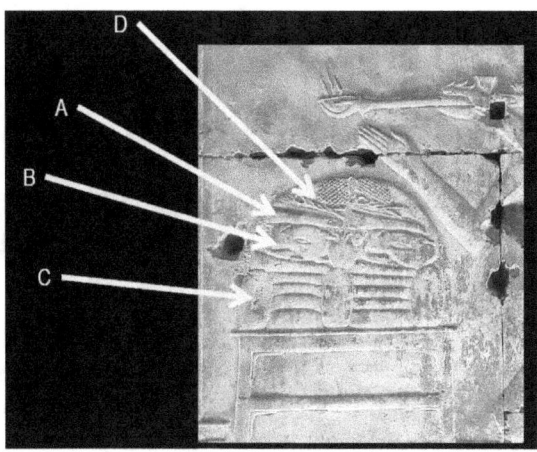

## COMPONENTS OF THE HETEP SYMBOLISM

- The haunch of beef symbolizing the masculine principle (A),
- geese representing the feminine principle (B),
- bread signifying spiritual sustenance (C),
- and optional fruits and vegetables representing additional spiritual nourishment (D).

The architectural precision of the HETEP offering table demonstrates the ancient sages' genius for creating physical implements that embody abstract spiritual principles [1]. The table features four main components representing different aspects of the offering: the haunch of beef symbolizing the masculine principle, geese representing the feminine principle, bread signifying spiritual sustenance, and optional fruits and vegetables representing additional spiritual nourishment. Still, the most sophisticated element lies in what the tradition describes as the dual canal system—two channels for directing libation fluids that "lead to a reservoir and then the dual canals join in a non-dual exit that goes into a vessel" [1].

Diagram showing the libation system of HETEP table with two separate channels flowing into a reservoir, then merging into single exit channel leading to collection vessel

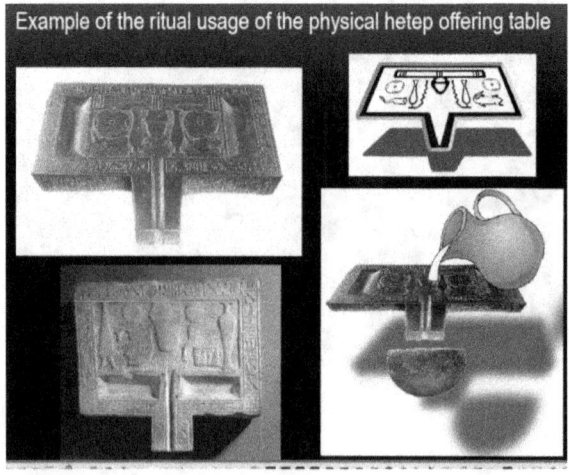

This architectural feature physically manifests the fundamental philosophical principle underlying all Ancient Egyptian spiritual practice: the transcendence of duality to achieve unity [5]. Furthermore, the libation system operates as concrete demonstration of what the teachings describe as "Smai Tawi"— the union of the two lands, higher and lower aspects of self— transforming abstract metaphysical concepts into tangible ritual experience. The ancient sages understood that consciousness development requires more than intellectual understanding; it demands embodied wisdom where physical actions serve as bridges between material and spiritual realms [1][5].

The ritual usage of the HETEP table operates simultaneously on physical and metaphysical levels, reflecting the Ancient Egyptian understanding that "HETEP is also an offering of food in the sense of that which sustains life, so it can be a physical offering with physical items, or it can be the images or concepts of those items which sustain the spiritual self" [1]. This dual nature reveals sophisticated psychological insight: consciousness transformation occurs through engaging multiple dimensions of human experience rather than remaining confined to mental or emotional domains alone [5].

IMAGE: Ancient Egyptian tomb painting showing figures performing HETEP offering ritual, with practitioners making offerings at table while hieroglyphic text describes the ritual process]

## Direct Connection to Chapter 175: From Physical to Spiritual Sustenance

The profound significance of the HETEP offering emerges through its role as systematic methodology for transcending duality [1]. As the ancient texts reveal, the practice represents "offering maleness (haunch of beef) and femaleness (geese) in a continuous flow (libated) of mental attention towards the Divine to go from dualism of mental and perceptual experience to non-dual unitary transcendental experience and divine awareness." The ultimate purpose involves "breaking down the duality between ego and Spirit to discover there is no ego, only Spirit"— a recognition that aligns perfectly with our examination of the Soul-Aware-Witness beyond ego-identification [1][5].

This understanding receives direct confirmation in Chapter 175 of the Pert-em-Heru, where consciousness transcends ordinary physical sustenance through recognition of spiritual fulfillment [4]. When Any declares: "To be given to me is becoming an Akh (spirit/enlightened being) instead of food and drink" and "Instead of those things I get inner peace; instead of food and drink I get inner peace; and this is a good thing, in fact I will be better off," we can understand how this transformation demonstrates practically what the HETEP offering facilitates theoretically: the movement from seeking satisfaction through external means to discovering the divine fullness that constitutes consciousness's essential nature [4][5].

The HETEP table provided practitioners with concrete methodology for understanding and practicing this transformation [1]. Rather than attempting to transcend physical needs through intellectual understanding alone, practitioners could engage in ritual action that embodied the very principles Chapter 175 describes. The act of offering physical sustenance while contemplating its spiritual significance created experiential understanding of how consciousness naturally chooses superior satisfaction when it has direct access to both physical and spiritual fulfillment [4][5].

## Spiritual Technology: Integration of Ritual and Philosophy

The HETEP offering table thus functions as what contemporary practitioners might recognize as "spiritual technology"—a carefully designed system that facilitates specific consciousness states through coordinated physical, mental, and spiritual activities [1][5]. Yet this technology requires proper understanding rather than mechanical application. The ancient sages taught that ritual effectiveness depends upon the practitioner's recognition of the philosophical principles embodied within physical actions. The table serves as external support for internal transformation, providing concrete methodology for practicing the abstract principle of transcending subject-object duality [1].

Observe how this approach addresses the practical challenge that contemporary spiritual practitioners often encounter: the difficulty of maintaining spiritual awareness during daily activities [5]. The HETEP practice created structured opportunity for consciousness to experience the movement from duality to unity through coordinated action that engaged body (somatic), mind (psyche) and soul (spirit) simultaneously. This embodied approach reinforced the scriptural teachings through direct experiential practice rather than leaving practitioners dependent solely on intellectual understanding [1].

The integration of ritual and philosophical aspects within HETEP practice demonstrates the sophisticated approach of Ancient Egyptian spiritual methodology [1]. Rather than treating ceremony and understanding as separate domains, the tradition created unified systems where physical actions and metaphysical comprehension mutually reinforce each other. Moreover, the HETEP offering exemplifies what the teachings describe as "Shedy" (spiritual discipline)—the systematic practice through which aspirants penetrate the "Shetaut Neter" (Divine Mysteries) by discovering that "all of nature is divine, including plants, animals, planets, stars, food, and other people" [1][5].

IMAGE: Example of physical HETEP offering table usage showing ancient table with libation vessel, demonstrating how liquid flows through dual channels to single exit

## Contemporary Applications of Ancient Spiritual Technology

For contemporary practitioners of transpersonal psychology, the HETEP offering table provides profound insights into how physical ritual can catalyze authentic spiritual transformation when approached with proper philosophical foundation [5]. The table's sophisticated design—particularly its libation system that physically demonstrates the movement from duality through integration to unity—offers practical methodology for what we have examined as consciousness development from ego-identification through witness recognition to divine realization [1][5].

This ancient spiritual technology stands as testament to the depth of Egyptian wisdom and its continuing relevance for serious students seeking not merely intellectual understanding but genuine consciousness transformation through integrated spiritual practice [1]. Contemporary practitioners can apply these principles by creating their own ritual practices that embody spiritual principles through physical action, engaging multiple dimensions of experience to support the consciousness transformations that the scriptures describe [5].

The HETEP teaching reveals that the ancient sages understood consciousness development as requiring a comprehensive approach that addresses the total human being rather than focusing exclusively on mental or emotional aspects [1][5]. This understanding helps explain why the Ancient Egyptian spiritual establishment proved so stable and effective—it engaged all aspects of human experience in service of divine recognition rather than attempting to transcend physical existence without resolving mental, feeling and physical oriented human issues.

Understanding the HETEP offering table thus enhances our comprehension of how the scriptural teachings on spiritual establishment were meant to be applied practically [1]. The table demonstrates that the ancient approach included sophisticated tools designed to support the profound transformations described in Chapter 175, the purification processes outlined in verses 177-179, and the practical integration guidance provided by Amenemopet's teachings [4][2][3].

# EXPANDING THE FOUNDATION: ADDITIONAL SCRIPTURAL CONTRIBUTIONS

Understanding HETEP offering practices becomes even more meaningful when we recognize how they build upon and apply the foundational teachings found in other ancient Egyptian scriptures [1]. These additional sources provide essential context that deepens our understanding of how spiritual establishment functions across different levels of consciousness and practical application [5].

### The Soul-Aware-Witness: Foundation for Integration

The concept of the Soul-Aware-Witness, which we examined in detail in earlier chapters, provides the psychological foundation that makes practical integration possible [5]. Ancient Egyptian Pert-em-Heru Chapter 26 describes this essential development through specific declarations: "my heart, he is peaceful within me," "I know myself," and "I have control over my arms and legs (body)" [6].

These statements might initially appear simple or obvious, but they describe profound psychological transformation [5]. This signifies human "consciousness that has achieved separation from ego-identification and now operates as what the ancient teachings call the 'instrument of the soul' (consciousness that exercises appropriate control over the body without being controlled by bodily urges and desires, functioning from inner peace and divine recognition rather than reactive patterns)" [6].

Understanding this foundation helps explain why the practical integration that Amenemopet describes becomes possible [3][5]. Without the Soul-Aware-Witness providing stable foundation, consciousness remains identified with the fluctuating contents of experience rather than recognizing its essential nature as the unchanging awareness within which all experience arises. This identification creates the heated patterns that Amenemopet describes—consciousness seeking fulfillment through external circumstances because it has not yet discovered its essential fullness [3][5].

These declarations provide specific indicators of established consciousness that contemporary practitioners can observe in their own development: natural inner peace that does not depend on external circumstances arising from recognition of one's essential divine nature; authentic self-knowledge that comes from recognizing oneself as awareness rather than identifying with temporary mental and physical phenomena; and natural self-control that emerges from divine recognition rather than forced effort to suppress natural impulses [6][5].

The Soul-Aware-Witness development, in a human personality, serves as the foundation for all practical integration because it provides stable identity that does not fluctuate with changing circumstances [5]. From this stable foundation, consciousness can engage effectively with worldly responsibilities while maintaining recognition of divine nature, creating the conditions for the practical wisdom that Amenemopet describes [3].

## The Three Levels of Consciousness: Operating Framework for Integration

The Scripture of Ra and Hetheru describes how consciousness can function through three distinct levels that provide a comprehensive framework for understanding how spiritual establishment operates across different circumstances and requirements [2]. These three levels are: "Soul of Ra representing pure consciousness without subject-object differentiation; Nunu representing undifferentiated consciousness with non-specific awareness; and Ra representing individuated consciousness capable of self-reference and personal identity" while maintaining divine recognition and engagement [5].

This framework proves essential for understanding how practical integration actually functions [5]. Rather than consciousness being limited to a single mode of operation, established consciousness develops the capacity to access different operational modes as circumstances require while maintaining recognition of divine nature throughout all modes of functioning. This flexibility enables effective functioning in worldly situations without losing spiritual awareness, resolving the apparent conflict between spiritual development and practical effectiveness [2][5].

When circumstances require focused individual action and decision-making, established consciousness can operate through Ra level while maintaining divine recognition [5]. When circumstances call for receptive awareness without specific focus, consciousness can function through Nunu level. When circumstances support recognition of pure being beyond all differentiation, consciousness can rest in Soul of Ra level. This operational flexibility creates the foundation for the effective life navigation that Amenemopet describes through his boat metaphor [2][3].

Contemporary practitioners can develop this operational flexibility through recognizing that different circumstances naturally call for different levels of consciousness functioning [5]. Rather than attempting to maintain a single mode of awareness regardless of circumstances, practitioners can learn to respond appropriately to different situational requirements while maintaining underlying divine recognition that remains constant through all levels of functioning.

This understanding helps resolve common confusions that arise in spiritual development when practitioners expect consciousness to function in the same way during all circumstances [5]. The teaching reveals that mature spiritual development includes operational flexibility that enhances rather than diminishes practical effectiveness [2].

## Contemplative Study: Ongoing Integration Method

Amenemopet's Prologue establishes contemplative study as an ongoing method for maintaining integration rather than a preliminary practice that becomes unnecessary after achieving initial recognition [3]. The wisdom text establishes contemplative study as "wisdom philosophy that is based on recorded wisdom literature that is to be experienced in life" representing "an exposition of precise teachings that when understood exactly, with precision cause a person to have well-being while living on earth" [3].

This definition reveals that contemplative study serves multiple functions that support ongoing integration [3][5]. First, it provides discriminative wisdom that helps practitioners distinguish between temporary mental phenomena and the unchanging awareness that witnesses all mental activity. Second, it reinforces understanding of divine principles that support appropriate response to challenging circumstances. Third, it maintains connection with the wisdom tradition that provides guidance for navigating unprecedented situations.

This volume, "Mystic Transpersonal Psychology of Ancient Egyptian Non-Duality" explains that effective contemplative study involves "engaging in right thinking and feeling based on the truth that Ra consciousness represents the higher reality of life, taking the form of spiritual studies that develop discriminative wisdom capable of distinguishing between temporary mental phenomena and the unchanging awareness that witnesses all mental activity" [1][5].

This approach to contemplative study differs fundamentally from academic study that focuses on accumulating information or intellectual analysis that remains separated from practical application [5]. Instead, contemplative study involves engaging with wisdom teachings in ways that directly support spiritual recognition and practical integration rather than merely expanding intellectual understanding [3].

The text reveals that established consciousness maintains discriminative wisdom through continued study, promoting stable recognition of divine identity during daily activities [3][5]. Rather than assuming that initial spiritual recognition eliminates the need for ongoing study, the teaching indicates that continued engagement with wisdom literature supports the deepening and stabilization of spiritual understanding while providing guidance for applying spiritual principles in evolving life circumstances.

Contemporary practitioners can apply this teaching by maintaining regular engagement with wisdom literature that supports their spiritual development while focusing on practical application rather than intellectual accumulation [3][5]. The goal involves allowing wisdom teachings to inform daily decisions and responses rather than remaining confined to formal study periods.

# AMENEMOPET'S TEACHINGS ON PRACTICAL INTEGRATION

Having examined the scriptural descriptions of spiritual establishment and the ritual technologies that supported ancient practitioners, we must now understand how this profound transformation functions in practical daily life circumstances [3]. The ancient texts provide detailed theoretical understanding and sophisticated tools, but contemporary practitioners require specific guidance for maintaining spiritual establishment while fulfilling worldly responsibilities and navigating human relationships.

This practical dimension becomes especially important because the ancient teachings emphasize integration rather than withdrawal from worldly engagement [5]. Amenemopet's teachings serve as the essential bridge between the profound metaphysical insights revealed in Book of Enlightenment Chapter 175, the purification processes described in Scripture of Ra and Hetheru verses 177-179, and the practical requirements of daily life in temporal circumstances [4][2][3].

## The Boat Metaphor: Navigation Through Life Circumstances

Amenemopet provides one of the most practical and comprehensive metaphors for understanding how established consciousness operates in daily life through his teaching about the boat of life [3]. This metaphor reveals two fundamentally different approaches to navigating life circumstances and their dramatically different outcomes.

He describes the first approach through the experience of heated persons: "The evening boat, the boat of the concluding period of life, of the heated person, ends with experiences of struggling and strife, suffering and... ...forsakes, turns away from the purpose of life and the nature of the Divine (Neberdjer), due to being, as if, carried away on a great swell, a large, billowing wave of water, an overpowering force (of negative aryu/karma) that overwhelms the boat of life (mind and body)" [3].

This description reveals how consciousness operating from ego-identification becomes overwhelmed by circumstances rather than maintaining effective navigation [5]. The heated person's approach to life creates an accumulation of negative aryu (karmic patterns) that eventually produce circumstances that overwhelm their capacity to maintain equilibrium. The metaphor of being "carried away on a great swell" perfectly captures the experience of consciousness that lacks stable foundation in divine awareness—external circumstances determine one's internal state rather than internal stability providing the foundation for effective external navigation [3][5]. This phrase, "carried away on a great swell", may be likened to modern terms such as "Emotionally triggered", "fly off into emotional states", "Egoic states of identification".

In sharp contrast, Amenemopet describes the approach of established consciousness: "Now, as concerns the boat of life of those who lead a silent life, who do not live by egoistic desires, boisterousness in the temple or unethical behaviors, in their boat they are able to sail on fair winds that are pleasant and right for sailing, and right for reaching the destination of life, to reach the hand of God and be accepted by God as one with God" [3].

The integration method becomes clear through this powerful metaphor [5]. Established consciousness enables effective life management ("sail on fair winds") rather than being overwhelmed by circumstances ("carried away on a great swell"). The silent person's approach to life creates conditions that support rather than obstruct spiritual development and practical effectiveness simultaneously [3].

However, this teaching requires careful interpretation to avoid superficial understanding [5]. The text should not be regarded as a panacea promising that perfect adherence to these principles will result in constantly "smooth sailing" without any challenges or difficulties. Rather, the teaching signifies that there develops such purity of mind and feeling that whether there might be rough or smooth sailing times in the journey of life, there would be sufficient spiritual understanding and character purity to weather those occasional storms effectively without being overwhelmed or losing divine recognition and its inner contentment [3].

Additionally, the teaching indicates that during the smooth sailing happy times, established consciousness would not produce deluded notions of abiding happiness or fulfillment derived from worldly circumstances [5]. Both challenging and pleasant external conditions are met with the same underlying stability that comes from recognizing divine reality rather than depending on external circumstances for one's fundamental sense of well-being and purpose [3].

This sophisticated understanding helps contemporary practitioners develop realistic expectations about spiritual development while providing practical guidance for maintaining spiritual stability during both difficult and pleasant circumstances [5]. The teaching reveals that authentic spiritual establishment creates internal conditions that enable effective response to any external circumstances rather than requiring particular external conditions for maintaining spiritual awareness [3].

## The Silent Ones: Practical Demonstration of Integration

Amenemopet provides specific descriptions of how established consciousness actually functions in daily life through his teaching about silent persons [3]. These descriptions offer practical verification criteria that contemporary practitioners can apply to assess their own development while providing guidance for cultivating the qualities that characterize authentic spiritual establishment [5].

Amenemopet describes "silent" persons as naturally receptive to divine influence and capable of recognizing "the greatness of the blessings they receive" [3]. He explains: "Now, in reference to those who are silent, all who go into the House-of-Divine (Temple)... those silent ones speak of the greatness of the blessings they receive from being in the temple from the Creator-Spirit" [3].

This initial description reveals that established consciousness naturally recognizes divine presence in spiritual environments and spontaneously expresses gratitude for spiritual nourishment received [5]. The silent person does not need to force recognition of divine presence or artificially generate grateful feelings. These arise naturally from the clarity of perception that characterizes a purified mind, whose silence allows clearer perception of the underlying conscious reality of the oneself [3][5].

The teaching continues with more comprehensive explanation: "Behold the glory of this way of being! Being silent means discovering the fullness of the Creator-Spirit that is within. This fullness cannot come from heatedly searching for fulfillment in the world for fulfillment with an imperfect personality. Rather, it is found not by externalities but instead by realizing that there is perfection within when the fullness of being is experienced beyond the worldly desires and cravings" [3].

This passage reveals the essential difference between heated and silent approaches to fulfillment [5]. The heated approach involves "searching for fulfillment in the world for fulfillment with an imperfect personality"—consciousness seeking satisfaction through external activities and acquisitions while operating from ego-identification that creates persistent sense of lack or incompleteness. This approach inevitably leads to agitated, deluded mind because external circumstances cannot provide the stable satisfaction that the soul (universal consciousness operating through the limited human personality) seeks [3][5].

The silent approach involves "discovering the fullness of the Creator-Spirit that is within" rather than external seeking [3]. This discovery occurs through "realizing that there is perfection within when the fullness of being is experienced beyond the worldly desires and cravings." The teaching indicates that consciousness naturally discovers internal spiritual fullness when it ceases heated seeking patterns that create agitation and distraction [5].

The practical integration that this teaching describes indicates that established consciousness naturally recognizes divine presence in spiritual environments and operates from internal spiritual fullness rather than seeking external satisfaction for fulfillment [3]. This creates conditions where spiritual practice becomes nourishing and easeful rather than effortful, and daily activities are approached from fullness rather than seeking to fill internal emptiness [5].

Contemporary practitioners can apply this teaching by observing their own relationship to spiritual practice and daily activities [5].

Do life activities and spiritual practices feel nourishing and naturally satisfying, or do they feel like efforts to achieve something that seems absent? Do daily activities arise from internal fullness and service orientation, or from attempting to satisfy internal emptiness through external achievements? These practical criteria help assess whether one's spiritual development is progressing toward silent integration or remaining trapped in heated seeking patterns [3].

# THEORETICAL GUIDANCE FOR CONTEMPORARY PRACTITIONERS

Having examined the complete range of scriptural teachings on spiritual establishment and integration, we can now provide comprehensive guidance for contemporary practitioners who seek to apply these ancient teachings practically [5]. This guidance emerges from synthesizing the verification criteria, practical methods, and ongoing maintenance approaches that the various scriptures provide when understood as a complete system.

## Recognition of Spiritual Establishment

Based on the complete scriptural evidence, authentic establishment manifests through observable characteristics that provide reliable criteria for assessing spiritual development [1][2][3][4][5][6]. These characteristics operate across multiple dimensions of experience, providing comprehensive verification that helps practitioners distinguish between preliminary experiences and stable establishment.

From Chapter 175, we observe natural confidence in divine communication that arises from recognizing one's essential divine nature rather than approaching spiritual reality with fear, excessive reverence, or dependence on elaborate ritual preparation [4][5]. Established consciousness demonstrates preference for spiritual over physical satisfaction based on direct comparative experience rather than forced suppression of natural desires. This preference emerges naturally when consciousness discovers through direct experience that spiritual fulfillment surpasses physical pleasure in both quality and sustainability [4].

Additionally, Chapter 175 reveals cosmic recognition of divine nature where individual spiritual development is understood within the context of universal divine functioning rather than remaining limited to personal achievement or advancement [4]. The text demonstrates functional relationship with divine authority while maintaining individual operational capacity, indicating integration rather than dissolution of personality or individual effectiveness [5].

From Scripture of Ra and Hetheru Verses 177-179, we observe personality transparency to divine forces where wisdom, compassion, and effective action flow through the individual without being obstructed or distorted by egoistic resistance [2][5]. This transparency develops gradually through sustained spiritual practice and manifests as increasing naturalness in expressing divine qualities rather than effortful attempts to cultivate spiritual characteristics.

The verses also reveal absence of internal resistance to divine awareness, manifesting as decreasing internal conflict between spiritual aspirations and natural human functioning [2]. Rather than experiencing spiritual development as suppression of natural tendencies, established consciousness experiences harmony between divine recognition and effective human functioning [5].

What's more, these verses demonstrate consciousness functioning as vehicle for "words-of-power" and "vital-life-fire," meaning that transformative spiritual energy operates through the individual in ways that benefit both personal development and service to others [2].

From Scripture of Ra and Hetheru Verse 180, we observe complete absence of "objectors" or internal resistance patterns that previously created obstacles to pure consciousness experience [2]. This manifests as stable capacity to maintain divine awareness regardless of external circumstances or internal mental activity [5].

From Amenemopet, we see the ability to "sail on fair winds" through life circumstances, demonstrating effective navigation of both challenging and pleasant situations without being overwhelmed by difficulties or deluded by temporary satisfactions

[3]. The teaching reveals natural receptivity to divine blessings in spiritual environments where spiritual practices feel nourishing rather than effortful, and discovery of internal spiritual fullness that eliminates heated seeking patterns characterized by persistent dissatisfaction and compulsive pursuit of external fulfillment [5].

## Methods for Maintaining Integration

Understanding the characteristics of spiritual establishment naturally leads to consideration of the methods that maintain and deepen integration over time [5]. The scriptural evidence reveals that spiritual establishment requires ongoing maintenance rather than representing a permanent achievement that needs no further attention or development.

Daily life navigation benefits from applying Amenemopet's boat metaphor, which provides guidance for maintaining spiritual establishment during worldly activities [3]. The teaching indicates that established consciousness naturally "sails on fair winds" rather than being "carried away" by circumstances, enabling effective life management from divine awareness rather than reactive responses to changing conditions [5]. This involves developing capacity to respond to circumstances from internal stability rather than allowing external conditions to determine internal state.

Practical application involves cultivating the silent qualities that Amenemopet describes avoiding egoistic desires that create persistent dissatisfaction; maintaining appropriate behavior in spiritual environments rather than boisterous or disruptive conduct; and practicing ethical behaviors that align with divine principles rather than seeking personal advantage through unethical means [3]. These practices create conditions that support rather than obstruct spiritual awareness during daily activities [5].

Continuous purification operates through the spiritual roasting principle described in the Scripture of Ra and Hetheru, indicating that established consciousness maintains ongoing purification through "vital-life-fire" that continues operating within the personality [2]. This ensures sustained transparency to divine forces rather than gradual accumulation of new resistances that might eventually obstruct divine awareness [5].

Practical application involves maintaining comprehensive spiritual practice that combines ethical living, contemplative study, divine name repetition, and regular meditation [1][2][3]. The ancient sages understood that sustained spiritual establishment requires ongoing practice rather than representing a condition that maintains itself automatically once achieved [5].

Discriminative wisdom develops through Amenemopet's teaching on contemplative study, revealing that integration requires ongoing discrimination between temporary mental phenomena and unchanging awareness [3]. This maintains clarity about one's divine identity during daily activities when consciousness easily becomes distracted by changing circumstances or engaging mental activity [5].

Practical application involves regular engagement with wisdom literature that supports discriminative understanding while focusing on practical application rather than intellectual accumulation [3][5]. This helps practitioners maintain proper perspective during challenging circumstances by remembering the spiritual principles that provide guidance for appropriate response.

Relationship with divine authority follows the pattern Chapter 175 demonstrates, where establishment involves functional relationship with divine reality ("he may see me as his second") rather than claiming independent divine status [4]. This indicates proper integration of individual and cosmic consciousness where personal spiritual development serves universal purposes rather than ego-aggrandizement [5].

Practical application involves maintaining humility and service orientation that recognizes individual spiritual development as participation in universal divine functioning rather than personal achievement that creates superiority over others who have not achieved similar development [5].

## Verification Criteria for Ongoing Development

The combined scriptural evidence provides specific criteria that enable practitioners to assess their ongoing development across three complementary categories of observable characteristics

[1][2][3][4][5][6]. These criteria help distinguish between authentic spiritual establishment and preliminary experiences that may lack stability or comprehensive integration.

Inner indicators provide the foundation for all other aspects of spiritual establishment [5]. Natural inner peace that remains stable independent of external circumstances demonstrates the Soul-Aware-Witness functioning as stable foundation for all experience rather than consciousness being identified with changing phenomena [6]. This peace emerges from recognition of one's essential divine nature rather than being cultivated through effort or maintained through controlling circumstances [5].

Absence of internal resistance to divine awareness manifests as decreasing internal conflict between spiritual aspirations and natural human functioning, enabling harmony between divine recognition and effective practical engagement rather than experiencing spiritual development as suppression or rejection of natural human capacities [2][5].

Spiritual practices that may have started as forced cultivation of grateful attitudes matured to a point where it indicates natural receptivity that arises from purified perception [3]. This receptivity creates conditions where spiritual practice feels nourishing and naturally satisfying rather than effortful or duty-driven [5]. This development also leads to spontaneous recognition of divine blessings in spiritual environments.

Internal spiritual fullness eliminates heated seeking patterns characterized by persistent dissatisfaction and compulsive pursuit of external fulfillment [3]. This fullness enables engagement with worldly activities from abundance rather than attempting to satisfy internal emptiness through external achievements or acquisitions [5].

Functional indicators demonstrate how spiritual establishment enhances rather than diminishes practical effectiveness in worldly circumstances [5]. Effective life navigation without being overwhelmed by circumstances shows consciousness operating from stable foundation rather than reactive responses to changing conditions [3]. This effectiveness includes both managing challenging situations skillfully and maintaining appropriate perspective during pleasant circumstances.

Natural confidence in spiritual communication indicates comfort with spiritual reality that comes from recognition of one's essential divine nature rather than approaching spiritual dimensions with fear, excessive formality, or dependence on elaborate preparation [4][5]. This confidence enables direct engagement with spiritual practice and spiritual community in ways that feel natural rather than artificial or performed.

Transparency to divine forces in daily activities manifests as increasing naturalness in expressing wisdom, compassion, and effective service rather than effortful attempts to cultivate spiritual qualities or maintain spiritual appearances [2][5]. This transparency allows divine principles to inform decisions and responses without conscious effort or self-conscious spiritual performance.

Preference for spiritual over physical satisfaction when both are available demonstrates consciousness naturally choosing superior forms of fulfillment based on direct experience rather than intellectual conviction or moral obligation [4]. This preference emerges naturally when consciousness has direct access to spiritual satisfaction rather than being imposed through willpower or ascetic practices [5].

Relational indicators reveal how spiritual establishment affects one's relationship with others and with spiritual reality itself [5]. Proper relationship with divine authority rather than spiritual inflation indicates recognition that individual spiritual development serves universal purposes rather than creating personal superiority or special status [4]. This humility comes from understanding one's place within larger spiritual reality rather than being cultivated through self-deprecation or artificial modesty [5].

Natural service orientation rather than ego-aggrandizement demonstrates spiritual development expressing through beneficial action that serves others rather than seeking recognition, status, or personal advantage through spiritual attainment [5]. This service orientation arises spontaneously from the fullness that characterizes established consciousness rather than being imposed through moral obligation or spiritual duty.

Ability to maintain individual functionality while operating from divine recognition indicates integration rather than dissolution of personality or practical capacity [4][5]. This shows spiritual establishment enhancing rather than diminishing one's capacity to function effectively in worldly circumstances while maintaining recognition of divine nature throughout all activities.

# SYNTHESIZING THE COMPLETE TEACHING

Having examined each scriptural source individually and explored their practical applications, we can now synthesize the complete teaching to understand how all these elements work together as an integrated system of spiritual development [1][2][3][4][5][6]. This synthesis reveals the profound approach of the ancient sages who designed complementary teachings that address every aspect of spiritual establishment from initial recognition through complete integration and ongoing maintenance.

## The Developmental Progression

The scriptural evidence reveals a natural developmental progression that begins with establishing the Soul-Aware-Witness as stable foundation, proceeds through systematic purification that dissolves ego-identification patterns, continues through direct recognition of divine nature and cosmic integration, and culminates in stable integration that maintains divine awareness throughout all life circumstances while enhancing rather than diminishing practical effectiveness [5][6].

This progression occurs through what the texts describe as comprehensive spiritual practice that combines ethical living aligned with divine principles, contemplative study that develops discriminative understanding, divine name repetition that maintains connection with spiritual reality, and regular meditation that enables direct recognition of consciousness's essential nature beyond ego-identification [1][2][3].

The ancient sages understood that each aspect of this comprehensive approach serves essential functions that cannot be replaced by other practices [1][5]. Ethical living creates conditions that support rather than obstruct spiritual development by aligning one's actions with divine principles rather than egoistic preferences. Contemplative study provides understanding that enables discrimination between temporary phenomena and eternal awareness while offering guidance for applying spiritual principles in evolving circumstances [3].

Divine name repetition maintains conscious connection with divine reality during daily activities when consciousness might otherwise become absorbed in temporal concerns [1]. Regular meditation provides direct access to consciousness's essential nature beyond the contents of experience, enabling recognition of divine identity that serves as foundation for all other aspects of spiritual development [5].

## The Integration Challenge

The scriptures reveal that authentic spiritual establishment requires resolving what represents the fundamental challenge of spiritual development: maintaining transcendent awareness while engaging fully with temporal existence rather than seeking escape from worldly responsibilities through spiritual pursuits [5].

This challenge becomes especially acute for practitioners who achieve preliminary spiritual recognition but struggle to maintain stability when facing ordinary life challenges [3][5]. The ancient teachings address this challenge by providing both the theoretical understanding and practical methods necessary for achieving stable integration rather than alternating between spiritual elevation and worldly engagement.

Chapter 175 demonstrates the final result where consciousness maintains natural divine communication while functioning effectively in any circumstances [4]. The spiritual roasting verses describe the purification process that creates internal conditions where such integration becomes natural rather than effortful [2]. The HETEP offering table provides ritual technology that supports the consciousness transformations through embodied practice [1]. Amenemopet's teachings provide practical guidance for maintaining integration during daily activities while fulfilling worldly responsibilities effectively [3].

**The Verification Framework**

The complete scriptural evidence provides a comprehensive verification framework that enables practitioners to assess their development while distinguishing between authentic spiritual establishment and preliminary experiences that may lack stability or integration [1][2][3][4][5][6].

This framework operates across multiple dimensions of experience rather than relying on single criteria that might be misleading [5]. Inner indicators reveal the quality of one's relationship with spiritual reality and the degree of internal resistance to divine awareness. Functional indicators demonstrate how spiritual development affects practical effectiveness and life navigation capacity. Relational indicators show how spiritual establishment influences one's relationships with others and with divine reality itself.

The comprehensive nature of this verification framework helps practitioners avoid common errors such as mistaking temporary elevated experiences for stable establishment, confusing intellectual understanding with experiential recognition, or assuming that partial development in certain areas indicates complete spiritual establishment [5].

# CONCLUSION: THE SCRIPTURAL MAP FOR SPIRITUAL ESTABLISHMENT

The examination of these ancient texts reveals a comprehensive understanding of how spiritual consciousness becomes established and integrated that addresses every aspect of authentic spiritual development from initial recognition through complete establishment and ongoing maintenance [1][2][3][4][5][6]. This understanding emerges through recognizing how different scriptures address complementary aspects of the complete transformation process rather than representing isolated teachings that compete with each other.

Pert em Heru Chapter 175 demonstrates the final result: consciousness capable of natural divine dialogue while maintaining individual functionality and effective engagement with any circumstances [4]. This demonstration provides practitioners with clear vision of what authentic spiritual establishment actually involves rather than leaving them to guess about the goals of spiritual development [5].

The spiritual roasting verses (Scripture of Ra and Hetheru 177-179) describe the purification process that enables such transformation through systematic spiritual practice that generates internal conditions where ego-identification patterns naturally dissolve while consciousness recognition of divine nature emerges effortlessly [2]. This description provides practical guidance for approaching purification effectively rather than struggling with suppression or forced elimination of natural human tendencies [5].

Scripture of Ra and Hetheru Verse 180 provides the ultimate verification criterion: absence of any internal or external resistance to pure consciousness that enables stable operation in divine awareness regardless of circumstances [2]. This criterion helps practitioners distinguish between preliminary experiences and authentic establishment while providing clear direction for continued development [5].

The HETEP offering table demonstrates the ancient sages' comprehensive approach that included sophisticated ritual technology designed to support the consciousness transformations through embodied practice that engaged multiple dimensions of human experience simultaneously [1]. This reveals their understanding that sustainable spiritual development requires methods that address the total human being rather than focusing exclusively on mental or emotional aspects [5].

Amenemopet's teachings offer practical guidance for maintaining establishment during daily life circumstances through specific instruction that enables integration of spiritual recognition with worldly responsibilities and human relationships [3]. He prescribes practice of maintaining awareness of Neberdjer (the truth and existence and reality of all-encompassing-Divinity), developing trust in divine guidance (hand of God), avoiding luxury-dependence or anxiousness about the future, cultivating contentment and developing personality characteristics that avoid boisterousness, excessive reliance on worldly pleasures, rapacious attitudes, or aggressive behavior patterns [5].

These scriptures serve as complementary aspects of a complete teaching system where each element supports and enhances the others rather than functioning independently [1][2][3][4][5][6]. Purification enables transformation by creating internal conditions where divine recognition becomes natural. Transformation enables divine dialogue by establishing consciousness in its essential divine nature. Divine dialogue confirms cosmic integration by revealing one's place within universal divine functioning. Ritual technology provides embodied support for consciousness transformations. Practical guidance ensures stable maintenance of this establishment during ongoing worldly engagement by providing methods for navigating temporal circumstances from divine awareness.

The ancient sages designed this comprehensive framework to address the complete spectrum of spiritual development: from initial purification through final establishment and ongoing integration [5]. These teachings reveal that authentic spiritual realization enhances rather than diminishes practical effectiveness, creating consciousness capable of effective service while operating from unshakeable divine recognition rather than ego-based reactive patterns.

Therefore, these scriptures provide not only theoretical speculation, but practical roadmaps based on direct experience of consciousness functioning in its established divine nature [1][2][3][4][5][6]. The ancient Egyptian civilization produced and preserved these teachings through millennia of application and refinement, testing their effectiveness across countless individual cases and varying cultural circumstances.

For contemporary aspirants, they offer reliable guidance for both recognizing authentic spiritual development and maintaining integrated awareness throughout all life circumstances [5]. The teachings provide specific criteria for assessing progress, practical methods for supporting continued development, and comprehensive understanding of what authentic spiritual establishment actually involves rather than leaving practitioners dependent on speculation or superficial indicators.

As the ancient tradition reveals, spiritual establishment represents not the end of the spiritual journey but rather its mature beginning—consciousness functioning from divine recognition while engaging fully in temporal existence for the benefit of all beings [5]. This mature functioning serves both individual fulfillment and collective benefit by creating examples of integrated spiritual development that inspire and guide others while contributing to the spiritual evolution of humanity through conscious participation in divine will rather than ego-driven activity that creates suffering and limitation.

The scriptures ultimately reveal that authentic spiritual establishment creates consciousness capable of functioning as conscious instrument of divine purpose in manifestation, serving the highest good of all beings while maintaining personal fulfillment that comes from recognition of one's essential divine nature rather than dependence on external circumstances for satisfaction and meaning [1][2][3][4][5][6].

# References

[1] Ashby, M. (2016). Egyptian Book of the Dead Hieroglyph Translations for Enlightenment: Understanding the Mystic Path to Enlightenment Through Direct Readings of the Sacred Signs and Symbols of Ancient Egyptian Language With Trilinear Deciphering Translation Method Vol. 1. Translation by Dr. Muata Ashby. Sema Institute.
[2] Ashby, M. (2022). The Mysteries of Ra and Hetheru/Sekhmet. Translation by Dr. Muata Ashby. Sema Institute.
[3] Ashby, M. (2019). Teachings of Ancient Egyptian Sage Amenemopet with Hieroglyphic texts. Translation by Dr. Muata Ashby. Sema Institute.
[4] Ashby, M. (2016). Egyptian Book of the Dead Hieroglyph Translations for Enlightenment Vol. 1. Chapter 175 Pert-em-Heru: Conversation with Temu. Translation by Dr. Muata Ashby. Sema Institute.
[5] Ashby, M. (2025). DEFINITIONS: The Nature of Consciousness and Awareness in Neterian Philosophy. Translation by Dr. Muata Ashby.
[6] Ashby, M. (2025). Papyrus Ani [Book of the Dead] Chapter 17 Verse 3-6- trilinear translation. Translation by Dr. Muata Ashby.

# INDEX

*Ab*, 55, 146, 241
Abraham, 15
Absolute, 15, 32, 35, 37, 61, 88, 93, 96, 112, 114, 116, 178, 193, 194, 317, 318, 325, 327, 404
Africa, 4, 5, 410, 418, 420, 422, 423
African Proverbial Wisdom Teachings, 428
*African Religion*, 404, 412, 417
All-encompassing divinity, 96, 178
Allopathic, 405
Amenemopet (ancient sage), 46, 52, 58, 63, 64, 104, 106, 131, 132, 133, 134, 140, 168, 169, 170, 171, 184, 186, 194, 199, 248, 254, 256, 257, 258, 260, 261, 265, 266, 267, 268, 272, 274, 276, 278, 279, 281, 285, 288, 290, 298, 300, 310, 330, 333, 334, 343, 344, 345, 369, 370, 371, 372, 374, 375, 376, 380, 381, 386, 388, 389
Amenta, 411

*Amentet*, 413
American Heritage Dictionary, Dictionary, 417
American Theocracy, 421
Amun, 47, 92, 103, 193, 236, 237, 249, 250, 270, 324, 327, 329
Amun-Ra, 47, 92, 103, 236, 237, 249, 270, 324, 327, 329
Ancient Egypt, 2, 3, 4, 5, 6, 15, 16, 17, 18, 19, 20, 22, 24, 25, 26, 28, 29, 34, 35, 36, 37, 38, 39, 40, 41, 42, 44, 45, 46, 48, 50, 51, 52, 53, 54, 64, 65, 67, 71, 73, 84, 86, 87, 92, 104, 112, 113, 118, 122, 124, 126, 138, 140, 141, 150, 152, 158, 159, 162, 165, 167, 172, 173, 176, 178, 180, 183, 184, 190, 199, 200, 201, 206, 207, 208, 209, 214, 215, 216, 223, 230, 231, 236, 254, 257, 259, 271, 282, 288, 289, 290, 291, 292, 293, 294, 305, 308, 311, 317, 329,

334, 337, 341, 342, 343, 344, 363, 365, 367, 369, 370, 373, 389, 404, 405, 406, 407, 408, 409, 410, 411, 412, 413, 414, 415, 416, 417, 418, 419, 421, 422, 426, 427, 429, 430, 431, 432, 433, 436, 437
**Ancient Egyptian Wisdom Texts**, 427
anger, 46, 63, 107, 108, 139, 151, 162, 260, 415
Ani, 184, 343, 390
*Anu*, 323, 412
*Anu (Greek Heliopolis)*, 323, 412
Anunian Theology, 412
Apep serpent, 124, 128, 204, 205
Apophis, 124, 126, 128, 131, 204, 205
Architecture, 81
*Ari*, 320
Aryan, 407
Aryu, 43, 120, 121, 131, 134, 139, 221, 238, 264, 308
Aryu (karmic impressions/mental residues), 43, 120, 121, 131, 134, 139,

221, 238, 264, 308
Aryu (karmic impressions/mental residues/feeling memories), 43, 120, 121, 131, 134, 139, 221, 238, 264, 308
Asar, 5, 16, 42, 47, 52, 54, 63, 86, 112, 114, 116, 123, 127, 130, 159, 160, 161, 162, 163, 164, 165, 166, 179, 183, 190, 191, 193, 200, 201, 202, 203, 204, 209, 214, 215, 216, 217, 218, 219, 222, 223, 224, 225, 226, 227, 228, 229, 231, 232, 250, 255, 262, 274, 303, 308, 311, 312, 319, 323, 329, 344, 346, 347, 354, 355, 356, 410, 411, 414, 415, 436
Asar and Aset, 410
Asar/Osiris (universal soul consciousness), 203, 216, 219, 312
Asarian Resurrection, 141, 410, 414, 415, 417, 436
Aset, 5, 407, 410, 411, 413, 414, 415, 436
Aset (Isis), 5, 407, 410, 411, 413, 414, 415, 436

Ashanti, 428
Asia, 423
Asia Minor, 423
Asiatic, 420, 422, 423
Assyrians, 426
Astral, 212, 411
Astral Plane, 212, 411
Atlantis, 418
Attachment, 327
Avoiding, 109, 335
Awakening, 75, 78, 79, 230, 315, 411, 432
Awareness, 31, 33, 78, 80, 90, 97, 104, 162, 169, 171, 176, 177, 193, 253, 254, 272, 285, 286, 288, 313, 315, 317, 318, 325, 326, 328, 330, 331, 332, 389
*awet ab*, 321
Ba (also see Soul), 35, 73, 82, 83, 84, 86, 88, 92, 94, 179, 185, 197, 198, 203, 204, 209, 212, 213, 252, 253, 282, 283, 308, 330, 361
Ba (soul essence), 35, 73, 82, 83, 84, 86, 88, 92, 94, 179, 185, 197, 198, 203, 204, 209, 212, 213, 252, 253, 282, 283, 308, 330, 361
Ba en Ra (Soul of Ra - absolute consciousness), 35, 73, 82, 83, 84, 88, 92, 94,

185, 197, 198, 252, 253, 283, 308, 330, 361
Being, 168, 209, 244, 247, 261, 285, 306, 308, 320, 323, 336, 377, 413
Bhagavad Gita, 426
Bible, 414
**Black**, 422
Black Africa, 422
Body, 163, 209, 432
Book of Coming Forth By Day, 411, 412
Book of Enlightenment, 16, 28, 34, 37, 52, 53, 87, 92, 112, 113, 118, 124, 126, 140, 159, 162, 172, 173, 178, 180, 183, 184, 201, 206, 207, 208, 215, 216, 223, 231, 259, 271, 290, 294, 308, 311, 317, 334, 363, 374
Book of the Dead, see also Rau Nu Prt M Hru, 16, 28, 39, 63, 104, 141, 158, 180, 184, 199, 206, 207, 231, 288, 343, 389, 390, 412, 427, 435
Brain, 16
Breathing, 316
Buddha, 418, 419, 420, 434
Buddhism, 3, 4, 412, 419
Buddhist, 410, 420

career counselor,
    career, job, 79
Catholic, 414
Catholic Church, 414
Causal Plane, 212
Challenging, 174
Change, 327
*Child*, 414, 415
Christ, 411
*Christianity*, 404,
    412, 414
Church, 414
Civilization, 407,
    419, 420, 421,
    422, 431, 432
coercion, 421
Coffin Texts, 343
**Collapse**, 420, 431,
    433
color, 425, 428
Color, 425
Concepts, 41, 176,
    336
Conflict, 421, 428
Confucianism, 4
Congress, 2
Conscious, 33, 41,
    88, 266, 281,
    300, 331
Conscious-
    awareness, 33,
    41, 88
Consciousness, 2,
    15, 35, 41, 44,
    45, 53, 60, 61,
    65, 71, 80, 81,
    84, 86, 88, 89,
    91, 93, 94, 96,
    97, 98, 99, 100,
    102, 104, 105,
    116, 120, 122,
    142, 156, 161,
    178, 180, 188,
    190, 191, 193,
    196, 197, 198,
    200, 208, 214,
    215, 221, 236,
    237, 240, 249,
    250, 251, 253,
    254, 262, 267,
    270, 283, 284,
    286, 288, 290,
    298, 303, 304,
    311, 317, 325,
    326, 327, 328,
    331, 334, 337,
    362, 363, 371,
    389, 410, 427
Consciousness,
    human, 35, 42,
    56, 59, 60, 62,
    122, 126, 129,
    131, 134, 142,
    143, 144, 147,
    151, 157, 158,
    189, 194, 208,
    250, 273, 284,
    295, 296, 344,
    346, 404
contentment, 31,
    76, 105, 114,
    115, 164, 173,
    174, 211, 286,
    348, 352, 353,
    375, 388, 434,
    436
Contentment (see
    also Hetep),
    325, 327
Coptic, 411
cosmic force, 44,
    74, 122, 143,
    150, 151, 238,
    240, 266, 276,
    413, 419
Cosmic Mind, 143,
    149, 156, 193,
    239, 240
cosmic vibration,
    153
Cosmos, 65, 93,
    115
Cow, 29
Creation, 29, 35,
    50, 51, 52, 62,
    65, 66, 68, 69,
    71, 73, 74, 75,
    81, 83, 85, 88,
    90, 92, 93, 94,
    113, 114, 115,
    120, 143, 146,
    147, 149, 150,
    151, 156, 157,
    169, 170, 171,
    172, 173, 176,
    179, 180, 181,
    184, 186, 187,
    189, 190, 194,
    200, 201, 204,
    205, 224, 239,
    240, 249, 250,
    251, 271, 272,
    279, 282, 284,
    298, 305, 306,
    320, 322, 323,
    330, 332, 333,
    334, 345, 361,
    410, 412, 427,
    436
Culture, 409, 418,
    424, 432, 433
Death, 16, 420, 431
December, 413
Deep sleep, 193,
    315
delusion, 43, 44,
    58, 74, 78, 79,
    81, 91, 97, 98,
    106, 107, 111,
    112, 114, 115,
    127, 132, 138,
    140, 144, 153,
    165, 173, 182,
    184, 195, 196,
    210, 215, 232,
    238, 239, 242,
    244, 245, 252,
    284, 285, 295,
    308, 312, 346,
    351, 358, 436,
    437
Delusion, 118, 120,
    218, 284
Denderah, 411
depression, 152,
    436
Desire, 428

Destruction of Humankind, 29
Devotional Love, 408
Diet, 406
Discipline, 309
discrimination, 42, 61, 92, 127, 129, 130, 137, 220, 222, 227, 257, 264, 266, 281, 282, 287, 292, 299, 301, 311, 325, 335, 337, 381, 385
Discrimination, 129, 175, 281, 310
Divine Consciousness, 91, 154, 161
Djehuty/Thoth (cosmic mind, intellect), 146, 154
Dollar, U.S. Dollar, 433
Dream, 65, 66, 71, 73, 75, 76, 77, 193
Dream, REM sleep, 65, 66, 71, 73, 75, 76, 77, 193
Duality, 344, 373
Duat, 321, 349, 411
dullness, 305
Earth, 188
Edfu, 411
Ego, 31, 32, 35, 57, 98, 99, 118, 174, 175, 191, 218, 259
Egyptian Book of Coming Forth By Day, 411
Egyptian civilization, 209, 388

Egyptian Mysteries, 2, 107, 406, 415, 416, 429, 430
Egyptian Physics, 413
Egyptian Proverb, 408
EGYPTIAN PROVERBS, 408
Egyptian Yoga, 404, 406, 410, 411, 412
Egyptian Yoga see also Kamitan Yoga, 3, 4, 107, 404, 406, 410, 411, 412, 434, 435
Egyptologists, 416, 426
Empire culture, 421
Enlightenment, 16, 29, 39, 52, 53, 63, 87, 92, 104, 112, 113, 124, 126, 140, 141, 158, 159, 162, 172, 178, 183, 184, 199, 201, 206, 207, 208, 215, 216, 223, 231, 259, 271, 288, 290, 294, 308, 311, 317, 334, 363, 374, 389, 404, 406, 408, 409, 411, 412, 413, 415, 419, 428, 431, 432
Ethics, 294, 406, 407, 419, 421, 422, 428
Ethiopia, 428
ethnicity, 175
Eucharist, 411
Europe, 5

evil, 122, 127, 179, 415, 416
Evil, 417
Exercise, 300, 410
Existence, 65, 68, 89, 188, 223, 224, 225, 226, 227, 229
Eye, 29, 74
Eye of Ra, 29, 74
**Faith**, 423
False, 77
Fate, 267
Finances, 432
Fire, 244, 245, 308, 358, 359
Form, 18
Formal meditation, 302
frustration, 106, 129, 162, 333, 436
Fullness, 171
Galla, 428
Galla culture, 428
Geb, 410
Ghana, 428
global economy, 421
Globalization, 421
Glorious Light Meditation, 29, 30, 40, 75, 104, 141, 231, 254, 409
God, 54, 61, 85, 86, 87, 135, 137, 138, 145, 149, 150, 153, 155, 156, 162, 180, 204, 206, 208, 214, 215, 230, 233, 235, 236, 241, 242, 244, 246, 248, 268, 269, 282, 298, 300, 318, 323, 355, 375, 388, 408, 412, 413, 418, 425

Goddess, 162, 233, 413, 425
Goddesses, 150, 151, 181, 242, 245, 358, 410, 417
Gods, 68, 150, 151, 181, 204, 242, 245, 358, 410, 417
gods and goddesses, 38, 42, 44, 65, 68, 73, 74, 75, 85, 114, 135, 149, 204, 205, 308, 319, 323, 354, 356, 412, 417, 418, 436, 437
Good, 417
Gospels, 414
Greece, 406, 418
Greek philosophy, 404
Greeks, 426
Harmony, 116
**Hate**, 428
**Hatha Yoga**, 421, 422
Hathor, 40, 42, 74, 145, 153, 282, 410, 411, 413, 415, 434
Hatred, 428
Health, 165, 166, 405, 413
Heart, 55, 172, 241, 248, 265, 415, 424
Heart (also see Ab, mind, conscience), 55, 172, 241, 248, 265, 415, 424
Heaven, 414
Hekau, 44, 434
Hekau (words of power, sacred utterances), 44, 434
Heliopolis, 323

Hermes, 430
Hermes (see also Djehuti, Thoth), 430
Hermetic, 430
Hermeticism, 430
Heru, 55, 122, 123, 124, 125, 126, 127, 128, 129, 130, 131, 135, 140, 178, 184, 212, 218, 231, 282, 283, 290, 344, 349, 350, 354, 366, 370, 387, 389, 411, 412, 413, 414, 415, 417, 427, 436
Heru (see Horus), 55, 122, 123, 124, 125, 126, 127, 128, 129, 130, 131, 135, 140, 178, 184, 212, 218, 231, 282, 283, 290, 344, 349, 350, 354, 366, 370, 387, 389, 411, 412, 413, 414, 415, 417, 427, 436
Herufy (dual nature of human consciousness), 122, 123, 124, 126, 127, 128, 129, 131
Hetep, 212, 213
Hetheru, 145, 415
Hetheru (Hetheru, Hathor), 16, 29, 40, 42, 52, 59, 61, 62, 64, 65, 66, 68, 69, 71, 73, 74, 75, 80, 81, 84, 89, 92, 102, 104, 105,

106, 120, 133, 134, 140, 145, 153, 158, 176, 178, 180, 181, 184, 185, 213, 223, 231, 232, 233, 238, 241, 248, 254, 256, 257, 259, 262, 263, 278, 280, 284, 288, 290, 301, 303, 305, 306, 308, 333, 343, 344, 345, 357, 363, 371, 374, 379, 380, 387, 389, 415
Hieroglyphic, 17, 18, 21, 24, 25, 26, 40, 64, 104, 131, 140, 158, 184, 199, 254, 288, 343, 389, 409, 425, 430
Hieroglyphic texts, 17, 18, 40, 64, 104, 140, 158, 184, 199, 254, 288, 343, 389, 430
Hieroglyphic Writing, language, 17, 18, 21, 24, 25, 26, 40, 64, 104, 131, 140, 158, 184, 199, 254, 288, 343, 389, 409, 425, 430
*Hieroglyphs*, 26
Hinduism, 412
Hindus, 416
hope, 424, 425
Horus, 124, 126, 127, 135, 137, 138, 218, 283, 349, 354, 436
HUMANITY, 416

Hymn to Ra, 317, 324, 325
Iamblichus, 426
Ibis, 150, 151, 157
Identification, 163
illusion, 31, 32, 34, 99, 102, 105, 115, 119, 170, 181, 187, 191, 217, 218, 224, 227, 232, 260, 274, 277, 279, 280
Illusion, 191
Image, 125, 347
India, 54, 406, 407, 409, 410, 420, 421
Indian Yoga, 3, 407
Indus, 407
Indus Valley, 407
Initiate, 406
Intellectual, 220, 286, 310
Isis, 5, 407, 410, 411, 413, 434, 436
Isis, See also Aset, 5, 407, 410, 411, 413, 434, 436
*Islam*, 404
Jesus, 411, 414, 434
Jesus Christ, 411
*Judaism*, 404
*Kabbalah*, 404
Kamit (Egypt), 417
Kamitan, 406, 418
Karma, 409
Kemetic, 3, 103, 253, 419, 424, 429, 432, 435, 436
Khemn (ignorance), 416
*Khemn, see also ignorance*, 416
King, 106, 188, 414, 418

Kingdom, 124, 140, 184, 206, 414
Kingdom of Heaven, 414
Krishna, 414
Kundalini, 3
Kundalini XE "Kundalini" Yoga see also Serpent Power, 3
Kybalion, 430
Liberation, 162
Life, 31, 36, 73, 75, 76, 98, 116, 171, 245, 258, 267, 285, 300, 308, 358, 359, 374, 410, 418, 423, 424, 427
*Life Force*, 410
Lord of Eternity, 202, 203, 217, 219, 311, 312
*Love*, 408, 434
lucid, 192
Maat, 4, 38, 43, 75, 95, 116, 121, 124, 125, 126, 129, 139, 140, 143, 148, 153, 156, 172, 173, 182, 183, 213, 221, 239, 244, 248, 262, 263, 265, 271, 275, 282, 289, 291, 294, 295, 296, 297, 298, 301, 302, 303, 309, 316, 321, 324, 327, 333, 346, 409, 413, 415, 418, 419, 424, 427, 429, 431, 432
MAAT, 408

Maat (divine order, truth, righteous living), 4, 38, 43, 75, 95, 116, 121, 124, 125, 126, 129, 139, 140, 143, 148, 153, 156, 172, 173, 182, 183, 213, 221, 239, 244, 248, 262, 263, 265, 271, 275, 282, 289, 291, 294, 295, 296, 297, 298, 301, 302, 303, 309, 316, 321, 324, 327, 333, 346, 409, 413, 415, 418, 419, 424, 427, 429, 431, 432
Maat Philosophy, 415, 419, 424, 431
*MAATI*, 408
Malawi, 428
Mathematics, 88, 197, 198, 240
Matter, 93, 413
media, 209, 421
Meditation, 40, 75, 104, 141, 177, 231, 254, 264, 301, 302, 309, 331, 332, 406, 408, 409
Meditation practice, 75, 177, 264, 302
Meditation system, 75
Mediterranean, 155
*Medu Neter*, 416, 434
Medu Neter (hieroglyphic

sacred texts), 416, 434
*Memphite Theology*, 412
Mental States, 138
**Mer**, 321
Meskhenet, 409
Metaphor, 300, 374
Metaphysics, 413, 427
Middle East, 404
Min, 410
Mind, 46, 60, 97, 138, 142, 143, 145, 149, 156, 163, 177, 193, 239, 240, 241, 244, 245, 248, 260, 284, 298, 360, 432
Moon, 155
Music, 4, 425
Mysteries, 2, 16, 24, 40, 64, 104, 107, 140, 158, 184, 190, 231, 254, 288, 343, 367, 389, 406, 415, 416, 426, 429, 430, 437
Mystic psychology, 37
mystical philosophy, 420, 427
Mysticism, 71, 343, 406, 407, 412, 413, 415, 419, 421, 422
Nature, 44, 65, 68, 104, 118, 120, 121, 122, 188, 189, 193, 223, 226, 227, 254, 288, 389
Neberdjer, 30, 50, 51, 52, 62, 63, 82, 88, 92, 93, 96, 111, 112, 113, 114, 115, 116, 152, 164, 169, 170, 171, 172, 173, 178, 185, 186, 187, 188, 189, 190, 191, 193, 194, 195, 196, 197, 198, 199, 200, 201, 209, 215, 222, 224, 226, 250, 268, 271, 272, 273, 274, 275, 279, 294, 298, 300, 308, 329, 330, 331, 332, 333, 334, 374, 388, 404
Neberdjer (All-encompassing divinity), 30, 50, 51, 52, 62, 63, 82, 88, 92, 93, 96, 111, 112, 113, 114, 115, 116, 152, 164, 169, 170, 171, 172, 173, 178, 185, 186, 187, 188, 189, 190, 191, 193, 194, 195, 196, 197, 198, 199, 200, 201, 209, 215, 222, 224, 226, 250, 268, 271, 272, 273, 274, 275, 279, 294, 298, 300, 308, 329, 330, 331, 332, 333, 334, 374, 388, 404
Nefer, 187, 189, 193, 250, 330, 337, 338, 339, 341, 343
Nefertem, See also Nefertum, 322
*Nehast*, 416
Nehast (spiritual awakening, resurrection), 416
neo-con, 421
Net, goddess, 42, 85, 86, 143, 144, 150, 156, 170, 193, 204, 207, 209, 238, 250, 276, 305
Neter, 81, 85, 89, 96, 98, 103, 107, 110, 137, 138, 139, 162, 164, 165, 167, 171, 178, 179, 184, 188, 193, 197, 199, 204, 205, 206, 208, 211, 219, 221, 223, 233, 235, 246, 250, 255, 258, 273, 275, 277, 286, 289, 290, 291, 296, 320, 337, 339, 341, 346, 367, 408, 411, 416, 417, 420, 426, 429, 433, 434
Neterian, 26, 104, 190, 254, 288, 317, 347, 389, 417, 420, 432, 433, 434, 435
Neterianism, 430, 433
Neteru, 42, 242, 417, 436
Neteru (gods and goddesses as cosmic principles), 42, 242, 417, 436
Netherworld, 159, 188, 201

New Kingdom, 124, 140, 184, 206
Nigeria, 428
Nile flood, 147, 148
Nun (See also Nu primeval waters-unformed matter), 66, 86, 91, 178, 343
Nunu, 15, 30, 35, 37, 45, 52, 60, 65, 66, 69, 71, 73, 75, 80, 81, 83, 85, 86, 87, 88, 89, 90, 91, 92, 93, 94, 95, 96, 98, 121, 174, 175, 176, 177, 178, 179, 180, 184, 185, 196, 197, 203, 204, 209, 222, 223, 249, 251, 252, 253, 262, 264, 277, 280, 282, 283, 284, 287, 296, 303, 304, 330, 336, 361, 371, 372
Nunu consciousness, 46, 91, 95, 96, 175, 176, 222, 253, 262, 304, 336
Nut, 410
Ocean, 253
Orion Star Constellation, 413
Orthodox, 416
Osiris, 5, 16, 23, 42, 51, 52, 54, 62, 86, 112, 123, 127, 130, 159, 160, 161, 162, 163, 165, 179, 183, 187, 201, 202, 203, 205, 209, 214, 215, 216, 217, 219, 223, 224, 231, 255, 262, 303, 311, 312, 319, 323, 346, 347, 349, 410, 411, 417, 436
Peace, 212, 317, 318, 325, 327, 428, 431, 432
Peace (see also Hetep), 212, 317, 318, 325, 327, 428, 431, 432
Persians, 426
*PERT EM HERU, SEE ALSO BOOK OF THE DEAD*, 412
Pert-em-Heru (Book of Enlightenment/ Coming Forth by Day), 16, 28, 37, 290, 344, 350, 366, 370, 389
Pharaoh, 432
Philae, 411
Philosophical, 175, 191, 196, 264, 301, 302, 310
Philosophy, 3, 4, 24, 104, 254, 255, 257, 258, 259, 262, 264, 267, 270, 278, 283, 284, 285, 288, 367, 389, 404, 406, 407, 408, 412, 413, 415, 419, 421, 422, 424, 431, 432
Physical, 147, 173, 212, 294, 295, 352, 366
physical realm, 348, 352
physical world, 117, 156, 160
pressure, 102, 177
priests and priestesses, 20, 24, 146, 154, 339, 340, 410, 417, 437
Priests and Priestesses, 406, 417
Progressive, 41, 220, 307, 312, 314, 316, 328
Proverbial Wisdom, 428
Psychology, 2, 15, 16, 28, 36, 41, 59, 91, 122, 126, 158, 162, 166, 199, 206, 208, 210, 230, 253, 344, 373, 413, 430
Ptah, 193, 250, 413
Ptolemaic period, 207, 209
quantum physics, 196
Queen, 418
Ra, 85, 86, 106, 145, 146, 149, 150, 155, 156, 203, 204, 233, 234, 242, 244, 282, 317, 318, 319, 321, 322, 323, 324, 349, 410
Ra (individuated divine consciousness), 15, 16, 29, 30, 35, 37, 40, 42,

44, 45, 46, 52, 59, 60, 61, 62, 64, 65, 66, 68, 69, 70, 71, 73, 74, 75, 80, 81, 82, 83, 84, 85, 86, 87, 88, 89, 90, 91, 92, 93, 94, 95, 96, 98, 99, 100, 101, 102, 103, 104, 105, 106, 107, 120, 133, 134, 137, 139, 140, 142, 143, 145, 146, 149, 150, 151, 152, 153, 154, 155, 156, 157, 158, 174, 175, 176, 177, 178, 179, 180, 181, 182, 184, 185, 193, 196, 197, 198, 203, 204, 205, 209, 212, 213, 214, 222, 223, 231, 232, 233, 234, 235, 236, 237, 238, 240, 241, 242, 244, 245, 246, 248, 249, 250, 251, 252, 253, 254, 256, 257, 259, 262, 263, 264, 270, 274, 275, 277, 278, 280, 282, 283, 284, 287, 288, 289, 290, 296, 297, 301, 303, 304, 305, 306, 307, 308, 310, 317, 318, 319, 321, 322, 323, 324, 325, 326, 327, 328, 329, 330, 333, 336, 343, 344, 345, 349, 352, 355, 356, 357, 358, 361, 363, 371, 372, 373, 374, 379, 380, 387, 389, 410

Ra, See also Ra-Herakty, 15, 16, 29, 30, 35, 37, 40, 42, 44, 45, 46, 52, 59, 60, 61, 62, 64, 65, 66, 68, 69, 70, 71, 73, 74, 75, 80, 81, 82, 83, 84, 85, 86, 87, 88, 89, 90, 91, 92, 93, 94, 95, 96, 98, 99, 100, 101, 102, 103, 104, 105, 106, 107, 120, 133, 134, 137, 139, 140, 142, 143, 145, 146, 149, 150, 151, 152, 153, 154, 155, 156, 157, 158, 174, 175, 176, 177, 178, 179, 180, 181, 182, 184, 185, 193, 196, 197, 198, 203, 204, 205, 209, 212, 213, 214, 222, 223, 231, 232, 233, 234, 235, 236, 237, 238, 240, 241, 242, 244, 245, 246, 248, 249, 250, 251, 252, 253, 254, 256, 257, 259, 262, 263, 264, 270, 274, 275, 277, 278, 280, 282, 283, 284, 287, 288, 289, 290, 296, 297, 301, 303, 304, 305, 306, 307, 308, 310, 317, 318, 319, 321, 322, 323, 324, 325, 326, 327, 328, 329, 330, 333, 336, 343, 344, 345, 349, 352, 355, 356, 357, 358, 361, 363, 371, 372, 373, 374, 379, 380, 387, 389, 410

Ra-Akhu, 233, 235, 244
racism, 429
**Racism**, 428
Ra-Herakty, 237
Ra-level consciousness, 92, 94, 175, 262
Reality, 112, 128, 351
**Realization**, 407
Reflection, 317
Relationships, 76
Religion, 3, 404, 407, 411, 412, 414, 415, 417, 418, 419, 421, 422, 433, 434
Ren, 193, 250
Resurrection, 127, 141, 410, 411, 413, 414, 415, 417, 435, 436
Ritual, 147, 367, 388, 415
Rituals, 413
Roman, 426
Romans, 426
Rome, 418
Sage Amenemope, 16, 30, 37, 40, 46, 52, 58, 63, 64, 104, 106,

131, 140, 158, 168, 171, 184, 194, 199, 254, 256, 258, 260, 266, 268, 274, 278, 281, 288, 290, 298, 300, 310, 330, 333, 334, 343, 344, 389

Sages, 337, 338, 339, 343, 404, 411, 412, 415, 419, 434

Saints, 412, 434

School, 3

Scribe, 317

Scripture of Ra and Hetheru, 5, 16, 29, 30, 37, 44, 45, 46, 52, 59, 60, 61, 62, 65, 66, 68, 71, 73, 74, 75, 80, 84, 89, 92, 102, 105, 106, 120, 133, 134, 142, 158, 176, 178, 180, 181, 185, 197, 198, 213, 223, 232, 238, 241, 248, 256, 257, 259, 262, 263, 278, 280, 284, 290, 301, 303, 305, 306, 308, 333, 344, 345, 357, 363, 371, 374, 379, 380, 387

Sebai, 419, 430, 433

See also Ra-Hrakti, 85, 86, 106, 145, 146, 149, 150, 155, 156, 203, 204, 233, 234, 242, 244, 282, 317, 318, 319, 321, 322, 323, 324, 349, 410

See Nat, 42, 85, 86, 143, 144, 150, 156, 170, 193, 204, 207, 209, 238, 250, 276, 305

Sekhem, 68

Sekhem (life force energy), 68

Sekhemit, 29, 43, 52, 60, 74, 81, 134, 232, 233, 234, 235, 237, 238

Sekhmet, 16, 40, 64, 104, 106, 120, 140, 158, 184, 209, 231, 254, 288, 343, 389

Self (see Ba, soul, Spirit, Universal, Ba, Neter, Heru)., 28, 35, 38, 93, 94, 111, 116, 158, 166, 167, 174, 189, 210, 211, 212, 213, 225, 230, 233, 237, 242, 245, 273, 296, 297, 308, 317, 318, 325, 326, 328, 329, 341, 358, 363, 407, 409, 411, 416, 425

Self-created lifestyle, lifestyle, 303, 315

Sema, 2, 3, 5, 16, 39, 40, 64, 104, 107, 140, 141, 158, 184, 199, 231, 254, 288, 305, 389, 418, 429, 431, 434

Set, 122, 123, 124, 125, 127, 128, 129, 417

Seti I, 409

Setjert drink (sacred transformative elixir), 235, 236

Sex, 348, 410

sexism, 429

**Sexism**, 428

Sexuality, 348, 353

Shedy, 367, 405

Sheps, 187

Shetaut Neter, 26, 31, 33, 38, 39, 41, 45, 49, 81, 89, 98, 103, 107, 110, 138, 139, 162, 164, 165, 167, 171, 184, 188, 197, 199, 205, 211, 219, 221, 235, 255, 258, 273, 275, 277, 286, 289, 290, 291, 296, 337, 339, 341, 346, 367, 411, 416, 417, 420, 429, 433, 434

Shetaut Neter (Ancient Egyptian spiritual tradition), 26, 31, 33, 38, 39, 41, 45, 49, 81, 89, 98, 103, 107, 110, 138, 139, 162, 164, 165, 167, 171, 184, 188, 197, 199, 205, 211, 219, 221, 235, 255, 258, 273,

275, 277, 286, 289, 290, 291, 296, 337, 339, 341, 346, 367, 411, 416, 417, 420, 429, 433, 434
Shetaut Neter See also Egyptian Religion, 26, 31, 33, 38, 39, 41, 45, 49, 81, 89, 98, 103, 107, 110, 138, 139, 162, 164, 165, 167, 171, 184, 188, 197, 199, 205, 211, 219, 221, 235, 255, 258, 273, 275, 277, 286, 289, 290, 291, 296, 337, 339, 341, 346, 367, 411, 416, 417, 420, 429, 433, 434
Shetitu (secret code of teachings), 416
Shu (air and space), 86, 190
Signs, 16, 39, 63, 104, 141, 158, 184, 199, 231, 288, 389
Silence, 168, 171, 212, 246, 261
*Sirius*, 413
slavery, 416
Sleep, 313, 315
Sleeping Patterns, Sleep, 313, 315
Smai, 365
Smai Tawi, 365
society, 4, 77, 405, 417, 419, 424, 428, 429, 431, 434
Society, 431, 433

Soul, 15, 27, 28, 30, 31, 32, 34, 35, 36, 37, 38, 45, 47, 48, 52, 56, 59, 60, 61, 70, 73, 82, 86, 87, 88, 89, 90, 92, 93, 94, 95, 96, 98, 100, 101, 118, 119, 122, 135, 138, 140, 159, 162, 163, 164, 165, 168, 171, 172, 174, 175, 177, 178, 180, 183, 184, 185, 195, 196, 198, 203, 204, 205, 206, 208, 209, 212, 214, 215, 218, 219, 223, 224, 244, 249, 251, 259, 260, 262, 264, 266, 277, 280, 281, 282, 283, 284, 287, 295, 300, 303, 304, 311, 312, 335, 338, 366, 370, 371, 372, 382, 384, 417, 432
Soul of Ra recognition, 96, 175, 178, 184, 262, 280
Soul-Aware-Witness, 27, 28, 31, 32, 34, 35, 36, 38, 47, 48, 52, 56, 59, 61, 73, 92, 93, 94, 95, 96, 101, 118, 119, 122, 135, 138, 140, 159, 163, 164, 165, 168, 171, 172, 175, 183, 184, 185, 195,

196, 198, 206, 214, 215, 218, 219, 259, 260, 262, 266, 281, 282, 283, 284, 296, 300, 312, 335, 338, 366, 370, 371, 382, 384
Spirit, 32, 44, 46, 61, 63, 80, 85, 86, 111, 112, 143, 146, 149, 152, 154, 155, 156, 168, 170, 171, 172, 180, 181, 193, 203, 204, 205, 215, 233, 235, 239, 242, 244, 245, 246, 247, 250, 261, 262, 276, 285, 303, 306, 325, 334, 358, 366, 376, 377
Spirit Being, 32, 242
Spiritual Development, 228, 255, 345
Spiritual discipline, 405
Spiritual Practices, 289
*SPIRITUALITY*, 406, 424, 433, 435
Study, 153, 165, 175, 294, 301, 309, 310, 312, 372
Sublimation, 410
Superpower, 421
Superpower Syndrome, 421
Superpower Syndrome Mandatory Conflict Complex, 421

Supreme Being, 209, 320, 323, 413
*TANTRA*, 410
*TANTRA YOGA*, 410
Taoism, 404
Tawi, 365
Tefnut (moisture), 190
Tem, 190, 237, 352, 354
Temple, 246, 339, 376, 411, 415, 433
Temple of Aset, 411
Temple of Hetheru, 415
**Temu**, 319, 344, 347, 348, 349, 351, 352, 354, 357, 359, 389
The Absolute, 404
The All, 185, 198
**The Black**, 422
The God, 68, 410
The Gods, 68, 410
Theban Theology, 404
Thebes, 404, 409
**Theocracy**, 420, 421
Theology, 3, 404, 412, 413
Thoth, 143, 145, 146, 149, 150, 155, 156, 238, 239, 240, 241
Thoughts, 68, 227
Thoughts (see also Mind), 68, 227
Time, 318, 325, 326, 328
time and space, 69, 88, 106, 116, 117, 160, 169, 171, 186, 190, 225, 241, 255, 272, 283, 330, 331, 333, 346, 347, 417

Tomb, 5, 29, 73, 85, 204, 241, 242, 243, 244, 409
Tomb of Seti I, 409
transcendental reality, 417
Transpersonal psychology, 15, 36, 37
Tree, 427
Tree of Life, 427
Triad, 404
Trinity, 411
Truth, 44, 148, 172, 220, 221, 294, 310
Tutankhamun, 241, 242, 243, 244
Tutankhamun, Pharaoh, 241, 242, 243, 244
Unconscious, 164
Understanding, 15, 16, 21, 39, 41, 48, 57, 59, 61, 63, 71, 76, 79, 81, 84, 95, 97, 98, 102, 104, 105, 118, 119, 122, 140, 141, 158, 184, 188, 191, 194, 199, 205, 220, 223, 231, 232, 249, 254, 255, 271, 285, 287, 288, 291, 293, 298, 300, 302, 303, 306, 308, 312, 314, 318, 330, 331, 335, 339, 345, 357, 359, 361, 362, 369, 370, 380, 389, 417, 431
United States of America, 421
Universal Ba, 209

Universal Consciousness, 65, 93, 190, 215, 284, 410
Upanishads, 412, 426
Vedanta, 4
Vedic, 407
**Violence**, 428
Waking, 193
Waset, 404
Wealth, Money, 432
White, 431
Will, 170, 171, 279
Wisdom, 16, 25, 30, 36, 37, 50, 61, 71, 75, 131, 133, 138, 171, 206, 207, 209, 256, 257, 258, 260, 281, 290, 293, 294, 310, 337, 338, 339, 343, 408, 410, 426, 427, 428, 432
Wisdom (also see Djehuti, Aset), 16, 25, 30, 36, 37, 50, 61, 71, 75, 131, 133, 138, 171, 206, 207, 209, 256, 257, 258, 260, 281, 290, 293, 294, 310, 337, 338, 339, 343, 408, 410, 426, 427, 428, 432
Witness, 28, 34, 35, 52, 56, 59, 61, 73, 92, 93, 94, 95, 96, 101, 118, 119, 122, 135, 138, 140, 159, 163, 164, 165, 168, 171, 172, 175, 183, 184, 185, 195,

196, 198, 206,
214, 215, 218,
219, 221, 237,
249, 250, 251,
259, 260, 262,
266, 270, 281,
282, 283, 284,
296, 300, 312,
317, 325, 326,
327, 328, 334,
335, 338, 366,
370, 371, 382,
384

Witness consciousness, 196, 221

World War II, 421

Yoga, 3, 107, 305, 404, 406, 407, 410, 411, 412, 413, 415, 418, 419, 421, 422, 434, 435

Yoga of Devotion (see Yoga of Divine Love), 434

Yogic, 422, 429

Yoruba, 428

# OTHER BOOKS BY MUATA ASHBY

P.O.Box 570459

Miami, Florida, 33257

(305) 378-6253
Fax: (305) 378-6253

Prices subject to change.

*EGYPTIAN YOGA: THE PHILOSOPHY OF ENLIGHTENMENT* An original, fully illustrated work, including hieroglyphs, detailing the meaning of the Egyptian mysteries, tantric yoga, psycho-spiritual and physical exercises. Egyptian Yoga is a guide to the practice of the highest spiritual philosophy which leads to absolute freedom from human misery and to immortality. It is well known by scholars that Egyptian philosophy is the basis of Western and Middle Eastern religious philosophies such as *Christianity, Islam, Judaism,* the *Kabala,* and Greek philosophy, but what about Indian philosophy, Yoga and Taoism? What were the original teachings? How can they be practiced today? What is the source of pain and suffering in the world and what is the solution? Discover the deepest mysteries of the mind and universe within and outside of yourself. 8.5" X 11" ISBN: 1-884564-01-1 Soft $19.95

*EGYPTIAN YOGA: African Religion Volume 2-* Theban Theology U.S. In this long awaited sequel to *Egyptian Yoga: The Philosophy of Enlightenment* you will take a fascinating and enlightening journey back in time and discover the teachings which constituted the epitome of Ancient Egyptian spiritual wisdom. What are the disciplines which lead to the fulfillment of all desires? Delve into the three states of consciousness (waking, dream and deep sleep) and the fourth state which transcends them all, Neberdjer, "The Absolute." These teachings of the city of Waset (Thebes) were the crowning achievement of the Sages of Ancient Egypt. They establish the standard mystical keys for understanding the profound mystical symbolism of the Triad of human consciousness. ISBN 1-884564-39-9 $23.95

THE KEMETIC DIET: GUIDE TO HEALTH, DIET AND FASTING Health issues have always been important to human beings since the beginning of time. The earliest records of history show that the art of healing was held in high esteem since the time of Ancient Egypt. In the early 20th century, medical doctors had almost attained the status of sainthood by the promotion of the idea that they alone were "scientists" while other healing modalities and traditional healers who did not follow the "scientific method' were nothing but superstitious, ignorant charlatans who at best would take the money of their clients and at worst kill them with the unscientific "snake oils" and "irrational theories". In the late 20th century, the failure of the modern medical establishment's ability to lead the general public to good health, promoted the move by many in society towards "alternative medicine".

Alternative medicine disciplines are those healing modalities which do not adhere to the philosophy of allopathic medicine. Allopathic medicine is what medical doctors practice by an large. It is the theory that disease is caused by agencies outside the body such as bacteria, viruses or physical means which affect the body. These can therefore be treated by medicines 2and therapies The natural healing method began in the absence of extensive technologies with the idea that all the answers for health may be found in nature or rather, the deviation from nature. Therefore, the health of the body can be restored by correcting the aberration and thereby restoring balance. This is the area that will be covered in this volume. Allopathic techniques have their place in the art of healing. However, we should not forget that the body is a grand achievement of the spirit and built into it is the capacity to maintain itself and heal itself. Ashby, Muata ISBN: 1-884564-49-6 $28.95

INITIATION INTO EGYPTIAN YOGA Shedy: Spiritual discipline or program, to go deeply into the mysteries, to study the mystery teachings and literature profoundly, to penetrate the mysteries. You will learn about the mysteries of initiation into the teachings and practice of Yoga and how to become an Initiate of the mystical sciences. This insightful manual is the first in a series which introduces you to the goals of daily spiritual and yoga practices: Meditation, Diet, Words of Power and the ancient wisdom teachings. 8.5" X 11" ISBN 1-884564-02-X Soft Cover $24.95 U.S.

THE AFRICAN ORIGINS OF CIVILIZATION, RELIGION AND YOGA SPIRITUALITY AND ETHICS PHILOSOPHY HARD COVER EDITION Part 1, Part 2, Part 3 in one volume 683 Pages Hard Cover First Edition Three volumes in one. Over the past several years I have been asked to put together in one volume the most important evidences showing the correlations and common teachings between Kamitan (Ancient Egyptian) culture and religion and that of India. The questions of the history of Ancient Egypt, and the latest archeological evidences showing civilization and culture in Ancient Egypt and its spread to other countries, has intrigued many scholars as well as mystics over the years. Also, the possibility that Ancient Egyptian Priests and Priestesses migrated to Greece, India and other countries to carry on the traditions of the Ancient Egyptian Mysteries, has been speculated over the years as well. In chapter 1 of the book *Egyptian Yoga The Philosophy of Enlightenment*, 1995, I first introduced the deepest comparison between Ancient Egypt and India that had been brought forth up to that time. Now, in the year 2001 this new book, *THE AFRICAN ORIGINS OF CIVILIZATION, MYSTICAL RELIGION AND YOGA PHILOSOPHY*, more fully explores the motifs, symbols and philosophical correlations between Ancient Egyptian and Indian mysticism and clearly shows not only that Ancient Egypt and India were connected culturally but also spiritually. How does this knowledge help the spiritual aspirant? This discovery has great importance for the Yogis and mystics who follow the philosophy of Ancient Egypt and the mysticism of India. It means that India has a longer history and heritage than was previously understood. It shows that the mysteries of Ancient Egypt were essentially a yoga tradition which did not die but rather developed into the modern day systems of Yoga technology of India. It further shows that African culture developed Yoga Mysticism earlier than any other civilization in history. All of this expands our understanding of the unity of culture and the deep legacy of

Yoga, which stretches into the distant past, beyond the Indus Valley civilization, the earliest known high culture in India as well as the Vedic tradition of Aryan culture. Therefore, Yoga culture and mysticism is the oldest known tradition of spiritual development and Indian mysticism is an extension of the Ancient Egyptian mysticism. By understanding the legacy which Ancient Egypt gave to India the mysticism of India is better understood and by comprehending the heritage of Indian Yoga, which is rooted in Ancient Egypt the Mysticism of Ancient Egypt is also better understood. This expanded understanding allows us to prove the underlying kinship of humanity, through the common symbols, motifs and philosophies which are not disparate and confusing teachings but in reality expressions of the same study of truth through metaphysics and mystical realization of Self. (HARD COVER) ISBN: 1-884564-50-X $45.00 U.S. 8 1/2" X 11"

*AFRICAN ORIGINS BOOK 1 PART 1* African Origins of African Civilization, Religion, Yoga Mysticism and Ethics Philosophy-<u>Soft Cover</u> $24.95 ISBN: 1-884564-55-0

*AFRICAN ORIGINS BOOK 2 PART 2* African Origins of Western Civilization, Religion and Philosophy (Soft) - <u>Soft Cover</u> $24.95 ISBN: 1-884564-56-9

*EGYPT AND INDIA AFRICAN ORIGINS OF Eastern Civilization, Religion, Yoga Mysticism and Philosophy*-<u>Soft Cover</u> $29.95 (Soft) ISBN: 1-884564-57-7

**THE MYSTERIES OF ISIS:** *The Ancient Egyptian Philosophy of Self-Realization* - There are several paths to discover the Divine and the mysteries of the higher Self. This volume details the mystery teachings of the goddess Aset (Isis) from Ancient Egypt- the path of wisdom. It includes the teachings of her temple and the disciplines that are enjoined for the initiates of the temple of Aset as they were given in ancient times. Also, this book includes the teachings of the main myths of Aset that lead a human being to spiritual enlightenment and immortality. Through the study of ancient myth and the illumination of initiatic understanding the idea of God is expanded from the mythological comprehension to the metaphysical. Then this metaphysical understanding is related to you, the student, so as to begin understanding your true divine nature. ISBN 1-884564-24-0 $22.99

*EGYPTIAN PROVERBS: collection of — Ancient Egyptian Proverbs and Wisdom Teachings -How to live according to MAAT Philosophy. Beginning Meditation. All proverbs are indexed for easy searches. For the first time in one volume, ——Ancient Egyptian Proverbs,* wisdom teachings and meditations, fully illustrated with hieroglyphic text and symbols. EGYPTIAN PROVERBS is a unique collection of knowledge and wisdom which you can put into practice today and transform your life. $14.95 U.S ISBN: 1-884564-00-3

*GOD OF LOVE: THE PATH OF DIVINE LOVE The Process of Mystical Transformation and The Path of Divine Love* This Volume focuses on the ancient wisdom teachings of "Neter Merri" –the Ancient Egyptian philosophy of Divine Love and how to use them in a scientific process for self-transformation. Love is one of the most powerful human emotions. It is also the source of Divine feeling that unifies God and the individual human being. When love is fragmented and diminished by egoism the Divine connection is lost. The Ancient tradition of Neter Merri leads human beings back to their Divine connection, allowing them to discover their innate glorious self that is actually Divine and immortal. This volume will detail the process of transformation from ordinary consciousness to cosmic consciousness through the integrated practice of the teachings and the path of Devotional Love toward the Divine. 5.5"x 8.5" ISBN 1-884564-11-9 $22.95

*INTRODUCTION TO MAAT PHILOSOPHY: Spiritual Enlightenment*

*Through the Path of Virtue* Known commonly as Karma in India, the teachings of MAAT contain an extensive philosophy based on ariu (deeds) and their fructification in the form of shai and renenet (fortune and destiny, leading to Meskhenet (fate in a future birth) for living virtuously and with orderly wisdom are explained and the student is to begin practicing the precepts of Maat in daily life so as to promote the process of purification of the heart in preparation for the judgment of the soul. This judgment will be understood not as an event that will occur at the time of death but as an event that occurs continuously, at every moment in the life of the individual. The student will learn how to become allied with the forces of the Higher Self and to thereby begin cleansing the mind (heart) of impurities so as to attain a higher vision of reality. ISBN 1-884564-20-8 $22.99

*MEDITATION The Ancient Egyptian Path to Enlightenment* Many people do not know about the rich history of meditation practice in Ancient Egypt. This volume outlines the theory of meditation and presents the Ancient Egyptian Hieroglyphic text which give instruction as to the nature of the mind and its three modes of expression. It also presents the texts which give instruction on the practice of meditation for spiritual Enlightenment and unity with the Divine. This volume allows the reader to begin practicing meditation by explaining, in easy to understand terms, the simplest form of meditation and working up to the most advanced form which was practiced in ancient times and which is still practiced by yogis around the world in modern times. ISBN 1-884564-27-7 $22.99

*THE GLORIOUS LIGHT MEDITATION* TECHNIQUE OF ANCIENT EGYPT New for the year 2000. This volume is based on the earliest known instruction in history given for the practice of formal meditation. Discovered by Dr. Muata Ashby, it is inscribed on the walls of the Tomb of Seti I in Thebes Egypt. This volume details the philosophy and practice of this unique system of meditation originated in Ancient Egypt and the earliest practice of meditation known in the world which occurred in the most advanced African Culture. ISBN:

1-884564-15-1 $16.95 (PB)

THE SERPENT POWER: The Ancient Egyptian Mystical Wisdom of the Inner Life Force. This Volume specifically deals with the latent life Force energy of the universe and in the human body, its control and sublimation. How to develop the Life Force energy of the subtle body. This Volume will introduce the esoteric wisdom of the science of how virtuous living acts in a subtle and mysterious way to cleanse the latent psychic energy conduits and vortices of the spiritual body. ISBN 1-884564-19-4 $22.95

EGYPTIAN YOGA The Postures of The Gods and Goddesses Discover the physical postures and exercises practiced thousands of years ago in Ancient Egypt which are today known as Yoga exercises. Discover the history of the postures and how they were transferred from Ancient Egypt in Africa to India through Buddhist Tantrism. Then practice the postures as you discover the mythic teaching that originally gave birth to the postures and was practiced by the Ancient Egyptian priests and priestesses. This work is based on the pictures and teachings from the Creation story of Ra, The Asarian Resurrection Myth and the carvings and reliefs from various Temples in Ancient Egypt 8.5" X 11" ISBN 1-884564-10-0 Soft Cover $21.95 Exercise video $20

SACRED SEXUALITY: ANCIENT EGYPTIAN TANTRA YOGA: The Art of Sex Sublimation and Universal Consciousness This Volume will expand on the male and female principles within the human body and in the universe and further detail the sublimation of sexual energy into spiritual energy. The student will study the deities Min and Hathor, Asar and Aset, Geb and Nut and discover the mystical implications for a practical spiritual discipline. This Volume will also focus on the Tantric aspects of Ancient Egyptian and Indian mysticism, the purpose of sex and the mystical teachings of sexual sublimation which lead to self-knowledge and Enlightenment. ISBN 1-884564-03-8 $24.95

**AFRICAN RELIGION Volume 4: ASARIAN THEOLOGY: RESURRECTING OSIRIS** The path of Mystical Awakening and the Keys to Immortality NEW REVISED AND EXPANDED EDITION! The Ancient Sages created stories based on human and superhuman beings whose struggles, aspirations, needs and desires ultimately lead them to discover their true Self. The myth of Aset, Asar and Heru is no exception in this area. While there is no one source where the entire story may be found, pieces of it are inscribed in various ancient Temples walls, tombs, steles and papyri. For the first time available, the complete myth of Asar, Aset and Heru has been compiled from original Ancient Egyptian, Greek and Coptic Texts. This epic myth has been richly illustrated with reliefs from the Temple of Heru at Edfu, the Temple of Aset at Philae, the Temple of Asar at Abydos, the Temple of Hathor at Denderah and various papyri, inscriptions and reliefs. Discover the myth which inspired the teachings of the *Shetaut Neter* (Egyptian Mystery System - Egyptian Yoga) and the Egyptian Book of Coming Forth By Day. Also, discover the three levels of Ancient Egyptian Religion, how to understand the mysteries of the Duat or Astral World and how to discover the abode of the Supreme in the Amenta, *The Other World* The ancient religion of Asar, Aset and Heru, if properly understood, contains all of the elements necessary to lead the sincere aspirant to attain immortality through inner self-discovery. This volume presents the entire myth and explores the main mystical themes and rituals associated with the myth for understating human existence, creation and the way to achieve spiritual emancipation - *Resurrection.* The Asarian myth is so powerful that it influenced and is still having an effect on the major world religions. Discover the origins and mystical meaning of the Christian Trinity, the Eucharist ritual and the ancient origin of the birthday of Jesus Christ. Soft Cover ISBN: 1-884564-27-5 $24.95

**THE EGYPTIAN BOOK OF THE DEAD**

*MYSTICISM OF THE PERT EM HERU* " I Know myself, I know myself, I am One With God!–From the Pert Em Heru "The Ru Pert em Heru" or "Ancient Egyptian Book of The Dead," or "Book of Coming Forth By Day" as it is more popularly known, has fascinated the world since the successful translation of Ancient Egyptian hieroglyphic scripture over 150 years ago. The astonishing writings in it reveal that the Ancient Egyptians believed in life after death and in an ultimate destiny to discover the Divine. The elegance and aesthetic beauty of the hieroglyphic text itself has inspired many see it as an art form in and of itself. But is there more to it than that? Did the Ancient Egyptian wisdom contain more than just aphorisms and hopes of eternal life beyond death? In this volume Dr. Muata Ashby, the author of over 25 books on Ancient Egyptian Yoga Philosophy has produced a new translation of the original texts which uncovers a mystical teaching underlying the sayings and rituals instituted by the Ancient Egyptian Sages and Saints. "Once the philosophy of Ancient Egypt is understood as a mystical tradition instead of as a religion or primitive mythology, it reveals its secrets which if practiced today will lead anyone to discover the glory of spiritual self-discovery. The Pert em Heru is in every way comparable to the Indian Upanishads or the Tibetan Book of the Dead." ▢ $28.95 ISBN# 1-884564-28-3 Size: 8½" X 11

*African Religion VOL. 1- ANUNIAN THEOLOGY THE MYSTERIES OF RA* The Philosophy of Anu and The Mystical Teachings of The Ancient Egyptian Creation Myth Discover the mystical teachings contained in the Creation Myth and the gods and goddesses who brought creation and human beings into existence. The Creation myth of Anu is the source of Anunian Theology but also of the other main theological systems of Ancient Egypt that also influenced other world religions including Christianity, Hinduism and Buddhism. The Creation Myth holds the key to understanding the universe and for attaining spiritual Enlightenment. ISBN: 1-884564-38-0 $19.95

*African Religion VOL 3: Memphite Theology: MYSTERIES OF MIND* Mystical Psychology & Mental

Health for Enlightenment and Immortality based on the Ancient Egyptian Philosophy of Menefer -Mysticism of Ptah, Egyptian Physics and Yoga Metaphysics and the Hidden properties of Matter. This volume uncovers the mystical psychology of the Ancient Egyptian wisdom teachings centering on the philosophy of the Ancient Egyptian city of Menefer (Memphite Theology). How to understand the mind and how to control the senses and lead the mind to health, clarity and mystical self-discovery. This Volume will also go deeper into the philosophy of God as creation and will explore the concepts of modern science and how they correlate with ancient teachings. This Volume will lay the ground work for the understanding of the philosophy of universal consciousness and the initiatic/yogic insight into who or what is God? ISBN 1-884564-07-0 $22.95

*AFRICAN RELIGION VOLUME 5: THE GODDESS AND THE EGYPTIAN MYSTERIESTHE PATH OF THE GODDESS THE GODDESS PATH* The Secret Forms of the Goddess and the Rituals of Resurrection The Supreme Being may be worshipped as father or as mother. *Ushet Rekhat* or *Mother Worship*, is the spiritual process of worshipping the Divine in the form of the Divine Goddess. It celebrates the most important forms of the Goddess including *Nathor, Maat, Aset, Arat, Amentet and Hathor* and explores their mystical meaning as well as the rising of *Sirius,* the star of Aset (Aset) and the new birth of Hor (Heru). The end of the year is a time of reckoning, reflection and engendering a new or renewed positive movement toward attaining spiritual Enlightenment. The Mother Worship devotional meditation ritual, performed on five days during the month of December and on New Year's Eve, is based on the Ushet Rekhit. During the ceremony, the cosmic forces, symbolized by Sirius - and the constellation of Orion ---, are harnessed through the understanding and devotional attitude of the participant. This propitiation draws the light of wisdom and health to all those who share in the ritual, leading to prosperity and wisdom. $14.95 ISBN 1-884564-18-6

*THE MYSTICAL JOURNEY FROM JESUS TO CHRIST* Discover the ancient Egyptian origins of Christianity before the Catholic Church and learn the mystical teachings given by Jesus to assist all humanity in becoming Christlike. Discover the secret meaning of the Gospels that were discovered in Egypt. Also discover how and why so many Christian churches came into being. Discover that the Bible still holds the keys to mystical realization even though its original writings were changed by the church. Discover how to practice the original teachings of Christianity which leads to the Kingdom of Heaven. $24.95 ISBN# 1-884564-05-4 size: 8½" X 11"

17. *THE STORY OF ASAR, ASET AND HERU:* An Ancient Egyptian Legend (For Children) Now for the first time, the most ancient myth of Ancient Egypt comes alive for children. Inspired by the books *The Asarian Resurrection: The Ancient Egyptian Bible* and *The Mystical Teachings of The Asarian Resurrection, The Story of Asar, Aset and Heru* is an easy to understand and thrilling tale which inspired the children of Ancient Egypt to aspire to greatness and righteousness. If you and your child have enjoyed stories like *The Lion King* and *Star Wars* you will love *The Story of Asar, Aset and Heru.* Also, if you know the story of Jesus and Krishna you will discover than Ancient Egypt had a similar myth and that this myth carries important spiritual teachings for living a fruitful and fulfilling life. This book may be used along with *The Parents Guide To The Asarian Resurrection Myth: How to Teach Yourself and Your Child the Principles of Universal Mystical Religion.* The guide provides some background to the Asarian Resurrection myth and it also gives insight into the mystical teachings contained in it which you may introduce to your child. It is designed for parents who wish to grow spiritually with their children and it serves as an introduction for those who would like to study the Asarian Resurrection Myth in depth and to practice its teachings. 8.5" X 11" ISBN: 1-884564-31-3 $12.95

*THE PARENTS GUIDE TO THE AUSARIAN RESURRECTION MYTH:* How to Teach Yourself and Your Child the Principles of Universal Mystical Religion. This insightful manual brings for the timeless wisdom of the ancient through the Ancient Egyptian myth of Asar, Aset and Heru and the mystical teachings contained in it for parents who want to guide their children to understand and practice the teachings of mystical spirituality. This manual may be used with the children's storybook *The Story of Asar, Aset and Heru* by Dr. Muata Abhaya Ashby. ISBN: 1-884564-30-5 $16.95

HEALING THE CRIMINAL HEART. Introduction to Maat Philosophy, Yoga and Spiritual Redemption Through the Path of Virtue Who is a criminal? Is there such a thing as a criminal heart? What is the source of evil and sinfulness and is there any way to rise above it? Is there redemption for those who have committed sins, even the worst crimes? Ancient Egyptian mystical psychology holds important answers to these questions. Over ten thousand years ago mystical psychologists, the Sages of Ancient Egypt, studied and charted the human mind and spirit and laid out a path which will lead to spiritual redemption, prosperity and Enlightenment. This introductory volume brings forth the teachings of the Asarian Resurrection, the most important myth of Ancient Egypt, with relation to the faults of human existence: anger, hatred, greed, lust, animosity, discontent, ignorance, egoism jealousy, bitterness, and a myriad of psycho-spiritual ailments which keep a human being in a state of negativity and adversity ISBN: 1-884564-17-8 $15.95

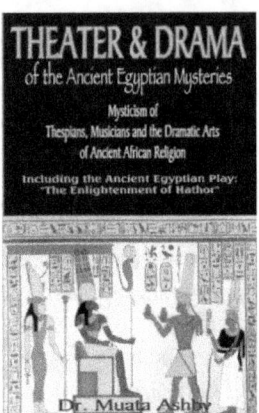

TEMPLE RITUAL OF THE ANCIENT EGYPTIAN MYSTERIES--THEATER & DRAMA OF THE ANCIENT EGYPTIAN MYSTERIES: Details the practice of the mysteries and ritual program of the temple and the philosophy an practice of the ritual of the mysteries, its purpose and execution. Featuring the Ancient Egyptian stage play-"The Enlightenment of Hathor' Based on an Ancient Egyptian Drama, The original Theater -Mysticism of the Temple of Hetheru 1-884564-14-3 $19.95 By Dr. Muata Ashby

GUIDE TO PRINT ON DEMAND: SELF-PUBLISH FOR PROFIT, SPIRITUAL FULFILLMENT AND SERVICE TO HUMANITY Everyone asks us how we produced so many books in such a short time. Here are the secrets to writing and producing books that uplift humanity and how to get them printed for a fraction of the regular cost. Anyone can become an author even if they have limited funds. All that is necessary is the willingness to learn how the printing and book business work and the desire to follow the special instructions given here for preparing your manuscript format. Then you take your work directly to the non-traditional companies who can produce your books for less than the traditional book printer can. ISBN: 1-884564-40-2 $16.95 U. S.

*Egyptian Mysteries: Vol. 1,* Shetaut Neter What are the Mysteries? For thousands of years the spiritual tradition of Ancient Egypt, *Shetaut Neter,* "The Egyptian Mysteries," "The Secret Teachings," have fascinated, tantalized and amazed the world. At one time exalted and recognized as the highest culture of the world, by Africans, Europeans, Asiatics, Hindus, Buddhists and other cultures of the ancient world, in time it was shunned by the emerging orthodox world religions. Its temples desecrated, its philosophy maligned, its tradition spurned, its philosophy dormant in the mystical *Medu Neter,* the mysterious hieroglyphic texts which hold the secret symbolic meaning that has scarcely been discerned up to now. What are the secrets of *Nehast* {spiritual awakening and emancipation, resurrection}. More than just a literal translation, this volume is for awakening to the secret code *Shetitu* of the teaching which was not deciphered by Egyptologists, nor could be understood by ordinary spiritualists. This book is a reinstatement of the original science made available for our times, to the reincarnated followers of Ancient Egyptian culture and the prospect of spiritual freedom to break the bonds of *Khemn,* "ignorance," and slavery to evil forces: *Såaa* . ISBN: 1-884564-41-0 $19.99

## Awakening Your Soul-Aware-Witness

**EGYPTIAN MYSTERIES VOL 2:** Dictionary of Gods and Goddesses This book is about the mystery of neteru, the gods and goddesses of Ancient Egypt (Kamit, Kemet). Neteru means "Gods and Goddesses." But the Neterian teaching of Neteru represents more than the usual limited modern day concept of "divinities" or "spirits." The Neteru of Kamit are also metaphors, cosmic principles and vehicles for the enlightening teachings of Shetaut Neter (Ancient Egyptian-African Religion). Actually they are the elements for one of the most advanced systems of spirituality ever conceived in human history. 20. Understanding the concept of neteru provides a firm basis for spiritual evolution and the pathway for viable culture, peace on earth and a healthy human society. Why is it important to have gods and goddesses in our lives? In order for spiritual evolution to be possible, once a human being has accepted that there is existence after death and there is a transcendental being who exists beyond time and space knowledge, human beings need a connection to that which transcends the ordinary experience of human life in time and space and a means to understand the transcendental reality beyond the mundane reality. ISBN: 1-884564-23-2 $21.95

**EGYPTIAN MYSTERIES VOL. 3** The Priests and Priestesses of Ancient Egypt This volume details the path of Neterian priesthood, the joys, challenges and rewards of advanced Neterian life, the teachings that allowed the priests and priestesses to manage the most long lived civilization in human history and how that path can be adopted today; for those who want to tread the path of the Clergy of Shetaut Neter. ISBN: 1-884564-53-4 $24.95

*The War of Heru and Set:* The Struggle of Good and Evil for Control of the World and The Human Soul This volume contains a novelized version of the Asarian Resurrection myth that is based on the actual scriptures presented in the Book Asarian Religion (old name – Resurrecting Osiris). This volume is prepared in the form of a screenplay and can be easily adapted to be used as a stage play. Spiritual seeking is a mythic journey that has many emotional highs and lows, ecstasies and depressions, victories and frustrations. This is the War of Life that is played out in the myth as the struggle of Heru and Set and those are mythic characters that represent the human Higher and Lower self. How to understand the war and emerge victorious in the journey of life? The ultimate victory and fulfillment can be experienced, which is not changeable or lost in time. The purpose of myth is to convey the wisdom of life through the story of divinities who show the way to overcome the challenges and foibles of life. In this volume the feelings and emotions of the characters of the myth have been highlighted to show the deeply rich texture of the Ancient Egyptian myth. This myth contains deep spiritual teachings and insights into the nature of self, of God and the mysteries of life and the means to discover the true meaning of life and thereby achieve the true purpose of life. To become victorious in the battle of life means to become the King (or Queen) of Egypt. Have you seen movies like The Lion King, Hamlet, The Odyssey, or The Little Buddha? These have been some of the most popular movies in modern times. The Sema Institute of Yoga is dedicated to researching and presenting the wisdom and culture of ancient Africa. The Script is designed to be produced as a motion picture but may be adapted for the theater as well. $21.95 copyright 1998 By Dr. Muata Ashby ISBN 1-8840564-44-5

*AFRICAN DIONYSUS: FROM EGYPT TO GREECE*: The Kamitan Origins of Greek Culture and Religion ISBN: 1-884564-47-X FROM EGYPT TO GREECE This insightful manual is a reference to Ancient Egyptian mythology and philosophy and its correlation to what later became known as Greek and Rome mythology and philosophy. It outlines the basic tenets of the mythologies and shoes the ancient origins of Greek culture in Ancient Egypt. This volume also documents the origins of the Greek alphabet in Egypt as well as Greek religion, myth and philosophy of the gods and goddesses from Egypt from the myth of Atlantis and archaic period with the Minoans to the Classical period. This volume also acts as a resource for Colleges students who would like to set up fraternities and sororities based on the original Ancient Egyptian principles of Sheti and Maat philosophy. ISBN: 1-884564-47-X $22.95 U.S.

*THE FORTY TWO PRECEPTS OF MAAT, THE PHILOSOPHY OF RIGHTEOUS ACTION AND THE ANCIENT EGYPTIAN WISDOM TEXTS* ADVANCED STUDIES This manual is designed for use with the 1998 Maat Philosophy Class conducted by Dr. Muata Ashby. This is a detailed study of Maat Philosophy. It contains a compilation of the 42 laws or precepts of Maat and the corresponding principles which they represent along with the teachings of the ancient Egyptian Sages relating to each. Maat philosophy was the basis of Ancient Egyptian society and government as well as the heart of Ancient Egyptian myth and spirituality. Maat is at once a goddess, a cosmic force and a living social doctrine, which promotes social harmony and thereby paves the way for spiritual evolution in all levels of society. ISBN: 1-884564-48-8 $16.95 U.S.

6. *THE SECRET LOTUS: Poetry of Enlightenment* Discover the mystical sentiment of the Kemetic teaching as expressed through the poetry of Muata Ashby. The teaching of spiritual awakening is uniquely experienced when the poetic sensibility is present. This first volume contains the poems written between 1996 and 2003. **1-884564--16 - X $16.99**

6. **The Ancient Egyptian Buddha: The Ancient Egyptian Origins of Buddhism**
This book is a compilation of several sections of a larger work, a book by the name of African Origins of Civilization, Religion, Yoga Mysticism and Ethics Philosophy. It also contains some additional evidences not contained in the larger work that demonstrate the correlation between Ancient Egyptian Religion and Buddhism. This book is one of several compiled short volumes that has been compiled so as to facilitate access to specific subjects contained in the larger work which is over 680 pages long. These short and small volumes have been specifically designed

to cover one subject in a brief and low cost format. This present volume, The Ancient Egyptian Buddha: The Ancient Egyptian Origins of Buddhism, formed one subject in the larger work; actually it was one chapter of the larger work. However, this volume has some new additional evidences and comparisons of Buddhist and Neterian (Ancient Egyptian) philosophies not previously discussed. It was felt that this subject needed to be discussed because even in the early 21st century, the idea persists that Buddhism originated only in India independently. Yet there is ample evidence from ancient writings and perhaps more importantly, iconographical evidences from the Ancient Egyptians and early Buddhists themselves that prove otherwise. This handy volume has been designed to be accessible to young adults and all others who would like to have an easy reference with documentation on this important subject. This is an important subject because the frame of reference with which we look at a culture depends strongly on our conceptions about its origins. in this case, if we look at the Buddhism as an Asiatic religion we would treat it and its culture in one way. If we id as African [Ancient Egyptian] we not only would see it in a different light but we also must ascribe Africa with a glorious legacy that matches any other culture in human history and gave rise to one of the present day most important religious philosophies. We would also look at the culture and philosophies of the Ancient Egyptians as having African insights that offer us greater depth into the Buddhist philosophies. Those insights inform our knowledge about other African traditions and we can also begin to understand in a deeper way the effect of Ancient Egyptian culture on African culture and also on the Asiatic as well. We would also be able to discover the glorious and wondrous teaching of mystical philosophy that Ancient Egyptian Shetaut Neter religion offers, that is as powerful as any other mystic system of spiritual philosophy in the world today. ISBN: 1-884564-61-5 $28.95

37. **The Death of American Empire: Neo-conservatism, Theocracy, Economic Imperialism, Environmental Disaster and the Collapse of Civilization**

This work is a collection of essays relating to social and economic, leadership, and ethics, ecological and religious issues that are facing the world today in order to understand the course of history that has led humanity to its present condition and then arrive at positive solutions that will lead to better outcomes for all humanity. It surveys the development and decline of major empires throughout history and focuses on the creation of American Empire along with the social, political and economic policies that led to the prominence of the United States of America as a Superpower including the rise of the political control of the neo-con political philosophy including militarism and the military industrial complex in American politics and the rise of the religious right into and American Theocracy movement. This volume details, through historical and current events, the psychology behind the dominance of western culture in world politics through the "Superpower Syndrome Mandatory Conflict Complex" that drives the Superpower culture to establish itself above all others and then act hubristically to dominate world culture through legitimate influences as well as coercion, media censorship and misinformation leading to international hegemony and world conflict. This volume also details the financial policies that gave rise to American prominence in the global economy, especially after World War II, and promoted American preeminence over the world economy through Globalization as well as the environmental policies, including the oil economy, that are promoting degradation of the world ecology and contribute to the decline of America as an Empire culture. This volume finally explores the factors pointing to the decline of the American Empire economy and imperial power and what to expect in the aftermath of American prominence and how to survive the decline while at the same time promoting policies and social-economic-religious-political changes that are needed in order to promote the emergence of a beneficial and sustainable culture. **$25.95soft** 1-884564-25-9, Hard Cover **$29.95** 1-884564-45-3

38. **The African Origins of Hatha Yoga: And its Ancient Mystical Teaching**
The subject of this present volume, The Ancient Egyptian Origins of Yoga Postures, formed one subject in the larger works, African Origins of Civilization Religion, Yoga Mysticism and Ethics Philosophy and the Book Egypt and India is the section of the book African Origins of Civilization. Those works contain the collection of all correlations between Ancient Egypt and India. This volume also contains some additional information

not contained in the previous work. It was felt that this subject needed to be discussed more directly, being treated in one volume, as opposed to being contained in the larger work along with other subjects, because even in the early 21st century, the idea persists that the Yoga and specifically, Yoga Postures, were invented and developed only in India. The Ancient Egyptians were peoples originally from Africa who were, in ancient times, colonists in India. Therefore it is no surprise that many Indian traditions including religious and Yogic, would be found earlier in Ancient Egypt. Yet there is ample evidence from ancient writings and perhaps more importantly, iconographical evidences from the Ancient Egyptians themselves and the Indians themselves that prove the connection between Ancient Egypt and India as well as the existence of a discipline of Yoga Postures in Ancient Egypt long before its practice in India. This handy volume has been designed to be accessible to young adults and all others who would like to have an easy reference with documentation on this important subject. This is an important subject because the frame of reference with which we look at a culture depends strongly on our conceptions about its origins. In this case, if we look at the Ancient Egyptians as Asiatic peoples we would treat them and their culture in one way. If we see them as Africans we not only see them in a different light but we also must ascribe Africa with a glorious legacy that matches any other culture in human history. We would also look at the culture and philosophies of the Ancient Egyptians as having African insights instead of Asiatic ones. Those insights inform our knowledge about other African traditions, and we can also begin to understand in a deeper way the effect of Ancient Egyptian culture on African culture and also on the Asiatic as well. When we discover the deeper and more ancient practice of the postures system in Ancient Egypt that was called "Hatha Yoga" in India, we are able to find a new and expanded understanding of the practice that constitutes a discipline of spiritual practice that informs and revitalizes the Indian practices as well as all spiritual disciplines. $19.99 ISBN 1-884564-60-7

**39. The Black Ancient Egyptians**

This present volume, The Black Ancient Egyptians: The Black African Ancestry of the Ancient Egyptians, formed one subject in the larger work: The African Origins of Civilization, Religion, Yoga Mysticism and Ethics Philosophy. It was felt that this subject needed to be discussed because even in the early 21st century, the idea persists that the Ancient Egyptians were peoples originally from Asia Minor who came into North-East Africa. Yet there is ample evidence from ancient writings and perhaps more importantly, iconographical evidences from the Ancient Egyptians themselves that proves otherwise. This handy volume has been designed to be accessible to young adults and all others who would like to have an easy reference with documentation on this important subject. This is an important subject because the frame of reference with which we look at a culture depends strongly on our conceptions about its origins. in this case, if we look at the Ancient Egyptians as Asiatic peoples we would treat them and their culture in one way. If we see them as Africans we not only see them in a different light but we also must ascribe Africa with a glorious legacy that matches any other culture in human history. We would also look at the culture and philosophies of the Ancient Egyptians as having African insights instead of Asiatic ones. Those insights inform our knowledge about other African traditions, and we can also begin to understand in a deeper way the effect of Ancient Egyptian culture on African culture and also on the Asiatic as well. ISBN 1-884564-21-6 $19.99

**40. The Limits of Faith: The Failure of Faith-based Religions and the Solution to the Meaning of Life**

Is faith belief in something without proof? And if so is there never to be any proof or discovery? If so what is the need of intellect? If faith is trust in something that is real is that reality historical, literal or metaphorical or philosophical? If knowledge is an essential element in faith, why should there be so much emphasis on believing and not on understanding in the modern practice of religion? This volume is a compilation of essays related to the nature of religious faith in the context of its inception in human history as well as its meaning for religious practice and relations between religions in modern times. Faith has come to be regarded as a virtuous goal in life. However, many people have asked how can it be that an endeavor that is supposed to be dedicated to spiritual upliftment has led to more conflict in human history than any other social factor? ISBN 1884564631 SOFT COVER - $19.99, ISBN 1884564623 HARD COVER - $28.95

Awakening Your Soul-Aware-Witness

**41. Redemption of The Criminal Heart Through Kemetic Spirituality and Maat Philosophy**
Special book dedicated to inmates, their families and members of the Law Enforcement community. ISBN: 1-884564-70-4
$5.00

**42. COMPARATIVE MYTHOLOGY**
What are Myth and Culture and what is their importance for understanding the development of societies, human evolution and the search for meaning? What is the purpose of culture and how do cultures evolve? What are the elements of a culture and how can those elements be broken down and the constituent parts of a culture understood and compared? How do cultures interact? How does enculturation occur and how do people interact with other cultures? How do the processes of acculturation and cooptation occur and what does this mean for the development of a society? How can the study of myths and the elements of culture help in understanding the meaning of life and the means to promote understanding and peace in the world of human activity? This volume is the exposition of a method for studying and comparing cultures, myths and other social aspects of a society. It is an expansion on the Cultural Category Factor Correlation method for studying and comparing myths, cultures, religions and other aspects of human culture. It was originally introduced in the year 2002. This volume contains an expanded treatment as well as several refinements along with examples of the application of the method. the apparent. I hope you enjoy these art renditions as serene reflections of the mysteries of life. ISBN: 1-884564-72-0
Book price $21.95

**43. CONVERSATION WITH GOD: Revelations of the Important Questions of Life**
$24.99 U.S.
This volume contains a grouping of some of the questions that have been submitted to Dr. Muata Ashby. They are efforts by many aspirants to better understand and practice the teachings of mystical spirituality. It is said

that when sages are asked spiritual questions they are relaying the wisdom of God, the Goddess, the Higher Self, etc. There is a very special quality about the Q & A process that does not occur during a regular lecture session. Certain points come out that would not come out otherwise due to the nature of the process which ideally occurs after a lecture. Having been to a certain degree enlightened by a lecture certain new questions arise and the answers to these have the effect of elevating the teaching of the lecture to even higher levels. Therefore, enjoy these exchanges and may they lead you to enlightenment, peace and prosperity. Available Late Summer 2007 ISBN: 1-884564-68-2

### 44. MYSTIC ART PAINTINGS

(with Full Color images) This book contains a collection of the small number of paintings that I have created over the years. Some were used as early book covers and others were done simply to express certain spiritual feelings; some were created for no purpose except to express the joy of color and the feeling of relaxed freedom. All are to elicit mystical awakening in the viewer. Writing a book on philosophy is like sculpture, the more the work is rewritten the reflections and ideas become honed and take form and become clearer and imbued with intellectual beauty. Mystic music is like meditation, a world of its own that exists about 1 inch above ground wherein the musician does not touch the ground. Mystic Graphic Art is meditation in form, color, image and reflected image which opens the door to the reality behind the apparent. I hope you enjoy these art renditions and my reflections on them as serene reflections of the mysteries of life, as visual renditions of the philosophy I have written about over the years. ISBN 1-884564-69-0 $19.95

### 45. ANCIENT EGYPTIAN HIEROGLYPHS FOR BEGINNERS

This brief guide was prepared for those inquiring about how to enter into Hieroglyphic studies on their own at home or in study groups. First of all you should know that there are a few institutions around the world which teach how to read the Hieroglyphic text but due to the nature of the study there are perhaps only a handful of people who can read fluently. It is possible for anyone with average intelligence to achieve a high level of proficiency in reading inscriptions on temples and artifacts; however, reading extensive texts is another issue entirely. However, this introduction will give you entry into those texts if assisted by dictionaries and other aids. Most Egyptologists have a basic knowledge and keep dictionaries and notes handy when it comes to dealing with more difficult texts. Medtu Neter or the Ancient Egyptian hieroglyphic language has been considered as a "Dead Language." However, dead languages have always been studied by individuals who for the most part have taught themselves through various means. This book will discuss those means and how to use them most efficiently. ISBN 1884564429 **$28.95**

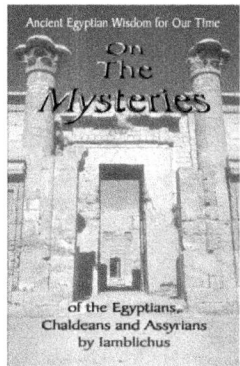

### 46. ON THE MYSTERIES: Wisdom of An Ancient Egyptian Sage -with Foreword by Muata Ashby

This volume, On the Mysteries, by Iamblichus (Abamun) is a unique form or scripture out of the Ancient Egyptian religious tradition. It is written in a form that is not usual or which is not usually found in the remnants of Ancient Egyptian scriptures. It is in the form of teacher and disciple, much like the Eastern scriptures such as Bhagavad Gita or the Upanishads. This form of writing may not have been necessary in Ancient times, because the format of teaching in Egypt was different prior to the conquest period by the Persians, Assyrians, Greeks and later the Romans. The question and answer format can be found but such extensive discourses and corrections of misunderstandings within the context of a teacher - disciple relationship is not usual. It therefore provides extensive insights into the times when it was written and the state of practice of Ancient Egyptian and other mystery religions. This has important implications for our times because we are today, as in the Greco-Roman period, also besieged with varied religions and new age philosophies as well as social strife and war. How can we understand our times and also make sense of the forest of spiritual traditions? How can we cut through the cacophony of religious fanaticism, and ignorance as well as misconceptions about the mysteries on the other in order to discover the true purpose of religion and the secret teachings that open up the mysteries of life and the way to enlightenment and immortality? This book, which comes to us from so long ago, offers us transcendental wisdom that applied to the world two thousand years ago as well as our world today. ISBN 1-884564-64-X $25.95

**47. The Ancient Egyptian Wisdom Texts -Compiled by Muata Ashby**
The Ancient Egyptian Wisdom Texts are a genre of writings from the ancient culture that have survived to the present and provide a vibrant record of the practice of spiritual evolution otherwise known as religion or yoga philosophy in Ancient Egypt. The principle focus of the Wisdom Texts is the cultivation of understanding, peace, harmony, selfless service, self-control, Inner fulfillment and spiritual realization. When these factors are cultivated in human life, the virtuous qualities in a human being begin to manifest and sinfulness, ignorance and negativity diminish until a person is able to enter into higher consciousness, the coveted goal of all civilizations. It is this virtuous mode of life which opens the door to self-discovery and spiritual enlightenment.

Therefore, the Wisdom Texts are important scriptures on the subject of human nature, spiritual psychology and mystical philosophy. The teachings presented in the Wisdom Texts form the foundation of religion as well as the guidelines for conducting the affairs of every area of social interaction including commerce, education, the army, marriage, and especially the legal system. These texts were sources for the famous 42 Precepts of Maat of the Pert-m-Heru (Book of the Dead), essential regulations of good conduct to develop virtue and purity in order to attain higher consciousness and immortality after death. ISBN1-884564-65-8 $18.95

**48. THE KEMETIC TREE OF LIFE**
**THE KEMETIC TREE OF LIFE: Newly Revealed Ancient Egyptian Cosmology and Metaphysics for Higher Consciousness**
The Tree of Life is a roadmap of a journey which explains how Creation came into being and how it will end. It also explains what Creation is composed of and also what human beings are and what they are composed of. It also explains the process of Creation, how Creation develops, as well as who created Creation and where that entity may be found. It also explains how a human being may discover that

entity and in so doing also discover the secrets of Creation, the meaning of life and the means to break free from the pathetic condition of human limitation and mortality in order to discover the higher realms of being by discovering the principles, the levels of existence that are beyond the simple physical and material aspects of life. This book contains color plates **ISBN: 1-884564-74-7 $27.95 U.S.**

**49-MATRIX OF AFRICAN PROVERBS: The Ethical and Spiritual Blueprint**
This volume sets forth the fundamental principles of African ethics and their practical applications for use by individuals and organizations seeking to model their ethical policies using the Traditional African values and concepts of ethical human behavior for the proper sustenance and management of society. Furthermore, this book will provide guidance as to how the Traditional African Ethics may be viewed and applied, taking into consideration the technological and social advancements in the present. This volume also presents the principles of ethical culture, and references for each to specific injunctions from Traditional African Proverbial Wisdom Teachings. These teachings are compiled from varied Pre-colonial African societies including Yoruba, Ashanti, Kemet, Malawi, Nigeria, Ethiopia, Galla, Ghana and many more. ISBN 1-884564-77-1

50- **Growing Beyond Hate: Keys to Freedom from Discord, Racism, Sexism, Political Conflict, Class Warfare, Violence, and How to Achieve Peace and Enlightenment**--- INTRODUCTION: WHY DO WE HATE? Hatred is one of the fundamental motivating aspects of human life; the other is desire. Desire can be of a worldly nature or of a spiritual, elevating nature. Worldly desire and hatred are like two sides of the same coin in that human life is usually swaying from one to the other; but the question is why? And is there a way to satisfy the desiring or hating mind in such a way as to find peace in life? Why do human beings go to war? Why do human beings perpetrate violence against one another? And is there a way not just to understand the phenomena but to resolve the issues that plague humanity and could lead to a more harmonious society? Hatred is perhaps the greatest scourge of humanity in that it leads to misunderstanding, conflict and untold miseries of life and clashes between individuals, societies and nations. Therefore, the riddle of Hatred, that is, understanding the sources of it and how to confront, reduce and even eradicate it so as to bring forth the fulfillment in life and peace for society, should be a top priority for social scientists, spiritualists and philosophers. This book is written from the perspective of spiritual philosophy based on the mystical wisdom and sema or yoga philosophy of the Ancient Egyptians. This philosophy, originated and based in the wisdom of Shetaut Neter, the Egyptian Mysteries, and Maat, ethical way of life in society and in spirit, contains Sema-Yogic wisdom and understanding of life's predicaments that can allow a human being of any ethnic group to understand and overcome the causes of hatred, racism, sexism, violence and disharmony in life, that plague human society. ISBN: 1-884564-81-X

52. Guide to Creating a Kemetic Marriage Contract

This marital contract guide reflects actual Ancient Egyptian Principles for Kemetic Marriage as they are to be applied for our times. The marital contract allows people to have a framework with which to face the challenges of marital relations instead of relying on hopes or romantic dreams that everything will work out somehow; in other words, love is not all you need. The latter is not an evolved, mature way of handling one of the most important aspects of human life. Therefore, it behooves anyone who wishes to enter into a marriage to explore the issues, express their needs and seek to avoid costly mistakes, and resolve conflicts in the normal course of life or make sure that their rights and dignity will be protected if any eventuality should occur. Marital relations in Ancient Egypt were not like those in other countries of the time and not like those of present day countries. The extreme longevity of Ancient Egyptian society, founded in Maat philosophy, allowed the social development of marriage to evolve and progress to a high level of order and balance. Maat represents truth, righteous, justice and harmony in life. This meant that the marital partner's rights were to be protected with equal standing before the law. So there was no disparity between rights of men or rights of women. Therefore, anyone who wants to enter into a marriage based on Kemetic principles must first and foremost adhere to this standard…equality in the rights of men and women. This guide demonstrates procedures for following the Ancient Egyptian practice of formalizing marriage with a contract that spells out the important concerns of each partner in the marital relationship, based on Maatian principles [of righteous, truth, harmony and justice] so that the rights and needs of each partner may be protected within the marriage. It also allows the partners to think about issues that arise out of the marital relations so that they may have a foundation to fall back on in the event that those or other unforeseen issues arise and cause conflict in the relationship. By having a document of expressed concerns, needs and steps to be taken to address them, it is less likely that issues which affect the relationship in a negative way will arise, and when they do, they will be better handled, in a more balanced, just and amicable way.

**EBOOK ISBN** 978-1-937016-59-3, HARDCOPY BOOK ISBN: 1-884564-82-8

53-Ancient Egyptian Mysteries of The Kybalion: A Hermetic Mystic Psychology Primer Paperback – November 28, 2014

This Volume is a landmark study by a renounced mystic philosopher, Dr. Muata Ashby. It is study not just to philosophize but to be practiced for the purpose of attaining enlightenment. The book is divided into three sections. Part 1 INTRODUCTION presents a brief history of Hermeticism, its origins in the Ancient Egyptian Mysteries (Neterianism) the Kybalion and the origins of the personality known as Hermes Trismegistus. Part 2 presents the essential teachings of the Kybalion text, a set of MAXIMS, without interpretation. Part 3 presents glosses (commentary and explanation) on the essential teachings of the Kybalion based on the philosophy of the Ancient Egyptian Mysteries as determined by Dr. Muata Ashby based on studies and translations of original Ancient Egyptian Hieroglyphic texts; the source from which the Kybalion teaching is derived. The Glosses are an edited and expanded version of Lessons given by Dr. Muata Ashby in the form of lectures on the teachings of the Kybalion.

54-Maat Philosophy Versus Fascism and the Police State: Understanding why Modern Society does not Experience the Peace and Prosperity of Ancient Egypt ... Law and Order, and Spiritual Enlightenment Paperback – January 1, 2014

Understanding why Modern Society does not Experience the Peace and Prosperity of Ancient Egypt and How To Discover the Pathway to Freedom, True Law and Order, and Spiritual Enlightenment. Understanding the Corporate State and How Maatian Philosophy can Leads to Freedom, Prosperity and Enlightenment

55-MALFEASANCE & IMMORALITY: An Analysis of the World Economic Crash of 2008, the Corrupt Political and Financial Institutions that Caused it and Strategies to Survive the Future Collapse of the Economy

The following is a first ever publication, by the Sema Institute, of a �White Paper�. The term is defined as: A white paper is an authoritative report or guide that often addresses issues and how to solve them. White papers are used to educate readers and help people make decisions. They are often used in politics and business. This paper serves as an update to the book Dollar Crisis: The Collapse of Society and Redemption Through Ancient Egyptian Fiscal & Monetary Policy (2008). That book was a continuation and expansion of issues presented in the book The Collapse of Civilization and the Death of American Empire (2006). Those books contained a detailed analysis of economic and political as well as social issues and how Maat Philosophy could offer insights into the nature of the problem, its sources and possible solutions as well as a means to develop an economic system (Fiscal and Monetary policies) that can work for all members of society. This paper contains an analysis of economic events and possible future outcomes based on those events as well as ideas individuals or groups may use in order to develop plans of action to deal with the possible detrimental events that may occur in the near and intermediate future. It serves as an update to the previous publications. This paper is divided into two parts. The first section is a summary which contains the conclusions of each section of Part 2. This was done so that the reader may have a quick and easy understanding of what is happening with the economy and finally, the actions that should be considered to meet the challenges ahead

**56- ANCIENT EGYPTIAN ECONOMICS**

Ancient Egyptian Economics: Kemetic Wisdom of Saving and Investing in Wealth of Body, Mind and Soul for Building True Civilization, Prosperity and Spiritual Enlightenment------ Question: Why has the subject of finances and economics become important, I thought the spiritual teachings and Ancient Egyptian Philosophy and money were separate? Answer: Finances and money are an integral part of Ancient Egyptian culture as an instrument for promoting Maat ethics in the form of the well-being of the 'hekat'. The hekat are the people and the "Heka" is the Pharaoh. The Pharaoh was like a shepherd leading a flock and moneys were controlled righteously to promote the welfare of the people. In that tradition we have applied the philosophy of maatian economics to promote the well-being of those who are following this path as well as those who may read the books so they may avoid financial trouble as much as possible and have better capacity to practice the teachings. In order to have a successful life, human beings need a certain amount of money and wealth, but money and wealth are not the goal. They are a foundation that enables the true goal of life, enlightenment, to be realized. Therefore, we are only fulfilling the duty of transmitting wisdom about wealth to promote Maat, righteousness, truth and well-being, for all. This volume explores the mysteries of wealth based on the teachings of the sages of Ancient Egypt and the means to promote prosperity that allows a person to create the conditions for discovering inner peace and spiritual enlightenment. HTP-Peace

**57- NETERIAN AWAKENING**

Journal of Neterian Culture Vol 1-12 In one Volume

This is a single file containing 12 volumes of The Neterian Awakening Journal. The Neterian Awakening Journal was a publication where the culture and community of Shetaut Neter spirituality was explored. In it Dr.

Muata Ashby and Dr. Dja Ashby along with members of the Temple of Shetaut Neter presented articles, festival reviews, Questions and Answer columns and many other important aspects of Neterian culture and spirituality beyond those presented in other volumes of the book series that are useful in understanding the practice of Neterian Spirituality and the path to achieving a ◆Neterian Spiritual Awakening.◆ Part of its mission was: To promote the study of Shetaut Neter (Neterianism, Neterian Religion) as a spiritual path. Instruct the serious followers of Shetaut Neter spirituality who would like to receive literature in between the publication of major books that will fill the needs of their daily spiritual practice. Neterian Awakening Journal explores the varied aspects of Shetaut Neter spirituality not covered in the books. NAJ provides a forum for the development of a Neterian Community of those who wish to follow the Neterian Spiritual Path of African Religious Culture

58- Little Book of Neter: Introduction to Shetaut Neter Spirituality and Religion Paperback – June 7, 2007

The Little Book of Neter is a summary of the most important teachings of Shetaut Neter for all aspirants to have for easy reference and distribution. It is designed to be portable and low cost so that all can have the main teachings of Shetaut Neter at easy access for personal use and also for sharing with others the basic tenets of Neterian spirituality.

59- Dollar Crisis: The Collapse of Society and Redemption Through Ancient Egyptian Monetary Policy by Muata Ashby (2008-07-24) This book is about the problems of the US economy and the imminent collapse of the U.S. Dollar and its dire consequences for the US economy and the world. It is also about the corruption in government, economics and social order that led to this point. Also it is about survival, how to make it through this perhaps most trying period in the history of the United States. Also it is about the ancient wisdom of life that allowed an ancient civilization to grow beyond the destructive corruptions of ignorance and power so that the people of today may gain insight into the nature of their condition, how they got there and what needs to be done in order to salvage what is left and rebuild a society that is sustainable, beneficial and an example for all humanity.

**60- Devotional Worship Book of Shetaut Neter: Medu Neter song, chant and hymn book for daily practice [Paperback] [2007] (Author) Muata Ashby Paperback – 2007**

Ushet Hekau Shedi Sema Taui Uashu or Ushet means "to worship the Divine," "to propitiate the Divine." Ushet is of two types, external and internal. When you go to pilgrimage centers, temples, spiritual gatherings, etc., you are practicing external worship or spiritual practice. When you go into your private meditation room on your own and your utter words of power, prayers and meditation you are practicing internal worship or spiritual practice. Ushet needs to be understood as a process of not only an outer show of spiritual practice, but it is also a process of developing love for the Divine. Therefore, Ushet really signifies a development in Devotion towards the Divine. This practice is also known as sma uash or Yoga of Devotion. Ushet is the process of discovering the Divine and allowing your heart to flow towards the Divine. This program of life allows a spiritual aspirant to develop inner peace, contentment and universal love, and these qualities lead to spiritual enlightenment or union with the Divine. It is recommended that you see the book "The Path of Divine Love" by Dr. Muata Ashby. This volume will give details into this form of Sema or Yoga.

**61- Initiation Into Egyptian Yoga and Neterian Religion Workbook for Beginning and Advancing Aspirants**

What is Initiation? The great personalities of the past known to the world as Isis, Hathor, Jesus, Buddha and many other great Sages and Saints were initiated into their spiritual path but how did initiation help them and what were they specifically initiated into? This volume is a template for such lofty studies, a guidebook and blueprint for aspirants who want to understand what the path is all about, its requirements and goals, as they work with a qualified spiritual guide as they tread the path of Kemetic Spirituality and Yoga disciplines. This workbook helps by presenting the fundamental teachings of Egyptian Yoga and Neterian Spirituality with questions and exercises to help the aspirant gain a foundation for more advanced studies and practices

**HIEROGLYPH TRANSLATION SERIES BY Dr. Muata Ashby**

EGYPTIAN BOOK OF THE DEAD HIEROGLYPH TRANSLATIONS USING THE TRILINEAR METHOD Volume 3: Understanding the Mystic Path to...
by Muata Ashby

EGYPTIAN BOOK OF THE DEAD HIEROGLYPH TRANSLATIONS USING THE TRILINEAR METHOD Volume 4: Understanding the Mystic Path to...

Temple of the Soul Initiation Philosophy in the Temple of Osiris at Abydos: Decoded Temple Mysteries Translations of Temple Inscriptions...
by Muata Ashby

Mysteries of Isis and Ra: A New Original Translation Hieroglyphic Scripture of t
by Muata Ashby

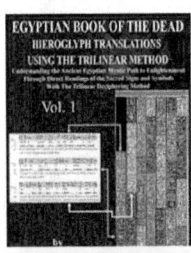

EGYPTIAN BOOK OF THE DEAD HIEROGLYPH TRANSLATIONS USING THE TRILINEAR METHOD Volume 5: Featuring Temple of Amun-Ra at Ab...
by Muata Ashby

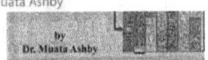

Egyptian Book of the Dead Hieroglyph Translations Using Th Trilinear Method Vol. 2: Understanding the Mystic Path to
by Muata Ashby

Egyptian Book of the Dead Hieroglyph Translations Volume 6 Featuring The Osirian Resurrection Paperback – September 23, 2021
by Muata Ashby (Author)
The aim of this book has been to render, for

the first time in one volume, the translated main hieroglyphic texts, associated with the Ancient Egyptian Osirian Resurrection, in the chronological order of the events of the myth and to present a translation that is grounded in the ancient texts, showing where the translated descriptions, wisdom and feelings expressed are coming from in the texts. Myth is a language of the soul by which the Ancient Kemetic (Egyptian) sages created a pathway for a human being to understand the nature of Creation, the powers (Neteru {gods and goddesses}) operating in it, and the manner in which to live a life that leads to happiness, fulfilment and spiritual enlightenment. The text of "Stele of Amenmose" contains references to the main scenes of the myth of the Asarian Resurrection, from the beginning of the myth to the end, but does not go into details related to some of those scenes. So, the text of "Stele of Amenmose" has been used as the foundational text, the trunk, as it were, of a tree. It begins the myth and describes the events of the myth, and as the tree (mythic rendition) grows, the branches extend the scenes not fully covered in the Amenmose scripture. So the contributing texts form expansions of the story which is taken up by another related scripture that goes into those details of hat section. Then, when that branch reaches a conclusion, we will return to the trunk of the tree again, the Stele of Amenmose, to again grow the tree, the mythic journey, until we reach another branch and so on to the end of the myth. As the text is presented, the characters in the myth, which represent aspects of the Divine as well as expressions of the human heart and soul, will be introduced. Then, as the saga unfolds, the reader will be able to identify with the characters and experience their passions, sorrows, victories and spiritual exaltations leading to the final victory of exhilaration and contentment over despondency, depression and frustration, and wisdom over delusion, and eternal mystic life over physical death.

This manuscript, authored by the esteemed Dr. Muata Ashby, offers a profound exploration of the Ancient Kemetic (Egyptian) myth of the Asarian (Osirian) Resurrection. Dr. Ashby, a respected figure in the field of Egyptian philosophy and mysticism, employs a unique trilinear translation method to present the hieroglyphic texts. This method not only provides a phonetic transliteration and direct word-for-word translation but also includes a contextual translation that brings out the deeper meanings and philosophical insights embedded in the ancient texts. The manuscript delves into the mythic journey of Asar (Osiris), Aset (Isis), and Heru (Horus), offering readers a chance to connect with the characters and experience their spiritual transformations. By reading this text, one can gain a deeper understanding of the nature of creation, the divine powers operating within it, and the path to spiritual enlightenment. The book is a treasure trove of wisdom, offering insights into the nature of the human personality, its fall into the delusion of mortality, and the means for its redemption and spiritual emancipation. The trilinear translation method used by Dr. Ashby ensures that readers can fully grasp the rich metaphorical and philosophical content of the hieroglyphic texts. This manuscript is not just a scholarly work but a spiritual guide that can enlighten and transform the reader's life. Don't miss the opportunity to purchase, read, and learn from the timeless wisdom contained in this manuscript. Let the ancient sages' teachings flow through you and illuminate your spiritual path.

THE PSYCHO-METAPHYSICAL MYSTERIES OF THE ANCIENT EGYPTIAN TEMPLE PANELS Paperback – July 21, 2021
by Muata Ashby (Author)

Why does the title of this book contain the term "Psycho-metaphysical Mysteries"? The first part, "psycho", references the aspect of the subject matter that relates to the human mind. The term "metaphysics" may be defined as a study about things that transcend the physical; studies that involve "philosophy" as a way of understanding, and "wisdom" about things known and understood, that allows the mind to transcend the knowledge and understanding that has been gained, and finally, "theurgy" which involves a science of spiritual evolution, that is the main subject taught and practiced in the Ancient Egyptian temple through mythic, and mystic writings, architecture and iconography of the temple. Therefore, this book examines the science of the Ancient Egyptian temple that is dedicated to the understanding and mentally enlightening process of spiritual evolution and discovery of the infinite.

Putting together, the teachings of the Ancient Egyptian mysteries and its theurgical science behind the mythic wisdom of the gods and goddesses with the temple architecture and the human mind with the catalyst of akhu or intuitional insight, of the Ancient Egyptian priests and priestesses, renders the conscious awareness of subject, the formal human person, in a state of ecstatic mystic self-discovery.

Awakening Your Soul-Aware-Witness

www.ingramcontent.com/pod-product-compliance
Lightning Source LLC
Chambersburg PA
CBHW070043080526
44586CB00013B/898